W9-ADR-299

WISH IN ONE HAND
SPIT IN THE OTHER

WISH IN ONE HAND SPIT IN THE OTHER

A COLLECTION OF PLAYS BY SUZAN ZEDER

Edited with Introduction and Critical Essays by

Susan Pearson-Davis

ANCHORAGE PRESS
Post Office Box 8067
New Orleans, Louisiana 70182

Anchorage Press, Inc.
Post Office Box 8067
New Orleans, Louisiana 70182

Cover art "Brightest Star" by Lynne Loshbaugh, Katie Gingrass Galley, 226
Canyon Road, Santa FE, NM

Book and Cover Design by Vivian L. Bradbury
Composition by Sans Serif, Inc., Ann Arbor, Michigan
Manufactured by Malloy Lithographing, Inc., Ann Arbor, Michigan

ISBN 0-87602-029-5

To Dan

Contents

Contents

Foreword

The first time I met Suzan Zeder was just after her parents embraced her. We were all in the lobby at the Dallas Children's Theatre where we'd enjoyed a production of her play *Step on a Crack*. I had marveled at the imaginative construction of her play and it's holding power. People of all ages, even the smallest children were glued to the stage. And this play was not short. It was complex, full of genuine emotions, hurts and worries with a recognition of true needs to be fulfilled and the resolve of good feelings at the end. Her parents were so very proud of her, and so was the entire audience. People lingered to catch a glimpse of the author and I waited till she was free so I could introduce myself and tell her how much I had enjoyed her play and had enjoyed the audience enjoying the play.

You get doubles at a Suzan Zeder play.

The next time I saw her, we were sitting side by side ready to begin a panel presentation at a New Orleans conference for international youth theatre sponsored by ASSITEJ. Susan Osteen, the renowned Swedish youth theatre playwright sat to my right and Suzan Zeder, the renowned American youth theatre playwright sat at my left. Suzan was leaning forward in her chair. Energy seemed to fly from her hair. Her eyes were flashing. She seemed to want to embrace the audience, to hold all three hundred people at once. She couldn't wait to begin. I could feel her muscles getting ready to leap forward, her imagination was churning, she was nervous but she was happy. Her eyes glowed and then her voice opened and she fired up the audience with her caring and her vision of theatre for young people. The audience was as pleased with her person and her words as that Dallas audience had been with her play. She is a dedicated and committed artist of the theatre.

Suzan Zeder can hold her own with any playwright in terms of quality and quantity. She uses all her intelligence, all her energy, all her unique humor and passion for her fellow creatures to inform her work. However, I believe her greatest contribution to dramatic literature is her focus on *the child as protagonist*. As she has said, "I'm fascinated by the possibilities of centering a play around the feelings and instincts and possibly heroic responses of a young person." She is able to do this because in her work she treats young people with the respect and artistic attention they deserve.

If she had only written *Mother Hicks*, or *Step on a Crack*, her work would be treasured, but consider the range of her output. *The Death and Life of Sherlock Holmes* is a challenging mystery for all ages. *In a Room Somewhere* breaks new ground for young audiences as five people must find their way out of a room with no doors or windows by taking a trip through their own pasts. *Mother Hicks*, an emotionally compelling play set during the great depression eloquently depicts three outsiders who find their way to themselves and each other via poetry and sign language. *Doors*, an insightful, emotionally true play deals with separation and divorce from the point of view of an eleven year old boy. *Ozma of Oz*, a warmly comic, imaginative, original play, loosely based on the Baum characters, shows how a young girl learns to look beyond the outward signs of aging and see the true worth of a beloved relative. *The Play Called Noah's Flood* is a fifteenth century medieval spectacle, offering the opportunity to involve a whole town on stage in a multi-media ensemble piece of comic delight. In *Step on a Crack*, Ellie, an engaging little girl tries to run away with her imaginary friends to escape her new stepmother, but when she is really alone she discovers how to come to terms with herself and her own need for a mother. *Wiley and the Hairy Man* celebrates the magic of the earth and the mud of the swamp and features an exciting dual of wits, as Wiley learns to rely on his own resources when he conquers the Hairy Man and his own fear.

There are no limits to Suzan Zeder's theatrical imagination, which is a boon to the field of theatre and to the young people and their families who are fortunate enough to experience her plays.

Megan Terry
Omaha, Nebraska

Acknowledgments

I would like to thank Anne-Denise Ford, Richard Greenblatt, Joan Lazarus, Jude Levinson, Bob Miller, and Gretchen Orsland for taking the time to write to me about their work with Suzan Zeder and her scripts; the designers with whom I have worked, especially Roy Hoglund, who helped me understand Suzan's rich visual metaphors; and the many actors who have showed me the real depth of her words. I greatly appreciate the moral support of my colleagues in the Theatre Arts Department at the University of New Mexico, especially Brian Hansen whose encouragement and guidance were particularly helpful. A very special thank you goes to Stacy Innerst for his understanding.

Most of the words in this anthology would not have been written had it not been for Charley Helfert of the Theatre Department at Southern Methodist University, who was both a mentor in the best sense of the word and the catalytic force behind the birth of both *Wiley and the Hairy Man* and *Step on a Crack*. Finally, I want to thank Suzan Zeder for her openness and generosity, both during the interviews that we had in preparation for this book and during our years of working together as playwright and director.

Photo by Gary Sweetman

Suzan L. Zeder

Introduction

The thousands of audience members who have had the privilege of meeting Ellie Murphy in *Step on a Crack* or Jeff in *Doors* or Girl in *Mother Hicks* will agree that Suzan Zeder is one of the most original, imaginative, and challenging playwrights currently writing for young audiences in the American theatre. One of Zeder's greatest contributions to contemporary theatre is her creation of compelling child characters, such as Ellie, Jeff, Girl, and the others you will meet in this volume. They are fully three-dimensional young people who grapple actively with the most difficult problems faced by children in our culture. Each of the worlds that Zeder has created for these young characters, and for a large array of fascinating adult characters as well, is highly theatrical and distinctive in structure. The title of this collection, *Wish on One Hand, Spit in the Other*, points to the tension in her plays between the wished-for and the real in people's lives, the sometimes dark distance between where we want to be and where we find ourselves at the moment. Although many of them deal with difficult and painful issues, they are also shot through with bouyant and earthy humor. The fact that her plays appeal to audiences of all generations is one of the hallmarks of her work.

Thus far, her greatest recognition has come from the field of professional theatre for young audiences, although her work is not at all limited to child audiences. The body of her work is distinguished by its variety both in form and content. In this collection you will find four adaptations of other works: a traditional American folk tale, a medieval mystery play, a well-known novel, and a famous series of mystery stories. There are also four completely original works, two of which take place in the present, one during the Great Depression, and one in a mixture of past and present. In her adaptations she has drawn from and built upon theatrical traditions of the past, but she has boldly changed the source material to make the plays original, timely, and universal. With her original works she has cultivated new ground in the field of theatre for young audiences, both in her choice of subject matter and in the theatrical structure she uses to bring that subject matter to life.

All of her works, taken together, serve as a major bridge over what has traditionally been a wide chasm between adult theatre and theatre for young audiences. In the scripts that dominated children's theatre in the first half of this century, issues of good and evil were clearly delineated, with good rewarded and evil punished. The difficult questions of greater or lesser good and evil were rarely found. Part of the bridging effect of her work is that some of Zeder's plays, especially her adaptations, are consonant with this traditional moral model, while others, including all of her original works, present moral ambiguities without easy answers.

The major supports for this bridge between adult and children's theatre, however, are her young protagonists. They stand out in high contrast to the passive, one-dimensional and sentimentalized children who were so prominant in traditional children's theatre. From the late 1800's until the 1960's, dramatic literature for young audiences consisted mainly of adaptations of fairy tales and favorite children's stories. The few professional playwrights creating original material for child audiences avoided depth of characterization, fearing it would confuse young theatregoers. Zeder's child protagonists, even those in her adaptations of favorite stories, are fully and richly drawn. They are forced to cope with contradictory thoughts and feelings. Their inner conflicts lead them to difficult, contradictory behavior, and the need to make tough decisions and take risky action.

Two of the eight plays in this volume, *Step on a Crack* and *Doors*, have been included in other collections of plays representing the trend toward depth of characterization and seriousness of themes in plays for young audiences.[1,2] She has been applauded in these anthologies and elsewhere for her imaginative use of theatrical styles and conventions. Her plays invite close personal involvement from even the youngest members of the audience without the typical distancing or insulating factors that have held sway during much of the history of theatre for young audiences. In spite of some people labeling her as a "social issue" playwright or an author of "today" plays, Zeder is far more than that. In works commissioned by particular theatre groups, she has been asked to adapt material with familiar titles that will attract large audiences and to craft material generated by actors and directors. But, she has also written works that spring from deep within herself, her interests, her passions, and her imagination, quite apart from the demands and limitations of particular commissions or a particular audience.

---

[1]Roger L. Bedard, ed., *Dramatic Literature for Children: A Century in Review* (New Orleans: Anchorage, 1984), p. 587.
[2]Coleman Jennings and Gretta Berghammer, eds., *Theatre for Youth: Twelve Plays with Mature Themes* (Austin: University of Texas Press, 1986), p. 410.

She has won numerous awards for her work. The Children's Theatre Association of America honored her with the Charlotte Chorpenning Cup for Outstanding Playwright of Plays for Young People in 1978 and gave her the Distinguished Play Award for *The Play Called Noah's Flood* in 1985. She won the American Association of Theatre for Youth's Distinguished Play Award for *Doors* in 1986 and the American Alliance for Theatre and Education's Distinguished Play Award for *Mother Hicks* in 1987.

Philosophy and Principles
That Have Guided Zeder's Writing

Zeder believes that the principles that have guided her work have grown out of what she has been doing instinctively as a writer, rather than being some sort of credo that has shaped her work from the outset. She has been quoted many times as saying that she writes *about* children rather than for them, not for any particular social or educational purpose, but because she finds children fascinating and dramatically dynamic. She points out that a hero if often defined as a character with stature and significance in a situation of life-threatening importance who valiantly tries to solve a problem bigger than himself. She maintains that child protagonists can function as heros in an action sense if not always in a symbolic sense.

In her doctoral dissertation in 1978[3], she investigated and categorized specific characteristics of child protagonists in a large sample of plays for young audiences. The dissertation was not completed until well after she had written major drafts of *Wiley and the Hairy Man* and *Step on a Crack*, and she feels that her research simply confirmed things she had already confronted in her treatment of her first two young protagonists, Wiley and Ellie Murphy.

> "There were many things that I was uncomfortable with in the way a lot of people were depicting children. Once I began a systematic investigation, I discovered that, in the vast majority of scripts for young audiences, child characters are passive, dependent, oversimplified and usually fall into sex-role stereotypes. Rarely do they have conflicting inner motivations—wanting two or more things at the same time that are diametrically opposed. Even more rarely do any decisions they make have any effect on the outcome of the plot, even if they are

---

[3]Suzan L. Zeder. "A Character Analysis of the Child Protagonist as Present in Popular Plays for Child Audiences," Diss. Florida State University 1978.

ostensibly the play's protagonist. Although the dissertation is in no way a formula, I think it does help me diagnose what's wrong with a character and gives me labels for what I don't want to do."

Zeder states that her primary relationship as an artist is with the material rather than with any set of rules or with any presumed audience. She feels strongly that too much theatre for young audiences has been written with an underlying assumption that children are somehow different or "other," and that many writers have mistakenly felt they had to alter the craft of playwriting for children.

Until the 1960's playwrights and producers for young audiences not only avoided depth of characterization, but they also stayed away from contemporary subject matter and controversial themes. They did not want to alienate parents and teachers during a time period when very narrow limits were set on what was considered appropriate for children. Escapist and fantasy subject matter, sex-role stereotyping, moralistic messages, bumbling rather than threatening antagonists, and inevitable happy endings permeated the literature because they were thought to be necessities for preserving a child's natural optimism and innocence.[4] Playwrights of this era also limited themselves stylistically to realism and the well-made play structure, thinking it was all that children could understand.

In contrast, Zeder speaks for and with a new generation of playwrights, producers, and directors of theatre for young audiences who have been influenced by the social and political upheaval of the last three decades. They have also been influenced by the impact of television. It has made problems such as war, nuclear proliferation, famines, terrorism, political scandals, drug abuse, and even child abuse part of everyday life for children and adults alike. In view of the fact that children are exposed to these problems daily through the media, even if they are not experiencing them in their own lives, Zeder emphasizes the need for adults to respect the child's perceptions and emotions.

"We condescend to children in real life, trivialize their emotional traumas and diminish the gravity of their situation, often in an attempt to protect them, or ourselves, from the inevitable pain involved in living. The results can be serious, sometimes as serious as suicide. I feel respect must be accorded to young audiences in the theatre. We owe the audience the right of coming to a performance and taking away

---

[4]Jed Davis and Mary Jane Evans, *Theatre, Children, and Youth* (New Orleans: Anchorage Press, 1982), p. 93, 97.

with them what they choose and responding to it in the way they choose. We shouldn't try to do their job for them."

The experimentation with theatrical forms and styles that marked the 1960's did not happen as quickly or boldly in theatre for young audiences as it did in adult theatre. There were still relatively few completely original plays that broke the old "rules" even into the early 1970's, leaving a small but growing vanguard of professional and university theatres for young audiences hungry for new material. It is not surprising that, in 1976, the appearance of Zeder's first published play, *Step on a Crack*, created such a wave of excitement in the field.

While Zeder rapidly gained the admiration of many, there were those in the field who felt (and still feel) that *Step on a Crack* and other of her plays, like *Doors, Mother Hicks,* and *In a Room Somewhere* aren't "really for children." Others try to pin her down about the specific age groups for which she intended them. But Zeder finds herself increasingly reluctant to categorize children in audiences by age groups and developmental levels. She feels that if she deals honestly with the characters and situations, most of her plays will hold all ages.

"I've read statements about children not paying attention to what they don't understand. I don't agree. There's a great deal about the world that young children don't understand, but that doesn't mean they always get up and walk out on those things. I think children will pay attention in the theatre when there is emotional truth on stage. I've seen pre-schoolers sit in rapt attention through both *Mother Hicks* and *In a Room Somewhere,* neither of which was written for young audiences at all, let alone pre-schoolers. I've come to have more faith in the audience and less feeling that we need age-group specific categories. In any event, I must deal with the demands of the material and leave it to directors and producing groups to decide what, if any, limitations there should be on the age of audience members."

Her belief has resulted in works that have expanded the field's notion of what is "really for children." Children stay involved in her plays through sections that many adults would expect to "go over their heads." Adults in the audiences of her plays find themselves just as emotionally involved, intellectually stimulated, and thoroughly entertained as the younger audience members. Both children and adults in the audience can identify with and respect her young characters because she has written them in a way that validates the child's perceptions and emphasizes the universal presence of the child within the adult and the adult within the child.

Family, Childhood, and Educational Influences

Zeder's initial interest in writing about young characters springs, at least in part, from her own easy access to the child space within herself. People occasionally ask her if she had to cope with a new stepmother, or with her parents getting a divorce, or with any of the other crises that many of her young protagonists face. She is quick to let people know that her childhood was a very stable and happy one and that her parents were extremely supportive of her and her brothers and sisters. As a result, she feels she didn't build up any serious blocks to childhood memories.

> "I really don't think of my childhood as something in the distant past. I'm becoming more and more convinced that within us is the child that we always are. Not always were, but always *are*. Conversely, I think we have within us, as children, the men and women we become."

Zeder can pinpoint a number of influential events during her childhood and adolescence that motivated her to work in the theatre and that are still very much a part of her writing. Even though her plays are not autobiographical, the reader will find traces of these pivotal events in the characters, themes, and even in the structuring of the plays in this volume.

Zeder knew from the time she was five years old that she would have some kind of life in the theatre. She grew up just outside New York City in Greenwich, Connecticut. For her fifth birthday her parents took her to see *Happy Hunting* with Ethel Merman and Fernando Lamas. Although, in retrospect, she admits it was "not all that great a show," she recalls it as

> "a galvanic experience that imprinted itself on me forever. To this day I can remember all the lyrics to all the songs, as well as specific scenes, costumes, sets, and even lighting effects. I cut my teeth on things like *The King and I, L'il Abner, My Fair Lady*, and *Camelot*. By the time I was a teen-ager, I was able to go into New York by myself for matinee performances. My father worked in New York and I would save my allowance and buy a theatre ticket, take the train in, see the show, then meet my Dad, and we would come back home together on the train. It became a passion."

Zeder's mother was a writer and Suzan has vivid memories of the many hours her mother spent at her desk surrounded by books and papers. That image of her mother working away at a desk had a lasting impact on her. "I knew from the beginning that writing was hard work with many revisions, and my mother's writing prepared me and let me know what I was in for." She admits that she never consciously thought about being a writer herself until well into her college years. She says that, as a child, "What I really wanted to be was a fabulously successful Broadway musical star." But even more than the childhood dream of fame, Zeder felt that being in plays was her most important means of expression and crucial to her sense of self-worth.

> "I always felt, as a kid, that I didn't quite fit in. I was never a good student in my younger years. I really had some serious problems with spelling and I had broken my right arm when I was quite young, so I always had terrible handwriting. I never felt like I was really any good at anything. But I compulsively did plays. Looking back on my drama activities, I call it a sort of 'backyard Nazi theatre.' I bossed everybody around. I got to play all the roles I really wanted and I forced everyone else to take the other parts. We did things like *The Sound of Music* in lip-sync to the record."

She was also in plays at school and vividly remembers being thrown out of a production of *H.M.S. Pinafore* because she had bad grades.

> "I can remember saying to myself 'That's never going to happen again.' I never felt more outside in my life as to be outside of that production, to be outside the theatre. To me the theatre was one thing that I could do, one place where I belonged. To this day, I think this feeling of not quite fitting in and the pain of being an outsider still show up a lot in my work."

Zeder recalls another experience that was very formative in terms of her continuing love of theatre and her particular interest in writing about young characters. When she was 14, she went backstage at a Broadway theatre and met actress Beatrice Lillie. She had gone with her parents to see the British comedienne in *High Spirits*, a musical version of *Blythe Spirit*. Zeder, who by that time was quite a sophisticated young theatregoer says:

> "I absolutely fell in love with the genius of this woman's comedy. I was determined to meet her. I wrote her quite a business like letter requesting an interview for an article in my school paper. I enclosed a self-addressed card with three possible responses: 'Yes, I will see you,' 'No, I won't see you,' and 'Forget it, kid.' Something must have tickled her. The card returned with the 'yes' box checked. I went into seventh heaven. I also went into action. I read everything my school library and the Greenwich Public Library had on Beatrice Lillie. I even went to the

Performing Arts Library in New York. I knew everything about her life that I could find out in those three weeks before the interview.

"Finally the great day came. I saw a matinee and went backstage, trembling with nervous anticipation. The first sight of a Broadway backstage was incredible! Scenery hung, props laid out on tables, costumes in the wings for quick changes. The magic dismembered was somehow even more magical.

"I arrived at her dressing room and the great lady herself ushered me into the back, the private section. At first I was petrified, but her kindness and humor put me at ease. She took me and my quest oh, so seriously. She treated my interview with complete professionalism. She sang me songs. She told me stories of her early days in the theatre. In a half an hour, I fell in love with her forever.

"And from that time it was like an obsession. I followed *Variety* to see how the show was doing at the box office all through the run. When I read that *High Spirits* was to close at a loss, I was very upset. I knew that Bea Lillie was in her late sixties, that this show was at the end of her career, and I took this very much to heart. I bought a ticket for the closing performance. I told my parents I was staying overnight with a friend and snuck into New York on the train to see the show. When I got there, I sent a final letter backstage. The passion of that letter was incredible—talk about 14 year old purple prose! It said something like 'you have given me something precious . . . a memory is imperishable gossamer and will dwell in the heart forever.' After the show I went back to see if the letter had been delivered. The stage manager said, 'You're Suzan. She wants to see you.' She came from the dressing room as I was headed across the stage. We met midway and just hugged each other and wept on that bare stage.

"That experience imprinted me in a number of important ways. There's something about 14 year old passion that is white hot, very serious, and completely mature, not in its target but in its velocity. I don't think I'll ever feel a passion as innocent or uncompromising again. I also realized the power of the theatre form to be life-transforming. There's something about the depth of that experience that has impelled me to write about young people, to give that time of life the respect it is due."

Another influence that is easy to see in Zeder's work is her long time admiration for the works of Thornton Wilder. Again, the beginnings of this admiration started when she was very young.

"The movie version of *Our Town* was on television and I thought it was a horror movie! What terrified me was Emily in the third act going back and not being able to talk to her mother. It haunted me that she was not being able to make contact."

Zeder's interest in Wilder resurfaced in high school when she did her major senior paper on him. In researching it, she read every play he wrote, including early plays that Wilder wrote at Lawrenceville, copies of which Wilder himself sent her after she wrote him a letter telling him of her project.

> "Seeing the continuity of his work and the structure of how it was put together fascinated me even then. I've always been intrigued by the structure of things and 'how' they mean. All of his plays have been very influential to me in terms of their manipulation of time and their concentration on the family."

Zeder's continuing passion for theatre led her to study theatre when she enrolled in Bennett College in upstate New York in 1967, but she still had no intention of becoming a playwright. In fact, she got herself into a sticky situation in which she was forced to write a play almost by accident. During her freshman year at Bennett, she lied to one of her acting teachers, telling her that she did not have her audition piece prepared on time because she was rushing to finish writing a play from which the audition piece was to be taken. When the teacher accepted the excuse but wanted to see the play, Zeder had to produce something in a hurry. She quickly adapted a chapter of a favorite novel and was astonished to find that her acting teacher felt the work had merit. This teacher, Barbara Curtin, made her finish the play and supervised her work on it for the next year. It was during this time that Zeder discovered that writing fulfilled her more than acting did. She realized that with acting she was always dependent on somebody else's estimation of who she was and she was tired of playing "old women and loud-mouthed aunts."

Zeder did not take a formal playwriting class until she transferred to Trinity University in San Antonio, Texas her junior year. In that class she wrote a play called *And the Trees were Filled with Angels* (which eventually had some influence on *Mother Hicks*) and *The Wizard Hills of Glass* which was somewhat diasterously produced. But she did not feel she knew who she was as a playwright yet and had not found her own voice.

It was not until she entered the M.F.A. program at Southern Methodist University in Dallas that she decided she would concentrate on playwriting. At that time she felt she was writing like the most recent work she'd read. "If I read Williams, I would write dialogue and characters reminiscent of Laura, Amanda, and Blanche. If I read Beckett, things got a little avant garde." It was at SMU that she wrote her first play for young audiences. In 1972 she was asked by faculty member, Charley Helfert, if she would be willing to help structure a piece he and a group of actors were putting together improvisationally based on the folk tale, "Wiley and the Hairy Man." She took on the job, not because it was a play for young audiences, but because it was a mainstage show and a real opportunity to get her work produced. It turned out to be an important turning point. It was the play during which she found her own voice as a writer. Indeed, *Wiley and the Hairy Man* is a microcosm of many of the forces that manifest themselves through the next 17 years of her writing.

Although she still did not consider young audiences as a major focus of her writing, her first professional playwriting job after earning her M.F.A. was with Anne Elgood at the Flint Youth Theatre in the summer of 1972. There she wrote the first draft of *The Play Called Noah's Flood* for the teen-age actors in the Flint program. After Flint, more opportunities presented themselves, each centered around children or youth. She spent 1972–73 as a Fulbright Scholar in England researching British Theatre-in-Education companies. In 1974 she taught a Theatre-in-Education class at Southern Methodist University based on her Fulbright studies. During that time another chance to write a play presented itself. I was a graduate student director at SMU at the time and needed a small-cast show with good roles for women that was suitable for touring to elementary schools. Zeder was eager to write another script and *Step on a Crack* was born. Her interest in working for children and youth continued, and in the fall of 1974 she entered the doctoral program at Florida State University on a full fellowship, studying with Moses Goldberg and serving as the playwright-in-residence for the Asolo Touring Theatre, which primarily serves young audiences.

After earning her Ph.D. in 1977, Zeder headed the Child Drama M.F.A. Program at the University of Washington for four years, during which time she continued her writing and her focus on plays for young audiences. So, without ever intentionally setting out to write works for young audiences, her own commitment to the significance of childhood, together with many demands for her scripts by producers of theatre for young audiences, led her quietly, but insistently, along the path for a decade.

She is currently living in Tampa, Florida and is married to Jim Hancock, Chairman of the Theatre Department at the University of South Florida. She credits her husband, a therapist, director, and teacher of stage movement, with bringing her to a new and higher level in her writing.

"I think Jim has helped me find the adult perspective. I was always fairly comfortable with the child's perspective because I was always comfortable with that child space within myself. But coming to terms with myself as a woman in an adult relationship, I began to trust myself with adult characters more fully."

It is hard to tell what Zeder's next step as a writer may be. The last three plays in this anthology, *Mother Hicks*, *In a Room Somewhere*, and *The Death and Life of Sherlock Holmes*, were written without any assumption that they would be for child audiences, and the last two do not have a major child character. Her most recent work, a new translation and adaptation of Moliere's *The Miser*, which is not included in this collection, is also intended for an adult audience.

"I'm finding that the texture and focus of my work is changing. I will only know if I am moving out of the focus on the child when I see the next two or three plays that come through me. I have come to believe that the writing shapes me much more than I shape it."

The Plays

The way Zeder shapes her plays is worthy of close examination. Most people who have worked on a production of one of Zeder's scripts discover that they provide a rich and exciting artistic challenge for actors and designers as well as directors. They require a great deal of imagination and a strong sense of theatricality to match her complexity and sophistication. Her scripts also demand the sensitivity to read between the lines to find the full depth of subtext in character interactions.

Content

When one looks beneath any particular topical or timely issue in these scripts, such as divorce or being a step parent, it is clear that Zeder's major concerns as a writer, and the themes that arc back and forth through the body of her works, focus on problems that are universal for both children and adults.

As mentioned above, one of these major concerns is creating child characters with magnitude and depth. Although each of her child protagonists is a unique individual, they do share some characteristics. They are all bright and imaginative, but full of conflicting emo-

xxvi *Wish in One Hand, Spit in the Other*

tions, doubts, and fears about themselves and their parents. Their active imaginations and vivid fantasies both help and thwart them in coping with their problems. They are aware whenever adults withhold information or affection from them and are hungry to have a voice in the decisions adults make for them. They are head strong and rebellious; their behavior is often far from likeable, but they grow in self-awareness through the plays to understand the effects that their behavior has on other people. All of them make the discovery that they have to face their fears and solve their problems alone.

Some of her protagonists end up literally alone; namely Wiley in *Wiley and the Hairy Man*, whose mother and dog are turned to stone leaving him facing the Hairy Man alone, and Girl in *Mother Hicks*, who has no parents. But, the issue of aloneness is also present even in plays in which the child protagonist is portrayed in a family setting with supportive parents. Ellie in *Step on a Crack* and Jeff in *Doors* are both struggling with shifting relationships between their parents; both have to sort out lots of internal conflicts alone before they are able to confront their parents.

Most of Zeder's young protagonists struggle to overcome a sense of incompleteness; often because they feel powerless, or because they lack a sense of identity. This is partly due to the fact that they are children and their sense of identity is still in a formative phase. However, this feeling of incompleteness is not a problem unique to children. Its universality is reflected in the adult protagonists in *In a Room Somewhere* who are having to confront the same kinds of questions about identity and power. The adult characters in *The Play Called Noah's Flood*, *Mother Hicks*, and *The Death and Life of Sherlock Holmes* also seek to complete themselves and affirm their identities, but do so through creative activities or efforts to nurture others.

The fact that many of Zeder's protagonists feel like they are alone and incomplete is reinforced by another major motif in Zeder's works—the difficulty people have in communicating with each other. Repeatedly in her work, communication breaks down for one of two reasons. The first is that her characters often refuse to listen to each other. Sometimes this is because one person assumes what the other says has little merit and simply tunes it out, like Dorothy and Uncle Henry in *Ozma of Oz*. Other times characters refuse to listen as an outright denial of what the other has to say, like John Talbot refusing to listen to his son Ira in *The Play Called Noah's Flood*. Communication also breaks down because characters purposely withhold information from each other. Usually this happens when a parent tries to protect a child. Whether it is well-intentioned, based on underestimating the child's ability to understand, or the result of simple self-interest, with-holding information only serves to increase the problem.

As Zeder's protagonists cope with their problems, imagination and fantasy are crucial elements. Sometimes the protagonists' fantasies compound their problems, as in *Mother Hicks* when Girl's elaborate fantasies about her real parents make the truth even harder for her to bear. Sometimes, fantasies seem to delay the solution of the problem, as in *Doors*, when Jeff uses them to put off finding out what is really happening. However, a character's ability to use the imagination is usually an important means to rehearse various options for action and a catalyst for growth.

A final recurring motif in these plays is the plight and perception of outsiders. Zeder has a particular sensitivity to the feelings of outsid-ers and to those who are somehow disenfranchised, in a real or meta-phorical sense. In a way, all her child protagonists fall into this cate-gory since they are struggling for the power to influence the adults who make decisions for them. Zeder has also created several memo-rable adult characters who have been forced to live outside the main-stream and who provide insights and observations about the society that does not include them.

The first of these is Uncle Henry in *Ozma of Oz*, who is neither used to, nor accepting of, the fact that old age and illness have forced him into a wheelchair. During the course of his adventure in Oz, he proves to Dorothy that being old and wheelchair-bound does not mean he is helpless or useless. He provides an image of a strong, spirited old man that runs counter to many stereotypes of old age that still prevail in society, in theatre, and particularly in theatre for young audiences.

Then there is Mother Hicks who has been forced out of town due to the fear and prejudice of those who use her as a scapegoat. Her wisdom grows out of her connection to the earth, to nature, and to its healing powers. The pain of being ostracized and of losing her child has taught her some of nature's most difficult lessons about the importance of letting go and not claiming ownership of other people.

The last two outsider characters are similar in that each has a dis-ability which makes communication difficult; Pipe, in *The Play Called Noah's Flood*, stutters, and Tuc, in *Mother Hicks*, is deaf. Although the two plays differ radically in style and come at widely different times in Zeder's career, both characters are highly perceptive about others. Both Pipe and Tuc bring other people together, in spite of being rejected and belittled by them. Because of their disabilities, other characters assume they are stupid, but both are more sensitive to what is going on inside and between people than anyone else. Pipe and Tuc also serve as literal saviours of something or someone that the other characters have begun to care about. The audience discovers the real ability behind the apparent disability in each of these young men and does so before the other characters on stage discover it. This makes both characters extremely sympathetic and compelling.

Form

Zeder's originality in structuring her plays, so that they are highly theatrical and rich with visual metaphors, can be described as falling into two general areas. First, is her innovative use of time and space, which she manipulates to juxtapose multiple planes of reality on stage at once. Time and space in Zeder's writing often overlap and influence each other and should not be thought of as having hard and fast boundaries. Second, is her own unique and imaginative way of using traditional theatrical conventions.

Zeder's innovative use of space is revealed in the psychological structures that form the inner landscape and architecture of her protagonists' minds. Several of her plays are set completely within, or move rapidly in and out of, the mind of her central character. As these characters enact their fantasies, inner, psychological space becomes external, physical space on the stage. In two plays, *Step on a Crack* and *Doors*, this inner space is represented by the character's bedroom, which is transformed into a variety of locations by the power of the protagonist's imagination. In *In a Room Somewhere* one room becomes a mutual inner space for five different adults.

The externalized inner life of her characters is not always represented by the character's own room. Sometimes the character's nightmares and imaginings spill out to become the world of the play, taking over the entire stage space. This happens in *Wiley and the Hairy Man* when Wiley's nightmares, enacted by the chorus, menace him both in his own room and in the swamp. It also happens in *Mother Hicks* in the graveyard when Hosiah spanks Girl. All of the other characters freeze, Girl steps out of Hosiah's grasp and shouts at the frozen characters. The audience is catapulted into a departure from reality in which Girl's subjective experience of being punished by the entire village takes over the stage space. During much of *The Death and Life of Sherlock Holmes*, the stage space represents the inner, imaginative world of Sir Arthur Conan Doyle. The seamlessness of the shifts from Doyle's imaginative world to the "real" world is a crucial and fascinating element in Zeder's structuring of this mystery.

Zeder is also inventive in her handling of the shifting and passage of time. One example is the witching ritual in *Mother Hicks*. Zeder condenses a whole week's worth of Girl's activities into a single short scene by placing several events on stage at one time. Girl reads aloud from a book on witchcraft, describing magic spells she plans to do, in one area of the stage; at the same time, the audience sees those spells being carried out on various townspeople, in other areas of the stage. In *Doors* large scrim wall posters in Jeff's bedroom are lit from behind to frame his parents enacting moments from marriage counseling sessions that took place in the past; simultaneously and in counterpoint, Jeff, in present time, tells his friend what he thinks is going on between his parents. *In a Room Somewhere* has characters stepping in and out of subtly intertwined planes of reality. Time moves backwards and stops for characters while they relive events from their pasts; at the same time, other characters on stage experience time moving forward as usual. These techniques of manipulating time and space make exposition very active, add layers of depth and texture to characterization, and build increased tension.

In addition to her unusual uses of time and space, Zeder also puts her own unique stamp on one of the more traditional theatrical conventions. For example, in *Wiley and the Hairy Man* and *Mother Hicks*, Zeder uses the ancient convention of the chorus in two very different ways. In *Wiley* a chorus of actors plays various types of animal and vegetable matter in the swamp, brings to life the magic forces conjured by Mammy and the Hairy Man, creates important sound effects, and narrates the story. In *Mother Hicks*, chorus members play specific and, in some cases, multiple roles as townspeople. They also take turns voicing the words of the deaf character, Tuc, as he narrates the story in sign language.

Zeder's use of language is also distinctive. Her fascination with verse, strong rhythms, rhyme, and an almost musical use of sound in her choice of words is evident in most of her plays. It is particularly important in *Wiley and the Hairy Man* and *Mother Hicks*. In both of these plays the chorus parts are written almost exclusively in verse, characterized by strong folk-ballad rhythms and lines repleat with alliteration, onomatopoeia, and repetition of individual words and short phrases that drive forward with great power. In *The Play Called Noah's Flood* Zeder uses an adaptation of the Chester and Townley Noah cycle plays which are written in verse. The rest of the play that frames it is in prose. She takes added care to blend rhyming couplets and strong, regular rhythms, echoing the medieval verse, into the prose sections, so that the ear will not be jarred when the play-within-the-play begins.

But even in plays that do not include verse, Zeder's love of sounds, rhythm, and rhyme is still apparent. In *Step on a Crack* it appears in the children's games and jump-rope rhymes in the opening sequence of the play and in Ellie's fantasies and dreams. In *Doors* the sounds of the parents arguing behind the door is a major factor that builds tension. The use of rhythmically repeated short sentences is alternately comforting and threatening, reinforcing Jeff's mood swings in a visceral, kinesthetic way.

Another important aspect of Zeder's use of language is the spareness and brevity of her dialogue. Very rarely do her characters have monologues or speeches that are longer than one or two sentences. Most of the time, in her non-verse plays, the dialogue moves along in what appears to be quite naturalistic conversation made up of short sentences. However, Zeder has given much attention to paring her writing down so that most of the action is taking place between the lines in the subtext rather than in the lines themselves. As Zeder says herself:

> "I have seen productions of my plays in which directors found only what was in the surface of the lines. My scripts just don't work that way. There must be action going on within the characters and between the characters, beneath the words and behind the silences."

This is especially true of her more recent scripts. She explains:

> "Early on, I don't think that I trusted in the emotional power of stillness. I think I had some confusion between action and activity. I felt that unless there was a great deal of activity on stage that nothing was happening. *Step, Wiley,* and *Ozma* are incredibly full of activity. I think it was in *Doors* that I began to trust that dramatic action could be internal emotional action within a character and interpersonal action between characters without a lot of physical activity. In the process of writing *Mother Hicks* it became even clearer to me that some of the most compelling action can happen in absolute stillness. When there is really something happening between actors in stillness, when there is emotional truth, even the youngest audience members will be held."

What the reader will find in this volume are eight plays in which there is always something very real going on between the characters. There is also plentiful humor and fantasy, but the reader will discover that the humor and fantasy deepen the internal action within and between characters and serve the emotional truth of the moment. In most of these plays the reader will also find Zeder's deep concern for the child—both for the child as an individual whose viewpoint and feelings have magnitude and significance and for the inner child that is a potentially life-enhancing part of every adult. Even in plays in which childhood is not the focus, the reader will find Zeder's continuing concern with families, with self-created or societal walls that inhibit communication and growth, and with the individual's or the larger community's search for identity and completion. She writes plays about people who have come through hard times and have made decisions to take responsibility for their own lives, no matter how old or young they may be.

Zeder's voice and vision, coming as they do at a time when affirmations are difficult to find in the society around us, are stronger because they acknowledge the brokenness from which the seeds of new growth must spring. Her vision includes a deep concern for and appreciation of the day-to-day struggles of ordinary people, both children and adults. Zeder combines this concern with her still white-hot passion for theatre as an art form that has the potential to transform lives. She uses her skill in shaping her plays to create a unique and highly theatrical way of meaning that finds the universal values within the everyday and makes the ordinary quite surprisingly extraordinary.

Wiley and the Hairy Man

Zeder based this play on a folktale of the same name which appeared in a manuscript of the Alabama Federal Writer's Project. In adapting it for the stage, Zeder changed the original in two significant ways: how the major problem in the story is solved and who solves it. The original folktale ends with Mammy saving the day. Zeder knew fairly soon after the first production that she wanted to have Wiley solve his problem himself. However, it took her several years to figure out exactly how Wiley could to it. These changes, as well as several other important variations from the original, make Zeder's version unique among other adaptations and give it greater archetypal resonance — greater even than the original folktale.

In Zeder's version, as in the original, the Hairy Man haunts the swamp, is out to get Wiley, and can only be stopped if three tricks can be successfully played on him. In the original folktale Wiley manages the first two tricks, but the last one is done by Mammy. She puts a pig in Wiley's bed in place of Wiley when the Hairy Man comes to snatch him. In Zeder's version Wiley must manage the three tricks all by himself, in spite of the fact that he seems far too inept at conjuring to succeed on his own. To heighten the tension, Zeder has the Hairy Man turn both Mammy and Dog to stone, leaving Wiley completely on his own. The last and most crucial trick, which Wiley devises all by himself, involves no real magic. Instead, he bravely confronts the Hairy Man and saves the day by using the very aspects of his personality — courage, wits, and skill — that he, Mammy, and the audience thought were deficient earlier in the play. These changes allow Zeder to preserve the action packed structure of the folktale, while shifting the thematic emphasis in a more internal, psychological direction. In her adaptation, Wiley's fears become more of an obstacle than the Hairy Man. The story becomes one not only of good triumphing over evil, but also of a young boy coming of age, overcoming his fear, and discovering his own power.

Zeder's only intention, in making these changes from the original, was to make Wiley an active, rather than a passive, protagonist; thus, making him more interesting dramatically and a better role model. However, these changes accomplished more than that. By making him more active, she also, serendipitously, gave Wiley many of the qualities of the "child savior" — one of the major archetypal figures that appear repeatedly throughout literature and mythology, as described by Jung.[1] Wiley differs from the pure archetype in not being divinely inspired, but he resembles it in many other ways.[2] He has no father; he seems small and insignificant; he is protected by animals (his beloved Dog); he has a vulnerable mother and faces abandonment (when Mammy has been turned to stone); and he is able to miraculously overcome the dark forces that oppose him. He saves his mother, his dog, and himself. Zeder's Wiley resembles the archetype more than the Wiley in the original tale, and, in that sense, her version makes Wiley's journey symbolic of a personal inner journey that all people must make at some point in their lives.

While changing and adding to the story, Zeder has managed to honor the spirit of the original. In good folktake form, she uses objects and events in threes. The plot is characterized by repetition of events, but there is plenty of variety within the repetition. This allows the audience the satisfaction of anticipating what will come next, while surprising them with how the expected event unfolds.

In spite of the fact that this is one of Zeder's earliest scripts, her gift for creating works that appeal to both the ear and eye of the spectator is already apparent here. Her use of language with strong folk rhythms, her almost musical repetition of rhyming words and phrases, and her skillful manipulation of sound have a primitive sensory appeal that is well suited to the primal nature of Wiley's conflict. Repetition also contributes to the delicate balance of fun and fear that characterizes this play. It provides both moments of safe predictability ("The Hairy Man sure can't stand no dogs") and moments that announce danger and build suspense ("He done got your pappy and he's gonna get you . . ."). The rhythmic dialogue Zeder has created for the chorus provides the narrative structure of the original.

Zeder's chorus is the major element contributing to the play's visual spectacle. It serves as a scenic element that creates the swamp and allows her to externalize the "inner landscape" of Wiley's mind. Through the chorus we can see how Wiley's imagination turns the environment into the very things he fears. The chorus members' physical transformations also create the magic spells cast by Mammy, the Hairy Man, and Wiley. The fact that all the chorus'

---

[1] Carl G. Jung and C. Kerenyi, *Essays on a Science of Mythology*, Bollingen Series XXII. (Princeton: Princeton University Press, 1971). p. 72.

[2] Alma D'Heurle, "The Image of the Child in Popular American Films", *Et cetera*, Spring, 1983. p. 49.

magic transformations are obviously not magic underscores one of the play's deep meanings—that it is the "magic" which one creates by using one's own mind, heart and imagination which ultimately counts the most.

Wiley and the Hairy Man

by Suzan L. Zeder

From the Playwright

The original Wiley was born somewhere deep in the swamp near the Tombigbee River. His tale of *Wiley and the Hairy Man* was passed down from generation to generation in the backwaters of Alabama and Mississippi; and his story has taken many forms: a legend set down by Donnell Van de Voot in a manuscript of the Federal Writer's Project of Alabama, an excellent drama-choir by Jack Stokes, and a recent book by Molly Garrett Bang. In this scripted version I have tried to do something a bit different with the story. I have given it a new ending and have written a play about a small boy with a big fear who learns to overcome his own problems himself. I wanted to write a play about the kinds of fears that children face, alone, in the dark. I wanted to write a play about magic—good magic and bad magic—and, most importantly, the magic that all of us have somewhere deep inside us.

I have seen this play produced by a number of different companies. The first production, in 1972 at Southern Methodist University, involved a great deal of improvisation by the company; and I am indebted to them for many of the ideas in this script. I have learned from subsequent productions and have revised the script accordingly. I have seen all white casts, all black casts, and racially mixed casts; and I feel that each approach can work equally well. But each approach has different implications and I would urge potential directors to be aware of these implications and to use them deliberately and carefully. To my mind this is not a play about any particular culture or race. It may be set anywhere where there are swamps, and magic, and small frightened boys. Whether it is set in Alabama or Appalachia, the world of the play is within Wiley's mind. The magical elements are the extensions of the very real fears and foolery of Wiley's world. I would caution you to avoid the "cute," the "tricky," and the "superficial." The magic of this play is not fairy dust. It is soil. This magic is of the earth and mud of the swamp; it is the magic of survival.

I feel that this play is particularly influenced by the director. I offer it to you as a map of an experience, not as a formula. I have given you the words, but it is up to you to find the rhythms, the tones, and the counterpoint. It is a play about fear, but it also a play about fun; the fun of a boy and his dog, the fun of words and how they wind into rhymes, and the fun of how a boy discovers that he is bigger than his fears.

Suzan Zeder
Seattle 1978

Dedication

To Charley

The premiere production of *Wiley and the Hairy Man* was presented on March 14, 1972, at Southern Methodist University, Dallas, with the following cast:

Wiley	Randolf Pearson
Mammy	Beki Rogers
The Hairy Man	Steve B. Read
Dog	Terry Lacy
Chorus	David Nance
	Deborah Hardee
	Jory Hingson
	Melody Ruhe
	Leslie Evans

The production was directed by Charles Helfert

The first professional production of *Wiley and the Hairy Man* was presented on October 17, 1977, by the Asolo Touring Theatre in Sarasota, Florida.

CHARACTERS

Wiley
Mammy
The Hairy Man
Dog
Chorus
(Four suggested but more may be used)

SETTING

Mammy's House
The Swamp

TIME

Any Time

Wiley and the Hairy Man

As the audience enters they find themselves in the gloomy mysterious atmosphere of the swamp. The set suggests a rough lattice-work of boards which reach out at angles forming odd tree-like structures. One section of the set suggests Mammy's house which is merely an extension of the environment. Several sharply raked platforms are covered with vines and moss. The theatre is filled with strange swamp sounds: moans and creaks and rattles and wind sounds are made by the CHORUS. The lights are dim and cast strange shadows.

WILEY lies sleeping in a single shaft of light. Around him the CHORUS lie in various positions on the set. They are formless creatures, part of the swamp made up of moss, vines, and odd bits of swamp grass.

The swamp sounds grow louder and the CHORUS begins to move in an eerie, rhythmic nightmare. WILEY tosses and turns, caught in his dream. The sounds, strange and abstract at first slowly form themselves into words.

CHORUS I: Wiiiiiiley . . . . Wiiiiiiley . . . .

CHORUS II: Haaaaaairy Man! Haaaaaairy Man!

CHORUS III: Look out Wiley! Wake up Wiley!

CHORUS IV: He done got your Pappy and he's gonna get you!

CHORUS III: He done got your Pappy . . . .

CHORUS I: . . . And he's gonna get you!

CHORUS II: Haaaaaairy Man! Haaaaaairy Man!

CHORUS IV: He done got your Pappy and he's gonna get you!

CHORUS I: Wiiiiiiley . . . Wiiiiiiley . . . .

CHORUS IV: He done got your Pappy . . . .

CHORUS I: . . . And he's gonna get you!

(*A shrouded FIGURE with a candle enters and slowly walks toward WILEY.*)

CHORUS III: Look out, Wiley. Wake up, Wiley.

CHORUS II: Haaaaaairy Man! Haaaaaairy Man!

CHORUS IV: He done got your Pappy and he's gonna get you!

CHORUS I: He done got your Pappy . . .

CHORUS III: . . . And he's gonna get you!

(*FIGURE reaches out toward WILEY.*)

FIGURE: Wiley!

CHORUS I: (*Echo*) Wiiiiiiley . . . .

CHORUS IV: He done got your Pappy and he's gonna get you!

CHORUS II: He done got your Pappy . . .

ALL CHORUS: . . . AND HE'S GONNA GET . . .

FIGURE: WILEY! Wake up, Wiley!

(*WILEY wakes up with a bolt, sees the FIGURE and dives beneath the covers with his bottom in the air.*)

WILEY: Go 'way Hairy Man. Leave me alone Hairy Man. Don't touch me Hairy Man!

MAMMY: (*Taking off the hood*) I ain't no Hairy Man. I is your Mammy!

(*MAMMY punctuates her sentence with a swat on WILEY'S rear.*)

WILEY: (*Up and rubbing his bottom*) Owwweeeee. That sure is my Mammy. No Hairy Man kin hit that hard.

MAMMY: Wiley, you was just havin' a bad dream.

WILEY: I saw him. I saw the Hairy Man and he was comin' for me. I was trying to run but I couldn't, and there I was starin' right into the Hairy Man's hairy eye ball.

MAMMY: You ain't got no cause to fear. There ain't no Hairy Man not nowheres near.

WILEY: But I saw Him! I saw his hairy hands, and his hairy teeth and his horrible hairy breath.

MAMMY: You know your Mammy's got more magic than any old Hairy Man.

WILEY: But he done got my Pappy and . . .

MAMMY: Looks like I gots to do a magic spell to get that Hairy Man outta your head.

(*MAMMY assumes the conjure position and holds WILEY's head between her hands. CHORUS makes "conjure sounds."*)

MAMMY: (*Conjuring*) Hairy Man, Hairy Man, git outta his head. Go scare yourself a tree toad instead. Hairy Man, Hairy Man, git outta his eyes. Listen to me while I conjurize. Hairy Man, Hairy Man, git outta his mouth. Git away from here. Go way down south!

(*Pause*)

MAMMY: Well, is he gone?

(*CHORUS IV waves his arms.*)

WILEY: What's that?

MAMMY: Just a shadow on the wall. Sun's comin up that's all.

WILEY: It's the Hairy Man.

MAMMY: I better hurry up the day and get some light in here.

(*MAMMY assumes the conjure position and throws a quick spell.*)

MAMMY: Rumble, Bumble, Snider, Rup. Sun, sun hurry it up!

(*CHORUS I hoists a colored sun up one of the structures and CHORUS II crows like a rooster.*)

WILEY: What's that?

MAMMY: Jest some old rooster.

WILEY: It's the Hairy Man!

MAMMY: (*Conjuring*) Beetle, tweedle, sneedle, sneak. Rooster, rooster shut your beak!

(*CHORUS II stops mid-crow.*)

WILEY: I gonna get my dog and bring him right here in bed with me!

MAMMY: You are gonna do no such thing.

WILEY: But the Hairy Man cain't stand no dogs, everybody knows that.

MAMMY: Wiley, I am the best conjure woman in the whole southwest county. I kin make the sun come up and the moon go down. I kin do spells an' conjures, an' charms, an' chants; I kin cure a cold or heal a wart fifty miles away. But there are two things I cannot do; I cannot get that fear outta your head, and I cannot stand that Dog slobbering up my house!

WILEY: Mammy, how did the Hairy Man git my Pappy?

MAMMY: He just did Wiley.

WILEY: People say my Pappy was a bad man and a no count.

MAMMY: People say.

WILEY: People say he slept while the weeds grew higher than the cotton, that he used to git himself hog drunk and chicken wild, and that he never even spit lessen someone else did it for him.

MAMMY: People say.

WILEY: Was my Pappy a bad man?

MAMMY: (*With respect*) Wiley, he was your Pappy!

WILEY: But people say he'd never cross the Jordan, cause when he died the Hairy Man'd be there waitin' for him. When he fell into the river near Tombigbee they never did find him. They jest heard a big man laughin, across the river.

MAMMY: He done got your Pappy.

CHORUS I and II: Said Mammy, said she . . .

MAMMY: And you better be keerful.

WILEY: Or he's gonna get me.

MAMMY: Now git yourself up and dressed, it is time for breakfast.

WILEY: Do I gotta go to the swamp today?

MAMMY: You have got to build a hound house for that dog of yours.

WILEY: I'm jest gonna sit here and do nothin' jest like my Pappy.

MAMMY: (*Angry*) Wiley, don't you ever say that! Now get yourself up and wash.

(*MAMMY crosses into the kitchen area. WILEY dives back under the covers.*)

WILEY: I'm tired. That Hairy Man scared all the restin' outta me.

MAMMY: Breakfast . . .

(*She conjures a quick off-handed spell.*)

MAMMY: Ashes, embers, soot on my face. Make me right there a fireplace.

(*CHORUS form a fireplace with a cauldron.*)

MAMMY: Wiley, I want to hear feet on that floor and washin' in those ears right now!

WILEY: (*In a gruff voice*) There ain't no Wiley here. He's been ete all up by the Hairy Man.

MAMMY: I ain't foolin'.

WILEY: (*Lumping about*) I tol' you Mammy there ain't no Wiley here. Jest an old ugly Hairy Man with fourteen toes and a bone in his nose.

MAMMY: You get up and put on your clothes!

WILEY: Hairy Man, Hairy Man, comin' through the trees; stampin' and a-squishin' everything he sees.

   (*Realizing what he has just said.*)

WILEY: Hairy Man?

   (*WILEY dives under the covers.*)

MAMMY: What are you doing?

WILEY: (*In a small voice*) I jest skeered myself all over again.

MAMMY: There is only one way to get you outta that bed, and boy you asked for it!

   (*MAMMY storms into WILEY's room and douses him with a wash basin full of water.*)

MAMMY: Now git up!

WILEY: I am up, I'm up, I'm up!!!

   (*MAMMY scrubs him with the cloth.*)

MAMMY: I swear you are the dirtiest boy I ever laid eyes on. Open up them ears. Hold still. Now come eat!

   (*MAMMY returns to the kitchen.*)

MAMMY: Now where was I? Breakfast.

   (*She conjures.*)

MAMMY: Tables and chairs . . . Right over theres . . .

(*CHORUS become table and chairs.*)

MAMMY: (*Conjuring*) Pot, pot, get yourself hot!

(*CHORUS with cauldron make bubbling sounds, WILEY enters kitchen.*)

MAMMY: What do you want to eat this morning?

WILEY: Not much. Jest some flap jacks an' lasses, and taters an' lasses, and biscuits an' lasses, and eggs an' lasses, and catfish an' grits, an' lasses.

(*As he says each one MAMMY scoops some out of the cauldron into a bowl.*)

MAMMY: (*Concerned*) What's the matter Wiley? Ain't you hongry? I never knew you to eat so skimpy.

WILEY: The Hairy Man musta skeered the hongries outta me.

(*WILEY gobbles his food.*)

MAMMY: Don't forget to drink your milk.

WILEY: (*Turning the glass upside down*) There ain't no milk in here.

MAMMY: I forgot.

(*MAMMY wordlessly snaps her fingers and points to WILEY'S glass.*)

WILEY: There still ain't . . . . . ooops.

(*WILEY turns the glass again this time there is milk which spills.*)*

MAMMY: Dumbhead! When I say there's milk, there's milk!

WILEY: Yasum.

(*Pause.*)

---

*A trick glass is used for this; one with a wide lip inside one half of the glass. When you pour this glass on one side nothing comes out, when you pour it from the other the contents spill out. These are available at magic stores.

WILEY: Mammy, I think tomorrow's a better day for goin' to the swamp for wood for my hound house . . . .

MAMMY: No! Today is the day. I told you that. But maybe I ought to teach you a conjure or two to keep you safe from the Hairy Man.

WILEY: You know I ain't no good at conjurin' no way no how.

MAMMY: Wiley, you hesh and come here now.

   (*WILEY crosses to MAMMY.*)

MAMMY: Wiley, you knows I's the best, the best conjure woman in the whole southwest county.

CHORUS II: The best conjure woman in the whole southwest.

   (*MAMMY shoots a look at WILEY.*)

WILEY: I didn't say nothin'.

MAMMY: You are my son and my only child and you are gonna learn. This here's a spell for changin' stickers and prickers and bonkers and briars into rubber so's they cain't hurt you.

WILEY: I cain't learn it.

MAMMY: Yes you can. It jest goes . . "Chip chop, chum, blubber. Turn this tree trunk into rubber."

WILEY: (*Carelessly*) Chip, champ, chomp, grubber. Blubber, drubber scrubber, flubber . . .

MAMMY: (*Furious*) Wiley! You gotta listen to the conjure words, cause when they are outta your mouth there is no takin' them back!

WILEY: But I cain't keep it all in my head. Powders, 'n potions, 'n magic, 'n charms. An' raisin' the spirits, 'n wavin' my arms. An' screechin' an' stampin', an' mutterin' low! I jest cain't do it, the answer is no!

MAMMY: Well someday you gotta learn.

WILEY: Well someday ain't today!

MAMMY: You better get yourself goin' ya hear? If'n you take your hound Dog you got nothin' to fear.

WILEY: Cause the Hairy Man sure cain't stand no Dogs . . .

MAMMY: Everybody knows that.

(*WILEY turns to go and MAMMY stops him.*)

MAMMY: Take this here bag. It's got some magic on it. It'll catch up the wind and hold it for you till you let it go.

WILEY: (*Taking the bag*) Thanks. Mammy.

(*WILEY turns to go.*)

MAMMY: And Wiley, take some of this here powder. Jest a pinch will make every livin' creature your friend . . . except the Hairy Man.

WILEY: (*Taking the powder*) Thanks Mammy.

(*WILEY turns to go.*)

MAMMY: And Wiley? You be sure to take your hound Dog.

WILEY: Yasum . . . YASUM!

(*WILEY crosses out of the house and MAMMY watches.*)

MAMMY: (*Muttering to herself*) He done got his Pappy.

CHORUS I and II: Said Mammy, said she . . .

MAMMY: . . . And he better be keerful . . .

WILEY: Or he's gonna get me.

(*As WILEY crosses down the house disappears. MAMMY exits and CHORUS comes to life.*)

CHORUS IV: So Wiley . . .

CHORUS II and III: Wherever he goes . . .

ORUS I: Takes his Dog.

LEY: (*Calling*) Dog!

ORUS IV: Cause the Hairy Man sure cain't stand no dogs . . .

CHORUS I: Everybody knows that. Everybody knows that.

WILEY whistles and DOG enters in a bound. He is extremely fierce looking but he moves with the lumbering playfullness of an overgrown puppy. He looks about ready to spring and then flops over asleep. WILEY laughs.)

WILEY: Hey there, Dog, what'cha doing there sleeping in the sun? Come on boy, let's have some fun.

(*DOG opens one eye and rolls over.*)

WILEY: I know what'll get you.

(*WILEY creeps up beside DOG and meows, DOG leaps up wide awake and growls, then he licks WILEY'S face.*)

WILEY: Good Dog, O.K. Boy, fetch . . .

(*WILEY throws a stick, DOG watches it go and sprawls out asleep.*)

WILEY: DOG? Hey, Boy, I know what let's do. I gotta game for you. Now, I'm going to hold my breath for a full minute and hold real, real still; and you gotta come over here and try to make me move. You gotta make me flinch, or move, or blink, or somethin'. If you do I'll give you something to eat.

(*At this promise DOG is interested. WILEY takes a deep breath and strikes a pose. DOG snifs him, tugs at his pants, barks at him, and finally climbs up and stands balancing his paws on WILEY'S shoulders and slobbers in his face. WILEY surpresses a smile and finally exhales. They laugh and play.*)

WILEY: I won! You didn't make me flinch, or move, or blink, or nothin'. Now, Dog, Mammy says we gotta go to the swamp and cut down a tree. 'Cause I'm gonna make you a hound house. But we gotta be careful of the Hairy Man, see! 'Cause he done got my pappy and he's tryin' to get me! Come on you old hound DOG!

(*DOG barks twice and they set off.*)

CHORUS IV: So Wiley . . .

CHORUS ALL: He takes up his axe. And he goes to the swamp, but he don't leave tracks. 'Cause the Hairy Man's hiding somewhere you see. And he done got his pappy . . .

WILEY: . . . and he's tryin' to get me.

CHORUS: But the Hairy Man sure cain't stand no Dogs . . . Everybody knows that. Everybody knows that. Everybody knows that.

(*On this line the CHORUS become the swamp, WILEY and DOG make their way cautiously. CHORUS make swamp sounds.*)

WILEY: Here we are, Dog, the deepest part of the swamp. Now this here's a mightly dangerous place cause the Hairy Man lives somewhere's near and everything's magic . . . Hairy Man magic. You stay close . . . Come on Boy . . .

(*Swamp sounds are louder and become words.*)

CHORUS I: Oh the sun never shines . . .

CHORUS II: . . . And the wind never blows,

CHORUS III: And the mud turns to slime,

CHORUS IV: The deeper you goes.

(*CHORUS becomes mud which oozes around WILEY'S feet and makes a slurping sound as he moves through it.*)

WILEY: Gulp.

DOG: Gulp.

CHORUS I and III: And the branches reach, And the vines twine around,

(*CHORUS become reaching branches and vines.*)

CHORUS IV: And the stumps and the stickers stick up through the ground.

(CHORUS becomes a huge sticker bush.)

WILEY: Lookee there DOG! I never seen that sticker bush there before. It must be Hairy Man magic. Maybe it's a trap! We gotta be keerful and jest kinda wiggle in and squiggle out. Now look here Dog and I'll show you, cause I am the best at wigglin' and squigglin' in the whole southwest county.

(DOG zips right through the bush.)

WILEY: Hey that's not the right way! You gotta kinda squinch yourself down and . . .

(DOG zips through again as WILEY tries to squeeze through the sticker bush. CHORUS pinch him and stick him with the briars.)

WILEY: Owwwww oweeeeee Owwwwweee Ouch, Ouch, Ouch!

(DOG bounds in and pulls WILEY through.)

WILEY: I made it. Hairy Man didn't get me, no siree. But Dog, I gotta bottom full of briars. Oww, ow, ow, Ouch.

(DOG helps WILEY pull out the stickers. CHORUS dissolves sticker bush.)

CHORUS: Shhhh, shhh, shhh, shhh. The Hairy Man listens and the Hairy Man sees; He's got eyes in the bushes and ears in the trees . . .

(WILEY and DOG move on.)

CHORUS: Cause the skeeters and the flies, is all his spies. And they's setting up a trap for sure, for sure. So's you better watch your step for sure.

(CHORUS becomes a bubbling pool of quicksand.)

WILEY: Dog! Don't move. Lookee there! That's a pool of quicksand. That's Hairy Man magic for sure and we gotta be keerful elsewise it'll swaller us up for sure.

(DOG growls at the quick sand.)

WILEY: We got to leap-frog ourselves right over it. Now git down and . . .

(DOG crouches and WILEY leap-frogs; they do it several times and DOG finally leap-frogs over the quicksand. WILEY is still on the other side.)

WILEY: Dog, that ain't no good. Now you gotta come back so's I kin leap frog over you.

(DOG leaps over the pool and he and WILEY repeat the leap frogging until WILEY leap-frogs over the quicksand. WILEY looks puzzled because DOG is on the other side.)

WILEY: Now I gotta come back so's you kin leap-frog over me.

(WILEY tries to leap over the quicksand but falls a bit short and lands in it.)

WILEY: Ooooops.

(He starts to sink.)

WILEY: Dog, Dog! I'm sinkin'! Help! The Hairy Man's got me. Help!

(DOG bounds over the pool and leans forward. WILEY takes hold of his collar and CHORUS slowly rolls away as if WILEY is being pulled out. CHORUS moves off and forms the tree.)

WILEY: Good Dog! Good Boy! That stuff almost swallered me up. Now let's go and find ourselves a tree.

(CHORUS makes "Hairy Man" sounds heard in the nightmare.)

CHORUS I and IV: There's some mighty scarey sounds, When the Hairy Man's around.

WILEY: Gulp!

DOG: Gulp!

WILEY: *(Coming upon the tree)* Hey Dog, what do you see? Ain't that there the finest tree you ever laid eyes on? Now you stay right there and don't move; 'cause when I start swinging them chips is gonna fly.

("Hairy Man" sounds are louder. WILEY sizes up the tree.)

WILEY: This here's a good tree. Jest look at that trunk.

(*From off stage a huge bone tied to a string is thrown directly in front of DOG. DOG watches as the bone is slowly pulled off stage. WILEY sees none of this, he has his back to DOG.*)

WILEY: Now, Dog, you stay right here; 'cause as long as you do we ain't gonna have no trouble with the Hairy Man.

(*Bone is thrown on again. DOG sniffs it but does not move.*)

WILEY: 'Cause the Hairy Man sure cain't stand no dogs. Everybody knows that.

(*Bone is thrown on a third time, this time bonking DOG on the head. DOG barks loudly and bone zips off. DOG bounds off after it.*)

WILEY: (*Turning*) Hey, Come back . . . Hound Dog don't chase no bones. CHASE NO BONES? Oh me oh my I never did see no bone in the sky. The Hairy Man must be nearby.

(*WILEY goes back to the tree.*)

CHORUS I: Keerful, Wiley . . .

(*WILEY chops.*)

CHORUS: Whack.

(*WILEY lifts axe.*)

CHORUS II: Look out, Wiley.

(*WILEY chops.*)

CHORUS: Whack.

(*WILEY lifts axe.*)

CHORUS III and IV: Lookee there, Wiley.

(*WILEY turns slowly.*)

CHORUS: (*Starting at a whisper and building*) Stampin', Stompin', Comin' through the trees, Shufflin' through the swamp grass, Blowin' in the breeze. Bounding, Pounding, Fast as he can, What did Wiley see? . . . . He saw the HAIRY MAN!

(*The HAIRY MAN enters slowly stalking WILEY. WILEY yelps and climbs the tree.*)

WILEY: (*Terrified*) THE HAIRY MAN?

CHORUS: The Hairy Man! (*Echoing*) Hairy Man . . Hairy Man . . Hairy Man . . Hairy Man.

(*CHORUS makes "Hairy Man" sounds.*)

(*HAIRY MAN slowly approaches the tree where WILEY tries to hide.*)

CHORUS I: (*Wailing*) Wiiiiiiley . .

HAIRY MAN: (*Echoing*) Wiiiiiiley.

WILEY: You get away from me Hairy Man. You go on. I'll sic my hound Dog on you.

HAIRY MAN: Wiley.

WILEY: Hairy Man, I tol' you . . . Hound DOG!!! Here, DOG!

HAIRY MAN: There ain't no hound Dog not nowhere's here.

WILEY: Say's you Hairy Man, I know he's near.

HAIRY MAN: He's chasin' my magic miles from here.

WILEY: (*Desperate*) HOUND DOG!

HAIRY MAN: What'cha doin' up in that tree?

WILEY: Climbin'.

HAIRY MAN: But it's only me.

WILEY: I know, that's why I'm climbin'.

HAIRY MAN: Why don't'cha come home with me for supper.

WILEY: I ain't even had lunch yet.

HAIRY MAN: Neither have I Wiley . . .

WILEY: My Mammy she tol' me don't you never have no conversation with no Hairy Man. So you get away from here.

HAIRY MAN: If you come on down I'll give you a nice piece of sugar cane.

WILEY: If'n you is so hongry you eat it yourself.

HAIRY MAN: I am tryin' to be nice Wiley, but you is gonna get me riled. If'n you don't come down, I is comin' up.

WILEY: You cain't, cause you got the ugliest, slimiest, no tree climbinest feet in the whole county.

HAIRY MAN: (*Wiggling his feet in the air*) Why don't you come down for a closer look?

WILEY: I don't need no closer look. I kin smell 'em all the way up here. P. U.! Hairy Man, you got smelly feet.

HAIRY MAN: (*Angry*) WILEY! I'm gonna cast a spell on this tree, boy, gonna be your end.

WILEY: No siree, this tree's my friend.

HAIRY MAN: Look out Wiley! There are snakes in that tree.

WILEY: No there ain't.

HAIRY MAN: There is now.

(*HAIRY MAN shakes all over and throws a wild conjure at the tree.*)

HAIRY MAN: I shakes, I shakes, That tree's full of snakes.

(*CHORUS become snakes and wind all over WILEY.*)

WILEY: Oh No, OOOOOOOH NOOOOOO! Oh snakes, nice snakes. Hey, Mammy's powder!

(*WILEY takes the powder and blows it on the snakes.*)

WILEY: Snakes, snakes be my friend. Sic HIM.

(*WILEY pats the snakes on the head, points to the HAIRY MAN. They turn and hiss at the HAIRY MAN.*)

WILEY: Dumb ole Hairy Man, even snakes like me better'n you.

HAIRY MAN: GO WAY snakes! Now I'll show you not to fool with the Hairy Man.

(*HAIRY MAN throws himself into another wild conjure.*)

HAIRY MAN: Branches, Branches, Brittle as ice. Snap in two when I clap twice.

(*HAIRY MAN claps twice. Branches snap under WILEY; but he manages to catch himself.*)

HAIRY MAN: I got you WILEY!

WILEY: Oh no you don't.

HAIRY MAN: Then I'll blow you out.

(*He conjures.*)

HAIRY MAN: Wind, wind, rise and howl. Make those branches creak and growl.

(*A huge wind blows the tree. CHORUS make the branches bend, WILEY grabs up the bag.*)

WILEY: Mammy's WIND BAG!! Bag, bag, do your charm. Keep me, keep me safe from harm.

(*WILEY opens the bag. It inflates as the wind sound dies down.*)

WILEY: Hairy Man, I always knew you were a wind bag. How do you like this here?

(*WILEY opens the bag. It deflates. CHORUS makes a rushing sound. The HAIRY MAN is blown over.*)

WILEY: Hairy Man, I am as safe as I kin be; sitting here in this old tree.

HAIRY MAN: (*Recovering*) Wiley! Now I am gonna do something terrible.

WILEY: You ain't so scarey now.

(*HAIRY MAN spies the axe, and picks it up, brandishing it.*)

HAIRY MAN: I AIN'T?

WILEY: OH, you is, you is, you is, you is!

HAIRY MAN: (*Advancing*) Lookee here what I found.

WILEY: Gulp.

HAIRY MAN: Now I am gonna chop you to the ground.

(*HAIRY MAN starts chopping slowly. As he does the tree shakes.*)

WILEY: Ohhhhh Nooooo!

CHORUS: Chop.

WILEY: Ohhh! Mammy tried to teach me a conjure for this.

CHORUS: Chop.

WILEY: What are the words, the words, the words?

CHORUS: Chop.

WILEY: Chip, yes . . . . chip, chip chop. Chip chop, chip chop.

CHORUS: Chop.

WILEY: Chip chop chump, that's it . . . Chip chop chump . . .

CHORUS: Chop.

WILEY: Chip, chop, chump, blubber. Turn this tree trunk into rubber.

CHORUS: BOINK.

WILEY: Chip, chop, chump, blubber. Turn this tree trunk into rubber.

CHORUS: BOINK.

(*On the "Boink", the HAIRY MAN'S axe bounces off the tree. HAIRY MAN speeds up chopping. WILEY speeds up chanting.*)

WILEY: Chip, chop, chump, blubber. Turn this tree trunk into rubber. Chip, chop, chump, blubber. Turn this tree trunk into rubber. Chip, chop, chump, blubber. Turn this tree trunk into rubber. Chip, Chop, chump, blubber. Turn this tree trunk into rubber.

CHORUS: Boink, Boink, Boink, Boink, Boink.

(*HAIRY MAN falls exhausted, but still chopping. DOG is heard barking in the distance.*)

WILEY: HOUND DOG!!!

HAIRY MAN: (*Gasping*) W . . . W . . . Wiley, don't you call no . . .

WILEY: DOG.

(*DOG'S barking gets closer.*)

WILEY: Run, Hairy Man. My Dog's gonna bite you like you never been bit before.

HAIRY MAN: I cain't stand no DOGS.

WILEY: (*Delighted*) Everybody know that . . . DOG.

(*DOG enters in a bound. HAIRY MAN grabs the axe. There is a moment of face to face confrontation. HAIRY MAN advances.*)

WILEY: Git him DOG. Git him.

(*They circle each other. CHORUS III slowly rolls out of the tree and lies down in back of the HAIRY MAN.*)

WILEY: Hairy Man. Look out for that old LOG behind you. You is about to fall over it.

HAIRY MAN: Hesh up, Wiley, I ain't fallin' for no dumb tricks.

WILEY: You is about to, Hairy Man.

HAIRY MAN: Yeeeeeowwwww.

(*HAIRY MAN falls over the log, drops the axe and exits at a run chased by DOG. WILEY comes down.*)

WILEY: Git him, Dog, Get him.

HAIRY MAN: (*Off stage*) Yeeeeeooowwwww.

(*DOG returns with tuft of hair.*)

WILEY: You alright DOG? Good Boy, Thank you Boy. We got him that time, but he'll be back. Let's go see Mammy, she'll know what to do. Oh Dog, Oh Boy, she's jest got to.

CHORUS: Cause when the Hairy Man gets mad . . . THAT'S BAD.

(*MAMMY'S HOUSE*)

(*WILEY and DOG run back through the swamp to the house. CHORUS sets up house as before. MAMMY enters with cauldron and gazes into it intently.*)

WILEY: (*Outside the house*) Dog, you go down to the hen house and you make sure that Hairy Man ain't nowhere's near here.

(*DOG exits, barking. WILEY enters house.*)

WILEY: Mammy? Mammy! Come here! You gotta help me Mammy!

MAMMY: Don't hurry me boy, I'm comin'.

WILEY: (*Excited*) He tried! He tried! He got me up a tree. He done got my Pappy and he's gonna . . . .

MAMMY: No he ain't, Wiley!

WILEY: He came for me. I saw his hairy eyes, and his hairy teeth, and his horrible hairy feet. So I climbed a tree and there he was lookin' up at me.

MAMMY: (*Quietly*) I know, Wiley.

WILEY: (*Acting it out*) And HE said . . . "Wiley!" and I said . . . "Hairy Man, you better leave me alone." And HE said . . . "Wiley!"

MAMMY: I know, Wiley.

WILEY: Oh, it was terrible, terrible. But I remembered the conjure and . . . .

MAMMY: I know, Wiley.

WILEY: How do you know lessen I tell you?

MAMMY: I looked in my conjure pot and saw the whole thing. Wiley, we got trouble.

CHORUS I: Cause when the Hairy Man gets mad . . .

CHORUS IV: That's Bad!

WILEY: Mammy! Why don't you do a conjure to turn the Hairy Man into a mosquito and I'll . . . .

   (*CHORUS makes a buzzing sound and WILEY slaps an imaginary insect.*)

WILEY: No more Hairy Man!

MAMMY: You think the Hairy Man would be dumb enough to let you squish him like that?

WILEY: (*Flicking it off his hand*) Nope.

MAMMY: We gotta be smart to fool the Hairy Man.

WILEY: We are in a mess of trouble . . . I know, why don't you conjure up a big pit filled with slimey grimies and the Hairy Man'll fall in and . . .

MAMMY: Wiley, I cain't conjure up a way to protect you from the Hairy Man.

WILEY: But my Dog! I'll get my Dog and he'll . . . Dog! Dog!

MAMMY: Wiley! There ain't no magic nor no dog strong enough to keep you safe every every minute. You gotta learn how to do it yourself.

WILEY: But that ain't fair. He's bigger than me.

MAMMY: Yep.

WILEY: What are we gonna do?

MAMMY: I am gonna try just once more to teach you how to conjure. Boy, you gotta fight magic with magic!

WILEY: I cain't.

MAMMY: Hesh up and pay attention. You gotta listen to what I tell you and you gotta say just what I say, cause once the conjure words is spoke they's spoke forever. Now stand here like this and put your feet apart . . . .

WILEY: Apart from what?

MAMMY: From each other! Now concentrate! Hard!

   (*WILEY closes his eyes and squinches up his face.*)

MAMMY: (*Exasperated*) Open your eyes.

WILEY: I'm concentrating, Mammy. I'm concentrating.

MAMMY: How are you gonna see what I'm doin' lessen you got your eyes open?

   (*WILEY opens his eyes and stares.*)

MAMMY: Now this is jest to practice . . . say . . . Snagle Blume . . .

   (*MAMMY makes small controlled circles with her hands as she says the magic words.*)

WILEY: (*Jumping up and down and making wild circles*) SNAGLE BLOOOO.

MAMMY: What you jumpin' around like a tree toad for? Anyone would hear you conjuring fifty miles away! Now a conjure is a QUIET thing! Snagle Blume.

WILEY: (*Whispering and making microscopic circles*) Sngl Blm.

MAMMY: You couldn't conjure up a hiccup with that. Now start small and grow gradual.

WILEY: (*Following her but mixing up the words*) Snnoooooooble gluuuume . . . snubble Bloooooom . . . Snooooo gleeeeee Bloooooom . . . . Snooooooo Gooooo Bloooooo. Snooooow Gooooooo Blooooow. Snow go Blooooooooow.

(*At the first mention of the words "Snow go blow" CHORUS makes wind sounds and begin building a snow storm. As WILEY chants the storm grows and snow starts falling and blowing.*)

WILEY: Snooooooow Gooooooo Blooooooow . . . Snooooow Goooooooo Blooow. Mammy it's getting cold in here. Snoooo Gooooo Blooooooow.

(*MAMMY looks up and sees what is going on.*)

MAMMY: Wiley! It's snowing in here!

WILEY: Snooooooowwww Gooooooo Blooooooow.

MAMMY: You got the words all mixed up!

WILEY: Snoooooow Gooooo Blooooww.

MAMMY: (*Clapping her hand over his mouth*) Stop it!

WILEY: (*Delighted*) Look what I did!

MAMMY: I know, Dumbhead, now I gotta get rid of it!

WILEY: But I did it all by myself!

MAMMY: (*Conjuring*) Snow Goooo Way! Snow Goooo Way! And don't come back no other day!

(*Storm stops instantly.*)

WILEY: That was fun. I want to do it again.

MAMMY: Oh no you don't!

WILEY: Maybe we could freeze the Hairy Man.

MAMMY: Ain't we got trouble enough without having snow storms in the house? My Son, my son! The son of the best conjure woman in the whole southwest county can't even do a simple conjure. What can you do?

WILEY: Well . . . I kin wiggle in and squiggle out of all sorts of places. I kin leap frog better'n the tree toads, AND I kin hold my breath for a full minute and not even flinch, or move, or blink, or nothing!

MAMMY: That ain't gonna help you with the Hairy Man. That's a conjure man, and when you face to face with him, you better have magic working for you.

WILEY: What are we gonna do?

MAMMY: (*Seriously*) There is only one thing we can do. We've tried everything else.

WILEY: (*Stunned*) You mean?

MAMMY: Yes Wiley, Git . . .

CHORUS: (*Whispering*) The BOOK!

WILEY: (*In awe*) The book?

(*MAMMY nods and they ceremoniously move to a trap in the floor.*)

CHORUS: Oh the screech owl howled . . .

CHORUS II: The sun went beneath a cloud.

CHORUS III: And the breeze in the trees . . .

CHORUS IV: . . . Whispered low.

CHORUS: Cause when Mammy takes a look, In the magic book, Then there's trouble up ahead for sure, for sure. Wiley better stay in bed for sure.

(*MAMMY and WILEY remove the Book from the trap and carry it to the center of the room.*)

MAMMY: The last thing my Mammy ever said to me was "Mammy, don't you never use this book lessen you got big trouble." And Wiley, we got big trouble.

(*CHORUS makes magic sounds.*)

MAMMY: (*Turning pages carefully*) Let's see now . . . B . . . Boogy Men, no we ain't got no Boogy Men here . . . . YET! Devils . . . no not Devils . . . E . . . Ear wax.

(*MAMMY looks in WILEY'S ears.*)

MAMMY: I'll get to that later . . . Hmmmmm Ghosts . . . Weirwolf . . . . whoops I went too far . . . H . . . Here we are . . . Hellfire . . . Hairy Man!

WILEY: That sure is HIM!

MAMMY: Hairy Man . . .

WILEY: (*Sneezing all over the page*) Achoooooooooo!

MAMMY: (*Furious*) Dumbhead! You spit all over Hunchback! You cain't hardly read it no more.

(*MAMMY wipes the book with her sleeve and continues reading.*)

MAMMY: "You cain't out magic the Hairy Man when he's mad . . . too bad."

WILEY: Gulp.

MAMMY: "You cain't out fight him."

CHORUS: Nope.

MAMMY: "You cain't out lick him."

CHORUS: Nope.

MAMMY: "You cain't out bite him."

CHORUS: Nope.

MAMMY: "You cain't out kick him."

CHORUS: Nope.

MAMMY: "You cain't out run him,"

CHORUS: Nope.

MAMMY: "And you cain't out fun him."

CHORUS: Nope.

MAMMY: But you CAN . . .

CHORUS: Ahhhhhhhh!

MAMMY: Out fox him.

WILEY: I'll go and get a fox.

MAMMY: That ain't what it is talking about. Sit down, there's more. "If you can trick the Hairy Man three times in a row he'll go away and never bother you no more . . . Good Luck" . . . Now I know just what to do!

   (*MAMMY puts the book away.*)

MAMMY: Wiley, What'cha going to do the next time you see the Hairy Man?

WILEY: I'm gonna run and climb the biggest tree I can find.

MAMMY: Oh no you ain't.

WILEY: Oh yes I am!

MAMMY: You are gonna stay right there on the ground and say "Hello, Hairy Man."

WILEY: Oh no I ain't.

MAMMY: Oh yes you are. And then you are gonna look him right in the eye and say "What you got in that croaker sack?"

WILEY: And then I'm gonna run.

MAMMY: Oh no you ain't! Wiley, you gotta trick him three times and you cain't do that if'n you keep running away!

WILEY: I cain't trick him if'n I'm dead!

MAMMY: That ain't gonna happen, Wiley. Not if'n you face to face with him and trick him.

WILEY: But how?

MAMMY: Listen . . .

    (*MAMMY whispers to WILEY and CHORUS makes whispering sounds.*)

MAMMY: You understand?

WILEY: Yasum. I think so.

MAMMY: Remember you gotta trick him three times. Now let me hear you say "Hello Hairy Man."

WILEY: (*Weakly*) Hello Hairy Man.

MAMMY: STRONGER! You gotta be fierce! You gotta show no fear.

WILEY: (*Stronger*) Hello Hairy Man.

MAMMY: Come on boy, Stronger! Louder!

WILEY: (*Flexing his muscles*) Hello Hairy Man!

MAMMY: GOOD! Now I'll pretend to be the Hairy Man and you come say "Hello."

WILEY: Hello Hairy Man. HELLO HAIRY MAN. HELLO HAIRY MAN!

MAMMY: (*Sneaking up behind*) Hello Wiley!

WILEY: (*Crumbling in terror*) Ahhhhhhhhhhh!

MAMMY: I sure do hope that Hairy Man is dumber than you are.

WILEY: I cain't do it.

MAMMY: Yes you can, and I don't want to hear no never mind! Now go get a rope.

WILEY: A rope? Do I gotta tie up the Hairy Man?

MAMMY: No, your Dog.

WILEY: Oh, my Dog . . .

(*Dawns on him.*)

WILEY: MY DOG?

MAMMY: Yep.

WILEY: But Mammy, cain't I take him with me? The Hairy Man cain't stand no dogs. Everybody knows that!

MAMMY: That Hairy Man won't come anywhere near you if you got that Dog. Wiley you gotta seek out the Hairy Man. You are hunting him now, boy! You gotta face to face and trick him three times just like I told you.

WILEY: But my Dog . . .

MAMMY: Tie him up good and tight.

WILEY: Yasum.

MAMMY: And Wiley, be keerful.

WILEY: Yasum.

MAMMY: You can do it Wiley . . .

WILEY: (*Not so sure*) Yasum.

(*WILEY takes a piece of rope, shivers, looks back, and crosses down.*)

MAMMY: (*Looking after him*) Leastwise I hope you can.

WILEY: Hello Hairy Man. Hello Hairy Man. Hello Hairy Man . . . Hello Hairy Man . . . Hello . . .

(*MAMMY exits and the scene shifts to the swamp. CHORUS moves to Swamp positions and makes swamp sounds. As WILEY passes through the swamp they reach for him menacingly.*)

(*THE SWAMP*)

CHORUS I: Oh the Hairy Man listens . . .

CHORUS II: . . . And the Hairy Man sees.

CHORUS III: He's got eyes in the bushes . . .

CHORUS IV: . . . . And ears in the trees . . .

CHORUS ALL: There's some mighty scary sounds, 'cause the Hairy Man's around.

(*CHORUS form themselves into the tree.*)

WILEY: Hello Hairy Man . . . Hello . . . Gulp.

CHORUS I: Keerful, Wiley.

WILEY: Gulp.

CHORUS II: Look out, Wiley.

WILEY: Gulp.

CHORUS III and IV: Lookee there, Wiley . . .

(*CHORUS point to a spot where the HAIRY MAN enters slowly with his croaker sack.*)

CHORUS: Stampin', Stompin', Comin' through the trees, Shufflin' through the swamp grass, Blowin' in the breeze. Bounding, Pounding, Fast as he can, What did Wiley see?

CHORUS IV: He saw the Hairy Man!

WILEY: The Hairy Man?

HAIRY MAN: The Hairy Man!

CHORUS: Hairy Man, Hairy Man, Hairy Man, Hairy Man.

(*WILEY tries to climb the tree but CHORUS pushes him back to the ground.*)

WILEY: (*High and squeeky*) H . . h . . hello, Hairy Man.

HAIRY MAN: (*Grinning*) Well, Hello Wiley.

WILEY: Hello, Hairy Man.

HAIRY MAN: I said, Hello Wiley.

WILEY: Uhhhhh Hello Hairy Man.

HAIRY MAN: Cain't you say nothin' but "Hello Hairy Man?"

WILEY: What you got in that croaker sack?

HAIRY MAN: I ain't got nothin' . . . yet! I aims to carry home my supper in it.

WILEY and CHORUS: Gulp!

WILEY: Hairy Man, my Mammy says she is the best at castin' spells in the whole southwest county.

HAIRY MAN: Your Mammy is a gabby woman.

WILEY: My Mammy says you's a gabby Hairy Man.

HAIRY MAN: I is the best at conjuring in the whole southwest.

WILEY: P . . . P . . . Prove it! My mammy she can turn herself into something she ain't.

HAIRY MAN: Shoot, that ain't nothin'.

WILEY: I reckon you cain't.

HAIRY MAN: I reckon I can.

WILEY: You cain't!

HAIRY MAN: I can!

WILEY: Cain't!

HAIRY MAN: CAN! I bet your Mammy cain't change herself into no Alligator! Ahhhhhhhhhhhhliiiiiiigaaaaaator.

(HAIRY MAN makes a dreadful hissing roar and throws himself into a conjure. CHORUS join him in wild gesticulations and finally throw themselves to the ground and form themselves into a gigantic Alligator with huge crude snapping jaws. They advance on WILEY.)

WILEY: *(Bravado)* Ohhh, That ain't much.

(The jaws snap at him.)

WILEY: My . . . mmmmm . . . My mammy does that all the time. That's how she chops kindlin'.

(WILEY tosses a stick into the Alligator's mouth and snaps the stick.)

(CHORUS and HAIRY MAN come out of the conjure and return to their own forms.)

HAIRY MAN: What do you mean that ain't no good?

WILEY: My mammy kin do that easy.

HAIRY MAN: You jest tell me something your Mammy cain't do and by durn I'll do it!

WILEY: There is jest one thing, Hairy Man, try as she will my Mammy ain't never changed herself into something smaller than she is.

HAIRY MAN: She ain't?

WILEY: No she ain't and I reckon you cain't neither. I reckon you cain't change yourself into no . . . Bat.

HAIRY MAN: Jest you watch. Baaaaaaaaaaatttttt. Baaaaaaaaaaattttttt.

(HAIRY MAN assumes conjure position and bellows. CHORUS form a tight circle around him and all sink down as small as possible. There is a puff of smoke and the CHORUS fall away and a Bat, held by one CHORUS

member on a pole and string flies out of the group. WILEY reaches and catches the Bat in his hat and stuffs the Bat into the Hairy Man's croaker sack.)

WILEY: I got you Hairy Man! I'm gonna throw you in the river!

(WILEY runs down stage and tosses the sack off and there is a splash.)

WILEY: I fooled you Hairy Man! I fooled you one time! Two more times and you'll leave me alone. Good–bye Hairy Man. So long Hairy Man!

(CHORUS makes "Hairy Man" sounds.)

CHORUS I: Keerful Wiley.

WILEY: Good bye Hairy Man.

CHORUS II: Look Out Wiley.

WILEY: So long Hairy Man.

CHORUS III and IV: Lookee there Wiley.

(WILEY turns in disbelief.)

CHORUS: (*Whispering*) Stampin', Stompin', Comin' through the trees, Shufflin' through the swamp grass, Blowin' in the breeze. Bounding, Pounding, Fast as he can, What did Wiley see?

(HAIRY MAN enters swinging from a vine.)

HAIRY MAN: He saw the Hairy Man!

WILEY: The Hairy Man?????

HAIRY MAN: (*On the backswing*) The Hairy Man.

(WILEY climbs the tree frantically.)

WILEY: HOW did you get outta that croaker sack?

HAIRY MAN: I turned myself into a cyclone and blewed myself out!

WILEY: What are you gonna do now, Hairy Man?

HAIRY MAN: Why Wiley, I am plum tuckered out. So I am gonna sit right down here till your belly gets the hongry grombles and you fall outta that tree. Wiley there ain't nothin' that can save you now, not your Mammy and not your Dog.

WILEY: (*Gets an idea*) I still says that my Mammy is better at conjurin' than you.

HAIRY MAN: No she ain't.

WILEY: After all you did fail the test.

HAIRY MAN: I turned myself into a bat jest like you said.

WILEY: Did not. That bat was much too pretty to be you.

HAIRY MAN: Were not.

WILEY: Were too.

HAIRY MAN: Not!

WILEY: Too!

HAIRY MAN: Wiley you gonna get me riled.

WILEY: I bet you cain't take a thing that's really here and make that thing plum disappear.

HAIRY MAN: I can!

(*Tree toad starts croaking.*)

HAIRY MAN: You see that tree toad? GONE!

(*Sound stops mid-croak.*)

WILEY: I didn't see no tree toad! You is cheatin'.

HAIRY MAN: Well take a look at your hat! . . . GONE!

(*CHORUS snatches WILEY'S hat.*)

WILEY: (*Lamely*) What hat? I wasn't wearin' no hat. Hairy Man you cain't do it.

HAIRY MAN: (*Throwing a tantrum*) I can! I can! I can! I can!

WILEY: You see this rope round my pants? I know it's here! Make this rope disappear!

HAIRY MAN: I kin make all the rope in the whole county disappear; cause this is my county and what I say goes!

(*HAIRY MAN conjures.*)

HAIRY MAN: Rope, rope, Wherever you are. Go away I don't know whar. Rope disappear, git away from here!

WILEY: I reckon that means rope holdin' pants up?

HAIRY MAN: I said All rope!

(*WILEY'S pants fall down.*)

WILEY: I reckon that means rope danglin' buckets in wells?

HAIRY MAN: I said ALL rope!

(*CHORUS drops a bucket.*)

WILEY: I reckon that includes ropes that ties DOGS up?

HAIRY MAN: I said . . . .

WILEY: I said, I reckon that includes ropes that ties DOGS up?

HAIRY MAN: (*It sinks in*) Uh oh . . . .

WILEY: (*Calling*) Heeeeeeeahhhhh DOG!

(*Off stage we hear DOG barking.*)

WILEY: Run, Hairy Man, or my Dog's gonna bite you again.

(*HAIRY MAN confused runs right into DOG as he enters. DOG stands his ground and growls.*)

HAIRY MAN: I'll get you Wiley, you see if I don't. You tell your Mammy I'm comin' for you!

WILEY: Git him Dog.

(DOG takes off after HAIRY MAN who runs offstage.)

HAIRY MAN: *(Off)* Yeoooooowwwwwww.

(DOG returns with another tuft of Hairy Man hair in his mouth. WILEY scrambles out of the tree and hugs DOG.)

WILEY: We got him! We got him! That's the second time we tricked him Dog! One more time and he'll leave me alone.

(DOG barks happily.)

WILEY: *(Thinks twice)* One more time! Oh Dog, he's comin' for me now!! And it sure is gettin' dark here. We gotta get some help. Now we need MAGIC! We never been in trouble like we's in now! Let's go home!

(WILEY and DOG run home. Scene shifts back to MAMMY'S house. MAMMY enters and sits center stage gazing intently into a candle on a small table.)

(MAMMY'S HOUSE)

(WILEY and DOG enter house area. WILEY stations DOG outside the house.)

WILEY: Now Dog you stay right here and don't move.

(WILEY enters the house and MAMMY does not break her concentration.)

WILEY: *(Panicked)* Mammy! I done it! I fooled the Hairy Man twice! But I cain't fool him again. He's more than mad; he's got fire in his eyeballs and he's spittin' sparks!

(MAMMY does not move.)

MAMMY: *(Quietly)* Hesh Wiley.

WILEY: He's comin' for me!

MAMMY: I know. I kin feel it in my bones.

(*CHORUS makes "magic" sounds.*)

WILEY: Do a spell! Do magic! Conjure up a storm! DO SOME-THING!

MAMMY: I am.

(*CHORUS sounds increase and MAMMY falls into a deep trance.*)

WILEY: Mammy, Mammy? MAMMY! You gone to sleep? Mammy help me!

MAMMY: (*In her trance*) Wiiiiiiley.

WILEY: (*Startled*) Oh My!!!!

MAMMY: Wiley!

CHORUS: Wiley, Wiley, Wiley, Wiley.

MAMMY: Put . . .

CHORUS I: . . . Your . . .

CHORUS II: . . . Dog . . .

CHORUS III: . . . In Your . . .

CHORUS IV: . . . Little Bed . . .

MAMMY: And Cover . . .

CHORUS I: . . . Him Up . . .

CHORUS II: . . . From . . .

CHORUS III: . . . Tail . . .

CHORUS IV: . . . To Head!

WILEY: I sure will Mammy.

(WILEY gets DOG and places him in bed.)

WILEY: Boy, I gotta put you in my bed. I don't know why but Mammy's got a powerful conjure workin'.

(WILEY covers DOG with a sheet.)

WILEY: I done it Mammy, now what do I do?

MAMMY: *(Still in trance)* Get yourself under the table and make yourself as small as you are able.

WILEY: But why, Mammy?

MAMMY: *(Out of the trance)* 'Cause I said so!

(They both duck under the table. CHORUS makes "Hairy Man" sounds.)

CHORUS I: Stampin', Stompin', Comin' through the trees . . .

CHORUS II: He done got your Pappy and he's gonna get you.

CHORUS III: . . . Shufflin' through the swamp grass . . .

CHORUS IV: He done got your Pappy . . .

CHORUS I: . . . Blowin' in the breeze . . .

CHORUS II: . . . and he's gonna get you.

CHORUS ALL: Bounding, Pounding, Fast as he can. What did they see?

(HAIRY MAN enters and comes to the door.)

HAIRY MAN: They saw the Hairy Man. Mammy! I has come for your child!

(He listens.)

HAIRY MAN: I said I has come for your child! And I is comin' IN.

(He makes a rush for the door and finds it is unlocked. He looks cautiously about.)

HAIRY MAN: Wiiiiiiley. There ain't no way out 'ceptin' with me, now. Wiley? Mammy?

WILEY: (*Peeking out*) Snore, Dog, Snore!

(*DOG starts snoring and HAIRY MAN notices the shape in the bed and moves toward it.*)

HAIRY MAN: SO there you are, Wiley. Sleepin' and a dreamin'. Well, boy I is your bad dream come true. And now, I gotcha . . .

(*HAIRY MAN pulls the blanket away and DOG leaps at him snarling. DOG chases him out the door where the Hairy Man throws the blanket over Dog's head and throws a wild conjure.*)

HAIRY MAN: Howl, growl, moan, groan. Turn this hound Dog into stone.

(*DOG freezes mid-attack.*)

HAIRY MAN: I gotcha Dog! That dumb trick was Mammy's idea and it don't count. I'm comin' for Wiley now and there ain't nothing you can do about it.

(*MAMMY and WILEY have not heard this. They come cautiously out of hiding.*)

WILEY: What happened Mammy?

MAMMY: I dunno, but I think we won.

WILEY: (*Looking about*) Dog! Dog? Mammy, where is my Dog?

HAIRY MAN: (*Shouting from outside*) Mammy! I give up. Looks like I lost. Looks like I better go away and never come back. Looks like I gotta find myself a new territory.

MAMMY: (*Not so sure*) Let me hear you say . . . "Mammy you is the best at conjuring in the whole southwest county."

HAIRY MAN: (*Nearly choking*) You is the best at conjuring in the whole southwest . . .

MAMMY: . . . County.

HAIRY MAN: County!

MAMMY: We won Wiley.

WILEY: I dunno . . . Mammy what about my dog?

(*WILEY is looking frantically for DOG while MAMMY is pre-occupied with her success.*)

HAIRY MAN: I know when I am licked, and just to show you, I'm gonna put all my magic right here in this croaker sack. Now you is the best conjure person in the whole county and you is gonna need all the magic you can get.

(*HAIRY MAN puts himself into the sack and chuckles.*)

HAIRY MAN: Good bye Mammy . . . Good bye Wiley . . .

(*HAIRY MAN closes the sack.*)

MAMMY: (*After a pause*) He's gone.

WILEY: You sure?

MAMMY: You heared him say that I'm the best conjure woman in . . .

WILEY: I don't trust him.

MAMMY: I'll show you.

(*She starts for the door.*)

WILEY: Don't go out there!

MAMMY: Oh, Wiley . . . hesh.

(*MAMMY and WILEY slowly go outside. MAMMY goes right for the sack, but WILEY is horrified to see his DOG turned to stone.*)

WILEY: DOG!

MAMMY: (*Looking at the sack*) Now ain't that nice.

WILEY: DOG! Oh No! MAMMY! He turned my Dog to stone.

MAMMY: What?

WILEY: Look at my Dog! Oh No.

MAMMY: Now Wiley it's all right. Now that I got all his magic I kin unconjurize that dog like nothin'.

WILEY: Do it now!

MAMMY: First help me get this inside.

WILEY: No, now!

MAMMY: It's heavy . . . He must'a left me all his magic.

   (*Reluctantly WILEY helps her push the sack into the house as they do so the CHORUS makes "Hairy Man" sounds.*)

MAMMY: Now let's just have a little look-see. I wonder what all this can be.

CHORUS: Guess what Mammy?

   (*She opens the sack and Hairy Man stands up.*)

HAIRY MAN: It's the Hairy Man!

MAMMY and WILEY: The HAIRY MAN???

HAIRY MAN: The Hairy Man! I fooled you Mammy. You ain't no kind of conjure woman. I has come for your child.

MAMMY: Well you ain't getting him.

HAIRY MAN: Says who?

MAMMY: Says me!

   (*MAMMY picks up the book.*)

HAIRY MAN: Oh yeah?

CHORUS: Think ugly things, Hairy Man.

HAIRY MAN: Well s'posen I have a look in this here book.

(*HAIRY MAN lunges for the book.*)

CHORUS: Think fast Mammy.

(*MAMMY tosses the book to WILEY. They toss it several times keeping it away from the HAIRY MAN, who finally intercepts it.*)

MAMMY: You wouldn't do that. Why that's plum underhanded.

HAIRY MAN: Well I's a plum underhanded Hairy Man. How about a "Mammy Whammy?"

(*HAIRY MAN flips open the book and throws a wild conjure.*)

HAIRY MAN: Fliminy, Flaminy . . . Al-a-ca-zaminy . . . Mammy Whammy!

(*MAMMY tries to get away but is frozen in her tracks.*)

WILEY: You cain't do that!

HAIRY MAN: I jest did. Come on now, Wiley . . . come with me!

WILEY: I ain't goin' nowhere till you un-whammy my Mammy!

HAIRY MAN: Wiley!

WILEY: (*Too mad to be scared*) You cheat, Hairy Man! You is one big cheater. You may be bigger'n me and stronger'n me, but you cain't do nothin' without cheating.

HAIRY MAN: Come on, Wiley.

WILEY: I'll fight you, Hairy Man. I'll fight you myself.

HAIRY MAN: You? You's just a kid.

WILEY: Come on, fight me!

HAIRY MAN: (*Toying with him*) O.K. Wiley. I'll give you one chance boy. If you kin git yourself out of that there sticker bush . . .

(*HAIRY MAN conjures the CHORUS into a sticker bush which surrounds WILEY.*)

HAIRY MAN: You kin go free.

WILEY: I can do that! 'Cause if there is one thing that I am good at it is wigglin' in and squigglin' out.

(*WILEY wiggles and squiggles and almost makes it out, but at the last minute the HAIRY MAN throws a sneaky conjure.*)

HAIRY MAN: Stickle him. Prickle him.

(*The sticker bush closes in around WILEY and traps him.*)

WILEY: Owwweeeeeee.

HAIRY MAN: You lose.

WILEY: You did that! You magicked them stickers.

HAIRY MAN: (*All innocence*) I didn't do nothin'. Why I am all the way over here.

WILEY: You cheat, Hairy Man. That weren't no kinda chance.

HAIRY MAN: (*Knowing he has him and playing with him*) Why then I'll give you another chance. If'n you can leap frog,

(*HAIRY MAN conjures the CHORUS into a line of stumps.*)

HAIRY MAN: over all of these stumps . . . I'll let you go.

WILEY: I know I kin do that because I kin leap frog better'n the tree toads.

(*As WILEY leaps over them the HAIRY MAN conjures them higher and higher.*)

HAIRY MAN: Git up . . . Git up . . . Git up . . .

(*WILEY falls.*)

HAIRY MAN: Awww shucks.

WILEY: (*Furious*) You magicked them up. Hairy Man that ain't fair.

HAIRY MAN: (*Grinning*) I never said I was fair, Wiley.

WILEY: (*Desperate*) Hairy Man, you want magic? I'll fight you with magic!

HAIRY MAN: You cain't do no magic.

WILEY: I can too, 'cause I'm the son of the best conjure woman in the whole southwest county.

HAIRY MAN: Come on Wiley.

WILEY: I can . . . I can turn my whole self into . . . STONE, and you cain't make me flinch, or move, or blink, or nothin'.

HAIRY MAN: Come on now Wiley . . .

WILEY: Come and get me Hairy Man.

   (*WILEY throws a desperate but totally fake conjure.*)

WILEY: Eeny, meany, miney, moan . . . Turn my whole self into stone.

   (*WILEY freezes but his expression tells us it is a fake.*)

HAIRY MAN: (*Amused, at first*) Wiley . . . . .

   (*WILEY does not move.*)

HAIRY MAN: I said, Wiley . . .

   (*WILEY does not move.*)

HAIRY MAN: Now cut that out!!! You ain't really . . .

   (*HAIRY MAN does all sorts of things to make WILEY move, much in the same way as the game seen earlier with DOG. He waves his hands in front of his face, pretends to poke his fingers at his eyes, etc.*)

HAIRY MAN: Is you?

   (*HAIRY MAN turns his back on WILEY and we see him gasp for breath but he resumes his pose the moment the HAIRY MAN turns back. Finally the HAIRY MAN walks right up to WILEY and stands with both hands on his shoulders and breathes in his face. WILEY trembles but does not break.*)

HAIRY MAN: (*Breaking away*) Now I'm through foolin' with you. There's just one thing that I can do. A conjure that will unfroze you!

(*WILEY'S face brightens but he does not move.*)

HAIRY MAN: (*Conjuring*) Statue, Statue, Turned to stone. Unfroze you now to flesh and bone.

(*WILEY springs to life and DOG slowly comes out of his spell.*)

WILEY: Wooooooooeeeeeee. Hairy Man, I'm free! I weren't no stone, no way no how. You just unfroze my hound Dog now! Hound DOG!!

HAIRY MAN: Wiley, that ain't fair.

WILEY: Oh yeah! Hound DOG!

(*HOUND DOG enters and HAIRY MAN makes a final lunge for WILEY who dives under his legs and trips him. DOG chomps down on the HAIRY MAN'S hair.*)

HAIRY MAN: Let Go. Let go . . . Let Go . . . .

(*HAIRY MAN pulls away leaving his hair in DOG's mouth. DOG looks slightly astonished.*)

HAIRY MAN: He got my Hairy Hair!

WILEY: You ain't so scarey now. You ain't so hairy now! You is bald. Now disappear, git away from here.

CHORUS: Well the Hairy Man yelled.

(*HAIRY MAN yells.*)

CHORUS: And the Hairy Man raged.

(*HAIRY MAN rages.*)

CHORUS: And the Hairy Man stomped.

(*HAIRY MAN stomps.*)

CHORUS: And the Hairy Man G-nashed his teeth.

(*HAIRY MAN G-nashes his teeth.*)

WILEY: I said GIT!

(*HAIRY MAN storms out followed by DOG. Mammy becomes unconjurized.*)

WILEY: Mammy, we did it. We fooled the Hairy Man three times. We did it!

MAMMY: No Wiley, we didn't do it . . . YOU did it.

WILEY: Yasum. Hey DOG . . Come here.

(*DOG enters with the blanket.*)

WILEY: Good boy. He ain't never comin' back no more.

MAMMY: No, we saw the last of him.

(*DOG barks happily.*)

MAMMY: Come on Wiley, time for bed.

WILEY: Awww Mammy, I got too many things going on in my head.

MAMMY: The least little thing happens and you want to stay up all night. Git to bed.

(*DOG whimpers.*)

WILEY: Kin Dog sleep here with me tonight?

MAMMY: Yes.

WILEY: (*As he gets in bed*) Dog. You and I are goin' down to the swamp tomorrow to get some wood for a hound house.

MAMMY: (*Tucking him in*) Go to sleep now.

(*MAMMY starts out.*)

WILEY: Thank you, Mammy.

MAMMY: (*Smiling*) G'night Wiley.

   (*SHE starts out again and then stops.*)

MAMMY: Wiley?

WILEY: Yasum?

MAMMY: We is the best conjure people in the whole southwest county.

WILEY: I know it, Mammy. Good night.

   (*MAMMY exits, WILEY starts to lie back but the "Hairy Man" sounds begin.*)

CHORUS I: Keerful, Wiley . . . .

   (*WILEY looks around.*)

CHORUS II: Look out, Wiley . . . .

CHORUS III: Lookee there, Wiley . . .

CHORUS: (*Starting at a whisper*) Stampin', Stompin', Comin' through the trees, Shufflin' through the swamp grass, Blowin' in the breeze. Bounding, Pounding, Fast as he can . . . What did Wiley see?

   (*WILEY looks around and CHORUS disappears.*)

WILEY: I didn't see nothin'!

   (*WILEY flips over and goes to sleep.*)

THE END

The Play Called Noah's Flood

The Play Called Noah's Flood, set in a tiny English village in the 1400's, is a delightful blend of medieval and modern theatre traditions. The convergence between its subject matter — a group of enthusiastic amateurs struggling to put on a play — and its genesis in a summer youth theatre program contribute to a spirit of joy and exuberance that stands out among other Zeder scripts.

Zeder freely admits that she has taken liberties with medieval theatrical conventions and historical fact, especially in the play that frames the pageant. In the original pageant cycles, each episode of the Bible was produced by members of a particular craft guild. However, Zeder has all the inhabitants of her medieval village working on the same episode, regardless of their craft guild affiliation. Having women in pageants was unheard of in medieval times, but Zeder gives them a prominent role in her play. She also sprinkles the play liberally with modern concepts about human relationships and freely uses contemporary language.

However, she succeeds in capturing the spirit and essence of the period by establishing a balance between medieval and modern elements in several aspects of the play. First of all, most of the characters practice some sort of craft which allows each one to make a unique contribution to the pageant. This preserves some link to the historical role of the crafts guilds in producing the medieval cycles.

Secondly, in using contemporary language, Zeder takes great care to intermix it with selected vocabulary, syntax, rhythms, and rhymes characteristic of medieval English. The resulting blend of contemporary and ancient sounding language is consistent within the world of the play, maintains the energy of the pageant's medieval verse, and establishes the distant time frame without making it seem obscure.

Finally, her handling of relationships between characters also achieves an effective balance of old and new. For example, Eleanor's protest of negative lines about women in the pageant is very much a product of the twentieth century. But, it is also related to the larger battle between the sexes which is very much evident in the original Noah cycle plays and a major part of the Noah pageant in this play. Likewise, the manner in which the Ira rejects his father's plans for his education has a distinctly modern flavor. However, it grows out of what is a universal conflict between fathers and sons. So Zeder's references to the contemporary concern with rights of women and young people is grounded in issues that transcend particular time periods.

A careful look at medieval art, especially those paintings depicting the work of craft guilds and the staging of the cycle plays, will reassure even the purist that Zeder's blending of modern and medieval element is very much in keeping with the style and spirit of the original cycle plays. Zeder's minor characters are unabashedly one-dimensional and drawn with bold strokes, to the point of being as cartoon-like and humorous as the medieval paintings of crafts-people.

The structure of the plot also adds to the play's medieval flavor. The original cycles were performed on wagons pulled through the town, surrounded by viewers on all sides, with each wagon devoted to a single Bible episode. In her play Zeder calls for the actors to enter through and address the audience in the opening sequence of the play. During the first two-thirds of the play leading up the presentation of the Noah pageant, Zeder has the numerous short scenes shift rapidly among a variety of locations in and around the town square. Although the play can be staged effectively on a procenium stage, this plot structure invites alternative types of staging that place acting areas amidst sections of the audience or otherwise increase the closeness of audience to actors as the medieval pageant wagons did.

Having the audience involved in the experience of putting on the pageant is very much in keeping with the themes of this script. On one level, Zeder has created a good fable with a moral—that people should work together instead of being mean and selfish. This level of meaning is obvious in the variety of little conflicts that arise among the minor characters as they try to put on the pageant about Noah. But the conflicts of the more fully drawn characters, John, his son Ira, and the handy man, Pipe, carry this simple moral to a deeper level and keep it from being simplistic.

When the pageant is finally performed, the pageant itself becomes a means through which both small and large problems are solved. Just as the story of Noah focuses on punishment, cleansing, and a fresh start, the doing of the pageant has the power, at least for a moment, to cleanse all the pageant's cast members by transforming their individual selfishness and weakness into something with meaning and merit. In the broadest sense, playing—in this case the theatrical kind—has the power to heal and rejuvenate.

Zeder's description of the way the character Pipe came into being, based on a student actor in that first youth theatre production, suggests some of the creative excitement and belief in the power of theatre to transform lives that informed this play from its beginnings.

"Pipe came from a boy in the summer program who really stuttered and was a convenient target for the jibes of his classmates. He wanted to try out for the role of God, one of the largest speaking parts. To my astonishment and to the surprise of his peers, when he read, he had this beautiful voice. I asked him if he would give me permission to reflect that experience in the writing. He did and Pipe was born."

The Play Called
Noah's Flood

by Suzan L. Zeder

From the Playwright

The medieval mystery play dates back to a time when the world was just waking up from the Dark Ages. As cities and towns sprang to life from feudal fiefs; the plays were developed to teach Bible stories to an illiterate population. The plays began piously as lessons, but by the fifteenth century had blossomed into full blown theatrical extravaganzas with dazzling special effects and slapstick comedy. Actors, designers and directors were untrained amateurs infused with the love of doing. Scripts were shaped through performance and roles were handed down from generation to generation.

My own odyssey with the development of this play parallels its historical development. In 1972 Ann Elgood and the Flint Youth Theatre gave me my first professional job in the theatre as playwright in residence and director of this play. I was barely out of graduate school and the challenge of bringing theatre history to life fascinated me. I adapted the 'pageant' from the original Chester and Townley cycle plays, maintaining the rhyme scheme, but taking the language out of Old English. The plot of the play which surrounds the pageant was created improvisationally by the teenagers in the summer company.

In the past eleven years there have been three formulative productions of this script, two by the Flint Youth Theatre and one at the University of Washington, under the direction of Susan Pearson. In all three productions, relatively young casts have worked to help give the script the shape you see here. It is fitting that these young people have helped to create a play about a time when the theatre was still in its youth.

I encourage you to be bold in your approach to the staging of this play. It will work in a regular proscenium auditorium space; but it cries out to be staged in a large open space, surrounding an audience, as in the medieval courtyards. It might also work outdoors, in a church, community hall, or in an interesting architectural environment.

I have departed from many of the actual conventions of medieval staging including having women take roles in the pageant. I have done so because I feel the essence of the play lies in what it says about theatre as a community collaboration rather than an historical portrait.

I give you this new/old play as a celebration of the power of the theatre to entertain, educate, energize and to hold a mirror up to our timeless selves.

Suzan Zeder
Dallas 1984

Dedication

To the Flint Youth Theatre, Flint Michigan,
who took the first chance with this play . . . twice!

and

To Susan Pearson and Judith Levinson
who helped keep the Ark on course.

The Play Called Noah's Flood was commissioned by the Flint Youth Theatre, Flint Michigan in July 1972 and was performed with the following cast:

John Talbot .... (Noah) .... Rick Morse
Petula Talbot .... (Mrs. Noah) .... Ann Hamilton
Ira Talbot .... (Shem) .... Bill Price
Henry Wainwright .... (Ham) .... Mike Allman
Nicholas Falconer .... (Japeth) .... Scott McKenzie
Yerna Covetine .... (Mrs. Shem) .. Cynthia Sopheia
Eleanor Wainwright .... (Mrs. Ham) ...... Lori Gottlieb
Jennifer Andrews .... (Mrs. Japeth)
Pipe Mandel .... (God) .... Tyson Curtis
Gossips .... (Gossips) .... Vicki Lehman
                                                Chris Wilcox

Makers of Thunder and Lightning: .... Leslie Elgood
                                                Peter Federoff
                                                Jill Gapper
                                                Debbie Gyenese
                                                Mike Kalanquin
                                                Paula Patrick
                                                Dennis Perez

Animals and Dancers: .... Sue Manley
                                                Paula Patrick
                                                Sharon Pomaville
                                                Molly Sapp
                                                Jan Schreiber
                                                Stan Simmons
                                                Dawn Swidorski
                                                Sharon Walls

This production was directed by Suzan Zeder and produced by Ann Elgood. Revised versions were presented by The University of Washington in 1978, directed by Susan Pearson and again by the Flint Youth Theatre, in 1982, directed by Judith Levinson. Original score for the pageant of *Noah's Flood* was composed by Daniel P. Davis and is available through the composer.

CHARACTERS

John Talbot	Blacksmith	(Noah)
Petula Talbot	His wife	(Mrs. Noah)
Ira Talbot	His son	˙(Shem)
		(Anger)
Henry Wainwright	Carpenter	(Ham)
Eleanor Wainwright	Wood cutter	(Mrs. Ham)
Nicholas Falconer	Shoemaker	(Japeth)
Jennifer Andrews	Seamstress	(Mrs. Japeth)
Yerna Covetine	Weaver	(Mrs. Shem)
		(Envy)
Pipe Mandel	Laborer	(God)
Hester Mountamous	Baker	(Gluttoney)
Laggard Slog	Town Layabout	(Sloth)
Enoch Thornscrew	Money-Lender	(Greed)
Stephen Fitz-Stephens	Scribe	(Pride)
Lavidia Sly	Fruit Seller	(Lechery)
Verba Mandible	Brewer	(Gossip)
Loquilla Finn	Fishmonger	(Gossip)
Page	Page to Crinch	
Sir Criticus Crinch	The Pageant Master	

If cast need be expanded, others can serve as animals, musicians, extra townspeople, etc.

If cast need be reduced, sins can play animals and waves. But the 18 listed characters and roles are a minimum.

SETTING

The town square and surrounding shops in Frodsham,
a tiny town near Chester, England.

TIME

A bright June morning in 1491.

The Play Called Noah's Flood

The market place of the small medieval village of Frodsham. The time is early June in 1491. In Portugal, Columbus is still raising money for his voyage, but that is of no concern here in England. King Henry is stirring up another of the endless wars with France, but life in this sleepy little hamlet near Chester is peaceful to the point of indolence.

Center stage is the town square featuring a tall pole with a.bell on it, used to assemble the townspeople in times of peril or celebration. Surrounding the square are a number of small shops, each with an awning or a banner, raised to signify that the shop is open. The shops are as follows: a blacksmith's forge, with anvil and hammers; a shoemaker's shop, with cobbler's bench; a carpenter's shop, with saws and wood; a tailor's shop, with a spinning wheel, colorful bolts of fabric and the unfinished beginnings of costumes. The awnings are closed.

Music begins, lights come up, the town wakes. PIPE MANDEL enters first; he looks around to see if anyone is awake, knocks on the platform bearing the blacksmith's shop, and gets no response. He crosses to the tall pole, unrolls a scroll bearing the words "Rehearsal Today! Be There!" and tacks it to the pole. He rings the bell.

One by one the awnings open and the townspeople enter and begin to work in rhythmic activity. The work rhythms build in a kind of overture with the music. NICHOLAS taps at bench; HENRY saws wood; JENNIFER spins; JOHN joins in last at the anvil. Each craftsman greets PIPE.

While this is taking place, others enter from the house, hawking their wares as they come down the aisles toward the stage. Music builds with the sounds of the craftsmen and the cries of the vendors. HESTER MOUNTA-MOUS approaches the stage, she is a very large Baker with a cart heaped with breads and pastries.

HESTER: Bread! Buy my hot bread! Fresh from the oven, a nice tasty loaf!

(She continues as VERBA MANDIBLE enters, selling wine.)

(She continues selling and calling as LOQUILLA FINN enters with a tray of assorted fish.)

LOQUILLA: Fish! Fish! Fresh from the sea.

(She continues as LAVIDIA SLY enters with fruit.)

LAVIDIA: Fruit! Fruit! The finest you'll see! A nice bunch of cherries.

LOQUILLA: And I've a fresh herring.

HESTER: A rich cornish pasty.

LAVIDIA: Crisp apples so tasty.

VERBA: Drink fit for the Gods!

LOQUILLA: And I've a nice cod.

ALL: Come buy from me!

(Sellers continue and craftsmen work rhythmically. Some speak to PIPE, others do not. VERBA waves to LOQUILLA.)

VERBA: Yoo Hoo! Loquilla, Loquilla Finn!

LOQUILLA: Yoo Hoo! Verba Mandible!

(They cross to greet each other.)

VERBA: Loquilla! Pray tell me what does that notice say? I swear it is writ so small that I can hardly see it with these eyes!

LOQUILLA: Verba, my dear, it says, "Rehearsal Today. Be There!"

VERBA: Rehearsal!

LOQUILLA: Today!

VERBA: Oh La! Isn't it exciting? A play done by our little village of Frodsham in the Corpus Christie Festival at Chester!

HESTER: Is it all decided then? Are we really going to Chester?

VERBA: We won't know for certain until after the Pageant Master sees our play.

HESTER: I have heard in Chester they have custard tarts as big as your fist!

(*LAVIDIA SLY approaches the women.*)

LAVIDIA: Would any of you . . . ladies . . . care for some fruit?

HESTER: (*Self-righteous*) Lavidia Sly, we are God-fearing women!

LAVIDIA: God doesn't like fruit?

VERBA: Have you never heard of Eve and a certain apple?

(*All women except LAVIDIA laugh as LAVIDIA moves on shaking her head.*)

LOQUILLA: (*To VERBA*) That was good, dear, very good!

VERBA: That Lavidia Sly!

LOQUILLA: Imagine, the nerve!

(*HESTER nods in agreement as PIPE approaches the women.*)

PIPE: (*Stammering*) G-G-G-G-good day, Ladies.

VERBA: G-G-G-G-G-good day, to you too!

(*VERBA and LOQUILLA laugh as PIPE turns away.*)

HESTER: Verba, you're terrible!

VERBA: Did I s-s-s-say something w-w-wrong?

(*They laugh again and move on. JOHN sees PIPE, stops working and gestures to him.*)

JOHN: Pipe! Pipe Mandel, come here a minute! What do you think of that?

(*He holds up a small metal hoop with points on it.*)

Well, what do you think?

PIPE: What is it?

JOHN: Can't you tell? It's a crown for God. I'll have Henry cover it with golden paint and it will look ever so much more crownly! Here, try it on.

(*PIPE puts it on and it falls over his ears.*)

It's for Will Thyxill and his head's bigger than yours!

PIPE: W-W-W-will Will be at the rehearsal today?

JOHN: No, I told him he could take his pigs to the Chester market! As Prompter it's your job to read in his lines.

PIPE: I know them by heart. G-G-God's my favorite part!

JOHN: Now, we have only five days left before the Pageant Master comes on the second Tuesday before Witsunday! Five days, and five thousand things still left to be done.

(*ENOCH THORNSCREW enters, looking like his name. He carries a money box.*)

ENOCH: Good day to you, Gentlemen, in the name of God and of profit!

JOHN: (*Stiffly*) Good day, Enoch Thornscrew, and what brings you to my shop?

ENOCH: I am inquiring as to young Master Ira. When he wasn't at the rehearsal yesterday I thought he might have left the village.

JOHN: He's around here . . . somewhere!

ENOCH: Would you be so kind as to tell him I called.

JOHN: May I also tell him the nature of your visit?

ENOCH: Beg to be forgiven, but I never discuss the affairs of my clients with anyone, even a father.

JOHN: (*Angry*) Does that boy owe you money?

ENOCH: Good day, in the name of God and of profit!

(*ENOCH exits and JOHN is clearly upset by his visit.*)

PIPE: Will Ira be at rehearsal today?

JOHN: Yes! . . . yes, he will, Pipe. Now, you see to the costumes.

(*PIPE salutes him and exits. JOHN returns to work. PETULA enters with a full load of laundry. She sits and sorts.*)

PETULA: God be praised, you're working.

JOHN: I'm always working.

PETULA: And this time is it real work or something for that . . . play?

JOHN: It's a crown for God.

PETULA: John, the wheel for Stephen Fitz-Stephens' wagon is over two weeks late.

JOHN: It will be done, after Corpus Christie Day.

PETULA: After Corpus Christie Day? After Corpus Christie Day? I swear if I were to drop down dead you'd prop me up and tell me to wait until after Corpus Christie Day!

JOHN: Petula, I need you.

PETULA: (*Touched*) Oh, John.

JOHN: Who would play Mrs. Noah?

PETULA: John!

JOHN: Come sit with me a while.

PETULA: I've too much work to do.

JOHN: Oh, come!

PETULA: We can't all be idle in this flock.

JOHN: Petula . . .

PETULA: I've the washing, and there's kindling to be cut, and the eggs . . .

JOHN: Now, stop your clucking, Mother Hen, and roost with me a while.

(*Reluctantly PETULA sits, she sighs. There is a pause.*)

JOHN: Shall I tell you what it will be like?

PETULA: What?

JOHN: At Chester?

PETULA: Ever since you and Henry went to Corpus Christie Festival last year, you've talked of nothing else!

JOHN: Oh, Petula, see it with me, now.

PETULA: John . . .

JOHN: (*Ignoring her protest*) The plays begin at dawn, but long before the streets are packed with people waiting. At first light, the trumpet sounds . . . TA DAH! The festival begins; and then the cries, "The wagons! The wagons are coming!" And there they are with flags and banners bright. Wagon after wagon, with players, and the scenes, and all the costumes glittering.

First, there is Creation of the World, with God and all his angels; and a world below filled with birds and trees and flowers so real I swear they smell; and then Lucifer in Hell, with fire, real fire, burning! It stopped my heart. On and on, they come all day, until the Crucifixion; and you would weep to see it, Petula. I did, and Henry too.

From dawn till long past dark, all through the town, are miracles. If just the seeing be that grand, to do plays must be wonder!

PETULA: No one here knows how to do a play.

JOHN: But we're working together, the whole village. Petula, it will be such an honor to be chosen.

PETULA: We haven't been chosen yet.

JOHN: That's why everything must be perfect when the Pageant Master comes!

PETULA: There has been trouble in this town ever since this started.

JOHN: Not trouble, excitement, there is a difference.

PETULA: (*Affectionately*) My silly man, your head is in the clouds, but there is soot all over the rest of you. Give me your apron, I'm doing the washing.

(*JOHN hands her his apron.*)

JOHN: Will you wash the waves as well?

PETULA: Wash the waves?

JOHN: For the flood, for the play.

PETULA: That play again, as if I don't have enough to do with you and Ira.

JOHN: (*Quickly*) Is Ira home yet?

PETULA: He didn't come home all last night, John, I think there's something wrong.

JOHN: He's not ill is he?

PETULA: I don't think so.

JOHN: Good, I need him to play Shem.

PETULA: And what if he doesn't want to play Shem?

JOHN: Shem's a good part!

PETULA: Not if he doesn't want it.

JOHN: It is all settled. I am playing Noah and you are playing Mrs. Noah. Ira, our son, plays Noah's son, Shem! We are doing this as a family, together.

PETULA: I am your wife everyday; must I also be your wife in this play?

JOHN: What would you play?

PETULA: The sin of Lechery, I think; she wears a pretty dress and doesn't have to speak.

(*She pats him on the cheek, just a little too hard, gathers up the laundry and leaves the shop as JOHN returns to work. Just outside the door, she catches sight of IRA sneaking into the house. She waits until he is almost upon her and steps into his path.*)

PETULA: Something lost?

IRA: Mother! I didn't see you.

PETULA: Nor I you, for at least a day or two. Where in creation have you been?

IRA: Out.

PETULA: And if I were to ask, would you tell me where?

IRA: I'd tell you something.

PETULA: Would it be the truth?

IRA: I've ridden all night, to the Chester Market . . .

PETULA: Chester?

IRA: To fetch this . . . kerchief, for you!

(*He hands her the kerchief, but she is suspicious.*)

PETULA: The truth, Ira!

IRA: It be true, if you let it be true. You have the kerchief.

IRA: Brother Benedictus says that you haven't been to lessons in three days.

IRA: Does Father know?

PETULA: Not yet.

IRA: Please Mother, don't tell him, not just now, there are things, things I have to do and . . .

PETULA: Ira, is something wrong?

IRA: No, Mother. Everything will be well, soon, I promise. What did you tell Benedictus?

PETULA: I told him you had a chill.

IRA: More like, his Greek and Latin made me ill.

PETULA: Oh, Ira! Go easily around your Father, he's angry.

IRA: Because I stayed out all night?

PETULA: Because you missed rehearsal.

IRA: That play!

PETULA: After Corpus Christie Day, maybe then all our lives will start again. Now, help your father in the shop; he's well behind in all his work.

IRA: Peace be with you, Mother.

PETULA: And with you.

(*PETULA exits, IRA sneaks around the back of the shop and disappears. JOHN works unobtrusively in his shop during the next scene. LAVIDIA SLY enters with her fruit, NICHOLAS FALCONER leaves his shop. LAVIDIA crosses to him seductively. She startles him.*)

LAVIDIA: Good day, Nicholas Falconer.

NICHOLAS: Oh, good day to you, Lavidia Sly.

LAVIDIA: Would you care for some . . . fruit?

NICHOLAS: Uhhh no, no thank you.

LAVIDIA: (*Sensuously*) But look, see how . . . ripe it is.

(*She bends to show the fruit and shows her decolletage. As she bends, VERBA and LOQUILLA enter and listen to the following.*)

NICHOLAS: YES! They certainly are ripe! That's what they are alright . . . RIPE!

LAVIDIA: The fruit!

NICHOLAS: Oh Yes, I mean NO, I mean . . . I'll take a melon.

(*VERBA and LOQUILLA bustle past in their usual moral outrage.*)

VERBA: The nerve!

(*They exit and NICHOLAS crosses to John's shop. He enters and strikes a dramatic pose.*)

NICHOLAS: (*Reciting*) "And I can well right make a pin, and with a hammer knock it in, and smooth it down as smooth as skin, for I am ready bound."

JOHN: (*Pleased*) Ahh good, you know your lines.

NICHOLAS: And listen. . . . "Father, I am ready bound an axe have I and by my crown, as fine as any in this town for I have work to do."

JOHN: But that's not your speech; Shem says those lines.

NICHOLAS: I know them, all of them!

JOHN: Ira is playing Shem.

NICHOLAS: He hasn't been at the last three rehearsals and I thought maybe I could play both Shem and Japeth!

JOHN: They're in the same scene.

NICHOLAS: I've thought of that as well . . . I could use this voice for Shem . . .

(*Changes his voice.*)

. . . and this little pinched up voice for Japeth.

JOHN: No.

NICHOLAS: Or perhaps, I could play Shem very tall and Japeth very short.

(He demonstrates.)

Or perhaps, I could wear two hats, one like this for Shem and another like this for. . . .

JOHN: Nicholas!

NICHOLAS: Or you could pen a prologue and tell the audience when I hold my face like this . .

JOHN: You will play Japeth and IRA will play Shem.

NICHOLAS: But he hasn't been at the last three rehearsals.

JOHN: He'll be there today!

(John tries to guide him out but another thought strikes NICHOLAS.)

NICHOLAS: How about an animal? I could be a panther or a . . . . .

JOHN: No.

NICHOLAS: A mouse! Surely there were mice on the ark and I can make ever such a little mouselike face.

JOHN: Nicholas?

NICHOLAS: Yes?

JOHN: No.

NICHOLAS: But . . .

JOHN: No.

(NICHOLAS crosses back to his shop practicing animal sounds as he goes. JOHN goes back to work. STEPHEN FITZ-STEPHENS enters grandly. Everything about him suggests vanity.)

STEPHEN: Salute, omnes, populo populorum!

(NICHOLAS makes a sound of a donkey as he passes STEPHEN and continues into his shop.)

JOHN: Stephen!

STEPHEN: Preggo?

JOHN: A word with you?

STEPHEN: A word, for I am on my way to see Jennifer Andrews about the final fitting for my costume.

JOHN: Stephen, tell me one more time what the Festival Council told you in Chester.

STEPHEN: But I have already told you that, Dolce Directorio, a thousand times or more! The Festival Council told me quite plainly, and I quote, "The Pageant Master will see your play, Two Tuesdays afore Witsunday."

JOHN: You're quite sure that's what they said?

STEPHEN: There hasn't been a mistake in the Fitz-Stephens family for over 100 years.

JOHN: I just don't want anything to go wrong!

STEPHEN: Semper Fidelus, John! And now, I must be on my way, tempus fugit, and so must I.

   (*STEPHEN enters the tailor's shop NICHOLAS pokes his head out of the window of his shop and makes the sound of a cock crowing.*)

NICHOLAS: That sounded just like a cock, didn't it!

JOHN: No.

NICHOLAS: Surely there were roosters on the ark.

JOHN: Nicholas, I said, NO!

   (*JOHN returns to his shop and lights come up on STEPHEN in the tailor's shop. JENNY and YERNA are in the shop busily at work.*)

STEPHEN: Stephen Fitz-Stephens is here for his fitting.

JENNY: I've just finished your costume.

YERNA: Oh, it's such a beautiful costume, Master Fitz-Stephens. I wish I had one just like it.

STEPHEN: Of course you do, my child.

JENNY: All done but the final hemming.

(*They help him into an elaborate costume.*)

YERNA: There are still a few pins in the pourpoint but if you're careful. . . .

STEPHEN: A Fitz-Stephens *is* always careful. Now, I trust that you used the silk I ordered, all six colors!

YERNA: Oh yes, Sir!

STEPHEN: And I trust that you followed my measurements and my instructions exactly!

YERNA: But of course!

STEPHEN: And I trust that you have sewn it all together with fine hand stitching and none of those wide sloppy basting stitches!

(*JENNY, somewhat annoyed by his pretensions, "accidentally" sticks him with a pin.*)

Owwww!

JENNY: Pardon, Sir.

YERNA: Oh, Sir, it looks WONDERFUL.

(*YERNA holds a looking glass for him.*)

STEPHEN: SPIRITUS SANCTUS! What is the matter with this liri-pipe?

JENNY: Nothing.

STEPHEN: And the pourpoint, it pinches; and the hoopelande hangs like a sad old sack.

JENNY: It does not!

STEPHEN: And the poulaines, why, they are positively puny.

JENNY: If they were longer, you'd trip on them and fall on your face.

STEPHEN: A Fitz-Stephens never falls on his face! It will have to be redone!

JENNY: It will not!

YERNA: I think it looks very nice. It's ever so much nicer than my costume.

STEPHEN: Well, of course it is, but it will not do for me! I cannot wear this in public!

JENNY: Then go naked!

STEPHEN: Ignorati!! You know nothing of style!

JENNY: And you know nothing of manners.

STEPHEN: I'll not pay you until it is done correctly!

JENNY: Out of my shop!

STEPHEN: Not a penny until it's redone!

JENNY: Out do you hear me? OUT!

(*He starts to say something, she snips the scissors dangerously and STEPHEN exits.*)

JENNY: Who does he think he is, the Archbishop of Everything?

(*PIPE approaches the shop. YERNA sees him and runs behind JENNY.*)

YERNA: Oh, he's coming, he's coming! You talk to him!

JENNY: What in the . . .

YERNA: I can't talk to him.

JENNY: Why it's only Pipe. Whatever is the matter with you?

YERNA: Whenever I talk to him, I'm always afraid that I'll s-s-s-stammer . . . SEE! I just did it?

JENNY: Don't be a goose.

(*PIPE enters the shop and YERNA ducks behind JENNY.*)

PIPE: G-G-G-G-Good Day to you, Jenny.

JENNY: Good Day to you, Pipe Mandel.

(*HESTER enters and barges her way into the shop, in her fist is a large garment, she also carries her tray of pastries.*)

HESTER: Everybody out of my way! Jennifer Andrews I need a word with you.

JENNY: You'll have to wait until I'm through with Pipe.

HESTER: I haven't got all day. It takes him forever to get to the end of a sentence.

PIPE: I can wait, Jenny.

HESTER: This costume is too small! I can't fit my big toe in this kirtle.

JENNY: It was made to your exact measurements last week.

(*She examines the garment.*)

The seams, they're all split.

HESTER: Really, Jenny! I expected better workmanship!

JENNY: No, Hester Mountamous! You've gained weight!

HESTER: Me? Gained weight?

JENNY: Yerna, see what you can do with it!

YERNA: Oh, what lovely little cakes.

HESTER: Yes, they are, aren't they?

(*HESTER pops a cake into her mouth as she exits with YERNA.*)

YERNA: (*On her way out*) I wish I had one.

PIPE: John wanted me to see how the costumes are coming.

JENNY: Don't ask! . . . I know, five days is all we have left. Tell him I'll be ready! If God made the world in seven days, I should be able to make costumes for Frodsham in five. Go in grace, Pipe Mandel.

PIPE: And you t-t-t-too, Jenny.

(*PIPE exits. JENNY joins YERNA and HESTER. JOHN leaves his shop and crosses to the carpenter's shop where HENRY is working on a small model. He covers it when JOHN enters.*)

JOHN: Henry, I have come to see the pageant wagon.

HENRY: Sit down, sit down, Brother John, and let me show you the plans.

JOHN: Never mind the plans, I want to see what you've completed.

HENRY: Look here a moment. The wagon is wonderous large with two levels, one here for Earth, and this here for the Heavens, where God shall sit with painted cloud and moons and shining stars.

JOHN: Good, Henry, just like we saw at Chester.

HENRY: And over here is Hell-mouth . . .

JOHN: Henry . . .

HENRY: . . . with dragon jaws a-yawning, belching smoke . . .

JOHN: Henry . . .

HENRY: . . . flames shooting forth from spirits of nitrate and gun-powder and tongues of fire lashing at the devils.

JOHN: HENRY! There is no Hell mouth in this play.

HENRY: Are you sure?

JOHN: The plays must be done exactly as written down. Come, let me see what you have built.

HENRY: Don't you want to hear about the flood? Look, here are copper sheets for thunder and barrels filled with nails for sounds of tempest and the gale. Then, at the moment of the flood, these ropes will pull over rain barrels placed atop the wagon. Down will come the water, down the aqueducts here and here, down the little channels, down upon the stage!

JOHN: BRAVO, Henry! Let me see it, now!

HENRY: There it is in all it's glory!

(*HENRY wisks aside the apron and reveals the model.*)

JOHN: Henry, this is but a model.

HENRY: But it is perfect in every detail. See here, the tiny heavens where sits the tiny God; and here, the tiny barrels to make the tiny flood. . . .

JOHN: How much of this is built to man size now?

HENRY: How much is built?

JOHN: How much?

HENRY: None.

JOHN: Nothing built? NOTHING?

HENRY: The hard part is the planning, the rest is but carpentry.

JOHN: But we have only five days left!

HENRY: 'Tis only carpentry.

(*ELEANOR enters carrying a very large pile of cut logs.*)

ELEANOR: Oh John, John Talbot, I must have a word with you!

JOHN: Later, Eleanor, now Henry . . .

ELEANOR: Now, John!

JOHN: What is the matter, Eleanor?

ELEANOR: I cannot say those words!

JOHN: Which words?

ELEANOR: When Ham's wife says, "And we shall trim the timbers too, for there's nothing else to do. Women are too weak it's true, for any great travail."

JOHN: What's wrong with those words?

ELEANOR: "WOMEN ARE TOO WEAK, IT'S TRUE"??

JOHN: So?

ELEANOR: Henry, when there's timber to be cut, who does it?

HENRY: Why you, Eleanor.

ELEANOR: When there's slash to be cleaned and burned, who does it?

HENRY: Why you, Eleanor.

ELEANOR: When there are logs to be hauled, and trimmed, and planed?

HENRY: You do it, Eleanor.

JOHN: What about you, Henry? What do you do?

HENRY: I do the planning.

ELEANOR: We must change the line.

JOHN: We can't.

ELEANOR: Why not?

JOHN: Because that's the way it's written.

ELEANOR: Well, it's written very stupid!

JOHN: We must do the play exactly as it's written or we won't be selected to perform in Chester!

ELEANOR: I give you fair warning, John, I'll not say those words!

(*PIPE enters at a run.*)

PIPE: J-J-J-J-John, come quick.

JOHN: What's the matter?

PIPE: It's Laggard Slog. He's fallen asleep in the hog wallow and says he won't play S-S-Sloth.

JOHN: But he promised!

PIPE: Y-Y-Y-Y-You'd better come.

JOHN: Henry, I need that wagon!

HENRY: You'll have it, 'Tis but carpentry.

(*PIPE and JOHN exit in a hurry. HENRY and ELEANOR return to their shop. Lights up on NICHOLAS, he is working in his shop and practicing animal sounds. After a beat IRA enters. He carries a large broadsword.*)

IRA: So, the boredom in this tiny town has finally driven you mad!

NICHOLAS: Oh, Ira, I didn't see you there. I was just practicing.

IRA: For a conversation with a goat?

NICHOLAS: For the play. Are you going to be in it, Ira? If not, can I have your part? I've learned all your lines as well as my own.

IRA: I give it to you, gladly! I won't be here for the play.

NICHOLAS: Thank you, Ira . . . Why not?

IRA: Nicholas, I'll show you something, but you have to swear not to tell anyone, especially not my Father.

NICHOLAS: What is it?

IRA: Swear?

NICHOLAS: I swear!

(*IRA shows him the broadsword.*)

IRA: Just look at that!

NICHOLAS: IRA!

IRA: Isn't it beautiful? Look at that blade, sharp as sin, and the handle, just feel that balance. Watch the swing!

(IRA swings and NICHOLAS jumps.)

NICHOLAS: Where did you get it?

IRA: I bought it in Chester. I've ridden all night.

NICHOLAS: It must have cost . . .

IRA: Fourteen crowns. I've been saving for a year and I borrowed the rest from Enoch Thornscrew.

NICHOLAS: Ira, you didn't.

IRA: That I did, and that's why I need your help, my friend.

NICHOLAS: How much?

IRA: Four crowns, but just until tomorrow. They'll pay us before we leave.

NICHOLAS: Leave?

IRA: I've joined King Henry's legion. We're going to fight in France!

NICHOLAS: Ira, you're not.

IRA: Yes I am, little Nick, and there's not a soul in this town who can stop me.

NICHOLAS: But, you're being trained for the University.

IRA: Nick, I'm nearly mad with Greek and Latin; and my mind's full up with useless facts. The only adventure I'll get this way is to read about it in books. I'll not read another word, it's time I had some adventure of my own.

(ENOCH has entered and overheard.)

ENOCH: But adventure is expensive, my dear Ira.

IRA: Enoch! I just need some more time.

ENOCH: But of course, time is no problem, but time is costly. Life is so short that even minutes are dearly bought.

(VERBA and LOQUILLA enter.)

IRA: You'll have your money, Thornscrew! Four crowns before the day is out!

ENOCH: Not to hurry, by tomorrow it will be six.

IRA: Four crowns! You'll have it today!

ENOCH: I have no doubt. Master Ira, I have no doubt.

(*IRA exits angrily. ENOCH turns to NICHOLAS.*)

ENOCH: Good Day to you, Nicholas, in the name of God and of . . .

NICHOLAS: Don't say it, Mr. Thornscrew, just go!

(*NICHOLAS watches him go and makes the sound of a snake.*)

VERBA: Poor Petula!

LOQUILLA: Poor, dear, Petula!

VERBA: Poor, dear, unsuspecting Petula! I'd hate to be around when John discovers that Ira owes Enoch Thornscrew four crowns.

LOQUILLA: Four? I thought it was fourteen.

VERBA: Or was it forty?

LOQUILLA: I think it was four hundred!

VERBA: Let's go find her and see!!

(*They exit, nattering to each other, after a beat JOHN and PIPE enter carrying a very heavy, very lazy, LAGGARD.*)

JOHN: Come now, Laggard, please wake up!

LAGGARD: Good fellows, let me be! Is it a crime to sleep in the sun?

PIPE: In the hog w-w-w-wallow?

LAGGARD: It is soft and warm in there, and hogs be good companions!

JOHN: But we need you for the play.

LAGGARD: What?

PIPE: W-W-W-We need you to play a part.

LAGGARD: Part of what?

JOHN: We need you take a role.

LAGGARD: Is it a nice crusty roll, with jam and butter?

PIPE: To play a r-r-r-role in the play for C-C-C-Corpus Christie Day?

LAGGARD: Oh, I'm too old to play, Pipe, and so are you.

JOHN: You don't understand.

LAGGARD: And you too John, now is that anything for a grown man to be doing?

JOHN: Laggard Slog, I'll explain it one more time! Now, a play is when you dress up in someone else's clothes and pretend to be something you're not and say words another person wrote. . . . .

(*They continue to talk with him as they exit. NICHOLAS leaves his shop and crosses to the tailor's shop. He carries the melon and a small leather pouch.*)

NICHOLAS: Good day to you, Jennifer Andrews.

JENNY: And to you, Nicholas.

NICHOLAS: And how, may I ask, are you?

JENNY: Busy.

NICHOLAS: I brought you a melon.

JENNY: I see.

NICHOLAS: It's ripe.

JENNY: I know.

NICHOLAS: You do?

JENNY: I can see the color, and I can tell you by the feel, and listen here, when you thunk it, that means it's ripe; and when you smell here by the stem, that means it's ripe too.

NICHOLAS: I surely thought it was ripe.

JENNY: Well, it is, nice and ripe.

(*There is an awkward pause.*)

Nicholas, I have to get back to my work now.

NICHOLAS: Oh.

(*She starts to turn away, but NICHOLAS stays.*)

I brought this for you too.

(*He hands her the small pouch, she opens it and finds what appears to be a handful of tacks.*)

JENNY: What is it?

NICHOLAS: It's a necklace.

JENNY: Ohhhhh.

NICHOLAS: I made it from tacks and shoe laces. See how I bent the tacks to look like tiny animals? And look, here is a little shoe and right next to it a tiny thimble, that's for our two crafts.

JENNY: Why, Nicholas . . .

NICHOLAS: I thought you might wear it at Chester, in the play. Of course when we're up there on the pageant wagon, no one will be able to see it, but we'll know.

JENNY: It's lovely.

NICHOLAS: Well . . . that's all.

JENNY: Thank you, Nicholas.

NICHOLAS: You better get back to work.

JENNY: Yes, I better.

NICHOLAS: Do you like it?

JENNY: Very much.

(*He starts to go.*)

Nicholas? Thank you.

(*He starts to go again.*)

Nicholas? I'll wear it.

NICHOLAS: Be careful you don't stab yourself on it.

(*He exits back to his shop. JOHN and PETULA enter from the direction of the river with the clean washing. They cross toward the shop. IRA enters the shop and paces as they approach.*)

JOHN: Petula, I'll find out how much he owes and why; but it can't be four hundred crowns, why there isn't that much gold in all of Frodsham.

PETULA: But Verba and Loquilla said they heard. . . . .

JOHN: If it's those two dragons, I'll not believe a word.

PETULA: They know everything that goes on in this town.

JOHN: And what they don't know, they make up I'll talk to Ira.

PETULA: But listen as well.

JOHN: I will, if I can find him.

(*They enter the shop and run right into IRA. PIPE enters and overhears the following.*)

IRA: Father, I want to talk to you.

JOHN: So there you are, sit down, boy, you have some explaining to do.

IRA: I am tired of slipping in and out of shadows, it's time we talked.

JOHN: Very well, you talk, I'll listen.

IRA: I don't know how to tell you this . . .

JOHN: You might start by explaining your absence at rehearsal for the last three nights.

IRA: The easy thing would have been just to run away . . .

JOHN: Then, you might explain why you borrowed money from Enoch Thornscrew.

IRA: . . . but I just couldn't do that.

JOHN: And finally, you might tell us where you were all night.

IRA: I'm trying to, Father.

JOHN: Well go ahead, boy, who's stopping you?

PETULA: John, sit down and be quiet!

(*JOHN sits.*)

IRA: I had hoped to stay until after the play and then to slip away in all the excitement in Chester, but they are leaving tomorrow and I must go tonight to join them.

JOHN: Go where?

PETULA: Join who?

IRA: The legion.

PETULA: What legion?

IRA: King Henry is raising an army to fight in France.

JOHN: And what concern is that of yours?

IRA: I am going with them.

PETULA: (*Crossing herself*) Oh no.

IRA: I've been all the way to Chester to buy my broadsword, that's why I borrowed the money.

JOHN: You will turn over the sword to Thornscrew in forfeit of the debt and we will consider this conversation at an end.

IRA: Say what you will, Father, but I am joining the legion.

JOHN: (*Ignoring him*) The wheel for Stephen Fitz-Stephen's wagon needs fixing.

IRA: Father . . .

JOHN: Will Thyxill left a broken plow blade . . .

IRA: Listen to me!

JOHN: And there is kindling to be cut for your Mother . . .

PETULA: John . . .

IRA: Father! I am talking to you!

JOHN: I won't listen to nonsense!

(*JOHN starts to exit.*)

IRA: You won't stop me from going!

JOHN: Never before has anyone, anyone from this village been selected to go to the University. Brother Benedictus says you will be chosen and, by God, you are going!

IRA: But I want . . .

JOHN: You don't know what you want.

IRA: I do, Father! Oh, I do! Everyday I sit on a stool and I read and I read and I read, and the words mean nothing, just scratches on the paper.

JOHN: Most of the people in this town can't even read.

IRA: They're lucky.

JOHN: Don't you dare speak like that! Your mind is a gift from God. You will be a scholar.

IRA: And sit forever on a stool and teach people to teach people to teach people . . . what?

PETULA: Ira, scholars are respected, scholars are gentlemen, scholars are . . .

IRA: Men who can do nothing else with their minds or bodies! Mother, I won't do it! I want to . . .

JOHN: What you want is not important!

IRA: The legionaires tell me there are fortunes to be made!

PETULA: What do you know of war, Ira? Soldiers die.

IRA: So do blacksmiths.

JOHN: I have work to do. This talk is at an end.

IRA: At least let me have my chance.

JOHN: What chance? The soldiers come here with drums and ducats and dreams beyond all reason. They fill you full of glories and they'll bring us back your body, nothing more.

IRA: I'd rather die on the field than slowly rot to nothing here!

PETULA: Ira . . .

IRA: You're a frightened old man, Father, and I'll be damned before I end my days like you!

(*JOHN raises his hand to slap him, there is a frozen moment as IRA places his hand on his sword hilt.*)

PETULA: Stop it, both of you!

JOHN: Now, Ira, you are my son and you will do as I bid you. You will get this foolishness out of your head and will work at the forge all day until it is time for the rehearsal of the play . . .

IRA: I am talking about my life and all you can think about is that foolish play?

JOHN: We will not discuss this or anything else until after Corpus Christie Day.

PETULA: And are we supposed to stop our lives until then?

IRA: By Corpus Christie Day, I will be sailing to Calais.

JOHN: Then go, damn you, go and throw it all away! But if you leave, don't you ever dare come back!

PETULA: John!

(*IRA exits angrily. PETULA is furious.*)

JOHN: I have much to do before rehearsal.

PETULA: That play will be an end of all of us.

JOHN: Petula, I hoped it would bring us together.

PETULA: No, John, you're doing it for yourself, by yourself, and you're using all of us.

(*She exits. JOHN strikes the anvil with the hammer. He sits and buries his head in his hands. PIPE enters, starts to approach, sees JOHN is upset. After a beat, JOHN speaks.*)

JOHN: Dear God, I only meant to do thee honor, but I have harmed everyone I love. Now help me, please. I know not what to do. Dear God in Heaven, what more can go wrong now?

(*PIPE exits as the PAGE enters. JOHN prays silently.*)

PAGE: Hullo there, Sirrah!

JOHN: (*Startled*) Who are you?

PAGE: Them that needs my name calls me Tom Tip; but mostly they say, "Boy" or "Page" or "You there in the corner." Tell me, Sirrah, am I near Frodsham?

JOHN: If you were any nearer, you'd be past it.

PAGE: Then could you tell me where I might find a blacksmith by name of Talbot, John Talbot?

JOHN: If you were any nearer, you'd be past him too, that is my name.

PAGE: Then I am sent to tell you to ready your play, the Pageant Master will be here later today.

JOHN: WHAT?

PAGE: My Master, Sir Criticus Crinch, will be here within the hour, he is but a league or two from here.

JOHN: But he's not coming for five more days.

PAGE: That will be a great surprise to him; he's been on a horse all night to get here by the Third Thursday afore Witsunday.

JOHN: THIRD THURSDAY?

PAGE: Afore Witsunday . . . . that's today!

JOHN: (*Bellows in rage*) STEPHEN FITZ-STEPHENS!

PAGE: No, Tom Tip, I already told you that.

JOHN: Can you stop him, Tom?

PAGE: I don't think so.

JOHN: Could you slow his pace, stop to water the horses, lead him around in circles, find some excuse to slow him down?

PAGE: Not without a beating.

   (*JOHN takes money from a pouch and hands PAGE a few coins.*)

JOHN: Here's a crown or two to ease the bruises.

PAGE: My Master has a fearful temper.

JOHN: Three crowns . . .

PAGE: And a heavy hand . . .

JOHN: Alright, four crowns!

PAGE: Oh, what a shame it will be when my Master's horse suddenly goes lame, and when I drop all his saddlebags into the stream, and when we take the wrong turn in the road, and . . . .

JOHN: Good lad, Tom. Give us all the time you can.

PAGE: And so I will. We have an afternoon in store!

JOHN: And so have we. Go now swiftly, but get you back here like a snail.

PAGE: The slowest snail in all the world!

(*PAGE laughs and exits. JOHN lifts his eyes heavenward and gives a little cry and runs to the bell. Lights up on the Carpenter Shop, Henry is fiddling with the medieval equivalent of fire-crackers. JOHN rings the bell, PIPE enters at a run.*)

PIPE: W-W-What's the matter, John?

JOHN: He's coming! The Pageant Master is on his way, today is the day he'll see our play!

PIPE: B-B-B-B-But . . .

JOHN: No time for talk, gather all the props and bring them here, and spread the word for everyone to meet here in the square.

PIPE: B-B-B-But . . .

JOHN: No time, Pipe, no time for any words!

(*During the next few scenes PIPE will quietly gather props and set up as best he can for the play. JOHN crosses to HENRY. HENRY drops a fire-cracker into the barrel and slams down the lid.*)

JOHN: HENRY!

HENRY: Stand back, John!

(*Both men crouch . . . nothing happens.*)

It's a new idea I have for thunder. We drop these little crackers here and they go off with a thunderous roar!

JOHN: No time for that. I must have the wagon, or the ark, or any part that's built.

HENRY: Easy John, I told you, 'tis but carpentry, and Eleanor has begun out back . . .

JOHN: No time. We must have anything that's built, we need it right away!

HENRY: It will be done before he comes.

JOHN: The Pageant Master comes today!

HENRY: That is not a good joke.

JOHN: He's on his way.

HENRY: I'm not laughing.

JOHN: Nor am I!

HENRY: It will be done when it is done and no made up story . . .

JOHN: I swear it's true!

HENRY: Oh John, I am ashamed of you. Now get you gone outside my door. It will be done when it is done and not a day before!

(*HENRY escorts JOHN out of the shop just as STEPHEN appears in the street.*)

JOHN: (*Bellowing*) STEPHEN FITZ-STEPHENS!!!

STEPHEN: Who misuses my name so loud and rude?

(*JOHN crosses down to him just as HESTER enters with her cart.*)

JOHN: Stephen, tell me one LAST time when the Pageant Master comes!

STEPHEN: John, John, John, can you remember nothing, Dolce Duncico?

JOHN: (*Through his teeth*) Say it, Stephen!

STEPHEN: "The Pageant Master will see your play, Two Tuesdays . . .

JOHN: No, Stephen! It's the THIRD THURSDAY!

STEPHEN: Third Thursday? . . . Why, that's today.

JOHN: And he's on his way.

STEPHEN: There must be some mistake!

JOHN: Yes, and you made it!

STEPHEN: Sacre Fumare!

(*HESTER, who has been listening crosses to them.*)

HESTER: What, what, what's this I hear?

STEPHEN: The Pageant Master is on his way, I fear.

HESTER: Oh my Lord!

(*VERBA and LOQUILLA enter.*)

VERBA: What rumpus is a-rumping here?

JOHN: Ladies, gather up your costumes, or whatever's ready for the play. The Pageant Master will be here today!

STEPHEN: (*Headed for the tailor's shop*) Jennifer Andrews, I need to talk to you about my costume!

VERBA: And so must I.

LOQUILLA: And so must I.

HESTER: And so must I!

(They all troop into the shop. IRA enters and sneaks across the stage without being seen by JOHN. PIPE sees him and watches him go. NICHO-LAS comes running from his shop and crosses to JOHN.)

NICHOLAS: John . . . John . . .

JOHN: Nicholas, the Pageant Master . . .

NICHOLAS: I know, I heard!

JOHN: Fetch Laggard Slog and Enoch Thornscrew.

NICHOLAS: Does this mean I'll play both Shem and Japeth too?

JOHN: You can play every bloody part for all I care! Now, go and bring the others to the square.

(PIPE approaches JOHN, just as PETULA enters upset.)

PETULA: John, it's Ira. He's taken his clothes and all his things.

JOHN: Pipe, tell the others to meet in the square immediately.

(PIPE exits same way as IRA.)

PETULA: John, we have got to stop him before he gets too far.

JOHN: What do you expect me to do? Go after him and bring him back with a rope? Haul him home and lock him in his room.

PETULA: We can't just let him go!

JOHN: He made a choice.

PETULA: And you are going to do nothing?

JOHN: No, Petula, we're going to do a play!

(JENNY exits from her shop as pandemonium breaks loose. She crosses to JOHN.)

JENNY: John Talbot, what is going on around here?

JOHN: The Pageant Master comes too soon to see the play. He comes TODAY!

(JENNY tosses a bolt of fabric in air and screams, PETULA sinks down on the stoop of the shop. VERBA and LOQUILLA come out of the shop and swoop down to JENNY just as LAVIDIA enters.)

VERBA: But my costume, it's not done!

LOQUILLA: And mine's not even begun.

LAVIDIA: I've an extra cloak or two.

VERBA: Not from you, Lavidia Sly. I'd rather die!

JOHN: *(Sharply to VERBA)* Then do so, Madam, quickly pray! I've got more important things to do today!

(VERBA and LOQUILLA are mortally offended, they cross to PETULA and all three exit in a huff. NICHOLAS enters with LAGGARD and ENOCH.)

NICHOLAS: I found them, John, and brought them here, quick as I could.

JOHN: Good, Nicholas, very good!

ENOCH: What, in the name of profit and loss is going on here?

JOHN: The Pageant Master is on his way . . . here . . . today!

(There is a general hub-bub from all assembled.)

JOHN: Quiet! Everybody! Everybody be QUIET!

(They are.)

Now get you home and ready for the show. Assemble when you hear the bell . . . Now, Go . . Go . . . Go!

LAGGARD: *(In a daze)* Who . . . where . . . when?

JOHN: GO!

(NICHOLAS helps LAGGARD off and all exit in various directions. As soon as the stage is clear, there is a shift of lighting and IRA enters in the downstage area which indicates the space away from town. IRA stops to lace his boot, and PIPE enters very out of breath.)

PIPE: Ira! W-W-W-Wait!

IRA: Pipe, I know why you're here, but you won't change my mind. I'm leaving.

PIPE: The Pageant Master comes to see the play.

IRA: But he's not due for five more days.

PIPE: He comes today!

IRA: (*Hesitates briefly*) That is none of my concern.

PIPE: C-C-C-Come back, just for today.

IRA: Just because my Father . . . .

PIPE: I'm a-a-asking you for all of us.

IRA: All my life, I have done what other people wanted, but not this time!

  (*IRA turns away.*)

PIPE: Ira?

  (*IRA turns back and PIPE tosses him a pouch.*)

IRA: What's this?

PIPE: Four crowns. It's a b-b-b-bribe!

IRA: (*Tossing it back*) I can't take your money, Pipe.

PIPE: If you w-w-won't d-d-do it for your Father, and you w-w-won't do it for me, then do it for yourself.

IRA: For myself?

PIPE: Your Father n-n-needs you. Do the play and be free of that n-n-n-need forever.

IRA: He doesn't need me! He can do it all by himself!

PIPE: No, he can't, and he knows it. I heard him when he was alone, he was . . . weeping.

IRA: (*Astonished*) My Father?

PIPE: Come with me, Ira.

IRA: But I want to go to France.

PIPE: You can g-g-g-go later t-t-tonight.

IRA: I want to go now!

PIPE: (*Explodes*) Then go! Go on and never mind! Just go and we'll manage somehow! I have too much to do to waste more time on you!

(*PIPE starts to go and IRA stops him.*)

IRA: Pipe, Pipe, wait a minute. You're not stammering.

PIPE: I never do when something's r-really important.

IRA: Let's go.

PIPE: You're c-c-coming?

IRA: Just for today. I'm leaving as soon as . . .

PIPE: B-B-B-But you're really coming?

IRA: Just for today.

(*They exit together. After a beat, JOHN enters and rings the bell. STEPHEN, NICHOLAS, JENNY, HESTER, ENOCH, YERNA, LAG-GARD, LAVIDIA, enter ad-libbing remarks and gathering together pieces of costume, etc.*)

JOHN: Now I'll call the roll to see if everyone's here!

(*As he calls a name the appropriate person responds.*)

Henry, you and Eleanor for Ham and wife, and Nicholas and Jenny for Japeth and his spouse . . .

NICHOLAS: Yo!

JOHN: And Yerna's here for Envy and she plays Mrs. Shem as well . . . now where is Shem!

JENNY: That's Ira.

NICHOLAS: Oh John . . John . .

(*NICHOLAS waves his arms and makes his presense very obvious.*)

JOHN: Alright! Alright! Nicholas, you play Shem too. I don't know what else to do!

STEPHEN: Stephen Fitz-Stephen's here for Pride.

LAGGARD: And Laggard Slog for Sloth.

ENOCH: And Enoch Thornscrew's here for Greed.

LAVIDIA: Lavidia Sly for Lechery.

HESTER: Hester Mountamous, as Gluttony, will do what she must do.

NICHOLAS: And nobody's here for Anger, so can I play that too?

JOHN: Alright, Nicholas!

HENRY: Where's Petula for Mrs. Noah?

(*Everyone does a long take.*)

YERNA: She's not here!

(*NICHOLAS starts jumping up and down and waving his arms.*)

JOHN: That's where I draw the line, Nicholas, go and find her!

NICHOLAS: But I know the lines.

JOHN: You can't play Mrs. Noah, Nicholas, that's just too odd!

(*He gestures and NICHOLAS exits.*)

JENNY: Just a moment everyone, where's God?

JOHN: God, William Thyxill? God . . .

HESTER: Oh my Lord, God's not here!

JOHN: Gone to take his pigs to the Chester Market!

STEPHEN: Who told him he could go?

JOHN: I did!

ALL: You did?

ENOCH: When you knew the Pageant Master was coming?

JOHN: But I didn't! Stephen, tell them the message you gave me from the Chester Council?

STEPHEN: If I told you once, I told you a hundred times, "the Pageant Master would see our play on the THIRD THURSDAY afore Witsunday!"

JOHN: WHAT?

HENRY: You told us the wrong day, John.

JOHN: But that's not true!

ENOCH: We would have been ready if it wasn't for you!

JOHN: Stephen, tell them the truth!

STEPHEN: You doubt my word? How absurd!

VERBA: We'll never get to Chester, John, all because of you!

LOQUILLA: You've ruined our play!

(*They all begin talking at once. Some side with JOHN, others with STEPHEN. John tries unsuccessfully to quiet them. Some shout at JOHN and advance on him. PIPE and IRA enter. IRA stands behind his father and draws his sword. The crowd sees him before John does.*)

IRA: What seems to be the trouble here?

(*The crowd backs off.*)

JOHN: Ira, you're back! Thank God!

IRA: That's Pipe's doing.

JOHN: Thank you, Pipe, and thank you Ira.

JENNY: I know what we can do. Someone can sit in that tree and read God's lines.

JOHN: Who here can read?

(*There is a general hubbub.*)

PIPE: I know the l-l-l-lines.

JOHN: (*Not listening*) Just a minute, Pipe.

PIPE: B-B-B-But I know them all!

JOHN: I said, just a minute!

IRA: Why not have Pipe play God? After all, he is the prompter.

(*All laugh derisively except JOHN, IRA and PIPE.*)

JOHN: Could you do it, Pipe, I mean without . . .

PIPE: I n-n-n-never s-s-stammer when it's really important.

VERBA: He n-n-n-never s-s-s-stammers when he knows what to s-s-s-say!

(*All laugh again.*)

ENOCH: I have a cloak of gold, so I should play God!

STEPHEN: A Money-Lender, God? You must be mad! We're sorely pressed, but not that bad!

ELEANOR: I'll play God for I can speak as well as any man!

HESTER: But I can show God's bounty, I swear I can.

YERNA: God is good and God is great, but you can't play God with all that weight.

LAVIDIA: Then I shall play God, for God is loving and giving and so am I.

HESTER: YOUR kind of woman, play GOD?

LAVIDIA: What do you mean by that, you big bag of dragon droppings?

HESTER: Well, I NEVER!!!!

(*HESTER hits LAVIDIA with a pie. All Hell breaks loose; all fight! PETULA, VERBA, and LOQUILLA enter to see what is going on. They sit at one side of the stage and drink and watch.*

(*At the height of the melee the PAGE enters with a trumpet and blows. No one notices.*)

PAGE: Hear Ye! Hear Ye! My Leige Sir Criticus Crinch . . . . . Hear Ye! Hear Ye! The Pageant Master of the Festival of Corpus Christie . . . . Hear Ye! Hear Ye!

(*PIPE notices and fights his way to the PAGE and bows to SIR CRITI-CUS.*)

PIPE: W-W-W-Welcome Sirrah. Welcome to Frodsham!

SIR CRITICUS: What is going on here?

PIPE: Uhhhhhh. . . WARM-UPS!

(*PIPE seats SIR CRITICUS on a small stool to one side of the stage. He desperately tries to get someone to notice. HENRY finally notices and lights a firecracker.*)

(*PIPE mounts the platform in the tree and puts on an article of clothing to signify God's costume, and starts the play.*)

PIPE: I . . .GOD!

(*Everyone looks up at him. PIPE points down at SIR CRITICUS and the light begins to dawn. One by one they slip into their costume pieces and slink*

into positions for the beginning of the play. From this point on, the pageant
will be played absolutely straight, except when noted.)

GOD: (*PIPE*) I, God, who all the world hath wrought,
Heaven and Earth and all of nought,
I see my people in deed and thought
Are foully set in sin.

   (*YERNA, STEPHEN, HESTER, IRA, ENOCH, LAGGARD, and LAVI-*
DIA assume poses for the dance of the Seven Deadly Sins.)

GOD: All mankind, both day and night,
Sins in deed or word or sight.
They turn their faces from my light
And set their paths on wrong.

For . . . For . . . For!

   (*Stephen nudges YERNA who realizes it is her cue.*)

YERNA: Envy,

STEPHEN: Pride,

HESTER: And Gluttony,

IRA: Anger,

ENOCH: Greed . . .

   (*Both ENOCH and LAVIDIA elbow LAGGARD who belches loudly.*)

SLOTH: 'Scuse . . . Sloth,

LAVIDIA: Lechery.

GOD: Seven sins, which I abhor
Corrupt their beings to the core
And lo, it wounds my heart.

   (*Music begins and the SINS dance a seductive dance with JOHN as*
NOAH. They try to tempt him with each of their individual corruptions but
he stays resolutely incorruptible. At the end of the dance, drums rumble for
thunder.)

GOD: Man that I made I will destroy,
Beast and worm and fowl to fly.
For on Earth, they do me deny,
All folk that are thereon.

DESTROYED BY RAIN THE WORLD SHALL BE!

Forty days and forty nights,
It shall rain for man's unrights.
To drown the earth of all I see,
And wash the world of pain.

Save, NOAH, thy wife, and children three,
And their three wives, preserved shall be.
For thou has never strayed from me
And kept thyself from sin.

Therefore, Noah, my servant free,
A righteous man thou art, I see.
BUILD THOU A SHIP FOR ALL THY FAMILY
Of timbers dry and light.

NOAH (*JOHN*): Ah, Lord, I thankest thee loud and still
That to me thou art in such will
And sparest my house not to kill
From out of all mankind.

But Lord, how shall I this ship make?
For I am old, my bones shall break.
I know not stem from stern or fore from aft.
I fear I cannot build this craft,
Without thy help combined.

GOD: And so it shall be done.
Go, fetch about thee all thy sons.

(*NOAH whistles and SHEM [IRA], HAM [HENRY], MRS. SHEM [YERNA], MRS. HAM [ELEANOR], and MRS. JAPETH [JENNY] enter. Just in time for his cue, NICHOLAS enters as JAPETH and points to PETULA who stands to one side between VERBA and LOQUILLA.*)

NOAH: Oh Lord, my sons are now with me.

SHEM: Shem.

HAM: Ham.

JAPETH: And Japeth.

NOAH: My sons three,
And they have brought their wives to thee
To listen to thy word.

  (*During the next several verses, NOAH and his children will measure out
the dimensions of the Ark using their bodies to form its outline.*)

GOD: Three hundred cubits it shall be long
And fifty wide to make it strong
And thirty high and all around,
Thus, measure it about.

  (*The next three verses are spoken as a round.*)

SHEM: Three hundred cubits it shall be long
And fifty wide to make it strong
And thirty high and all around,
Thus, measure it about.

HAM: Three hundred cubits it shall be long
And fifty wide to make it strong
And thirty high and all around,
Thus, measure it about.

JAPETH: Three hundred cubits it shall be long
And fifty wide to make it strong
And thirty high and all around,
Thus, measure it about.

GOD: With tar and pitch seal it stout
To keep the raging waters out.
And three roofed chambers in a row,
A door, a window, there I show,
For to come in and out.

And let there other chambers be
And fill with hay and grain and seed

And food for every kind of breed,
For therein beasts must dwell.

NOAH: Beasts?

SHEM: Beasts?

HAM: Beasts?

WIVES: BEASTS?

(*They all look at each other horrified and more than a little amazed.*)

GOD: Yes, beasts, of each kind and two therefore
Male and female, but no more.
Of every make, of every kind,
And mark you leave not one behind,
'Ere thou put up thy sail.

Noah, to thee and thy fry
My blessings grant I.
For ye shall wax and multiply
And fill the earth again.

(*Light out on GOD. NOAH turns to his children and claps hands loudly.*)

NOAH: Have done ye men and women all!
Help for all that may befall
To build this ship, this chamber, hall.
As God has bidden us do.

(*During the next sequence the Ark will be built. Pieces of the set, boards from the shops, benches, pieces of fabric, will be assembled to indicate the Ark. It is also possible to build the Ark around the audience, if platforms have been built out in the house. At any rate, the audience must have a good view of the inside of the Ark as the whole flood scene will be played from inside the boat. During the next several stanzas, NOAH and his children build the Ark in front of the audience.*)

SHEM: Father, I am ready bound.
An axe have I, and by my crown,
As sharp as any in this town.
For I have work to do.

HAM: I've a hatchet wonderous keen
To bite well, as may be seen,
A better blade has never been
No, not in all this town.

JAPETH: And I can well right make a pin
And with this hammer knock it in
And smooth it down, as smooth as skin,
For I am ready bound.

MRS. SHEM: And I will go and gather slitch
For the ship to caulk and pitch.
Painted must be every stitch,
The stem, the stern, the sail.

MRS. JAPETH: Here's a solid chopping block.
On this we may hew and knock.
None are idle in this flock.
And now, no man may fail.

(*ELEANOR as MRS. HAM comes forward, pauses, clears her throat and looks right at JOHN as she delivers her speech.*)

MRS. HAM: Ahhhhhhem!
And we shall trim the timbers too
Give the women now their due
For they are strong enough, it's true
For ANY great travail.

(*HENRY and JOHN break character as they respond to what ELEANOR has just said. ELEANOR is enormously pleased with herself. HENRY pulls her back out of view of SIR CRITICUS.*)

HENRY and JOHN: ELEANOR!

(*SIR CRITICUS notices the change. He gestures to the PAGE, who scribbles something down on a long scroll.*)

SIR CRITICUS: Page, make a note!

NOAH: (*Back in character*) Of this tree, I'll make a mast
Tied with cables that will last,

Sturdy ropes against the blast.
This ship is at an end.

(*The ship is completed and all look skyward.*)

For the coming of the flood.

(*There is an ominous rumble of thunder on the drums. All are frightened.*)

ALL: For the coming of the flood!

GOD: Noah, Noah, take thou and thy family
Into the ship where thou must be.
For the beasts do come here presently.
Go fetch thee now thy wife.

(*JOHN crosses to where PETULA is sitting with VERBA and LOQUILLA. They sit on large pillows and pretend disinterest in everything. He makes a grand gesture for her to enter and she turns her back on him.*)

JOHN: (*Under his breath*) Petula!

GOD: Go fetch thee now, thy wife!

(*JOHN tries again to no avail, he returns to the playing area.*)

NOAH: Lord, I will haste fast as I may.
I fear though what my wife might say.
I am afraid there might be a fray
Between the both of us.

For she is often testy
And easily angry.
If anything wrong be
She'll shout and rage and fuss!

(*PETULA, still refusing to go along, makes an indignant sound and turns her back on him again.*)

PETULA: HA!

GOD: Go fetch thee now, thy wife!

(*JOHN crosses back to PETULA and tries again, this time sweetly.*)

NOAH: Good wife, dear wife, how fare thee?

PETULA: Better before I looked on thee!

(*JOHN crosses over to PIPE and whispers to him.*)

JOHN: Was she supposed to say that?

PIPE: (*Whispering*) No.

(*SIR CRITICUS notices that something unusual is going on.*)

SIR CRITICUS: Page, make a note!

(*PAGE scribbles onto the scroll. During the next two speeches it is obvious that PETULA is improvising and JOHN is getting panicky.*)

PETULA: Don't tell me now what thou has done!
All day you laze in the sun.
But woman's work is never done,
No matter what you think!

ELEANOR: (*Breaking character*)That's right!

HENRY: Eleanor!

(*SIR CRITICUS gestures and PAGE makes another note.*)

PETULA: For I have cooked and washed for thee,
Kept thy house and family,
With narry, no never, a thought for me.
With my gossips I shall drink!

VERBA: Yes, let us drink, 'ere we depart.

LOQUILLA: For often we have done so.

VERBA: Yes, let us drink another quart.

PETULA: And so I will, before I'll go!

(*JOHN turns to PIPE AND whispers.*)

JOHN: Are they supposed to be saying that?

PIPE: (*Whispering*) No. Make something up!

(*JOHN crosses to PETULA and improvises the following speech.*)

NOAH: Good Wife, the rains come soon and all will drown
To wash the sin from out this town.
So, come in this ship, or by my crown,
I'll carry you within.

PETULA: Good Husband have thee no doubt
That I shall stand right here without.
Though you might stand all day and shout,
I'll n'ere do as thy bid!

VERBA: We women may curse all ill husbands,
For loud they shout their brash demands.

LOQUILLA: And we must stand and wring our hands.

ALL THREE: And do just as we will!

NOAH: (*ROARING*) Oh Lord, that women are crabbed aye!
And never are meek, that dare I say!
This is well seen by me today,
In witness of each of you!

   (*PETULA picks up a pillow and swats him with it.*)

For when she wants to strike,
She is fast to strike.
In faith, I'll hold none of the like.
I'll give her now her due!

   (*JOHN picks up another pillow and swats PETULA. The following lines underscore their pillow fight.*)

NOAH: Good Wife, inside this ship, get in!

PETULA: No.

NOAH: To deny your husband is a sin.

PETULA: NO!

NOAH: Thinkest thou art Master and will win?

ALL THREE: YES!

(*They all clobber him.*)

NOAH: And so thou art, by St. John!

(*SIR CRITICUS rises.*)

SIR CRITICUS: None of this is in the text, pray, what is going on here?

GOD: NOAH!!!!

(*JOHN crosses back to the boat, PIPE catches his eye and shakes his head. JOHN gestures to IRA.*)

NOAH: Shem, thy Mother doth bellow.
Forsooth such another, I do not know.

SHEM: I shall fetch her, here I go,
Without any fail.

(*SHEM crosses to PETULA.*)

Mother, my Father to you sends me
And bids into the ship get thee.
Look, the rains have come you see,
And we are ready to sail.

MRS. SHEM: (*Back in the boat*) Good Mother, come in, for all is overcast.

MRS. HAM: And soon the winds begin to blast.

MRS. JAPETH: The flood it comes and quickly runs.

WIVES: Therefore, Mother, come in!

MRS. NOAH: I fear I cannot heed your call,
Unless you save my Gossips all!

SHEM: In faith, Mother, yes you shall,
Whether you will or not!

(*SHEM picks her up and carries her to the boat. The family cheer and encourages him to toss her to them inside the Ark. He does, and they all wind up in a heap with NOAH underneath and MRS. NOAH on top.*)

MRS. NOAH: Oooooo I am undone, my family's a wonder.

NOAH: How can she groan while I lie under?

SHEM: Now, cease you both this quarreling blunder.

NOAH: My back is broke in two.

MRS. NOAH: And I am black and blue.

NOAH: Welcome, Wife, into this boat!

MRS. NOAH: And have you that, and do not gloat!

(*SHE tweaks his cheek. Drums rumble and lights are back up on God.*)

GOD: Noah, hurry thyself, thy children, thy wife.
Make ready the ship for fear of thy life.

(*More drums for thunder.*)

And beasts and fowl with thee thou take
He and she and mate to mate.
For look, the flood draws nigh.

(*More drums for thunder.*)

Forty days and forty nights
Rain shall fall for man's unrights.
All I have made with all my might,
I seek now to destroy.

NOAH: Have done ye men and women all!
Hurry you lest this water fall
Before each beast is in its stall
And into the ark is brought.

(*MUSIC begins and NOAH and family look out front in disbelief. From the rear of the house, other townspeople come carrying simple animal heads or masks on long poles. They dance down the aisles in time to the music and finally wind up in the Ark. If the whole house is used, Noah's children can cross down into the house and play the flood scene from positions in the aisles.*)

SHEM: Father!

HAM: Father!

JAPETH: Father!

ALL: FATHER!

MRS. SHEM: Look, they come, they run, they fly.

MRS. HAM: They cover the ground. They fill the sky.

MRS. JAPETH: They hop, they crawl, they swim, they climb.

SHEM: And two by two they form a line.

NOAH: As God has bidden them do.

JAPETH: Sir, sir, sir, here are lions, leopards fine.
Bears and sheep, oxen, swine.
Beasts of every manner and kind
Here coming thou may see.

HAM: Tigers, panthers men may find.
Buck and doe, hart and hind.

SHEM: See here, cats and dogs and calves
Otters, foxes and giraffes.

MRS. SHEM: Elephants with trunks and tails,
Fish and snakes, with all their scales.

MRS. HAM: Here are chickens, cocks and crows,
Rooks and ravens, many rows.

MRS. JAPETH: Swans and peacocks and who knows,
Just two of every kind.

(*There is a huge peal of thunder and the sound of rain.*)

NOAH: (*Humbly*) Thy will be done.
The flood's begun.

(*More thunder and family reacts to the rain.*)

ALL: Thy will be done.
The flood's begun.

(*As thunder peals and lightning flashes in the GOSSIPS are terrified. They react to the rising floods.*)

GOSSIP I: The flood comes fleeting in full fast.

GOSSIP II: Full fast!

GOSSIP I: On every side it builds, alas!

GOSSIP II: Alas!

GOSSIP I: For fear of drowning I am aghast!

GOSSIP II: Aghast!

BOTH: I fear we all shall drown!

(*They exit as lights dim and music for the flood begins. The music will continue throughout the scene and incorporate singing of the hymn "Eternal Father".*)

MRS. JAPETH: Father, Father, what's that sound
That shakes the ship from off the ground?

NOAH: It is the wind that's all around.
Methinks the ship has moved.

(*There is a violent lurch as the ship is moved by the waves. The movement of the tempest is mirrored in the bodies of the family. Sound and movement build, lightning flashes.*)

NOAH: Quick, bolt the windows, latch the doors!
Tighten the ropes 'till they're secure!
Cling to each other firm and fast
That we may ride safe through this blast.

(*All mime securing ropes, lashing down the animals, etc. as the storm builds to a crescendo.*)

SHEM: Father, the elephants have broken their chains!

HAM: The horses paw and thrash their manes.

JAPETH: I am full frightened of these rains.

SONS: The ropes are snapping from the strain.

MRS. NOAH: I fear, my Husband, for my life.

MRS. SHEM: This craft cannot withstand this strife.

MRS. HAM: The wind, it slices like a knife.

ALL WOMEN: I fear we all will drown!

NOAH: (*Trying to quell the panic*) Creatures, Wife, and children, sing!
And let your hearts and voices ring!
And trust the Lord for everything,
And we shall saved be.

Now raise your voices loud and strong!
Come join together in this song.
Let everyone now join this throng.
And sing, yes sing, for me.
SING! SING! SING!

(*As music swells into the hymn, the entire cast sings.*)

ALL: (*Singing*) "Eternal Father, strong to save
Whose arm doth bind the restless wave
Who bid'st the mighty oceans deep
Its own appointed limits keep
Oh, hear us when we cry to thee
For those in peril on the sea."

(*Gradually the storm abates some. The movement is less frantic, but the storm continues. NOAH surveys the damage and calls to his children.*)

NOAH: Children, children, hear my call

And tell me art thou well withall?
Hast thou safely stood this squall
And art thou safe and well?
Shem?

SHEM: My Father, I am well.

NOAH: And thy wife?

MRS. SHEM: No harm befell.

NOAH: And Ham?

HAM: My Father, I am fair.

NOAH: And thy wife?

MRS. HAM: I do forebear.

NOAH: And Japeth?

JAPETH: Japeth and his wife are safe.

NOAH: (*To MRS. NOAH*) And my dear Wife, art thou still chafe?

MRS. NOAH: My husband, I am fully grateful
And sorry am I that I was hateful.
For now I know, and now I see
How kind thou art in thy mercy.

NOAH: And the beasts, how did they fare?

SHEM: Nothing is damaged beyond repair.
The camels are quiet.

HAM: The birds, they do nest.

JAPETH: The cats and the camels, lie down for to rest
And give thanks abundant that we here are blessed.

(*Music for the storm is softer still. Gradually all quiet down; the family settles the animals. The rocking motion is still apparent but much gentler.*)

NOAH: The storm now is ending, the thunder is soft.
The rain falls more gently, but never so oft.

The wind blows more lightly, the ship now is still.
So, sleep now, my children, for such is God's will.

Yes, sleep now and pray that whenever we wake
A new light will shine and the first dawn will break
And we'll find before us a new world to make.
Now sleep, sleep and be still.

(*The animals and family huddle together and fall asleep. NOAH kneels in prayer as lights dim and a single spot comes on NOAH as the last sounds of the flood are heard. NOAH raises his hand to touch the light.*)

NOAH: Now, forty days are fully gone
And I shall send a raven on.
Then he will land on tree or stone.
If dry be any place.

(*All wake during this last speech. NOAH hands a bird to one of the townspeople outside the boat. The raven "flies" off stage.*)

SHEM: And if this bird comes not again.

HAM: Then it is dry on hill and plain.

JAPETH: Therefore, stoppeth now the rain.

WOMEN: And we have known some grace.

(*Noah looks for the raven, but it does not come.*)

NOAH: Oh Lord, wherever this raven be
Somewhere is dry, that well I see.
And yet, a dove I will set free
To make me double sure.

(*NOAH speaks to the dove.*)

Thou wilt return again to me,
For of all the fowls that may flee,
Thou are the most meek and rightfully
That thou should be the one to set us free.

(*Noah releases the DOVE and there is music as it "flies" around the stage and passes GOD who places a branch of olive in its beak. The DOVE returns to NOAH.*)

NOAH: Oh Lord, blessed be thou aye.
For thou has comforted me today.
For by this sight, I well may say
The floods begin to cease.

My sweet Dove to me has brought
A branch of olive that she sought
To show now what the world has wrought.
It is a sign of peace.

(*Drums beat and the spot comes up on GOD.*)

GOD: Noah, take thy wife anon
And thy children, every one,
Out of the ark where thou has gone
And all who are with thee.

Beasts, and all that can fly
Out into the world, now shall they hie,
On Earth to grow and multiply.
I will that it so be.

NOAH: Oh Lord, I see thee through thy might,
Thy bidding must be done in right
That I find honor in thy sight.
From out of the ark we go.

(*Part of the ark is removed and the people and animals move out into a fresh new world. As GOD speaks the following verses, a brilliant dawn breaks on the cyclorama.*)

GOD: Noah, to me thou are full able.
For I have found thee true and stable
And thou shall give the world this fable
To show the path to right.

GOD: So, forward, Noah, with thee I make,
And for thy seed, and for thy sake,
A vow, such vengence I will never take.
again, I never will smite.

And man and woman shall never more
Be wasted by water, as it was before.

For the sin that grieveth me so sore
Is fully washed away.

(*The whole company assembles in a long single line and slowly unfurls a beautiful rainbow colored banner which arcs across the whole stage. There is soft music.*)

GOD: This rainbow between you and me
In the firmament shall ever be.
And by this token you shall see
The love that I bear man.

The ends are turned toward you
And up toward me is bent the bow.
The colors bright shall always show
The gift I grant to thee.

My blessings now I give thee here
To thee, Noah, my servant dear
For vengeance no more will appear.
And now, farewell, my darling dear.

(*All hold in a final tableaux, which is broken only by the sound of the PAGE clapping.*)

IRA: We did it!

(*The townspeople explode in jubilation, totally forgetting about the Pageant Master. They hug each other and generally carry on until SIR CRITICUS rises and the PAGE trumpets for their attention.*)

PAGE: Hear ye! Hear Ye! My Leige, Sir Criticus Crinch, Pageant Master for the Festival of Corpus Christie, will deliver his decision in a few moments.

(*In a single long cross SIR CRITICUS exits without a word, followed by the PAGE.*)

HENRY: What does that mean, John?

JOHN: I don't know, but it doesn't bode well.

IRA: But we did it!

(*Crowd responds but not as enthusiastically.*)

JENNY: I think we were wonderful!

NICHOLAS: I think you were wonderful!

STEPHEN: I think I was wonderful!

(*PIPE is still up in the GOD tree.*)

PIPE: W-W-W-Well, how did I d-d-d-do?

ALL: You were wonderful!

(*All respond and help PIPE down just as PAGE enters and blows his trumpet. They are silent instantly.*)

PAGE: Hear Ye! Hear Ye! Attend Ye all! Sir Critcus Crinch will speak to you now!

(*SIR CRITICUS enters and takes forever crossing the stage. He pulls out a long long scroll.*)

SIR CRITICUS: Ahhhem. I shall now read, the list of your mistakes!

ALL: What?

SIR CRITICUS: Firstly the scenery, the costumes and the physical effects were all woefully underdeveloped!

ELEANOR: But we weren't ready!

HENRY: I could show you the plans!

SIR CRITICUS: Secondly, there was a rude sound during the dance of the Sins.

LAGGARD: This was my favorite part.

SIR CRITICUS: (*Plunging on, pedant that he is*) Thirdly, there were flagrant errors in the text and inexcusible changes.

ELEANOR: I like my way better.

SIR CRITICUS: Fourthly, there was all that nonsense between Noah and his wife. You know perfectly well that none of that is in the text . . .

JOHN: Sir Criticus, does this mean we'll not be going to Chester?

SIR CRITICUS: Chester is not a place for amateurs.

NICHOLAS: But we tried so hard.

SIR CRITICUS: (*The soul of condescension*) My dear little Sirrah, trying hard is not enough.

IRA: (*Angry*) Not so quick, Sirrah, yourself! We did more than try, we did it!

(*All respond in agreement.*)

SIR CRITICUS: But there were errors.

IRA: Improvements!

SIR CRITICUS: Blunders.

PIPE: Refinements!

SIR CRITICUS: You made many many mistakes!

IRA: A mistake is just another way of doing something.

SIR CRITICUS: Not at the Chester Festival!

IRA: Then we have no need of the Chester Festival!

ALL: What?

IRA: That's it! Come Corpus Christie Day, we'll have our own festival! We'll do the play just like you planned, right here!

SIR CRITICUS: But that's impossible.

PETULA: No, it isn't!

SIR CRITICUS: You can't just . . . do the play.

JOHN: Of course, Ira! Of course we can! And we'll do it our way!

HENRY: The wagon will be done by then.

JENNY: And the costumes too.

HESTER: I'll bake a score of cakes, my friends.

VERBA: And I'll supply the brew!

SIR CRITICUS: It won't be the same as the Chester Festival!

JOHN: No, Sir, it will be better for we won't have to listen to a committee full of chicken-heads like you!

SIR CRITICUS: I don't have to stay here and listen to this!

JOHN: Then I suggest you go!

(*SIR CRITICUS storms off, followed by the PAGE who gives them all the thumbs up sign before leaving.*)

PIPE: Hear Ye! Hear Ye! All hail the F-F-F-FRODSHAM FESTIVAL!

(*There is a communal gasp of joy and all freeze in postures of celebration. Music and blackout!*)

CURTAIN!

Step on a Crack

Step on a Crack is not only Zeder's first published play, but also the play which first brought her recognition as an innovator in scripts for young audiences. One of the major reasons for this is that *Step* is not an adaptation of some other story, like so many scripts for young audiences, but is completely original, both in concept and structure. The dramatic action, the setting, and the imaginary characters—indeed the play's entire structure—grow out of Ellie Murphy's mind and are revealed through the way she plays. The beneficial effect of play is a recurring theme in Zeder scripts, but here, more than in any of her other works, play takes central focus. Ellie's free flowing imaginative fantasy play and the more structured games, jokes, and rhymes that Ellie and Max share contribute both to Ellie's characterization and to the structuring of the play as a whole. The result is a child protagonist drawn with as much depth, dimension, and specificity as any in the literature and a play that flows in and out of reality with high theatricality.

The intrusion of a new stepmother into Ellie's relationship with her father brings out all of Ellie's insecurities, jealousies, and fears of abandonment. Ellie's primary means of coping is by playing out fantasies in the privacy of her room with her imaginary friends Lana and Frizbee and her alter-ego, Voice. All of these characters represent different parts of Ellie's personality.

Her fantasy play has both a positive and a negative side. On the one hand, it helps her work through conflicts. When we first move inside her mind in the early fantasies, we see Ellie casting herself in a role far superior to her stepmother, Lucille, and casting Lucille as a defeatable villain. This allows Ellie to express her anger about the changes Lucille has made in household routines. But these fantasies provide only temporary solace as Lucille's real life intrusions into Ellie's private world increase.

Ellie's fantasies also get in her way. As the deeper layers of Ellie's internal struggles unfold, we see that she cherishes the idea of having a mother, but it takes the trauma of running away to shake her out of her fantasy world enough to realize the depth of Lucille's concern and good will. Ellie finally discovers that Voice—her own dark side—doesn't always tell her the truth. Her symbolic burial of Voice and her desire to put away Lana and Frizbee signal a major growth step for

Ellie—a realization that her own view has been distorted by her feelings and that Lucille could be a "perfectly good" mother after all.

In contrast to the free form fantasy play that reveals the depths of Ellie's personality, Zeder uses structured forms of play—games, rhymes, and jokes—to give the script structural cohesion. The opening sequence of jump rope rhymes and games sets up the exposition quickly and establishes a convention used throughout the play to signal the shift into and out of Ellie's fantasies. Not only do these games provide unifying links structurally, but Zeder has chosen games that, when looked at on a metaphoric level, give us additional insight into how Ellie feels about her relationships to Max and Lucille. Red-light/Green-light is a game in which "it" attempts to control the inevitable approach of other players, much as Ellie tries to control Lucille's inevitable approach. The knock-knock jokes presume a closed door with an unknown stranger seeking admission, just as Lucille is constantly seeking admission to Ellie's life. Zeder's use of the knock-knock joke at the end of the play, to signify the beginning of Lucille's inclusion, is an effective inversion of that established pattern. It prevents the ending from becoming too pat by hiding Ellie's acceptance of Lucille in the subtext rather than stating it directly.

The set, as Zeder describes it, is also strongly reflective of Ellie's inner life. She indicates that it should be little more than a brightly colored framework to define Ellie's room which is to be decorated "outlandishly with old pieces of junk." Ellie's room is a visible manifestation of her state of mind. There are no real walls called for in Zeder's description—just a free standing door. This parallels the invisible walls Ellie has created in her mind to keep Lucille out and the barriers that she imagines exist in Lucille's mind.

Max and Lucille are the only aspect of the play which are not extensions of Ellie's mind, except when they appear in her fantasies. Because so much of the play is devoted to unfolding Ellie's inner life, less time is available for in-depth characterization of Lucille and Max. Though they are somewhat more thinly drawn than Ellie, they are not one-dimensional. Depths are possible to find in both characters, but they must be found between the lines in the subtext.

Step on a Crack has probably received the most critical attention and acclaim of all Zeder's plays. The field of theatre for young audiences, with a few notable exceptions, had been held in thrall for 60 years by adaptations of fairy tales and favorite children's stories, by accepted formulas for the "well-made" children's play and by stereotypic and one-dimensional characters. The importance of this play to dramatic literature for young audiences cannot be minimized. In the history of children's theatre moral values have been painted in black and white, with good rewarded and evil punished. In this play there are only degrees of good and bad, right and wrong, decisions that work and decisions that don't. There are no villains. *Step on a Crack* stands as a landmark that depth of characterization is fully as appropriate for young audiences as for adult audiences. Its enduring popularity with audiences and producers for more than a decade proves that young audiences are capable of accepting challenging theatrical structures, styles, and conventions that depart from realism.

Step on a Crack

by Suzan L. Zeder

From the Playwright

I offer this play to you with a profound respect for the complexity of childhood. As a writer, I have tried to confront the child within myself as honestly as possible in order to bring you a child of this moment. A funny, crazy, wildly imaginative child who arms herself with a full-blown fantasy life to fight her way through real life problems. Ellie's difficulty adjusting to her new stepmother is as classic as Cinderella and as timely as tomorrow.

I have been deeply gratified by audience reaction to this play. I remember one day after a matinee performance a child and a young woman sat quietly together in the empty lobby of the theatre. After a few moments the child turned to the woman and said, "That could have been about us." "Yes," the woman replied, "Do you want to talk about it?" The child thought for a moment and finally said, "Okay. Let's go home!"

Perhaps I might offer a bit of advice to potential producers and directors of this play. If a child actress with sufficient maturity, skill, and depth can be found; by all means cast her. But do not let this be a limitation. I have seen this play work equally well with a young adult in this role. Perhaps you might consider a college student with a bit of training behind her. I have even seen an impressive performance by a high school student.

If an adult actress is used I would urge her to spend some time with children; to notice how they move; to listen to the patterns of their laughter; to watch them closely in the whirlwind of temper tamtrums, in joyous flights of fantasy, and in quiet moments of frustration and despair. All of these things are part of Ellie. It is my sincere wish that Ellie be played as a real child and not as an adult comment on childhood.

Above all, please have fun with this script . . . I have!

Suzan Zeder

Dedication

To My Mother

The premiere production of *Step on a Crack* was presented on March 14, 1974, at Southern Methodist University, Dallas, Texas, with the following cast:

Ellie .... Martha LaFollette
Lucille .... Mary Jo Lutticken
Max .... Ron DeLucia
Lana .... Jackie Ezzell
Frizbee .... John Rainone
Voice .... Jennifer Glenn

The production was directed by Susan Pearson.

Set Design by .... John Tillotson
Costume Design by .... Nina Vail
Faculty Advisor .... Charley Helfert

A musical version of *Step on a Crack* was introduced by Seattle's Poncho Theatre in 1978, with a score by John Engerman and lyrics by Suzan Zeder. It is available through Anchorage Press.

CHARACTERS

Ellie Murphy: A ten year old girl
Max Murphy: Her father, about thirty-seven
Lucille Murphy: Her stepmother, about thirty-five
Lana: Ellie's imaginary friend
Frizbee: Another imaginary friend
Voice: Ellie's alter-ego

SETTING

Ellie's house
A bowling alley
The streets

TIME

The Present

Step on a Crack

The main playing space consists of two areas: ELLIE'S bedroom and a living room. A free standing door separates the two areas. The set should be little more than a brightly colored framework. Each space has a ladder which is hung with the various costumes and props used throughout the play.

ELLIE'S room is the larger of the two spaces. It is outlandishly decorated with old pieces of junk, flags, banners, old clothes etc. which have been rescued by ELLIE from her father's junk yard. The room is a mess, strewn with piles of clothes and junk. Up center is a larger box marked "TOYZ". At the far side of the room there is a stool surrounded by a simple frame. This frame indicates a mirror. This is VOICE'S area. VOICE never moves from this spot until the very end of the play. It would be helpful to have a microphone and P.A. speaker here. VOICE will make all of the sound effects used during the play.

The living room, MAX and LUCILLE'S space, is conspicuously neat. A coffee table and a few chairs indicate this area.

At Rise: ELLIE, MAX and LUCILLE and VOICE are onstage. MAX holds one end of a jump rope, the other end is tied to the set. VOICE sits on the stool. LUCILLE sits in the living room area. ELLIE jumps as MAX turns the rope for her. She jumps for a few seconds to establish a rhythm.

MAX: Cinderella . . . Dressed in yeller . . . Went downtown to meet her feller. Cinderella . . . Dressed in yeller . . . Went downtown to meet her feller.

(MAX continues to chant and ELLIE to jump as LUCILLE speaks.)

LUCILLE: Grace, Grace . . . Dressed in lace . . . Went upstairs to wash her face. Grace, Grace . . Dressed in lace . . . Went upstairs to wash her face.

VOICE: *(Joins in)* Step on a crack . . . Break your mother's back. Step on a crack . . . Break your mother's back. Step on a crack . . . Break your mother's back!

(*ELLIE jumps out of the rope and hops four times firmly.*)

ELLIE: CRACK! CRACK! CRACK! CRACK! Step on a crack, break your STEPmother's back!

VOICE: Red Light!

(*All freeze.*)

VOICE: Ellie Murphy used to be a perfectly good little girl. Green Light!

(*All come to life for a second MAX and ELLIE take a few steps toward each other.*)

VOICE: Red Light!

(*All freeze.*)

VOICE: Her mom died when Ellie was just four years old, and everybody felt so sorry for her. They said, "Oh you poor little girl." And they brought her extra helpings of cake and lots of presents. Ellie lived with her pop, Max Murphy, boss of Murphy's Wrecking and Salvage Company. Green Light!

(*During the next few lines MAX and ELLIE play a game of tag.*)

ELLIE: Not it!

MAX: Knock, knock . . .

ELLIE: Who's there?

MAX: Banana.

ELLIE: Banana who?

MAX: Knock, knock . . .

ELLIE: Who's there?

MAX: Banana.

ELLIE: Banana who?

MAX: Knock, knock . . .

ELLIE: Who's there?

MAX: Orange.

ELLIE: Orange who?

MAX: Orange you glad I didn't say banana?

VOICE: Red Light!

(*All freeze.*)

VOICE: They played tag and went bowling; they ate T.V. dinners and practiced baseball for six years and they were very happy. Green Light!

(*ELLIE and MAX mime practicing baseball.*)

MAX: Listen Midget, if I told you once I told you a million times, you gotta keep your eye on the ball.

(*He throws an imaginary baseball, ELLIE hits it and MAX follows the ball with his eyes and sees LUCILLE.*)

MAX: Fantastic!

VOICE: Red Light!

(*All freeze.*)

VOICE: About two months ago Ellie went to camp and Pop met a pretty lady who taught music. Green Light!

(*ELLIE and MAX hug goodbye. ELLIE moves up her ladder and scratches her bottom, she mimes writing.*)

ELLIE: Dear Pop, Today we went camping in the woods and guess where I got poison ivy?

(*MAX moves over to LUCILLE.*)

MAX: (*Shyly*) Hi, my name is Max, Max Murphy.

LUCILLE: Pleased to meet you Max, I'm Lucille.

VOICE: Red Light!

(All freeze.)

VOICE: And Pop liked Lucille and Lucille liked Pop. Green Light!

(ELLIE puts a blindfold over her eyes.)

ELLIE: Dear Pop, I can't go swimming today cause I got pink eye.

VOICE: Ellie came back from camp and everything in her whole life was different.

(ELLIE, MAX and LUCILLE play blind man's bluff.)

ELLIE: 5, 4, 3, 2, 1 . . . Ready or not here I come.

MAX: We're over here.

ELLIE: Where? Am I getting warmer?

MAX: Naw, you're a mile off.

ELLIE: Am I getting warmer?

VOICE: Red Light!

(All freeze.)

VOICE: Pop and Lucille got married. Green Light!

(MAX and LUCILLE move into wedding positions. They mime an exchange of rings and kiss.)

ELLIE: I said am I getting warmer? Hey Pop where did you . . .

(ELLIE takes off the blindfold and sees them kissing. She claps her hand over her eyes and giggles.)

VOICE: Red Light!

(All freeze.)

VOICE: Everything was different. Lucille cooked well balanced meals with vegetables. She kept the house neat and sewed buttons on all

Ellie's clothing. Pop liked Lucille a lot, he wanted Ellie to like her too but somewhere deep inside Ellie's head this little voice kept saying . . . Look how pretty she is . . .

ELLIE: Look how pretty she is.

VOICE: Look how neat she is . . .

ELLIE: Look how neat she is.

VOICE: Pop likes her much better than he likes you.

ELLIE: No!

VOICE: Oh yes he does!

   (*ELLIE turns away.*)

VOICE: Ellie Murphy used to be a perfectly good little girl. Green Light!

   (*MAX exits. ELLIE moves into her room and picks up a Whammo paddle-ball. LUCILLE moves into the living room area and sets up a music stand and practices singing scales. She has a beautiful voice.*)

ELLIE: (*Hitting the paddle-ball*) 235, 236, 237, 238, 239,240, 241, 242, 243, 244, 245, 246 . . .

   (*ELLIE misses, sighs, and starts again.*)

ELLIE: 1,2,3,4,5,6,7,8,9,10,11,12,13,14 . . .

   (*ELLIE misses, sighs, and starts again.*)

ELLIE: 1,2,3,4,5,6,7,8,9,10,11 . . .

   (*ELLIE misses.*)

ELLIE: I'll never make 300! 1,2,3,4,5,6 . . .

   (*ELLIE misses. She crosses to the mirror. VOICE mimes her gestures.*)

ELLIE: If I could make 300 I'd be famous. I'd be the world's champion. I'd be rich and famous and everyone in the whole world would come up to me and . . . How de do? Yes, it was very difficult, but I just kept practicing and practicing. No, it wasn't easy.

(*LUCILLE sings louder.*)

VOICE: Considering all the racket SHE was making.

ELLIE: Considering all the racket SHE was making.

VOICE: How could anyone expect to concentrate with all that toot toot de doot?

ELLIE: How could anyone expect to concentrate with all that toot toot de doot. . .

VOICE: What does she think this is Grand Opree or something?

(*ELLIE clutches her throat and mimics LUCILLE, she warbles off-key.*)

ELLIE: Laaaaa . . . Laaaaaaa, Laaaaaaa, Laaaaaaa.

(*LUCILLE hears her and stops.*)

LUCILLE: Ellinor? Did you call me?

ELLIE: No.

(*LUCILLE resumes the scales. ELLIE gets an idea. She crosses to the toy box and pulls out a weird assortment of junk: a couple of old hats, a black cloak, a deflated inner tube, silver shoes, and a set of Dracula fangs. ELLIE dresses herself and makes a couple of menacing passes at the mirror. VOICE mimics her action. ELLIE sneaks out of the room and up behind LUCILLE.*)

ELLIE: I am Count Dracula and I have come to suck your blood!

LUCILLE: (*Startled*) Oh my!

ELLIE: Did I scare you?

LUCILLE: You startled me.

ELLIE: What are you doing anyway?

LUCILLE: I am just running through a few scales.

ELLIE: Do you have to?

LUCILLE: Well, yes, the voice is just like any other instrument, you have to practice every day.

ELLIE: You call that MUSIC? All that toot toot de doot?

LUCILLE: Well, scales aren't exactly music but . . .

ELLIE: (*Singing very off-key*) "Everybody was Kung Fu Fighting." Uh . . uh . . . uh . . . uh . . . hu!**

LUCILLE: Well, ummm that's very nice but . . .

ELLIE: (*Lying on her back with feet in the air*) "I've got tears in my ears from lying on my back crying out my eyes over you."**

LUCILLE: Ellinor, what in the world are you wearing?

ELLIE: Pretty neat huh? I got this stuff from Pop. It's from the yard. He said I could keep it. You should go down there, he's got some great stuff.

LUCILLE: Oh Ellinor, you have such a nice room and so many lovely toys. Why do you keep bringing home all this junk?

ELLIE: This isn't junk! It's perfectly good stuff!

LUCILLE: But people have thrown it away.

ELLIE: That doesn't mean it isn't any good! How would you like to be thrown away?

LUCILLE: When I was your age I had a collection of dolls from all over the world. I used to make clothes for them and make up stories about them. You know I still have those dolls. I gave them to my brother for his children. Maybe I could write to him and we could . . .

ELLIE: Dolls! Ugghhh! I like this stuff better. Besides most of it isn't mine. Most of this belongs to Lana and Frizbee.

LUCILLE: Oh?

**These songs should be constantly changed to songs that are currently popular.

ELLIE: This tire is for Frizbee's motorcycle and these hats and beautiful shoes are for Lana. She's a movie star and she needs these things in her work.

LUCILLE: I thought you told me she was a Roller Derby Queen.

ELLIE: She's both! Oh, the Dracula fangs . . . they're mine.

LUCILLE: Just put them away when you are through. Have you finished cleaning up your room yet?

ELLIE: Ohhh I have been busy.

LUCILLE: You promised to do it before your father came home.

ELLIE: Pop doesn't care. He never used to make me clean up my room.

LUCILLE: Look, why don't I give you a hand. Together we can do it in no time.

ELLIE: No way! You'll just make me throw stuff out.

(*ELLIE walks back to her room and stands in her doorway.*)

ELLIE: Nobody gets in my room without a pass!

(*She slams the door. LUCILLE sighs and turns back to her music.*)

VOICE: Red Light!

(*All freeze.*)

VOICE: She doesn't like you.

(*ELLIE is drawn to the mirror.*)

ELLIE and VOICE: Pick up your room you messy little girl. Why don't you play with dolls like normal children? You're freaky and you like junk. You could have such a lovely room if it wasn't such a mess.

VOICE: She could never like a messy little girl like you. Green Light!

(*LUCILLE resumes her scales. ELLIE listens for a second and begins to mimic her.* ELLIE leaps to the top of the toy box and warbles in a high squeaky voice. FRIZBEE pops up from under a pile of dirty clothes.*)

FRIZBEE: Bravo! Bravo! What a beautiful voice you have! You sing like an angel! You sing like a bird, only better. I kiss your hand. May I have your autograph?

ELLIE: Why certainly young man!

(*ELLIE scribbles on his back.*)

ELLIE: "To Frizbee from Ellie, the world's greatest opera singer."

FRIZBEE: I will treasure this forever. Here this is for you!

(*FRIZBEE pulls a flower from nowhere and presents it to ELLIE.*)*

LANA: (*Her voice comes from the toy box*) Everybody out of my way.

(*ELLIE jumps off the box, the lid flies open and LANA pops out.*)

LANA: Ellie Murphy, the great opera singer, do you have anything to say to our viewers at home?*

ELLIE: How de do.

LANA: How did you get to be such a great opera singer?

ELLIE: Oh it was very difficult. The voice is just like any other instrument you have to practice every day.

(*FRIZBEE presents her with a bowling pin.*)

FRIZBEE: Ellie Murphy I am pleased and proud to present you with this singer of the year award.

ELLIE: Dear friends, I thank you and I have only one thing to say, I deserved it. I practiced every day . . .

---

*Cues for music and songs in the musical version of the play are indicated by single asterisks. The musical version of *Step on a Crack* is available through Anchorage Press.

(*LUCILLE starts to sing a beautiful melody. ELLIE moves toward the mirror.*)

ELLIE: I practiced until my throat was sore from singing and . . .

VOICE: Red Light!

(*All freeze.*)

VOICE: You'll never be as good as Lucille.

(*VOICE snatches the pin away from her.*)

VOICE: She's a much better singer than you are. Green Light.

ELLIE: (*Grabs for the pin*) This is MY prize and I deserve it!

(*They struggle with the pin.*)

ELLIE: (*To LANA and FRIZBEE*) Hey you guys!

(*They rush to her aid. The pin is tossed in the air and FRIZBEE catches it.*)

FRIZBEE: Ellie Murphy I am pleased and proud to present you with this singer of the year award.

ELLIE: Thank you for my prize. It is neat!

*(*There is the sound of thunderous applause. LUCILLE crosses to ELLIE's door and knocks. The applause stops instantly.*)

LUCILLE: Ellinor?

(*LANA and FRIZBEE freeze.*)

ELLIE: Who goes there?

LUCILLE: May I come in?

ELLIE: What's the password?

LUCILLE: Please?

ELLIE: (*Peeking out*) Have you got a pass?

(*LUCILLE enters and looks around.*)

LUCILLE: Who were you talking to?

ELLIE: Lana and Frizbee.

LUCILLE: (*Playing along*) OH! Are they still here?

(*Frizbee pops his head up and makes a rude sound, then disappears into the box.*)

ELLIE: Sure, Frizbee just did a raspberry.

LUCILLE: Oh?

(*LANA crosses in front of LUCILLE making ugly faces at her.*)

ELLIE: And Lana's making faces . . . like this and this . . . .

(*LANA goes into the toy box. LUCILLE crosses to the middle of the room crouches down and speaks into empty air.*)

LUCILLE: Were you two helping Ellie clean up her room?

ELLIE: Lucille, they're not here. They went into the toy box.

LUCILLE: (*Playing along a bit too much*) Oh I see. Do they live in the toy box?

ELLIE: (*Nonplussed*) It's too small to live in there. They just sit there sometimes.

LUCILLE: Oh. Please Ellie, let me help you. We'll have this place cleaned up in no time. Now where does this go?

ELLIE: No deal! You throw out too much!

(*ELLIE starts putting things away.*)

LUCILLE: Oh Ellinor, you've lost another button. I just sewed that one on too.

ELLIE: It is a scientific fact that some people are allergic to buttons.

(*ELLIE looks hard at LUCILLE.*)

Hey, Lucille, how old are you?

LUCILLE: (*A bit taken aback.*) Uhhh, well, I'm thirty-five.

ELLIE: (*Very serious*) Boy that's old.

LUCILLE: Well, it's not that old.

ELLIE: Do you use a lot of make-up?

LUCILLE: I use some.

ELLIE: A lot? Do you put that goopy stuff on your eyes to make them look big?

LUCILLE: Would you like me to show you about make-up?

ELLIE: Uhhhgg. NO! Make-up is for girlies and OLD people.

LUCILLE: Come on Ellinor, let's get this room done before your father gets home.

(*MAX enters with a football helmet and a feather duster for ELLIE.*)

MAX: Anybody home?

ELLIE: Too late!

(*ELLIE runs to greet him and jumps into his arms. He gives her the helmet and duster. As LUCILLE enters, ELLIE hides them behind her back and sneaks them into her room.*)

MAX: Hey Midget.

ELLIE: Neato. Thanks.

(*LUCILLE approaches to hug him.*)

LUCILLE: Hello dear, you're early.

MAX: Be careful, I'm a mess. I gotta wash up.

(*LUCILLE gets him a rag. He wipes his hands and then kisses her. He sits down to take off his boots. ELLIE enters with his house shoes.*)

MAX: Hey Ellie, what's the matter with your shirt?

(*MAX points to an imaginary spot on her shirt, ELLIE looks down and MAX tweaks her nose.*)

MAX: Ha! Hah! Gotcha! Can't have your nose back. Not till you answer three knock knocks . . . Let's see . . . Knock, knock . . .

ELLIE: (*With her nose still held*) Who's there?

MAX: Dwain.

ELLIE: Dwain who?

MAX: Dwain the bathtub I'm dwouning.

ELLIE: Hey, I got one. Knock, knock.

MAX: Who's there?

ELLIE: DeGaulle.

MAX: DeGaulle who?

ELLIE: (*Crossing her eyes*) De-gaulle-f ball hit me in the head and dats why I talk dis way.

MAX: Ohhhh.

ELLIE: Oh I got another one Pop. Knock, knock . . .

LUCILLE: (*Jumping in*) Who's there?

(*Ellie shoots her a nasty look and turns away.*)

ELLIE: Nobody.

LUCILLE: (*Puzzled*) Nobody who?

ELLIE: (*Insolently*) Just nobody that's all!

(*MAX and LUCILLE exchange a look.*)

MAX: I've still got your nose.

ELLIE: (*Back in the game*) Give it back you Bozo.

MAX: Nope you gotta get it.

(*MAX pretends to hold her nose just out of reach. ELLIE jumps for it. MAX tosses it to LUCILLE.*)

MAX: Here Lucille, catch!

(*LUCILLE, confused, misses it.*)

LUCILLE: Huh? Oh I'm sorry.

(*The game is over and Ellie scowls.*)

ELLIE: Pop, do I have to clean up my room? Can I get you a beer? Can I watch T.V.? Do I have to throw out all my good stuff?

MAX: Whoa! What's going on?

ELLIE: Can I watch T.V.?

MAX: Sure.

LUCILLE: Max, I have been trying to get her to clean up her room for days.

MAX: Awww it's Friday afternoon.

LUCILLE: Max.

MAX: Clean up your room Ellie.

ELLIE: Awww Pop, you never used to make me.

MAX : Sorry Midget, this ship's got a new captain.

ELLIE: Awww Pop!

MAX: Do what your mother says.

ELLIE: (*Under her breath*) She is not my real mother.

MAX: What did you say?

ELLIE: Nothing.

MAX: Hey, maybe later we'll do something fun.

ELLIE: Can we go bowling?

MAX: Maybe.

ELLIE: Oh please, oh please, oh please! We used to go all the time. Pop and me, we were practically professional bowlers. We were practicing to go on Family Bowl-O-Rama, on T.V.

MAX: Clean up your room and we'll talk about bowling later.

(*ELLIE trudges into her room. MAX sits down and LUCILLE massages his back.*)

LUCILLE: You're early.

MAX: Yep, and I have a surprise for you.

LUCILLE: For me, Max? What is it?

MAX: You gotta guess. It's something we've been talking about.

(*ELLIE interrupts. She is wearing a long black cape, a tall hat and a scarf. She holds a piece of metal pipe.*)

ELLIE: Ta Dah! Presenting the Great Mysterioso! You will see that I have nothing up my sleeve. See this pipe? See this scarf? Here hold this hat lady.

(*ELLIE hands the hat to LUCILLE.*)

ELLIE: Now I take this scarf, just an ordinary everyday magic scarf, and I put it over this piece of pipe. Now you both will blow on it.

(*MAX and LUCILLE blow on the scarf.*)

ELLIE: I say some magic words. OOOOOBLEEEDOOOO OBBBB-BLEEEDAY ZOOOOOBLEEEDA! Zap! Zap! Zap!

(*ELLIE flips the pipe over her shoulder, it lands with a loud crash. She grabs the hat and places the scarf in it.*)

ELLIE: Presto! No more pipe! Ta Dah!

(*ELLIE displays the empty scarf. MAX and LUCILLE clap.*)

MAX: I thought you went to . . .

ELLIE: I found this stuff while I was cleaning. Pretty neat huh?

LUCILLE: That was very nice Ellie.

MAX: Ellie, Lucille and I are talking.

ELLIE: What about?

MAX: ELLIE!

ELLIE: I'm going. I'm going!

(*ELLIE goes back to her room. MAX takes some folders out of his pocket.*)

MAX: Do you remember that travel agent I said I was going to talk to?

LUCILLE: Oh Max, do you mean you did it?

MAX: Did I talk to him? Ta Dah! Little lady, you and I are going on a honeymoon. We are going to Hawaii.

LUCILLE: Hawaii? Oh Max!

MAX: Just look at this, "American Express twenty-one day excursions to Honolulu and the islands." That's our honeymoon, that is if you want to go.

LUCILLE: Want to? I have always wanted to go to those places. But can we? I mean should we? Right now?

MAX: Why not? I've been saving for a trip and I think I can take about three weeks off. Now's as good a time as ever.

LUCILLE: I'm not so sure we ought to leave Ellie right now.

MAX: She'll be fine. I can get someone to stay with her and after all she's in school. There is this lady, Mrs. Dougan, she used to stay with Ellie when I'd go on hunting trips. I'll call her tomorrow.

LUCILLE: I just don't want her to think that we are running off and leaving her.

MAX: Don't worry, I'll talk to her.

LUCILLE: Right away . . . that is if you are serious.

MAX: You bet I'm serious. I got all this stuff didn't I? Look at some of these tour deals. You get everything: air fare, meals, hotel, an air conditioned bus . . .

LUCILLE: Oh look at that sun, and all that sand. What a beautiful beach.

(*ELLIE enters clutching a T.V. Guide.*)

ELLIE: Guess what? Midnight Spook-a-thon has a double feature tonight! *The Curse of Frankenstein* and the *Return of the Mummy's Hand!* Isn't that neat? Can I watch it Pop?

MAX: (*Hiding the folders*) Uhhh sure, why not.

LUCILLE: What time does it come on?

ELLIE: (*Nonchalantly*) Oh early.

LUCILLE: What time?

ELLIE: (*Quickly*) Eleven-thirty.

LUCILLE: That's awfully late.

ELLIE: Tomorrow's Saturday. And besides Pop said I could.

LUCILLE: We'll see.

ELLIE: You always say that when you mean no. What are you guys doing?

MAX: We're talking.

ELLIE: (*Seeing the folders*) What this?

(*LUCILLE starts to show them to her and MAX snatches them away.*)

MAX: Papers, papers of mine. Ellie is your room cleaned up yet?

ELLIE: No! Gee whiz! I'm going. I'm going!

(*ELLIE crosses back to her room.*)

LUCILLE: Max, why didn't you talk to her?

MAX: Oh I don't know, I just hate it when she yells.

LUCILLE: Yells! I thought you said it was going to be alright.

MAX: It is! I just have to kind of talk to her about it . . . when she's in a good mood.

LUCILLE: If you really think it is going to upset her, let's not do it now. We can always go later.

MAX: I said I was going to talk to her and I will . . .

(*MAX crosses to ELLIE'S room. LUCILLE follows slightly behind.*)

MAX: Ellie . . . uhhh . . .

ELLIE: I'm not finished yet but I'm cleaning!

MAX: Looks like you are doing a good job there. Want any help?

ELLIE: Huh?

(*ELLIE finds the duster and dusts everything and then starts dusting MAX.*)

MAX: Ellie, umm Lucille and I . . . uhhh we were thinking that it might be a good idea if . . . if . . . we went . . . bowling! Tonight!

ELLIE: Hey, neato!

MAX: After you clean up your room.

ELLIE: I'll hurry. I'll hurry.

(*MAX leaves the room with LUCILLE shaking her head.*)

LUCILLE: Why didn't you tell her?

MAX: Let's wait until we know exactly when we're going.

LUCILLE: I don't want her to think that we are sneaking around behind her back.

MAX: I'll tell her. I just want to pick my own time.

(*ELLIE starts out the door.*)

VOICE: Red Light!

(*ELLIE freezes.*)

VOICE: Something fishy's going on. They don't want you around. They're trying to get rid of you . . . Green Light.

(*ELLIE stares into the mirror.*)

MAX: So that's your surprise. How do you like it?

LUCILLE: Oh Max!

(*LUCILLE hugs him. Ellie enters.*)

ELLIE: Ahem!

MAX: What do you want?

ELLIE: I just came to get a shovel.

LUCILLE: What do you need shovel for?

ELLIE: I'm cleaning! I'm cleaning!

(*MAX turns her around and marches her back into the room.*)

LUCILLE: Please Max!

(*They all enter the room.*)

MAX: Ellie, I want to talk to you . . . . .

(*Ellie shines his shoes.*)

MAX: ELLIE!

(*ELLIE looks up at him and gives him a goofy look.*)

MAX: I just want to tell you . . . . I tell you what! If you clean up your room right now then we'll all go get ice cream or something!

LUCILLE: (*Exasperated*) I have to stop at the market anyway. I'll go make a list.

(*LUCILLE exits.*)

MAX: And now once and for all . . . listen here tough guy . . . you is gonna clean up that room. Okay?

ELLIE: (*Tough guy*) Oh Yeah? Who is gonna make me?

MAX: I am Louie, cause I am da tough cop in dis town. Now you is gonna get in dat cell and you is gonna clean it up, or else I is gonna throw you in solitary . . see?

(*They tussle for a moment, MAX pulls her cap over her eyes.*)

MAX: An I don't want to see you outta there till you is done.

(*MAX shuts the door and exits.*)

ELLIE: Darn! Lately this place is really getting like a prison.

VOICE: Red Light! She keeps you locked up like some kind of prisoner.

ELLIE: Yeah! A prison with walls and bars and chains. A dungeon with cold stones and bread and water and rats. Solitary confinement . . The walls are closing in. You gotta let me out . . . You gotta let me out . . .

VOICE: Green Light!

(*Suddenly the toy chest lid flips open and a shovel full of dirt comes flying out. A shovel appears and on the other end of the shovel is LANA.*)*

LANA: Hi yah, Sweetie!

ELLIE: Lana!

LANA: Who else? You think we wuz gonna let you take a bum rap? We dug this tunnel t'bust you outta here.

ELLIE: We?

LANA: Frizbee and me! Right Frizbee? Frizbee? He was right behind me in the tunnel. He must be here someplace.

(*They look for FRIZBEE. LANA looks in the toy chest and slams the lid.*)

LANA: Oh no!

ELLIE: What?

LANA: Don't look!

ELLIE: Why not?

LANA: Cave in! The tunnel's caved in.

ELLIE: Oh NO!

LANA: The whole thing . . . . Squash!

ELLIE: Poor Frizbee!

LANA: What are we gonna do?

ELLIE: There is only one thing we can do!

LANA: Yeah?

ELLIE: Blast!

LANA: Blast Boss?

ELLIE: It's the only way. You get the dynamite and I'll get the fuse.

(*They gather together junk to make a blasting box, fuse and plunger.*)

ELLIE: First you gotta make the box. Then you gotta put the dyna-mite in and then stick your fingers in your ears, and count down 10,9,8,7,6,5,4,3,2 . . . . 1 BARRROOOOOOOM.

(*VOICE makes the sound of the explosion. The lid flies open a puff of smoke comes out. FRIZBEE'S arms and legs hang out of the box.*)*

FRIZBEE: (*Weakly*) Hey you guys . . . . .

(*LANA and ELLIE rush to FRIZBEE and lift him out of the toy chest.*)

LANA: Are you alright?

FRIZBEE: Sure.

ELLIE: The tunnel collapsed on you.

FRIZBEE: I thought it got dark all of a sudden.

ELLIE: Okay. Youse guys we gotta blow this joint.

(*FRIZBEE pulls a handkerchief out of costume and blows his nose, as he pulls another handkerchief comes out and a whole string of handkerchiefs follow to FRIZBEE'S amazement.*)

ELLIE: Great idea Frizbee. Here Lana you take one end and go first, I'll hold this, and Frizbee, you bring up the rear. Goodby cruel cell.

*(*LANA and ELLIE dive into the box.*)

FRIZBEE: Goodbye cruel ceeeeeeee . . . . .

(*FRIZBEE is pulled in after them. LUCILLE enters wearing a police hat and badge.*)

LUCILLE: Calling all cars. Calling all cars. This is the warden speak-ing! Ellie-the-mess-Murphy has just escaped from solitary confine-ment. She is messy and extremely dangerous. After her! After her!

(*There is a chase. LANA and ELLIE crawl under the bed, and around the stage. LUCILLE crouches behind the bed.*)

LANA: We made it!

ELLIE: Free at last.

LANA: Wow that was close.

(*LUCILLE appears.*)

LUCILLE: Have you cleaned up your room yet?

ELLIE and LANA: EEEK!

(*There is a short chase. LUCILLE lassos ELLIE and LANA with the scarfs and drags them over to one side of the stage where she crouches down and VOICE makes the sound of a car. LUCILLE mimes driving the paddy wagon. FRIZBEE finally makes it out of the tunnel, sees what's going on, disappears for a second and reappears wearing the football helmet. VOICE makes the sound of a siren, FRIZBEE mimes riding a motorcycle. LUCILLE puts on the brakes. FRIZBEE gets off the motorcycle, pulls an imaginary pad out of his pocket, licks an imaginary pencil.*)

FRIZBEE: Okay girlie, where's the fire?

LUCILLE: I'm sorry officer, I . . . . just wanted her to clean up her . . .

FRIZBEE: Let me see your license. I'm gonna give you a ticket.

LUCILLE: But officer I . . . .

FRIZBEE: But first I'm gonna give you a . . . tickle.

(FRIZBEE tickles LUCILLE, she laughs helplessly, LANA and ELLIE escape.)

LUCILLE: You can't do that!

FRIZBEE: Oh yeah? I just did!

ELLIE: To the hideout!

(*LUCILLE chases them off. ELLIE, LANA and FRIZBEE race back to ELLIE'S room. They overturn the benches to make a barricade. ELLIE rifles through the toy chest throwing junk everywhere they put on guns and helmets.*)

ELLIE: Get the ammo and take cover.

VOICE: Come out with your hands up.

ELLIE: Let 'em have it.

(*Imaginary battle takes place. They throw things all over the room. FRIZ-BEE uses a toilet paper roll like a grenade. ELLIE clutches a grease gun like a tommy gun. All make sounds. LUCILLE enters dressed in regular street clothes. She is not part of the fantasy.*)

LUCILLE: (*Approaching the door*) Ellinor, are you ready?

ELLIE: You'll never take us copper!

(*LUCILLE opens the door. All sound effects stop. LANA and FRIZBEE freeze. The room is totally destroyed. ELLIE pretends to be oiling the bed.*)

LUCILLE: (*Dumbfounded*) Ellinor.

ELLIE: I . . . I . . . I. uh, was just cleaning my room.

LUCILLE: Ellinor.

ELLIE: I didn't do it all. Lana threw the grenade.

LANA: I did not!

LUCILLE: I certainly hope you don't mean to tell me that Lana and Frizbee made all this mess.

ELLIE: What are you hoping I'll tell you?

LUCILLE: Oh Ellinor.

ELLIE: They made most of it.

FRIZBEE: We did not!

LUCILLE: Are they supposed to be here now?

ELLIE: (*Gesturing with grease gun*) They're right over . . . .

LUCILLE: Ellinor, that's a grease gun . . . . . don't . . . . .

(*ELLIE squeezes a glop of grease on the floor.*)

VOICE: Glop!

ELLIE: Uh oh!

LUCILLE: The carpet! A brand new carpet! Grease is the worst possible stain. Oh my lord.

ELLIE: I thought it was empty.

LUCILLE: Now which is it hot water or cold? . . . . Oh my lord.

(*LUCILLE rushes off to get a rag.*)

LANA: Uhhhh so long Boss.

FRIZBEE: Be seeing you around.

ELLIE: Where are you going?

LANA: I just remembered something I gotta do.

FRIZBEE: Yeah and I gotta do it with her . . . . Whatever it is . . . .

(*THEY exit into the box. LUCILLE enters and rubs frantically at the spot.*)

LUCILLE: It just gets worse and worse . . . It's ruined. A brand new carpet.

ELLIE: Well, I'm your brand new kid.

LUCILLE: Ellinor I knew something like this would happen. This is the last time you bring junk into your room. Oh it just gets bigger and bigger.

(*MAX enters, and rushes to help.*)

MAX: What in the world . . . . . .

LUCILLE: Oh Max, Ellinor spilled grease on the carpet.

ELLIE: I didn't mean to.

LUCILLE: The more I rub the worse it gets.

ELLIE: It's not my fault.

MAX: Did you try cold water?

LUCILLE: No, it's hot water for grease.

ELLIE: Hey listen, I don't mind that spot.

MAX: No, I'm sure it's cold water.

ELLIE: Honest, I like that spot just the way it is.

LUCILLE: Max, it's hot water for grease and cold water for blood stains and ink.

MAX: I've got this stuff in my car.

LUCILLE: Oh it's no use!

ELLIE: (*Shouting*) Would you leave it alone! I like that spot.

   (*They both stop and stare at her.*)

This is MY room.

LUCILLE: But it is a brand new carpet.

ELLIE: BIG DEAL.

MAX: Ellie don't talk that way to your Mother.

ELLIE: She is not my real Mother.

   (*Still pause.*)

   (*To LUCILLE*)

You'll never be my REAL MOTHER.

LUCILLE: (*Angry but even*) You know, Ellie, you're absolutely right.

   (*Pause.*)

LUCILLE: (*Covering*) Well if we are going to the market I better get my coat.

(*LUCILLE exits. MAX is angry and very depressed.*)

MAX: That was nice . . . . that was really nice.

ELLIE: It's not my fault.

MAX: You hurt her feelings.

ELLIE: I have feelings too you know. Just because you're a kid doesn't mean you're junk!

MAX: Come off it Ellie.

ELLIE: That spot is almost out.

MAX: (*Really down*) Yeah!

ELLIE: Maybe we could put something over it.

MAX: Yeah.

ELLIE: With a sign that says "Don't look here."

MAX: (*With a slight laugh*) Sure.

ELLIE: (*Trying to get him out of his mood*) Knock, knock.

MAX: Not now, Ellie.

ELLIE: Let's wrestle.

MAX: Uh uh! You're getting too big for me.

ELLIE: Do you think I'm too fat?

MAX: You? Naw you're fine.

ELLIE: Hey Pop, do you remember the time we went camping and you drove all afternoon to get out to the woods? It was dark when we pitched the tent and we heard all those funny sounds and you said it was MONSTERS. Then in the morning we found out we were in somebody's front lawn.

MAX: (*Responding a bit*) I knew where we were all the time.

ELLIE: Or when we went to the Super Bowl and I got cold, and you said yell something in your megaphone.

MAX: Yeah, and you yelled "I'm cold and I want to go home."

(*They both laugh.*)

ELLIE: (*Tentatively*) Hey Pop, tell me about my real mother.

MAX: How come you want to hear about her all the time these days?

(*ELLIE sits at his feet and rests against his knees.*)

ELLIE: I just do. Hey do you remember the time it was my birthday and you brought Mom home from the hospital, and I didn't know she was coming that time? I remember I was already in bed and you guys wanted to surprise me. She just came into my room, kissed me good night and tucked me in, just like it was any other night.

MAX: (*Moved*) How could you remember that? You were just four years old.

ELLIE: I just remember.

MAX: Your mother was a wonderful person and I loved her very much.

ELLIE: As much as you . . . like Lucille?

MAX: Ellie.

ELLIE: Was she pretty?

MAX: She was beautiful.

ELLIE: Do I look like her?

MAX: Naw, you look more like me, you mug.

ELLIE: (*Suddenly angry*) Why does everything have to change?

MAX: Hey.

ELLIE: How come Lucille is always so neat and everything? I bet she never even burps.

MAX: She does.

ELLIE: HUH!

MAX: I heard her once.

ELLIE: Do you think I'd look cute with make-up on?

MAX: You? You're just a kid.

ELLIE: But Lucille wears make-up. Lot's of it.

MAX: Well she's grown up.

ELLIE: Hey do you know how old she is?

MAX: Sure. Thirty-five.

ELLIE: How come you married such an old one?

MAX: That's not old.

ELLIE: Huh!

MAX: Why I am older than that myself.

ELLIE: You are??

MAX: Ellie, you know how you get to go to camp in the summer. You get to go away all by yourself.

ELLIE: Yeah but I'm not going any more.

MAX: You're not?

ELLIE: Nope, look what happened the last time I went. You and Lucille get to be good friends, then as soon as I get back you get married. Who knows if I go away again I might get back and find out you moved to Alaska.

MAX: We wouldn't do that.

ELLIE: You might.

MAX: Ellie, kids can't always go where parents go. Sometimes parents go away all by themselves.

ELLIE: How come ever since you got married I am such a kid. You never used to say I was a kid. We did everything together. Now all I hear is, "Kids can't do this," "Kids can't do that," "Kids have to go to bed at eight-thirty." "Kids have to clean up their rooms." Why does everything have to change?

MAX: Nothing's changed. I still love you the same. Now there's just two of us who love you.

ELLIE: HUH!

POP: I just wish you'd try a little harder to . . . . .

ELLIE: To like Lucille? Why should I? She doesn't like me. She likes cute little girls who play with dollies.

MAX: Well she got herself a messy little mug that likes junk.

   (*ELLIE pulls away.*)

MAX: I'm just kidding. She likes you fine the way you are.

ELLIE: Oh yeah, well I don't like her.

MAX: Why not?

   (*LUCILLE enters and overhears the following.*)

ELLIE: Cause . . . Cause . . Cause she's a wicked stepmother . . . .

   (*ELLIE giggles in spite of herself. MAX is really angry.*)

MAX: That's not funny!

ELLIE: You shout at me all the time!

MAX: (*Shouting*) I'm not shouting!

LUCILLE: (*Breaking it up*) Is everybody ready to go?

MAX: Ellie get your coat.

ELLIE: I'm not going.

MAX: Get your coat. We are going for ice cream!

ELLIE: (*Pouting*) I don't want any.

MAX: Okay. Lucille let's go. Ellie you can just stay at home and clean up your room.

LUCILLE: Max . . . .

MAX I said let's go!

ELLIE: See if I care.

(*They leave the room. ELLIE pouts.*)

LUCILLE: Was it about the trip?

MAS: What?

LUCILLE: Were you two arguing about the trip?

MAX: Are you kidding, I didn't even get that far.

LUCILLE: Let's just forget it.

MAX: What?

LUCILLE: Forget the whole thing!

MAX: Oh no. I need this trip. We need it; we have got to have some time for US.

LUCILLE: If you want to go, then let's talk to her and we'll go. If not, let's just forget it!

MAX: Let me work this out in my own way.

LUCILLE: Why does everything have to be a game or a joke? Max, it really isn't fair to Ellie or me. Why can't we just talk?

MAX: This isn't easy for her.

LUCILLE: Well, it isn't easy for me either; and frankly, Max, I have just about had it.

MAX: Lucille . . .

LUCILLE: If we are ever going to be a family, we've got to be able to talk . . .

MAX: Not now! You're angry, she's angry. Let's go to the market, calm down, and we'll talk when we get home.

   (*They exit.*)

ELLIE: Hey, wait a minute . . . Wait, I changed my mind. I want to go.

   (*They have gone. ELLIE turns back.*)

VOICE: Red Light! It's all her fault! She didn't want you to go. SHE made it so you couldn't go.

   (*ELLIE is drawn to the mirror.*)

ELLIE and VOICE: Pick up your toys. Make your bed. Do what we say or you won't be fed.

ELLIE: I'll never be pretty. Ugly face, ugly hair and squinty little eyes. If I had my real mother I'd be pretty.

VOICE: You'll never be as pretty as Lucille. Green Light!

ELLIE: They dress me in rags. They make me work all day.

VOICE: Ugly Ellie.

ELLIE: Ugly Ellie, Ugly Ellie . . .

   (ELLIE sits on the bed and pulls her cap over her face dejectedly.)

FRIZBEE: (*Inside the toy box*) Cinderelli, Cinderelli, Cinderelli . . .

   (*Lid to the box opens and out pops FRIZBEE wearing Mickey Mouse ears and singing the Walt Disney song.*)

FRIZBEE: Cinderelli, Cinderelli, Cinderelli, Cinderelli . . . .

ELLIE: What are you supposed to be?

FRIBEE: I am just a little Mouse, who lives inside this great big house. Oh Cinderelli kind and dear, I see what's been going on right here.

Your wicked stepmother cruel and mean, makes you wash and wax and clean. Now she's gone to the ice cream ball, and left you here with nothing at all.

ELLIE: Dear little Mouse you've seen everything?

FRIZBEE: Oh Yes! Everything and more.
  Ever since your stepmother came to stay,
  I have seen you slave all day.
  She gives you crusts of bread to eat.
  She pinches your elbows and stamps on your feet.
  She gives you rags and paper towels to wear.
  She calls you names and tangles your hair.

ELLIE: But what are we to do? I want to go to the ball but I have nothing to wear, my hair is dull, dull, dull, and my face is blah!

LANA: (*From the toy box*) Perhaps there's something I can do.

  (Toy box opens again, we see LANA'S feet waving in the air. ELLIE and FRIZBEE pull her out, she is outlandishly dressed in a gold lamee dress, blond wig, tiara, and silvery shoes.)

LANA: I am your fairy godmother and I have come to make you a star. We have much to do, after all stars are made not born.

ELLIE: Are you going to do a spell?

LANA: Oh no, spells are old fashioned. Today we have something much better . . . money!

  (*LANA throws a fist-full of money in the air.*)

LANA: First we need a dress.

ELLIE: Hey, I got an idea. Come with me . . . . .

  (*ELLIE leads them out of her room to LUCILLE'S ladder where she gets an elaborate party dress.*)

LANA: Perfect!

FRIZBEE: But that's Lucille's.

LANA: Not anymore. We just bought it.

(*LANA spears a bill on the hanger and helps ELLIE on with the dress over her clothes.*)

LANA: And now the hair! Give her something that simply screams glamour.

*(*FRIZBEE becomes the hairdresser.*)

FRIZBEE: Would Madame care for a flip?

(*FRIZBEE does a flip.*)

LANA: The hair you dolt!

(*LANA clobbers him. FRIZBEE makes an elaborate production of messing up ELLIE'S hair.*)

LANA: Make-up!

(*FRIZBEE slaps make-up on ELLIE and shows her how to blot her lipstick by smacking her lips. He gets carried away with the smacking and gives LANA a big kiss.*)

LANA: Oh gross!

(*LANA clobbers him.*)

LANA: And now the coach.

(*FRIZBEE puts on the football helmet and jumps around being a coach.*)

LANA: THE CARRIAGE!!

(*FRIZBEE gets a broomstick horse.*)

LANA: And last but not least . . . your public!

(*LANA throws a fist-full of money in the air and there is tumultuous cheering.*)

(*ELLIE, FRIZBEE and LANA exit in procession. A fanfare is heard. FRIZ-BEE enters with a roll of paper towels which he rolls out like a red carpet. He stands at attention at the end of the carpet. LANA swirls on and down the carpet, she curtsies to FRIZBEE.*).

VOICE: Ladies and gentlemen, the Prince.

(*MAX enters dressed in a frock coat over his regular clothes. He bows and stands at the end of the "carpet."*)

VOICE: And now ladies and gentlemen, the moment we have all been waiting for, the star of stage, screen and television . . . the Princess Cinderelli!

(*Music plays the Sleeping Beauty Waltz, ELLIE enters, a spot light catches her, she sweeps down the carpet to MAX who bows. They dance.*)

LANA: (*As they waltz by her*) Remember darling, your contract is up at midnight.

(*VOICE begins to bang on a pot with a spoon, twelve times in all. On the stroke of twelve LUCILLE appears, sweeps down the "carpet." MAX turns and bows to her and dances off with her leaving ELLIE.*)

ELLIE: Hey wait a minute, what do you think you're doing?

(*LANA and FRIZBEE exit.*)

ELLIE: Hey, I'm supposed to be the Princess around here. Hey, I'm Cinderelli! Come back. Alright see if I care. I don't need any stupid old prince. I can have a good time all by myself.

(*ELLIE sings and dances all by herself. Music out, ELLIE, obviously upset, dances faster and faster. MAX and LUCILLE enter with groceries. They stop at her door and watch. MAX bursts out laughing. LUCILLE elbows him. ELLIE stops, mortified at being caught.*)

ELLIE: Well what are you staring at?

MAX: What is this, Halloween?

ELLIE: What's so funny?

LUCILLE: I think you look very pretty.

ELLIE: (*Defensive*) Well I wasn't trying to look pretty! I was trying to look dumb and funny, like this . . and this . . and this . . .

(*ELLIE makes faces.*)

ELLIE: Since I can't be pretty I might as well be funny and dumb.

(*ELLIE capers around wildly until she stubs her toe.*)

ELLIE: Owwwwwwwww!

LUCILE: What's the matter?

ELLIE: I stubbed my dumb toe.

(*ELLIE sits and buries her head in her hands. MAX starts to go to her. LUCILLE stops him by shoving her sack of groceries into his arms.*)

LUCILLE: Max, will you put these in the kitchen for me?

(*MAX gives her a look, she waves him away and he exits. LUCILLE goes to ELLIE and helps her out of the dress.*)

LUCILLE: You okay?

(*ELLIE pulls away and sits on the bed. She shrugs.*)

LUCILLE: Ellinor, if I asked you to help me with something would you do it?

ELLIE: I didn't clean up my room.

LUCILLE: So I see, but that's not what I am talking about. I want you to help me with something else.

ELLIE: Huh! I don't see what I could help you do.

LUCILLE: (*Tentatively*) Well, I've never had any children . . . and lots of times I'm not too sure what mothers are supposed to do. So I wanted you to help me.

ELLIE: How should I know? I never really had a mother, not one I remember real well.

LUCILLE: Well, maybe we could help each other.

(*ELLIE shrugs.*)

LUCILLE: You see, my mother was very strict. She made me pick up my room and practice my voice every day and I loved her.

ELLIE: She was your real mother.

LUCILLE: Yes.

ELLIE: That makes a difference. You have to love your real mother and your real kids.

LUCILLE: But you can choose to love your stepchildren.

ELLIE: But nobody can make you.

LUCILLE: (*Pause*) That's right.

ELLIE: Well I can tell you a couple of things mothers shouldn't do. They shouldn't try to make their kids different from the way they are. Like if the kid is messy, they shouldn't try to make them be neat. And mothers shouldn't make their kids go to bed at eight-thirty, especially when there's good movies on T.V.

LUCILLE: But what if the mother wants the child to be healthy and she thinks the child should get some sleep?

ELLIE: Who's supposed to be doing the helping around here, you or me?

LUCILLE: Sorry.

ELLIE: Mothers should love their kids no matter what. Even if the kid is funny and dumb and looks like a gorilla; Mothers should make them think they are beautiful.

LUCILLE: But what if the . . kid won't let the mother . . . .

ELLIE: Mothers gotta go first! That's the rules.

LUCILLE: Ellie . . . I . . . .

ELLIE: (*Turning away*) What's for supper?

LUCILLE: Huh?

ELLIE: I'm getting hungry. What's for supper?

LUCILLE: I thought I'd make a beef stroganoff.

ELLIE: What's that?

LUCILLE: It's little slices of beef with sour cream and . . . . .

ELLIE: SOUR CREAM! UHHHHHH! Mothers should never make their kids eat SOUR CREAM!

   (*ELLIE clutches her throat.*)

LUCILLE: (*Laughing*) You should try it.

ELLIE: I know, Why don't I make dinner tonight? I used to do that all the time. Pop and I had this really neat game we'd play. First we'd cook up a whole bunch of T.V. dinners and then we'd put on blind-folds and try to guess what we were eating.

MAX: (*Entering*) Did I hear somebody mention food?

LUCILLE: I just had a great idea! Why don't we eat out tonight?

ELLIE: Knock knock . . .

MAX: Who's there?

ELLIE: Uda.

MAX: Uda who?

ELLIE: (*Singing*) "You deserve a break today" . . . . . .

MAX: (*Joining in*) . . . "So go on and get away to MacDonalds."

   **(*MAX encourages LUCILLE to join in.*)

LUCILLE: But I don't know the words.

ELLIE: It's simple. But you can't sing it in that toot toot de doot voice. You gotta do it like this . . .

   (*ELLIE belts it out.*)

ELLIE: "You deserve a break today. So go on and get away to MacDonalds."

**This jingle should be constantly updated to any popular theme song of a fast food chain.

LUCILLE: (*Belting*) Like this? "You deserve a break today. So go on and get away to MacDonalds."

(*They all join in on the last line.*)

ELLIE: Not bad, for a beginner.

MAX: Let's go.

LUCILLE: Wait a minute, I have to put the meat in the freezer.

(*LUCILLE exits.*)

MAX: Hey Ellie, after supper how about a little . . .

(*MAX mimes bowling.*)

ELLIE: Great! Just you and me, like the old days?

MAX: Ellie?

ELLIE: Oh I bet Lucille doesn't even know how to bowl. I bet she thinks it is a dirty smelly sport.

MAX: Oh, come on.

ELLIE: Oh, I guess she can come.

MAX: If she doesn't know you'll have to teach her.

ELLIE: Yeah, I could. Cause if there is one thing I do know it is bowling.

(*LUCILLE enters.*)

MAX: Lucille, would you like to go bowling after supper?

LUCILLE: Oh Max, I was hoping we could all come back here and TALK.

MAX: (*Ignoring the hint*) Oh yeah, yeah. We can do that afterward.

LUCILLE: Maybe just you two should go. I've never bowled before and I wouldn't want to slow you down.

MAX: Baloney! There's nothing to it. We'll show you. Right Midget?

(*ELLIE shrugs and MAX elbows her.*)

ELLIE: Sure, sure, it just takes practice, to get good that is. I'll show you.

MAX: Let's go.

(*They start out.*)

ELLIE: Wait a sec, let me get my shoes.

MAX: We'll meet you in the car.

(*MAX and Lucille exit. ELLIE gets her bowling shoes from under the bed and starts out.*)

VOICE: Red Light!

(*ELLIE freezes.*)

VOICE: You aren't going to fall for all that stuff are you?

ELLIE: Huh?

VOICE: All that "Help me be a mother" stuff?

ELLIE: Well . . .

VOICE: Stepmothers always say that . . . to soften you up. They don't really mean that. And now she's going bowling with you. And after you teach her you know what will happen? She and Pop will go and leave you home . . . alone. Green Light!

MAX: *(*Off stage*) Come on Ellie!

(*ELLIE hesitates and exits. By minor adjustments in the set it switches to the bowling alley. The sound of balls rolling and pins falling can be heard all through the next scene. As soon as the scene is shifted ELLIE, MAX, and LUCILLE enter. ELLIE munches a bag of french fries, they cross to benches set up to indicate their alley. MAX sets up a score sheet, changes his shoes. All bowling should be mimed.*)

MAX: Why don't we take a couple of practice shots? Will you show Lucille how to hold the ball while I get us squared away?

ELLIE: (*Licking her fingers*) Okay, first you get a ball . . .

(*ELLIE points, LUCILLE looks a bit apprehensive but she gets a ball.*)

MAX: (*Under his breath*) Ellie, I want you to be nice.

ELLIE: (*Slaps on a huge smile*) I am being nice . . . SEE? Now you hold the ball like this with three fingers . . . That's good . . . very very good! And you look right at that center pin and bring your hand straight back . . like this and you just swing through . . . . See?

LUCILLE: (*Gamely*) Sure I think so . . .

ELLIE: Well go ahead . . . Try one.

(*LUCILLE follows all ELLIE's instructions but the unexpected weight of the ball throws her off balance. Finally she manages to bowl one ball but very badly. There is the sound of a gutterball.*)

ELLIE: (*Much too nice*) Good! VERY GOOD Lucille.

(*ELLIE smirks.*)

MAX: Lucille, that's called a gutterball, and it's not good. Ellie I'll show her. Why don't you take your turn?

ELLIE: Can I have a Coke?

LUCILLE: You just finished dinner.

ELLIE: Pop?

MAX: Yeah sure, here's fifteen cents.

(*ELLIE walks away a few steps. MAX moves over to LUCILLE and shows her how to hold the ball, very cozily. ELLIE returns.*)

ELLIE: AHEM! I believe it is MY turn.

(*ELLIE takes a ball and goes through a very elaborate warm-up.*)

MAX: (*Quietly*) Now you see you just bring the ball straight back and . . .

LUCILLE: Where is the aiming?

(*ELLIE bowls just as LUCILLE is talking, she slips a little and is thrown off. There is the sound of a few pins falling.*)

ELLIE: No fair! No fair! You're not supposed to talk! You threw me off!

MAX: (*Writing down the score*) Uhhh, three! A little to the left.

ELLIE. That's not fair.

MAX: Oh go on, you've still got another ball.

ELLIE: This time NO talking.

(*ELLIE bowls. All pins fall.*)

MAX: Fantastic.

LUCILLE: Nice aiming, Ellinor. That was a good shot wasn't it dear?

ELLIE: (*Cocky*) You bet. That's what you call a spare. It is just about the best you can do. Of course it takes hours and hours of practice.

MAX: Nice one Midget! Okay Lucille, it's all yours. Just relax and concentrate.

(*LUCILLE starts into the backswing.*)

ELLIE: Hold IT!

(*LUCILLE stops clumsily.*)

ELLIE: This is the foul line. If you step over it nothing counts . . . . I was just trying to help!

(*LUCILLE bowls, very awkwardly. Sound of ball rolling very slowly.*)

ELLIE: (*Watching the ball*) Don't expect too much, not right at first. After all there is only one thing better than a spare and that's a . . .

(*Sound of pins falling domino effect. ELLIE'S face contorts in utter amazement.*)

ELLIE: A STRIKE?????

MAX: Fantastic!

LUCILLE: Is that good?

Max: You bet it is!

ELLIE: I think I'm going to be sick!

LUCILLE: What does that little X mean up there?

ELLIE: (*Nasty*) It means a strike!

MAX: Not bad, old lady, not bad at all.

   (*ELLIE starts coughing real fakey.*)

LUCILLE: Beginner's luck.

MAX: Let's see. My turn now.

   (*ELLIE coughs.*)

MAX: What's the matter with you?

ELLIE: I don't feel so good.

MAX: Well lie down for a minute.

ELLIE: I don't exactly feel like bowling.

   (*MAX shoots her a look which silences her. MAX picks up the ball and lines up the shot, very machismo. Just as he bowls ELLIE coughs and throws him off. He gets a gutterball.*)

MAX: Ellie!

ELLIE: (*Innocently*) Sorry.

LUCILLE: What's the matter Ellinor?

MAX: Nothing's the matter. She's just got a bad case of fakeitus that's all!

ELLIE: By the way, Lucille, that's called a gutterball, it's not good.

MAX: Now, no more talking, noisemaking, sneezing, coughing or anything.

(*MAX lines up the shot and ELLIE yawns.*)

MAX: One more noise out of you and it's out to the car.

(*MAX takes his time lining up the shot, ELLIE picks up her Coke can which she opens just as he bowls. The can explodes in a spray of Coke. MAX tosses his ball over several lanes. He is furious.*)

ELLIE: Ooops!

MAX: ELLIE!

LUCILLE: Good Lord it is all over everything!

ELLIE: I couldn't help it.

MAX: You did that on purpose 'cause you're a rotten sport.

ELLIE: I did not.

MAX: Out to the car!

ELLIE: POP!

MAX: I said out to the car!

LUCILLE: Dear!

MAX: I am not going to have her wreck our game just because she's a lousy sport.

LUCILLE: Let's go home.

MAX: WHAT?

LUCILLE: I don't really care about bowling.

MAX: Well I do. Ellie out to the car. I said it and I meant it.

LUCILLE: You can't send her out there to wait in a dark parking lot.

MAX: Oh yes I can. We are going to finish this game, and Ellie is going to wait for us out in the car. If there is one thing I can't stand it is a rotten sport.

LUCILLE: I will not permit you to send that child out there alone.

MAX: It's just out to the car, do you want me to hire a babysitter?

ELLIE: (*Embarrassed*) POP!

LUCILLE: Max, keep your voice down. We'll settle this when we get home.

MAX: Are you telling me how to discipline my kid?

LUCILLE: You? You're a fine one to talk about discipline. Why you're a bigger kid than she is. Why we should all be sitting at home right now having a family discussion. But Oh no! We have to get ice cream. We all have to go bowling first . . . all because you can't even talk to your own child . . . .

MAX: (*Impulsive*) Oh you don't think I can tell her . . .

(*MAX crosses to ELLIE, LUCILLE tries to stop him.*)

LUCILLE: Max, not here and not now . . . Let's go home.

MAX: (*To ELLIE.*) Ellie, we are going to Hawaii!

(*To LUCILLE*)

There! Now are you satisfied?

(*LUCILLE is horrified. MAX realizes instantly that he has really blown it.*)

LUCILLE: Oh MAX!

ELLIE: What are you guys talking about?

MAX: (*Fighting his way out*) Uhhh, Ellie, we are going away . . . We're going to Hawaii.

ELLIE: HAWAII?

MAX: Yeah, for about three weeks.

ELLIE: Neato! Do I get to get out of school?

MAX: No Ellie, just Lucille and I are going. I was gonna tell you all about it when we got home tonight, well now you know.

ELLIE: What . . . What about me?

MAX: Well you kind of like Mrs. Dougan and I thought may be she'd come and . . .

ELLIE: You are going away and leaving me.

LUCILLE: Ellie . . .

ELLIE: (*Getting mad*) So that's what all that sneaking around was about! So that's what all those papers and secret stuff was about. You guys are going away and leaving me.

LUCILLE: Ellinor, that's not . . . .

ELLIE: (*Turns on her*) And YOU! All that "Help me be a mother" stuff! That was just to soften me up. Well I'll tell you one thing mothers shouldn't do, mothers shouldn't lie to their kids about all that love stuff and then dump them.

MAX: Ellie, stop shouting.

ELLIE: I should have known. I should have known you didn't really like me. You just wanted to have POP all to yourself. Well go ahead! See if I care!

MAX: Ellie, we are going home. Take off your shoes and wait for me in the car.

ELLIE: You can't just throw me out like the trash you know.

MAX: ELLIE OUT TO THE CAR!

  (*ELLIE starts to run out. MAX stops her.*)

MAX: Ellie, your shoes!

(ELLIE, furious, takes off her shoes and throws them at him and runs out. LUCILLE looks at MAX for a minute.)

LUCILLE: Well you certainly handled that one well.

MAX: Lay off! Oh I'm sorry, I didn't mean for this to happen.

LUCILLE: I should hope not. Max, discipline isn't something you turn off and on like hot water.

MAX: I know.

LUCILLE: *(Taking off her shoes and exiting)* We were just beginning. After two months we were just beginning.

(LUCILLE exits. MAX sits for a minute. He picks up the score sheet and crumples it. He starts out when LUCILLE enters at a run.)

LUCILLE: Max, she isn't there! She's gone!

MAX: What?

LUCILLE: She's run away. She left this note on the windshield.

(LUCILLE hands MAX a note.)

MAX: *(Reading)* "You win, Lucille."

LUCILLE: *(Panicking)* Where could she have gone?

MAX: Anywhere! Let's go, she can't have gotten too far.

(LUCILLE sees ELLIE'S shoes.)

LUCILLE: Oh Max, she hasn't even got her shoes on.

MAX: Come on.

(MAX and LUCILLE exit. Weird sounds begin, the recorded voices of LANA, FRIZBEE and VOICE are heard chanting "Run away." The following scene is a mixture of fantasy and reality. A sound collage of voices and scary music form the background.)

VOICE, LANA and FRIZBEE: Run away . . . Run away . . . Run away . . . Run away . . . .*

(*ELLIE enters at a run. LANA and FRIZBEE enter also but they appear as strange menacing figures, such as a stop sign that is knocked over, a staggering drunk, a car that nearly runs ELLIE down.*)

VOICE, LANA and FRIZBEE: Run away. Run away. Run away. Run away.
There's a fact you've got to face . . .
Run away. Run away.
That she's taken your place . . .
Run away. Run away.

VOICE, LANA and FRIZBEE: (*Recorded*) And there's nothing you can do . . . Run away, Run away. Cause he loves her more than you . . . Run away, Run away.

ELLIE: I'll show you. Boy will you be sorry! I'm never going home.

(*A cat yeowls and LUCILLE appears dressed in a long black cloak.*)

LUCILLE: (*Recorded*) Mirror, mirror, on the wall, who's the fairest of them all?

ELLIE: I am, you wicked old stepmother!

(*ELLIE runs into FRIZBEE who holds a newspaper in front of his face.*)

FRIZBEE: Go home little girl.

ELLIE: I'm never going home. I'll find some new parents.

(*ELLIE runs over to LANA who is wearing a farmer's hat and mimes churning butter.*)

ELLIE: Will you adopt a poor orphan child?

LANA: (*Malevolently*) My lands, who is this child?

ELLIE: I am just a poor orphan with no father or mother.

FRIZBEE: (*Also wearing a farmer's hat*) I see the mark of the princess Cinderelli upon her cheek. We will adopt you.

ELLIE: I am not the princess. I'm just Ellie, Ellie Murphy.

FRIZBEE: Well, if you are not the princess then get lost.

(*ELLIE staggers away from them.*)

ELLIE: I'm not scared. I'm not scared. I'm not scared. Oh, my feet are so cold.

(*MAX enters slowly with his back to the audience. He wears a raincoat with a hood. LUCILLE enters with her back to the audience, she too wears a long coat.*)

ELLIE: Pop! Is that you Pop? Hey!

MAX: (*Still with his back to her*) I beg your pardon?

ELLIE: Pop! it's me, Ellie.

MAX: I'm sorry but I don't believe I know you.

ELLIE: Pop, it's me, your daughter! Ellie!

MAX: Who?

ELLIE: Hey Lucille! It's me, Ellie.

LUCILLE: (*Still with her back to her*) I beg your pardon?

ELLIE: Look at me! It's Ellie!

LUCILLE: I don't believe I know you.

(*Slowly they turn to look at her. They wear half-masks which are transparent.*)

LUCILLE: Do you know this child?

MAX: No, I'm sorry little girl.

LUCILLE: Come dear, we have a plane to catch.

MAX: Oh yes, we mustn't be late.

LUCILLE: (*As they exit*) What a strange little girl.

ELLIE: Don't you know me? I'm your child!

(Strange music and recorded voices begin again. LANA and FRIZBEE step in and out of the shadows moving in slow motion.)

VOICE, LANA and FRIZBEE: *(Recorded)* You're alone . . . You're alone.

LANA: *(Like a cat yeowl)* Hi ya Sweetie . . . .

VOICE, LANA and FRIZBEE: *(Recorded)* Can't go home . . . Can't go home . . .

ELLIE: Doesn't anybody know me?

LANA: Hi ya Boss . . .

ELLIE: I'm not the Boss. I'm . . .

VOICE, LANA and FRIZBEE: *(Recorded)* You're alone . . . You're alone.

FRIZBEE: Singer of the year . . .

ELLIE: I don't want to be . . .

VOICE, LANA and FRIZBEE: Got no home . . . Got no home . . .

ELLIE: I don't want to be an orphan.

VOICE, LANA and FRIZBEE: You're alone . . . You're alone . . . All alone . . . All alone . .

ELLIE: I just want to go home.

(ELLIE runs around the stage, as she does the scene is shifted back to her house. ELLIE enters the living room area and looks around.)

ELLIE: I'm home! Hey Pop? Lucille? I'm home. I don't want to be an orphan. Pop? LUCILLE?

(ELLIE sighs and goes into her room. She throws herself down on her bed and falls into a deep sleep.)*

(*Soft music begins, a lullabye played on a music box. ELLIE dreams and in her dream MAX and LUCILLE enter wearing dressing gowns. LANA and FRIZBEE enter. They carry windchimes which tinkle softly. During this scene the words must tumble and flow like a waterfall, nothing frightening. It is a soft and gentle dream.*)

LUCILLE: Shhhhh. Don't wake the baby . . . .

FRIZBEE: What a beautiful baby . . .

LANA: What a good baby . . .

MAX: Daddy's beautiful baby girl.

ELLIE: (*Recorded*) I never had a Mother, not one I remember real well.

LANA: Sleep . . .

FRIZBEE: . . . Dream.

ELLIE: (*Recorded*) Mother? Mother? Where are you? It's dark. I'm scared.

(*LUCILLE billows a soft coverlet and covers ELLIE.*)

LUCILLE: Shall I tell you a story? Shall I sing you a song?

ELLIE: (*Recorded*) I can't see myself. I'm messy. I'm mean.

LANA: Sleep . . .

FRIZBEE: . . . Dream.

MAX: Daddy's pretty Ellie.

ELLIE: (*Recorded*) Mother tell me a story. Mother sing me a song.

(*LUCILLE begins to hum softly.*)

LANA: Sleep . . .

FRIZBEE: . . . Dream.

ELLIE: Can you be my mother?

LUCILLE: Sleep . . .

ELLIE: Please be my mother.

MAX: . . . Dream.

ELLIE: I want to have a mother!

LANA: Shhh. Don't wake the child.

FRIZBEE: What a beautiful child.

MAX: Daddy's beautiful girl.

LUCILLE: Pretty Ellie . . .

MAX and LUCILLE: (*Recorded*) Pretty Ellie . . . Pretty Ellie . . . Pretty Ellie . . Pretty Ellie.

(*All exit slowly as the recorded music and sound continue for a moment. ELLIE tosses and turns on the bed. The dream fades and the house returns to normal. MAX enters the house dressed as he was at the bowling alley. He is upset and in a hurry.*)

MAX: I know I have a recent photograph around here somewhere. Lucille you call the police; say you want to report a missing person.

(*LUCILLE enters.*)

LUCILLE: I just don't understand how she could have gotten so far so quickly. Oh Max, what are we going to do?

MAX: I know we had some pictures taken at Woolworths right before she left for camp. Where did I put them?

LUCILLE: She's been gone two hours. Anything could have happened.

MAX: Take it easy. We'll find her. She's probably just hiding in a restaurant or something. You call the police. I'll go back to the bowling alley.

LUCILLE: I can't help feeling this is all my fault.

MAX: Maybe they are in her room. Call the police.

(*MAX enters ELLIE'S room. He stops dead when he sees her asleep. He is unable to speak for a second and sighs in relief.*)

MAX: (*Very calmly*) Lucille.

(*LUCILLE crosses to him. He points to the sleeping figure. LUCILLE crouches by the bed.*)

LUCILLE: Thank God.

MAX: Let's let her sleep. She must be exhausted.

(*They leave the room and close the door behind them.*)

LUCILLE: She must have walked all this way.

MAX: She must have run.

LUCILLE: (*Still slightly hysterical*) Thank God she's alright. Anything could have happened to her. I don't know what I would have done if . . .

(*ELLIE wakes up, sits and listens.*)

MAX: Hey, calm down. Everything is alright now.

LUCILLE: She could have been killed. What if she'd gotten hit by a car?

MAX: (*Firmly*) Lucille, it is all over now. Take it easy. She's home. I'll get something to relax you, just a minute.

(*MAX exits. ELLIE gets out of bed and starts toward the door.*)

VOICE: Red Light!

(*ELLIE freezes.*)

VOICE: Where are you going?

ELLIE: Out there.

VOICE: Why?

ELLIE: To tell them I'm . . .

VOICE: You could have been killed and it's all HER fault. She almost got rid of you once and for all.

ELLIE: But she really sounded worried.

VOICE: You aren't going to fall for that stuff again are you? She just said that so Pop wouldn't be mad at her. She's trying to get rid of you.

ELLIE: Aww that's dumb.

VOICE: You could have been killed and she'd live happily ever after with Pop. That's how wicked stepmothers are you know.

ELLIE: But . . .

VOICE: You could have been killed and she'd live happily ever after with Pop. That's how wicked stepmothers are you know.

ELLIE: But . . .

VOICE: You could have been killed. Green Light!

(*MAX enters with a drink for LUCILLE.*)

MAX: Here, this will calm you down. Everything is going to be alright.

LUCILLE: Thanks. I've been thinking, Max, maybe I should go away.

MAX: What?

LUCILLE: Maybe I should just let you and Ellie work things out alone. I kept hoping it was just a matter of time . . . that gradually she would come to accept me.

MAX: You're just upset.

LUCILLE: I care for both of you too much to see you destroy what you had together. Maybe I should just leave for a while.

MAX: That's crazy. We are a family now and we are going to work through this thing, all of us, together. Your leaving isn't going to help.

LUCILLE: I don't know.

MAX: Well, I do.

LUCILLE: She must have loved her real Mother very much to hate me so.

MAX: She doesn't hate you. She's just mixed up right now. It's late and we are tired. Let's talk about this in the morning.

LUCILLE: No, I really think it would be better for me to leave you two alone for a while to work things out any way you can.

MAX: Let's go to bed.

(*MAX exits. LUCILLE picks up the note ELLIE left on the windshield and reads.*)

LUCILLE: "You win, Lucille."

(*She looks toward Ellie's room.*)

No, Ellie, YOU win.

(*She exits.*)

(*ELLIE is disturbed by this and she starts out the door after them.*)

ELLIE: Hey you guys . . .

VOICE: Red Light!

(*ELLIE freezes.*)

VOICE: Congratulations! You won!

ELLIE: But she's leaving.

VOICE: That's what you wanted isn't it? Now you and Pop can go back to having things the way they used to be.

ELLIE: Yeah but . . .

VOICE: After all, she wanted to get rid of you. She wanted you to get killed, and then you could have had a funeral.

ELLIE: A funeral?*

VOICE: Yeah a funeral. At funerals everybody is real sorry for all the mean things they ever did to you. Everybody just sits around and says nice things about you and they cry and cry and cry.

   (*FRIZBEE starts to sniffle.*)

ELLIE: What about Pop?

VOICE: He cries the loudest of all.

   (*FRIZBEE bursts into sobs.*)

ELLIE: What am I supposed to do?

VOICE: Well, first you gotta have a coffin.

   (*LANA and FRIZBEE move the toy box forward for the coffin.*)

VOICE: You just lie there.

ELLIE: Suppose I want to see what's going on.

VOICE: No, you gotta just lie there.

ELLIE: That sounds stupid. Hey, I got an idea. Why don't you lie there and be me in the coffin.

VOICE: No, I stay right here.

ELLIE: Get in that coffin!

VOICE: Okay . . . Okay . . . Green Light.

   (*VOICE lies on the box and ELLIE takes charge of the microphone.*)

ELLIE: Okay ladies and gentlemen. Let's get this show on the road. Ellie Murphy's funeral . . . Take One!

   *(*LANA and FRIZBEE clap their hands like a claque board.*)

ELLIE: Now the parade starts over there. I want a black horse with a plume.

(*FRIZBEE puts a plume on his head and neighs.*)

ELLIE: Fantastic! I want music, drums sad and slow! That's right.

(*LANA wearing a long black veil falls into a procession behind FRIZBEE and they both wail.*)

ELLIE: Now start with the nice things.

LANA: She was so young and so beautiful . . .

ELLIE: Cut! Lana, honey, more tears . . . that's right cry, cry, cry. Now throw yourself over the coffin. Preacher that's your cue.

(*FRIZBEE becomes the preacher.*)

FRIZBEE: Poor Ellie Murphy! Why didn't I tell her how cute she was and what nice straight teeth she had.

ELLIE: Come on preacher, nicer things!

FRIZBEE: Poor Ellie Murphy. Why didn't I tell her how pretty she was, what a good voice she had. She was the best bowler I ever saw!

ELLIE: Pop! You're on!

(*MAX enters wearing pajamas and a high silk hat, and black arm bands.*)

MAX: I'm sorry Ellie.

ELLIE: More feeling Pop!

MAX: I'M SORRY ELLIE!!!! How could I have been so blind? I never needed anyone but you. Now my life is empty, bleak, bland . . .

ELLIE: From the bottom of your heart, Pop!

MAX: What a fool I have been and now it is too late!!!

ELLIE: And now for the final touch! Lucille enters up right, rubbing her hand and laughing.

(*ELLIE indicates up right. Nothing happens.*)

ELLIE: I said, the grand finale . . . LUCILLE enters up right, rubbing her hands and laughing.

(*ELLIE indicates up right again and LUCILLE enters up left. She wears a coat and carries a suitcase.*)

LUCILLE: I have been thinking, Max, maybe I should go away.

ELLIE: No, CUT! Lucille enters up right, rubbing her hands and laughing.

LUCILLE: Maybe I should let you and Ellie work things out alone.

ELLIE: I said, up right!

LUCILLE: I kept hoping that it was just a matter of time.

ELLIE: Cut Cut! You are not supposed to be saying that!

LUCILLE: I kept hoping that gradually she would come to accept me.

ELLIE: You are supposed to be glad that I'm dead.

LUCILLE: I care for you both too much to see you destroy what you had together. Maybe I should just leave.

ELLIE: You are not supposed to be saying that!

LUCILLE: She must have loved her real mother very much to hate me so. So I'm leaving.

ELLIE: Hey wait, Lucille.

LUCILLE: No Ellie, YOU win.

ELLIE: Wait I didn't mean for it to go this far.

VOICE: Red Light!

(*ELLIE freezes.*)

VOICE: Don't call her back. You've won! Now things will be the way they always have been.

ELLIE: Why don't you shut up! You are supposed to be dead! I want a mother and she's a perfectly good one.

VOICE: But she's a wicked step. . . .

ELLIE: **RED LIGHT!**

(*VOICE freezes.*)

ELLIE: Lana, Frizbee, take that thing away. Green Light!

(*LANA and FRIZBEE move like puppets. They move VOICE back to the stool and move the toy box back into its place.*)

ELLIE: Now get in.

(ELLIE helps them both into the toy box. She closes the lid and sits on the box for a second.)

ELLIE: Lucille! Lucille! Come back!

(*ELLIE moves back into bed as LUCILLE and MAX enter her room. They both wear the dressing gowns seen in the dream scene.*)

MAX: (*Entering first*) Ellie? What's the matter?

ELLIE: Where is Lucille?

LUCILLE: (*Entering*) Right here. What's the matter?

ELLIE: (*Relieved*) Oh . . . uhhh, nothing. I must have had a bad dream.

MAX: Do you want to tell me about it?

ELLIE: I don't think you'd like it.

MAX: Is it alright now?

ELLIE: Yeah. I guess so.

MAX: Well, good night Midget.

(*MAX kisses her on the forehead.*)

ELLIE: Good night Pop.

(*MAX and LUCILLE turn to leave.*)

ELLIE: Uhhh Lucille?

(*MAX stays in the doorway and LUCILLE crosses to her.*)

LUCILLE: Yes?

ELLIE: I'm . . . sorry I ran away.

LUCILLE: So am I.

ELLIE: Well, I'm back now.

LUCILLE: I'm glad.

ELLIE: So am I.

(*Pause.*)

ELLIE: Uhhh Lucille, I'm cold.

LUCILLE: Well no wonder, you kicked your covers off.

(*LUCILLE billows the covers over her and tucks her in. ELLIE smiles.*)

ELLIE: Uhh Lucille, knock, knock . . .

LUCILLE: Who's there?

ELLIE: Sticker.

LUCILLE: Sticker who?

ELLIE: Sticker-ound for a while, okay?

LUCILLE: Okay. Good night Ellie. Sleep well.

*(*LUCILLE moves away a few steps and crouches.*)

LUCILLE: Good night Lana. Good night Frizbee.

ELLIE: Uhhh Lucille, they're not here.

LUCILLE: Oh.

(*LUCILLE crosses to MAX and turns back.*)

LUCILLE: Good night Ellie.

ELLIE: (*Pulling the covers up and turning over*) See ya in the morning.

BLACK OUT

Ozma of Oz
A Tale of Time

Zeder admits, in her notes introducing this script, that hers is not a faithful adaptation of the original book by Baum. Indeed, she has updated the story from the turn of the century to the present, radically changed many elements of the plot and given circumstances, and left out some characters. Most importantly, she has created a thematic focus on the relationship between Dorothy and Uncle Henry that is not even touched on by Baum. However, as in her other adaptations, she preserves the spirit of the original with its wildly eccentric characters and bizarre situations.

Zeder makes changes in many aspects of the Baum original, the most important being in the way she portrays the major characters. Baum's Dorothy is incredibly brave, strong, and positive, but thoroughly one-dimensional. By contrast, Zeder has made Dorothy a teen-ager with weaknesses and negative attitudes that sometimes get in her way.

In the Baum original Uncle Henry takes the Australia trip as a rest cure since he is weak, nervous, and not very well. Zeder, preserving Baum's intent, has Uncle Henry confined to a wheelchair following a stroke, but he is a man who has glimpsed his own mortality and has responded with the high-spirited determination to have an adventure.

Zeder also makes changes from the original in her handling of the character of Ozma. Zeder has given Ozma a new power—to see "behind the mind and into the heart." Ozma uses this power to help Dorothy free Uncle Henry from the rock crystal in which he's trapped, while freeing herself from her own limited view of him as a helpless old man. Zeder also makes a unique twist on the fact that the original Ozma was powerful, but not all powerful. In Zeder's version Ozma's virtues become faults under certain circumstances; for example, because Ozma cannot lie, she becomes more of an obstacle than a help in escaping Roquat's cavern. Not only does this create a layer of moral complexity not present in the original, but it allows Zeder to isolate the protagonists from outside help and force them to be active rather than passive. Uncle Henry and Dorothy display more courage, quick thinking, and physical stamina in solving their problems than either of them knew they had.

Zeder's treatment of thematic elements, like her treatment of the characters, both builds upon and diverges from Baum's book. On the level of the fantasy adventure story, Zeder's play is still about the battle between the forces of darkness and the forces of light that was part of the original novel. Zeder also takes the quality of courage, a thematic element that seemed dear to Baum's heart, but gives it added emphasis by having Dorothy learn that courage does not mean being without fear, but that it means being able to go on in spite of it.

Uncle Henry describes a new theme when he says, "It all depends on how you look at it." Zeder explores how one's view of a person effects how that person behaves. When Dorothy sees Uncle Henry as an invalid, her actions toward him make him seem more helpless than he is. When Uncle Henry sees himself as bold and brave, he manages to conquer the Wheelers, and ultimately, the evil Roquat. The difficulty of perceiving things clearly and of seeing beneath appearances, a related thematic pattern, is echoed throughout the story in repeated instances of the inhabitants of Oz not being what they seem.

Zeder also departs thematically from the original by subtitling her play, "A Tale of Time," and exploring the relationship between Dorothy and Uncle Henry against a background in which the passage of time is extremely important. She makes Oz a land in which time has stopped, and Dorothy and Uncle Henry accidentally start it moving forward again when they wind up Tic Toc. When time intrudes in the land where people never age, all the characters face major challenges, including Dorothy and Uncle Henry. The difference in their feelings about the passage of time and in life experience, which comes with time, are major elements that make it so difficult for them to understand each other. In adding this theme to the story, Zeder touches on a universal conflict that people face many times in life as they realize they are growing older.

The tender, growing relationship between Dorothy and Uncle Henry occurs in a world of bizarre characters and exotic, menacing settings. In addition, many of the characters from Oz are farcical, and Zeder has done some of her best comic writing for them. Bill the Chicken is the most noteworthy comic character. Bill's large size is matched by her monumental egg-laying and equally oversized one-liners. The ridiculous conversations between General and Army and Roquat's dialogue, liberally studded with geological puns, also provide comic relief. All of these characters are humorous in the Baum original, but Zeder's humor is bold and brazen compared to Baum's gentler, wry qualities.

This sometimes outrageous humor, the strangeness and larger than life quality of Oz and its inhabitants, and the external problems posed for Dorothy and Uncle Henry can easily overshadow their inner journey. Just as Zeder has symbolized all the liveness trapped within Uncle Henry's aging body as dancing colors trapped inside a crystal, she has tried to control the wild energy and kaleidoscopic images of Oz with the rather rarified and abstract concept of time. In the immediacy of the theatrical experience, relationships may be overwhelmed by spectacle and wild adventure. But, as long as the human relationships are kept in the forefront, the element of spectacle in this play can be a delight for designers, actors, and audiences as they chronicle the adventures of two human beings on an internal journey toward greater understanding of themselves and each other.

Ozma of Oz

A Tale of Time

by Suzan L. Zeder

Based on characters and events from
Ozma of Oz
by
L. Frank Baum

From the Playwright

For those of you who have long cherished L. Frank Baum's Ozma of Oz, and who have been searching for an absolutely faithful stage adaptation of the book, this may not be the play for you. But for those who read, or were read the Oz books as a child, (as I was), who delight in their zany characters and improbable situations, and who admire and respect the spirit of Baum's work, this may be the play for you.

In the process of adapting this work to the stage, I found myself looking for something more: something beyond story, something deeper than crazy characters, a theme or central core I could care deeply about. I found this, not in the book, but in the potential of a relationship between a contemporary teenaged Dorothy and her elderly, but magnificently spirited, Uncle Henry. So, I decided to depart from the book, to blow them both off the boat, and to whirl them away on an adventure of mutual discovery in the Land of Oz. Virtually all of the characters in this play appear in the book. Some of the events are the same but I have woven these glittering threads from Baum into a fabric of my own making. The theme of intergenerational caring and understanding has been my touchstone because, quite simply, that is what I care about.

I have seen four different productions of this script, and I have learned from all of them. I offer only one word of advice. This play tends to invite overproduction. I urge you to resist the temptation to pull out all the stops. Be simple, suggest, and allow the imagination of the audience to work for you. The world of Oz should be a wild and dazzling place, but the accomplishment of this theatricality can obscure the focus on Dorothy and her personal voyage to discover her equally dazzling Uncle.

Suzan Zeder
Seattle
1981

Dedication

To Claire
Who has the power to see behind the mind
And into the heart

The premiere production of *Ozma of Oz: A Tale of Time* was commissioned by The Poncho Theatre, Seattle and performed on October 5, 1979, with the following cast:

Sam .... Randy Hoffmeyer
Steve .... Ramone Marue
Dorothy .... Pamela Bridgham
Uncle Henry .... Edward Sampson
Bill .... Linda Hartzell
Tic Toc .... Paul Fleming
Wheeler I .... Randy Hoffmeyer
Wheeler II .... Pamela Pulver
Princess Langwidere .... Linda Hartzell
Nanda .... Diane Petrie
Guard .... Pamela Pulver
Ozma of Oz .... Gretchen Orsland
General .... Ramone Marue
Army .... Randy Hoffmeyer
Roquat of the Rock .... Ramone Marue
Feldspar .... Pamela Pulver
Rock People .... Diane Petrie
Randy Hoffmeyer

The production was directed by Jenifer McLauchlan

Set Design by .... Mark Sullivan
Custume Design by .... Susan Nininger
Music and Sound by .... John Engerman

CHARACTERS

Sam: A sailor*
Steve: A sailor*
Dorothy: Thirteen years old
Uncle Henry: Seventy-two years old
Bill: A giant hen*
Tic Toc: The time machine
Wheeler I: Spy of the Gnome King*
Wheeler II: Another spy*
Princess Langwidere: Woman with thirty heads*
Nanda: Servant to Langwidere*
Guard: Guard to Langwidere*
Ozma of Oz: The ruler of Oz
Army: Ozma's army*
Roquat of the Rocks: The Gnome King
Feldspar: The Gnome King's Servant*
Several Rock People: Gnomes*

* These roles may be double and triple cast to reduce the size of the company. This show may be done with a minimum of twelve actors to a maximum of eighteen to twenty depending on the number of Gnomes.

SCENES

Shipboard
In the Cabin
On the Raft
On the Beach of Oz
The Desert of Shifting Sand
Langwidere's Palace
In the Guard House
Outside the Guard House
A Pass in the Road
In the Gnome King's Cavern
Outside the Gnome King's Cavern
Shipboard

Ozma of Oz

Scene I: Shipboard

The play opens on board a cargo freighter bound for Australia. It is an open deck with several large crates marked "Sydney". The ship is old and somewhat rusty; there are a railing along one side of the deck, a couple of deck chairs, and a free-standing unit which indicates the entrance to the cabins. Sounds of gulls, water, and wind are heard. At opening the sky is light, but as the scene progresses the sky darkens and wind sounds build as a large storm approaches. The movement of the characters reflects the increasing roughness of the sea.

(*STEVE, a sailor, swabs the deck industriously; he whistles as he mops. In a moment SAM, another sailor, enters in a hurry.*)

SAM: Hey, Sailor, never mind about that deck! I got new orders for you!

STEVE: But Sir, I'm almost finished.

SAM: Radar's picked up a storm up ahead. We gotta get all this cargo stowed.

STEVE: All of it?

SAM: Lash down anything that can't be moved, and lash it good! Steel cables! Winds are up to seventy-five and we ain't got much time.

STEVE: (*Apprehensively looking at the sky*) Jeeze!

SAM: Jeeze is right, Sailor. Check those crates off the manifest and get that shipment of chickens below.

STEVE: Yes, Sir! But Sir, what about the passengers?

SAM: Passengers?

STEVE: You know, the kid and . . .

SAM: Oh yeah, the old guy. I don't know why they let them on this boat in the first place. Cargo ship's no place for kids and old people.

STEVE: Yes, Sir! I mean, no, Sir.

SAM: Tell 'em to stay in their cabin. I don't want to see them on this deck until we dock in Sydney.

STEVE: Yes, sir!

(*STEVE and SAM exit in opposite directions. DOROTHY and UNCLE HENRY enter from their cabin. UNCLE HENRY has had a stroke and is confined to a wheelchair throughout the play. DOROTHY pushes him as he reads along from "AUSTRALIA ON $15. A DAY."*)

UNCLE HENRY: "The original Australians were too isolated from the rest of the world to conceive of any chronological history."

(*DOROTHY pushes him to a spot on the deck, checks the sun and fixes the angle of the wheelchair. She places a blanket around his legs, and crosses to the deck chair. While he reads she makes an elaborate but silent production out of **not** listening to him.*)

UNCLE HENRY: "But all the legends of these early Australians contain the image of endless space; a world where time and distance really didn't matter."

(*DOROTHY turns on a small pocket radio; some music, but mostly static.*)

UNCLE HENRY: (*Louder, over the sound of the radio*) "In 1770 Captain James Cook sailed into Botany Bay and claimed the entire eastern seacoast of Australia for England."

(*DOROTHY pulls out a movie magazine and buries herself in it.*)

UNCLE HENRY: (*Still trying to get her attention*) "The men with watches, measuring rods, and muskets had arrived. The great continent, Terra Incognita Australius, had been discovered."

DOROTHY: You can go on reading until you are blue in the face, but I'm not going to listen to you anymore.

(*DOROTHY props her magazine on her knees and puts both hands over her ears. As he reads, UNCLE HENRY reaches out with one of his canes, hooks her arm, and pulls it from her ear.*)

UNCLE HENRY: "The first settlers of Australia were convicts . . ."

DOROTHY: Uncle Henry, PLEASE! We have been on this boat for two and a half weeks and I have listened to you read about Australia. If I hear one more word about koala bears or kangaroos I'm going to throw up.

UNCLE HENRY: But this is the good part, it's about convicts.

(*DOROTHY turns up the radio.*)

Dorothy, you can't get any music on that thing.

DOROTHY: There's nothing to do around here.

UNCLE HENRY: We are sailing to Australia, just like the explorers.

DOROTHY: On a cargo ship?

UNCLE HENRY: When Captain Cook was your age he was a cabin boy; sailed all over the North Sea.

DOROTHY: Good for Captain Cook.

UNCLE HENRY: Travel when you're young! If you wait till you're my age, you start falling apart and it's too late!

DOROTHY: When we land in Sydney . . .

UNCLE HENRY: Dock, we don't land, we dock.

DOROTHY: When we DOCK, we stay one week, then we catch the first plane right back to Kansas where we belong.

(*UNCLE HENRY lines up his chair next to a deck chair and struggles to lift himself onto his canes.*)

UNCLE HENRY: I don't know why you came along in the first place.

DOROTHY: You know perfectly well, Aunt Em couldn't leave the farm, so somebody had to come along to take care of you, so I . . .

UNCLE HENRY: I can take care of myself! (*He can't quite manage getting into the chair.*) Uhhhhh. Could you help me into that deck chair?

DOROTHY: (*Helping him*) Besides, I have to get back for school. We start in two weeks.

UNCLE HENRY: How can some piddly junior high school compare to an adventure on the high seas?

DOROTHY: Tommy is going to be on the football team, and I promised I'd get back in time to sign up for cheerleaders.

UNCLE HENRY: Tommy who?

DOROTHY: Tommy Gleason.

UNCLE HENRY: Tommy Gleason's a nurd.

DOROTHY: Uncle Henry!

UNCLE HENRY: I knew his grandfather, he was a nurd too; so's his father! Whole family of nurds.

DOROTHY: You shouldn't talk like that.

UNCLE HENRY: When you get to be my age you can talk any fool way you like.

DOROTHY: I really don't think it's any of your business.

UNCLE HENRY: When you're as old as I am, you haven't got any business of your own, so you gotta mess around in everybody elses' . . . . Let's talk about something interesting. In Australia they had these outlaws, bushrangers they called 'em. They were sort of like Robin Hood, except they stole from the rich and kept it. . . . No nurds there.

(*The ship lurches and STEVE enters.*)

STEVE: Hey, kid, you and your grandfather better get to your cabin.

DOROTHY: I'm not a kid and he's not my grandfather.

STEVE: Sorry, kid, but there's a big storm up ahead and we don't want anyone getting hurt.

DOROTHY: Did you say storm?

STEVE: That's right and it's a beaut!

UNCLE HENRY: (*Delighted*) Hot Damn!

(*SAM enters and exits quickly.*)

SAM: Get a move on Steve! Kid, Gramps, you gotta get to your cabin and stay there.

(*The ship lurches, wind sounds increase. Unnoticed, UNCLE HENRY tries to hook his wheelchair with his canes.*)

STEVE: Better do as he says.

DOROTHY: How big is this storm? Are we in danger, I mean could we turn over?

UNCLE HENRY: (*Taking wide swipes with his cane at the chair*) Capsize, they say capsize!

STEVE: You are perfectly safe as long as you stay in your cabin.

UNCLE HENRY: (*Hooking the chair and pulling it towards him*) I hope it's a regular typhoon!

STEVE: Just take him inside and take good care of him.

UNCLE HENRY: (*Struggling to his feet*) I can take care of myself.

(*His legs buckle, but he catches himself.*)

DOROTHY: Where are the life jackets? You do have life jackets?

STEVE: They're in the cabin, now go on!

(*UNCLE HENRY works his way carefully toward the wheelchair.*)

UNCLE HENRY: (*Delighted*) Maybe a waterspout! That would be a sight!

(*DOROTHY sees him. She and STEVE rush to help, upsetting his balance.*)

DOROTHY: Uncle Henry!

UNCLE HENRY: Watch it. I can manage!

STEVE: Careful Gramps.

UNCLE HENRY: I SAID, I CAN MANAGE! There are still some things I can do for myself.

(*With wounded dignity, he wheels off. Stage darkens and wind sounds build.*)

DOROTHY: I was just trying to help!

SAM: (*Off*) Get a move on, Steve!

STEVE: Gotta go! Take care, kid.

(*STEVE exits.*)

DOROTHY: I was just trying to help!

(*In frustration she kicks a crate; clucking sounds are heard.*)

DOROTHY: What are we doing on this stupid boat? He's just a crazy old man, crazy as a coot. Whenever I try to help he turns into an old grouch, an old grump, an old . . . I must be going nuts; talking to a chicken!

(*SAM enters, the ship lurches. Wind, lightning, thunder.*)

SAM: I thought I told you to get in your cabin!

DOROTHY: Where's my Uncle? I should never have let him out of my sight . . .

SAM: He's in the cabin! Now, Move!

(*DOROTHY exits to cabins. SAM exits shaking his head.*)

Kids and old people. I don't know why they let them on this boat!

Scene II: In the Cabin

The storm is in full swing; wind sounds and thunder crash. UNCLE HENRY is in the tiny cramped cabin; his chair moves with the rocking of the boat. He is delighted with the storm, peers out a porthole, and sings a sea shantey at the top of his lungs.

UNCLE HENRY: "As we poor sailors go skipping through the tops, While the land lubbers lie down below, below, below" . . . .

(The ship rocks and he slides.)

Whoooooeeee! That last wave must have been ten feet high!

(DOROTHY enters very sea sick.)

DOROTHY: Aaaaaaaaauuuuuuggggghhhhh!

UNCLE HENRY: If I could walk, I'd be out there with those sailors, winds lashing at my face, hauling in the top-sail.

DOROTHY: This is a cargo ship, there aren't any sails. Auuuuugghhh.

UNCLE HENRY: Think of the explorers who have ridden these waves! They thought that storms were sea monsters, churning up the waters with their long scaley tails.

DOROTHY: I don't feel very well.

UNCLE HENRY: I never thought I'd live long enough to see something like this!

(The ship lurches.)

DOROTHY: Ohhhhh, this is terrible!

UNCLE HENRY: No, it's not; it's wonderful. It all depends on how you look at it. Let's pretend we're explorers heading into unknown territory.

(DOROTHY puts on a life jacket.)

DOROTHY: I don't feel much like pretending anything.

UNCLE HENRY: Well you used to. We used to pretend all sorts of things.

   (*DOROTHY holds out a life jacket for him.*)

DOROTHY: You better put this on, just in case.

UNCLE HENRY: Remember the story you used to tell about going up in a tornado? Just imagine that you're up there now, going round and round and round . . . .

   (*He wheels his arms as DOROTHY is trying to put the jacket on him.*)

DOROTHY: I was just a little kid. I made it up. Now let me put this on you.

UNCLE HENRY: Don't want it!

DOROTHY: Come on, Uncle Henry, if anything happened . . . with your legs . . . you couldn't swim or anything.

UNCLE HENRY: I bet Captain Cook never wore one of those contraptions.

DOROTHY: (*Putting it on him*) It's for your own good.

UNCLE HENRY: You always say that when you're making me do something I don't want to do.

   (*The ship lurches.*)

DOROTHY: This ship's going under and we'll all be drowned.

UNCLE HENRY: Nonsense.

DOROTHY: Boats do sink you know!

UNCLE HENRY: At least this way's exciting. It beats popping off in your sleep or something.

DOROTHY: This cabin's so small. I can't breathe.

UNCLE HENRY: I'll open a porthole.

DOROTHY: Don't! We'll all be drowned for sure!

UNCLE HENRY: Dorothy, you are getting on my nerves.

(*DOROTHY tries to put her radio on a shelf.*)

DOROTHY: What are we doing on this stupid boat?

UNCLE HENRY: All my life I've wanted to see Australia, like the explorers.

(*She loses her balance, the radio falls.*)

DOROTHY: Everybody thinks you're cracked, going to Australia at your age.

(*They both go for the radio.*)

UNCLE HENRY: Before I die, I just want one adventure.

(*His wheelchair runs over the radio and pinches her fingers under the wheel.*)

DOROTHY: (*Hurt and very upset*) Why couldn't you stay home to die!

(*There is a frozen moment.*)

UNCLE HENRY: I need some air!

(*UNCLE HENRY, furious, wheels out the door.*)

DOROTHY: No! Stop! . . . . . I didn't mean . . .

(*DOROTHY bolts out the door.*)

UNCLE HENRYYYYYYY . . . . . .

(*DOROTHY struggles against the wind; she grabs a large crate as a gust hits her. Sounds and light create the effect of a water spout. Scenery for the boat swirls away. BLACKOUT.*)

Scene III: On the raft

It is morning. DOROTHY lies unconscious on a large raft-like structure which bears some resemblance to the chicken coop in the previous scene. Another figure is also on the raft covered with a tarpaulin. The raft is floating on a calm open sea; the sky is a strange non-sky color, and there is music.

DOROTHY: (*Wakes slowly*) Where am I? The boat? Where's the boat? Uncle Henry? UNCLE HENRY?????? . . . . There's nothing out there . . . Stay calm, Dorothy, just stay calm . . . there's bound to be a rescue ship. Just stay calm and wait . . . HELP! SOMEBODY HELP ME PLEASE!

(*The figure under the tarpaulin moves.*)

BILL: Kut-kut-kut-Ka Daw Kut!

(*The tarp falls away revealing BILL, a person-sized chicken.*)

BILL: What do you know, it's morning.

DOROTHY: (*Astonished*) What in the world?

BILL: Bill's the name, chicken's the game. Pleased to meet you.

DOROTHY You're . . . You're . . . a chicken?

BILL: You were expecting an armadillo?

DOROTHY: But you're so . . . big.

BILL: Yeah, I noticed that.

DOROTHY: And you can talk . . . You speak English.

BILL: How do you know you aren't speaking chicken?

DOROTHY: I must be dreaming; this is all a very strange dream.

BILL: Don't count on it, toots.

(*BILL pecks her.*)

DOROTHY: Ow! The name is Dorothy!

BILL: Did you wake up, Dorothy?

DOROTHY: No.

BILL: Then I guess we're here.

DOROTHY: Where are we?

BILL: How should I know, I just got here myself. One minute I was on the boat . . .

DOROTHY: You were on the boat? What happened?

BILL: First the storm hit, and I was sliding all over the deck. Then you came along and grabbed my coop. Then there was this big water-spout that sucked up everything on the deck.

DOROTHY: UNCLE HENRY! Did you see what happened to my Uncle? He was on the deck too!

BILL: Take it easy.

DOROTHY: If anything happened to him . . .

BILL: The old coot bobbed by here . . . .

DOROTHY: What if he drowned? Oh, my Lord, it's all my fault. He never would have gone out in that storm if I hadn't . . .

BILL: I said, the old grouch floated by in that . . . . . .

DOROTHY: He can't be dead, he just can't be . . . . .

BILL: HOLD IT! You don't listen too well, do you? I said, the old grump floated by in that wheelchair of his.

DOROTHY: Was he all right?

BILL: Sure.

DOROTHY: Thank God.

BILL: The old guy was just bobbing and smiling and singing, "Waltzing Matilda, Waltzing Matilda" at the top of his lungs. Crazy old man.

DOROTHY: Don't call him those things!

BILL: Why not? You did. Uh Oh! Look out! Here it comes. Man your battle stations. 10, 9, 8, 7, 6, 5, 4, 3, 2, 1 . . . Hit the deck! Uhhhhh.

(*BILL lays an egg.*)

DOROTHY: What are you doing?

BILL: Laying an egg.

DOROTHY: Do you have to make such a big deal out of it?

BILL: Have you ever laid an egg?

DOROTHY: No.

BILL: Then don't knock it.

DOROTHY: We have got to get out of here. We'll probably starve to death.

BILL: Here, you can have my egg.

DOROTHY: Don't you want it?

BILL: Oh, no! I just lay 'em and leave 'em.

DOROTHY: Thanks.

BILL: I sure wish you hadn't mentioned food. What I wouldn't give for a nice juicy order of grubs over easy with a side order of worms.

(*There is a clunk and the raft lurches.*)

What was that?

DOROTHY: Either we hit something or something hit us.

BILL: It's sharks!

(*There is a clunk and the raft lurches.*)

DOROTHY: There it is again.

BILL: It's a submarine.

(*DOROTHY peers over the back of the raft.*)

DOROTHY: It's a fish . . . a fish with sails or wings . . . and it's coming at us again.

(*The raft lurches and the fish leaps into DOROTHY's hands. It is a strange looking fish with a large key in it's mouth.*)

I've got it! I've got it!

(*BILL dives down head first. Suddenly the fish leaps out of her hands, disappears back into the water, leaving the key.*)

I had it. It's gone . . . . But it left this . . . . . .

BILL: (*Head up*) Is it a worm?

DOROTHY: No. It looks like a key or something; and look here, under the barnacles, it has something written on it.

(*DOROTHY scrapes away the barnacles and reads the inscription. As she does the lights change and magic music is heard.*)

DOROTHY: (*Reading*) "The power of this key is stronger than strength,
Wider than width and longer than length.
The holder of this key has power unshaken,
The key may be given but never taken.
S and T Incorporated."

What do you suppose it means?

BILL: Beats me, but then I'm just a chicken.

DOROTHY: This is weird.

BILL: I wish it was a worm.

DOROTHY: Really weird! I suppose we should keep it. Maybe it can help us get out of this mess.

BILL: (*Suddenly excited*) Uh Oh! Uh Oh! Look out! Here it comes!

DOROTHY: Don't tell me you are going to lay another egg?

BILL: Oh, no! Land Ho!

DOROTHY: Where?

BILL: There!

   (*DOROTHY and BILL are thrown forward as the raft lands upon the beach of OZ. Lights change and as they pull the raft off-stage, the scene shifts.*)

Scene IV: The Beach of Oz

   A large open space of rocks and bushes bearing wild and brightly colored flowers. It is like no place on this earth, the sky is a strange rainbow colored dawn, odd and wonderful music in the air. To one side of the stage is a large rock with vines and flowers growing on it. The rock bears a sign with the message "Beware of Wheelers." On the other side of the stage two ROCK PEOPLE sit in perfect stillness. They seem to be part of the scenery.

   (*DOROTHY and BILL enter, shaking the water off themselves and looking about in amazement. BILL begins to look intently at the ground.*)

DOROTHY: This is weird, really weird. Out there on the water it was bright daylight, but here it looks like dawn.

BILL: (*Not looking up*) Yeah.

DOROTHY: (*Checking her watch*) My watch has stopped. I wonder where in the world we are?

BILL: You got me. Hey, look there on the ground!

DOROTHY: A tire track! A track from a wheel of some kind. Maybe a wheelchair!

BILL: Not that, A WORM! Hot diggety, a worm!

   (*BILL pecks at the ground in joy.*)

DOROTHY: Maybe Uncle Henry washed up here just like we did. Maybe he's . . .

BILL: There goes a fat wriggly one!

(*BILL takes off after the worm. DOROTHY searches.*)

DOROTHY: Uncle Henry! Uncle Henry!

BILL: Oh goody, a slug. Gotcha!

DOROTHY: I wish you'd help me find my Uncle.

BILL: (*Oblivious to all but the feast*) Ants, slugs, juicy grubs! Heaven, I'm in heaven!

DOROTHY: Bill! You have got to help me find him. He's a very old man and he can't do anything for himself. We have got to find him before something terrible happens to him.

BILL: Dorothy, there's something written on that rock.

DOROTHY: What does it say?

BILL: How should I know? Chickens can't read.

DOROTHY: (*Reading*) "Beware of Wheelers." What's a Wheeler?

BILL: I don't know, but it sounds bad. Let's get out of here.

DOROTHY: Wheelers! Maybe that's why there are wheel tracks all over this place! Maybe these aren't Uncle Henry's tracks at all!

BILL: I wonder if Wheelers eat chickens or just run over them?

DOROTHY: Uncle Henry! Uncle Henry!

BILL: Quiet! Do you want to bring those Wheeler things?

DOROTHY: (*Discouraged*) What if he never even made it to shore?

BILL: Dorothy . . .

DOROTHY: What if he's still out there? What if he's . . .

BILL: Dorothy . . .

DOROTHY: This is all my fault. I said such terrible things to him back on the boat.

BILL: I hate to interrupt this moment of self-awareness, but don't you think we better get a move on?

(*BILL prods DOROTHY off.*)

DOROTHY: (*As she is going*) Uncle Henry, if you're alive, I promise never to be mean or nasty again. I promise I'll be sweet tempered and understanding and . . .

BILL: Go . . . . go . . . . go . . . .

(*They exit. All is still for a moment. UNCLE HENRY is heard off-stage.*)

UNCLE HENRY: (*Off*) Stroke . . . Stroke . . . Stroke . . . Stroke . . .

(*UNCLE HENRY enters, rowing and using his canes for oars. He wheels on backwards.*)

HA! Land Ho! What do you know, I made it!

(*He looks around a bit puzzled.*)

UNCLE HENRY: Hmmmmmmmm, what happened to the sun? Seems to be twilight or dawn here, but out there it was . . .

(*He checks his watch.*)

Stopped. Must be water in the works. I wonder where in the blue blazes I am? Unknown territory . . . Terra Incognito . . . Hot Damn!

(*He wheels about exploring.*)

I wonder what Captain Cook would do in a situation like this? Hello? Is anyone here? . . . . Uninhabited! I know . . . .

(*He wheels center-stage and raises a cane.*)

I, Henry S. Gale, claim this entire unknown territory in the name of Kansas and the United States of America!

(*He plants his cane in the ground and salutes.*)

DOROTHY: (*Off*) Over here, Bill.

UNCLE HENRY: Hot Damn!

(*DOROTHY enters at a run.*)

DOROTHY: Uncle Henry!

UNCLE HENRY: (*Astonished*) Dorothy! What in the world . . . .

DOROTHY: Uncle Henry, are you all right?

(*DOROTHY runs to him and hugs him.*)

UNCLE HENRY: Of course I'm all right.

DOROTHY: But how did you ever . . . .

UNCLE HENRY: I rowed!

DOROTHY: You're all wet.

UNCLE HENRY: Of course, I'm wet.

DOROTHY: Here, take my sweater. Are you sure you're all right? You must be freezing.

UNCLE HENRY: I don't need . . . . .

DOROTHY: (*Rubbing his arms*) Here, let me warm you . . .

UNCLE HENRY: I'M ALL RIGHT!

DOROTHY: I've been looking all over for you.

UNCLE HENRY: How the devil did you get here?

DOROTHY: I followed you out in the storm and blew off the boat.

UNCLE HENRY: (*Without malice*) That was a stupid thing to do.

DOROTHY: That's what happened to you.

UNCLE HENRY: At my age, people expect me to do stupid things.

DOROTHY: I was just trying to help!

UNCLE HENRY: I can take care of myself!

DOROTHY: (*Losing any vestige of self-imposed "control"*) Well, you certainly managed very well this time. Look at us, we're shipwrecked! Lost! If you hadn't gone out in that storm . . .

(*BILL enters singing.*)

BILL: "Hail, Hail, the gang's all here" . . . .

UNCLE HENRY: What in the world?

DOROTHY: That's Bill.

UNCLE HENRY: Looks like an overgrown chicken to me.

BILL: I'm very sensitive about my height.

UNCLE HENRY: It can talk! It speaks English!

BILL: What did you expect, pig latin? And I'm not an "it"; I'm a hen!

UNCLE HENRY: A hen named Bill?

BILL: Well, pardon me. I was named when I was an egg.

DOROTHY: This is a weird place, Uncle Henry. Out there on the water it was broad daylight, but here it's dawn, and the sun hasn't moved.

UNCLE HENRY: I noticed that too.

DOROTHY: And when Bill and I were out on the raft, there was this fish, it leaped right into my hands and dropped this key.

UNCLE HENRY: Key?

DOROTHY: Yeah, and it's got the weird inscription . . .

(*As she reads, lights change and there is magical music. The large rock directly behind them slowly turns.*)

"The power of this key is stronger than strength,
Wider than width and longer than length.
The holder of this key has power unshaken,

The key can be given but never taken.
S and T Incorporated."

BILL: (*Noticing the turning, vine-covered rock*) I hate to tell you this but the shrubbery is moving around.

DOROTHY: What?

(*They all jump back as the rock completes its turn, revealing TIC TOC, a robot-like creature, with dials and a clock face. He is immobile.*)

UNCLE HENRY: What's that?

BILL: It's a pressure cooker!

DOROTHY: It is not!

BILL: A deep fryer!

UNCLE HENRY: Nonsense.

BILL: Then what?

DOROTHY: There's a sign around its neck.

BILL: Yeah and it reads "Family sized bucket: wings, backs and thighs; cole slaw and a roll."

DOROTHY: It does not.

BILL: I told you chickens can't read.

UNCLE HENRY: (*Moving closer*) It says, "Do not touch by order of the Gnome King: Roquat of the Rock. This means You!"

BILL: (*Up and leaving*) That means us.

UNCLE HENRY: There's other writing too. "Smith and Tinker. Patent. Double Action Time Machine."

DOROTHY: S and T . . . . Just like on the key.

BILL: I'm going back to the coop. Drop me a post card and let me know how it all turns out.

UNCLE HENRY: Go ahead, ya big chicken!

(*He laughs at his own pun and DOROTHY stops BILL.*)

DOROTHY: Look, Bill, I want to go home, back to Kansas. I don't want to spend the rest of my life in a place where chickens talk, the plants move around, and the sun never rises. Maybe the power of this key can get us all home!

UNCLE HENRY: Here's some directions. Come on, Dorothy, let's wind him up and see what happens.

(*DOROTHY crosses to TIC TOC, and UNCLE HENRY reads the directions.*)

"For thinking, wind Clock Man in the head."

(*DOROTHY winds and TIC TOC opens his eyes.*)

"For speaking, wind the Clock Man in the neck."

(*DOROTHY winds and TIC TOC speaks.*)

TIC TOC: Tic Toc . . . Tic Toc . . . Tic Toc . . .

BILL: It's talking! It's talking!

UNCLE HENRY: "For time control activation, wind Clock Man in the chest and adjust time control activation dial. Caution, once you have started you cannot turn back."

DOROTHY: I don't want to turn back. I want to go forward. I want to go HOME!

(*DOROTHY turns the final crank and UNCLE HENRY turns the dial. TIC TOC shudders and moves. Lights change abruptly to brilliant colors, which flash during TIC TOC's chant. DOROTHY, BILL, UNCLE HENRY, and all of OZ experience a severe jolt and freeze in off-balance positions.*)

TIC TOC: (*Booming*) This is the power that's stronger than strength,
Wider than width and longer than length.
The holder of the key has power unshaken.
The key may be given but never taken.
Tic Toc . . . Tic Toc . . . Tic Toc . . . Tic Toc . . .

(*There is a loud and rapid ticking sound. All are thrown forward and move quickly, as if time were speeding. The stage darkens and lightens several times. The sun spins through the sky as day becomes night, and night turns to day.*)

DOROTHY: What's happening?

BILL: Make it stop! Make it stop!

UNCLE HENRY: My heart, it's beating too fast!

TIC TOC: Slow me down! Slow me down. On my chest, turn the dial!

(*DOROTHY manages to get to the dial and turns it. Movements return to normal and the sky is bright, in full daylight.*)

DOROTHY: Uncle Henry, are you all right?

UNCLE HENRY: I think so.

TIC TOC: I'm sorry if I gave you a start, but you gave me one.

DOROTHY: What happened?

TIC TOC: You have started me and you have started time. It's a good thing you slowed me down or years would have passed in minutes.

UNCLE HENRY: Who are you?

TIC TOC: I am Tic Toc, the Time Machine. I was made by the marvelous inventors Smith and Tinker.

BILL: I told you we shouldn't have messed with it.

TIC TOC: I am your most obedient servant and I shall serve you until the end of time; but right now we had best be getting out of here. They will be here any minute, perhaps any second.

DOROTHY: Who?

TIC TOC: Why the Wheelers, of course.

BILL: I told you!

(*BILL and TIC TOC start out.*)

UNCLE HENRY: Wait a minute.

TIC TOC: All right. 1, 2, 3, 4, 5, 6, . . .

UNCLE HENRY: What are you doing?

TIC TOC: Waiting a minute.

UNCLE HENRY: That's not what I meant. Where are we?

TIC TOC: You are in Oz.

UNCLE HENRY: Where's that?

TIC TOC: Right here.

DOROTHY: You're a Time Machine?

TIC TOC: Before I was invented there was no time in Oz. The sun always shone and it was always day. The people of Oz were forever young and no one ever grew older. When I was invented, time began. The people of Oz started to age and day was followed by night. In the darkness of the night a terrible thing happened.

DOROTHY: What?

TIC TOC: The earth rumbled and split wide open. Roquat, the Gnome King, and his evil Gnomes escaped from underground. There was a terrible battle. Roquat captured the forces of the Wheelers and forced them to fight for him. Then Ozma, the ruler of Oz, came from the Emerald City with her army. They fought all through the night.

UNCLE HENRY: Then what happened?

TIC TOC: Dawn broke and the sun began to rise. The Gnomes cannot stand the light of day; they started to crumble and turn to ash. As Roquat retreated back beneath the ground, he grabbed me and started to pull me down with him. Ozma caught my arm just in time and the rock began to close around me. At the last possible second, Ozma snatched away my key and threw it far out to sea. My time control will not work without the key; so it has been forever dawn, and time had stopped till now.

(*A rumbling is heard and all look around apprehensively.*)

BILL: Let's just turn him off and get out of here.

TIC TOC: Now that my key is back in Oz, and I am started, I cannot be stopped.

UNCLE HENRY: You can control time?

DOROTHY: But how?

TIC TOC: With this dial. You turn it this way for fast and that way for slow.

DOROTHY: You mean I just put the key here and turn?

(*DOROTHY gives the key a turn and lights change as the sun rises quickly and sets; the stage darkens.*)

TIC TOC: Be careful!

BILL: Look at the sun.

DOROTHY: What happened?

TIC TOC: You have made it night!

(*The earth rumbles and they are all jolted back.*)

UNCLE HENRY: What was that?

TIC TOC: An earthquake.

(*The TWO ROCK PEOPLE slowly come to life and move towards them.*)

BILL: The rocks! They're moving!

(*ROQUAT'S laugh is heard.*)

TIC TOC: Don't let them get my key!

(*DOROTHY grabs the key and tries to evade them. UNCLE HENRY tries to hold them off with his canes; all the while ROQUAT is laughing off-stage and making disgusting sounds.*)

UNCLE HENRY: I'll hold them off.

TIC TOC: Speed me up! Make it day!

(*As the ROCK people move toward them, BILL tries to escape and gets in the way. The ROCK PEOPLE grab BILL.*)

BILL: Hey! Not me!

TIC TOC: Now, turn the dial!

(*DOROTHY turns the key and the stage begins to lighten. The ROCK PEOPLE exit with BILL.*)

BILL: You got the wrong one! I'm an innocent byyyyyyyyyyy . . . . . .

(*Lights return to normal. ROCK PEOPLE and BILL are gone.*)

UNCLE HENRY: Hostile savages!

DOROTHY: They're gone!

TIC TOC: Gnomes cannot exist in the light.

UNCLE HENRY: Aborigines! Bushrangers!

DOROTHY: Where have they taken Bill?

TIC TOC: To Roquat's Kingdom underground. But it's me they are after, and you because you have the key.

DOROTHY: Here, take it. I don't want it.

TIC TOC: You must keep it. It can never be taken from you. Roquat will get it only if you give it to him and you must never do that.

UNCLE HENRY: Showing cowardice only encourages the savages.

TIC TOC: Now, you must take me to Ozma. She'll know what to do with me.

UNCLE HENRY: If I could just walk. If I could just get out of this chair!

(*There is a rumble and the voice of ROQUAT is heard.*)

ROQUAT: My time has come at last!

DOROTHY: Who's that?

TIC TOC: Roquat.

DOROTHY: But I thought . . .

TIC TOC: He is just below the surface.

UNCLE HENRY: (*Beats on the ground with his canes*) Come out you blasted Bushranger. Come out where we can see you.

ROQUAT: Not before night!

UNCLE HENRY: Come out and fight!

DOROTHY: Uncle Henry!

ROQUAT: Give me that key!

DOROTHY: No!

   (*She holds the key high above her head.*)

ROQUAT: You will give me that key or I will order my loyal subjects, the Wheelers, to attack!

UNCLE HENRY: Bring 'em on!

DOROTHY: Uncle Henry, don't make him mad!

ROQUAT: Wheelers . . . . .

   (*A weird "Wheeler" sound is heard.*)

TIC TOC: They are coming!

UNCLE HENRY: Hot Damn!

   (*DOROTHY grabs UNCLE HENRY's chair and starts off.*)

UNCLE HENRY: Don't give them an inch, men!

TIC TOC: We'll never out run them.

UNCLE HENRY: We'll stand and fight!

DOROTHY: We will not!

TIC TOC: Hide him in my cave.

UNCLE HENRY: Oh, no!

TIC TOC: Then we'll climb those trees over there. Wheelers can't climb trees.

UNCLE HENRY: But I want to . . .

(*DOROTHY shoves the chair into the cave.*)

DOROTHY: Now stay in there and don't make a sound.

UNCLE HENRY: Cowards!

DOROTHY: Promise me you won't make a sound.

UNCLE HENRY: Oh, Dorothy!

TIC TOC: Here they come!

(*DOROTHY and TIC TOC exit. UNCLE HENRY leans down low in his chair.*)

ROQUAT'S VOICE: WHEELERS, ATTACK!

(*The WHEELERS enter; they are strange looking creatures on roller skates. They have wheels for hands as well. They sweep in fiercely making a weird warbling sound. They wheel around in a wide circle growing less fierce and more confused.*)

WHEELER I: There's nothing here!

WHEELER II: The Gnome King will have our heads.

WHEELER I: Or our wheels, which is worse.

WHEELER II: Not our wheels!

WHEELER I: What did the order say?

WHEELER II: It said to attack.

WHEELER I: Attack what?

WHEELER II: It didn't say.

WHEELER I: But there's nothing here.

WHEELER II: If there's nothing here, then there's only one thing to do.

WHEELER I: What?

WHEELER II: Attack nothing!

WHEELER I: ATTACK NOTHING!

(*With renewed vigor, they race around attacking nothing. UNCLE HENRY can stand it no longer. He charges out of the cave.*)

UNCLE HENRY: Stand back, you savages!

WHEELERS: (*Terrified*) Ahhhhhhhhhh!

UNCLE HENRY: Stand back, or I'll give you a taste of gun powder.

(*They crumble in abject terror.*)

WHEELER I: Will you look at that?

WHEELER II: Look at his face.

WHEELER I: Look at his hair.

BOTH: Look at his WHEELS!

UNCLE HENRY: (*Nervously*) Sure wish I had a musket.

WHEELER I: Will you look at those wheels!

WHEELER II: Biggest I've ever seen.

WHEELER I: He must be a General at least. He must be . . .

(*As they advance on him, UNCLE HENRY lifts his cane and uses it like a musket.*)

UNCLE HENRY: BANG!

WHEELERS: (*Crumbling again*) Oh, noooooo. Don't hurt us. We've waited for you. And you've finally come.

UNCLE HENRY: Huh?

WHEELER I: We knew you at once from your wheels.

WHEELER II: Will you look at those wheels!

WHEELER I: We knew you had to be . . .

BOTH: The Big Wheeler!

UNCLE HENRY: Well I'll be . . .

WHEELER I: (*Groveling*) Oh, Big Wheeler, it's been terrible.

WHEELER II: The Gnome King has made all us Wheelers his spies.

WHEELER I: We have to do all his dirty work above the ground . . .

WHEELER II: Or he wrecks all our houses with earthquakes.

WHEELER I: Burns up our fields with volcanos.

WHEELER II: Clogs up our plumbing with sludge!

BOTH: Save us, Big Wheeler! Save us!

UNCLE HENRY: At ease!

(*They assume an at-ease position.*)

Now let me think. If we are going to fight this Gnome King, we need something big, something organized, something like an army.

(*He looks at them dubiously.*)

Attention!

(*They snap to.*)

Forward march! . . . . Halt! . . . . About face . . . .

(*They respond with as much precision as they can muster. UNCLE HENRY is delighted.*)

Good! Very Good! Now try some circles . . . . How about a figure eight?

(*As he puts them through their paces, DOROTHY and TIC TOC enter cautiously.*)

DOROTHY: Oh, No! They've captured Uncle Henry.

TIC TOC: How did he get out of the cave?

DOROTHY: He never does what I tell him to. We have got to save him. When I count three, run in and scream like crazy. 1 . . . 2 . . . 3. . .

(*They enter making a great deal of noise. WHEELERS cower behind UNCLE HENRY.*)

UNCLE HENRY: What in the blue blazes are you doing?

DOROTHY: We saved you; are you all right?

UNCLE HENRY: Of course I'm all right!

DOROTHY: (*Bravely to the Wheelers*) I demand that you release my Uncle at once!

(*WHEELERS advance on DOROTHY trying their best to be menacing.*)

WHEELER I: Oh, you do, do you?

WHEELER II: And who are you?

WHEELER I: (*Indicating Tic Toc*) And what is that?

DOROTHY: (*Nervous*) Uncle Henry . . . .

UNCLE HENRY: (*Trying to give her a high sign*) Uhhhh, Dorothy, they have guessed our secret.

DOROTHY: Secret?

UNCLE HENRY: They know who I am. They know I'm the . . . Big Wheeler.

DOROTHY: (*Bursts out laughing in spite of herself*) You? The Big . . .

WHEELER I: (*Sharply*) What's so funny?

DOROTHY: (*Quickly*) Nothing.

(*They continue to advance on her.*)

WHEELER I: Speaking of wheels . . .

WHEELER II: Yes, speaking of wheels . . .

BOTH: WHERE ARE YOURS?

WHEELER II: Yes, where are your wheels?

DOROTHY: Uncle Henry, do something!

UNCLE HENRY: Halt! She has no wheels because . . . she has no wheels! Don't question your superiors! This is Dorothy, my lieutenant; and that is Tic Toc the Time Machine.

WHEELERS: The Time Machine!

TIC TOC: All Hail the Big Wheeler!

(*WHEELERS snap to attention and salute.*)

WHEELERS: All Hail the Big Wheeler!

(*DOROTHY, mystified, salutes slowly.*)

UNCLE HENRY: Now, that's more like it!

(*There is a rumble and the earth shakes.*)

WHEELER I: We must leave here at once.

WHEELER II: The Gnome King knows where we are.

(*There is another rumble.*)

ALL: We must find Ozma!

TIC TOC: Ozma will know what to do with me!

UNCLE HENRY: Which way do we go?

TIC TOC: Forward, across the desert of shifting sand, then on to the Emerald City!

WHEELER I: (*Terrified*) Oh, no, not the desert!

WHEELER II: Please sir, not the desert!

WHEELER I: The desert is the domain of the Princess Langwidere. She hates Wheelers.

WIIEELER II: She hates everyone, except herself.

WHEELER I: She loves herself.

WHEELER II: She'll have our heads.

WHEELER I: She'll have YOUR heads.

DOROTHY: Is there any other way?

TIC TOC: No. To get to the Emerald City, we must cross the desert of shifting sand.

UNCLE HENRY: Then forward.

WHEELERS: Oh, please, Sir . . . . . .

UNCLE HENRY: Brace up, men!

(*They do . . . sort of.*)

Forward, March, and everybody hang on to your heads.

(*UNCLE HENRY starts off and DOROTHY takes his chair.*)

DOROTHY: Allow me. It would be an honor to push . . . the Big Wheeler.

UNCLE HENRY: Forward, March!

(They set off as sounds of the earthquake rumble.)

Scene V: The Desert of Shifting Sand*

Sounds change from the earthquake to a raging sand storm. Lights flicker strangely to give the effect of swirling sand. UNCLE HENRY, DOROTHY, and TIC TOC enter with the WHEELERS nervously bringing up the rear. All shield their eyes from the sand.

UNCLE HENRY: I can't see anything.

DOROTHY: Neither can I.

TIC TOC: Neither can I.

WHEELERS: Neither can we.

DOROTHY: Are we going the right way?

UNCLE HENRY: Who knows, but at least we're going.

DOROTHY: Look! Up ahead! I see something. There's someone coming.

WHEELERS: Who is it?

DOROTHY: (*Moving to the lead*) I can't see very well . . . there seems to be four, no five of them.

(She points.)

And they are coming this way!

WHEELERS: Oh, Noooooo!

UNCLE HENRY: I see them too. There's a girl in front and she's pointing at us.

---

*If time is a problem this scene can be cut. The transition to Scene VI is better with it included, but it is not absolutely essential to the action. At the conclusion of the previous scene have the Wheelers hesitate and take off in the opposite direction from the others.

DOROTHY: And there's a man in a chair.

TIC TOC: And a strange looking creature with clocks or something . . .

WHEELERS: And two Wheelers!

(*DOROTHY waves.*)

UNCLE HENRY: They've seen us! They're waving.

DOROTHY: It's us! Look, It's us! We're there!

WHEELER I: Funny, I thought we were here.

WHEELER II: Me, too.

TIC TOC: It is us, and we're headed this way.

UNCLE HENRY: HALT!

(*They stop.*)

DOROTHY: Look! We're still coming.

UNCLE HENRY: But we've stopped.

WHEELER I: No, we haven't; we're still coming!

TIC TOC: It's Langwidere's guards! They have shields made of mirrors and we are seeing our own reflections!

UNCLE HENRY: They are coming right for us.

WHEELER II: They're running!

TIC TOC: If Langwidere discovers that I have been started again we are all doomed!

DOROTHY: Why?

TIC TOC: Time is an enemy to Langwidere.

WHEELERS: They are still coming!

UNCLE HENRY: Tic Toc, you try to get through that way. Dorothy and the Wheelers and I will hold them off as long as we can. Come on, men . . . .

WHEELERS: Oh, nooooo, Sir. We aren't very fond of danger.

UNCLE HENRY: The only way is to face them down. Captain Cook never ran from hostile savages.

DOROTHY: But you're not Captain Cook.

UNCLE HENRY: Come on, men! Forward!

(*Before DOROTHY can stop him UNCLE HENRY charges forward. The WHEELERS grab onto each other.*)

WHEELERS: RETREAT!

(*The WHEELERS exit in the opposite direction.*)

DOROTHY: Uncle Henry . . . . Wait for me!

UNCLE HENRY: (*Off stage*) CHARGE!

(*DOROTHY races off after him. TIC TOC, left alone, shrugs and exits in another direction. In the distance we hear the WHEELERS making their weird WHEELER sound.*)

Scene VI: Langwidere's Palace

Langwidere's palace is made of mirrors; there is a dressing cubicle and a series of cupboards, each containing a head with an elaborate hairdo and makeup. At the opening of the scene LANGWIDERE is inside the cubicle. NANDA, her serving woman, sits wearily. It has not been a good day. As LANGWIDERE changes heads she also changes personality, accent, mood, and body posture.* NANDA also embodies this change, always playing to her mistress' present personality.

LANGWIDERE: (*French accent*) Non! Zis will not do! Fetch another head!

---

*The simplest and most effective way to stage this is to use a series of wigs, rather than full heads or masks. This allows the head changes to be suggested and leaves the actress' face visible to the audience.

NANDA: But Princess Langwidere, zis is zee twenty-sixth head today. What is wrong with zis one?

LANGWIDERE: Everything!

NANDA: But, Madam . . .

(*LANGWIDERE enters wearing a "French" head.*)

LANGWIDERE: C'est la meme chose! Zis head also has zee headache. Bring the mirror.

(*NANDA holds up a mirror.*)

LANGWIDERE: Sacre Bleu!

NANDA: What?

LANGWIDERE: Zee eye! Look under zee eye!

NANDA: It looks a little puffy perhaps, but . . .

LANGWIDERE: Zat is a bag! A bag under zee eye! Fetch another head. Vingt-huit! Vite! Vite!

(*LANGWIDERE goes back inside the cubicle. NANDA crosses to the cupboard and takes out a head which bears some resemblance to Dolly Parton.*)

NANDA: I do not understand what is happening today.

(*NANDA hands the head in to LANGWIDERE; in return she is handed the French head which she returns to the cupboard.*)

NANDA: Something very strange is going on, Madam. First zere is ze bang, zen everysing is light, zen everysing is dark, zen light, zen dark, now everysing is coo coo. I do not understand.

LANGWIDERE: (*From inside the cubicle, in a thick drawl*) Well I'll be.

NANDA: (*Also in a drawl*) How's that?

(*LANGWIDERE enters wearing the "Country Western" head.*)

LANGWIDERE: This little ole head ain't no better'n the rest. Why, it don't look good or feel right neither.

(*She snaps for the mirror, NANDA hands it to her.*)

NANDA: Why it looks right purdy, Mam.

LANGWIDERE: You lookee there! What do you see? You see that chin? Now you see this other one? Nanda, why does this head have two chins?

NANDA: I swan! I don't know.

LANGWIDERE: Girl, you better do somethin', quick.

NANDA: What can I do?

LANGWIDERE: Bring me number thirty.

NANDA: Please not number thirty. You always shout at me when you wear number thirty. You're always so short tempered when you wear number thirty.

LANGWIDERE: (*Like iron under the sweetness*) Nanda, sugar, baby, honey, darlin'; I couldn't be more short tempered than I am right now. Now, hustle me up number thirty!

(*LANGWIDERE stamps back into the cubicle.*)

NANDA: Yes, Mam. Right away, Mam. Anything you say, Mam.

(*NANDA hustles to the cupboard and removes head number thirty.*)

LANGWIDERE: (*From inside*) I said, NOW!

NANDA: I'm goin' as fast as my little legs can carry me.

(*NANDA hands the new head into the cubicle and is given the old one which she returns to the cupboard. A GUARD enters.*)

GUARD: Your Majesty, two prisoners were apprehended crossing the desert of shifting sand.

LANGWIDERE: (*Inside the cubicle, her voice is imperious and austere*) Dispose of them.

GUARD: Do you want me to interrogate them?

LANGWIDERE: Just bring me their heads.

GUARD: (*Quietly to NANDA*) Is she wearing number thirty?

(*NANDA nods and GUARD looks skyward.*)

GUARD: Very well, Madam.

(*GUARD starts out.*)

LANGWIDERE: Wait!

(*LANGWIDERE enters wearing a proud and haughty head.*)

LANGWIDERE: Strange things are happening today, and now you tell me there are strangers in my domain. I will see them. But tell them to bow.

(*GUARD exits.*)

LANGWIDERE: People who don't bow around here, don't keep their heads for very long.

(*NANDA bows.*)

LANGWIDERE: Nanda, arrange me!

(*NANDA primps and pats her mistress and the GUARD enters with DOROTHY and UNCLE HENRY.*)

GUARD: The Prisoners! Bow.

(*They bow, LANGWIDERE turns and faces them squarely. GUARD exits.*)

LANGWIDERE: You may rise.

(*They do so and LANGWIDERE gasps at the sight of UNCLE HENRY.*)

LANGWIDERE: What is the matter with your face?

DOROTHY: Mine?

LANGWIDERE: No, his! It's all rumpled!

UNCLE HENRY: Rumpled?

LANGWIDERE: (*Examining him with distaste and curiosity*) His eyes are so squinty, and his brow is all . . . bumpy. His cheeks, they sag, and all those lines. He has broken his face!

UNCLE HENRY: These are just wrinkles.

LANGWIDERE: Is that what you call them? How droll.

   (*She snaps and NANDA brings a magnifying glass. She peers at him through it.*)

LANGWIDERE: And his hair . . . What is that disgusting color?

UNCLE HENRY: Grey.

LANGWIDERE: Nanda, if you ever see any grey hair in any of my heads, pull it out at once!

NANDA: Yes, Mam.

LANGWIDERE: (*To DOROTHY*) I demand that you tell me what has happened to him!

DOROTHY: He's just old, that's all.

LANGWIDERE: Old?

DOROTHY: It's just something that happens as time passes.

LANGWIDERE: In Oz we do not allow time to pass. What does "old" feel like?

UNCLE HENRY: Inside I feel like I've always felt, but everytime I look in a mirror it gives me a jolt. I wonder how that old man got in there.

LANGWIDERE: Stand up.

DOROTHY: He can't.

LANGWIDERE: I command you to stand up!

DOROTHY: But he can't use his legs.

UNCLE HENRY: (*Struggling to raise himself on his canes*) I can try!

LANGWIDERE: If he cannot use his legs, then why does he have them? What good are they?

(*UNCLE HENRY is now upright, LANGWIDERE motions for NANDA to pull away the wheelchair.*)

LANGWIDERE: Remove it!

DOROTHY: No, he needs that!

LANGWIDERE: He does, does he? Let's see. WALK!

DOROTHY: But he can't!

(*UNCLE HENRY takes a few very shaky steps on his canes.*)

LANGWIDERE: Faster! Faster!

DOROTHY: He can't.

(*LANGWIDERE kicks one of the canes out from under him, he stumbles and DOROTHY rushes to catch him and helps him back into the chair.*)

LANGWIDERE: Helpless! How revolting!

DOROTHY: He's not helpless. He's just old, and it's not his fault!

LANGWIDERE: THEN WHO'S FAULT IS IT?

(*NANDA spies something on her mistress.*)

NANDA: Madam, hold still.

(*NANDA plucks a hair from LANGWIDERE'S head.*)

LANGWIDERE: OW!

NANDA: Got it.

LANGWIDERE: WHAT?

NANDA: One of those grey hairs.

LANGWIDERE: On me? You found one of those grey hairs on me? Nanda, how did this happen?

(*UNCLE HENRY laughs.*)

LANGWIDERE: (*Turns on him*) It's YOU! You SORCERER! What have you done to my HEADS?

UNCLE HENRY: (*Brandishing his watch in front of him*) It's not me! It's TIME!

LANGWIDERE: That's impossible. We do not allow time in OZ!

(*GUARD enters with TIC TOC.*)

GUARD: Your Majesty, we have apprehended another prisoner.

DOROTHY: Tic Toc!

LANGWIDERE: Tic Toc? Tic Toc? The Time Machine? You have started the TIME MACHINE? TURN HIM OFF AT ONCE!

(*LANGWIDERE makes a lunge for them, DOROTHY grabs the closest thing she has to a weapon, the key, to defend them. There is a flash of light and a magical sound. LANGWIDERE is repelled by the power of the key.*)

LANGWIDERE: The key! Where did you get the key?

DOROTHY: I found it.

LANGWIDERE: What have you done? Give me that key!

DOROTHY: (*Holding it high*) You can't take it. I have to give it to you and I won't!

UNCLE HENRY: That a girl, Dorothy!

TIC TOC: Hold fast, Dorothy!

LANGWIDERE: Silence! do you know what you have begun? I beg you, give me that key.

DOROTHY: No.

LANGWIDERE: Then turn him off; please, turn him off.

DOROTHY: I don't know how.

TIC TOC: Only Ozma knows.

LANGWIDERE: Fools! Take them to the Guard House immediately. Lock them up out there and starve them. You can't possibly know what you have started.

(*GUARD and NANDA lead DOROTHY, UNCLE HENRY, and TIC TOC off. LANGWIDERE moves frantically from mirror to mirror.*)

LANGWIDERE: We had a perfect balance here! Perfect! And now it's all out of joint.

(*She is alone and frightened.*)

I am growing older!

(*Music and Blackout.*)

Scene VII: In the Guard House

Lights come up on DOROTHY, UNCLE HENRY, and TIC TOC in the Guard House. It is a small space indicated by a bench and a door with bars. All are very depressed. TIC TOC peers out the door, DOROTHY sits with her head in her hands, UNCLE HENRY seethes with frustration and rage.

DOROTHY: Do you see anything out there?

TIC TOC: No. It's night, and night is a dangerous time in Oz.

UNCLE HENRY: I never felt so totally helpless.

DOROTHY: It's all right, Uncle Henry.

UNCLE HENRY: I wanted to stand up, walk over, and spit right in her eye.

DOROTHY: I know.

UNCLE HENRY: That's what I would have done, you know, that's what I would have done, if I just could have . . . .

DOROTHY: It's all right . . . .

UNCLE HENRY: But I couldn't.

DOROTHY: But you tried.

UNCLE HENRY: That's not enough!

DOROTHY: We've got to get out of here. I have got to get us home!

TIC TOC: If we could just get to Ozma.

DOROTHY: What could she do?

TIC TOC: Everything. And anything. She is beautiful and she is brave. She has the power to see behind the mind and into the heart. She can make you speak your truth, no matter with it is. It is a great power.

UNCLE HENRY: Tic Toc, can you really control time?

TIC TOC: Yes.

UNCLE HENRY: Make it start and stop, make it go faster and slower?

TIC TOC: With this dial.

UNCLE HENRY: Could there be a way . . . Could you make time go backward?

TIC TOC: Reverse?

UNCLE HENRY: Could you make me . . . could you make me young again?

TIC TOC: Once you have started you cannot turn back. I do not have a setting for reverse.

UNCLE HENRY: I only wondered.

TIC TOC: I'm sorry.

UNCLE HENRY: So am I.

DOROTHY: (*Reaching out to him*) Uncle Henry, back on the boat, I said some stupid and terrible things; but I didn't realize . . . I didn't understand . . . .

(*The GUARD enters abruptly.*)

GUARD: (*To UNCLE HENRY and TIC TOC*) You and you, come.

DOROTHY: What's happening? Are we free?

GUARD: You are summoned to the Princess.

(*DOROTHY starts out but the GUARD stops her.*)

GUARD: Only the Tic Toc Man and the Old One.

DOROTHY: What about me?

UNCLE HENRY: I'm not leaving without Dorothy.

GUARD: (*Forcing them out*) The Princess does not like to be kept waiting!

UNCLE HENRY: I said, I'm not leaving without DOROTHY! . . . . . DOROTHY!

(*They exit, leaving DOROTHY alone.*)

DOROTHY: Uncle Henry! Don't leave me here alone!

(*She throws herself down on the bench in despair. Lights fade, music indicates a passage of time.*)

Scene VIII: Outside the Guard House

It is now morning. The sky is light and DOROTHY is asleep on the bench. From the rear of the house there is a drum beat. DOROTHY stirs and wakes. As she rises, the strains of the "Ozma March" can be heard growing louder and louder.

DOROTHY: What's that sound? I see something . . . There's something coming cross the desert. Why it's a huge green carpet and . . . HELP! Save me! HELP!

(*From the back of the house OZMA enters on a litter carried by GENERAL and ARMY. As they march they sing.*)

ALL: The sun has the day
The moon has the night

And youth belongs to the stars
The sky has the way
The sea has the might
But the truth belongs to Ozma
Ozma of Oz
Defending the good and upholding the laws
Ozma, Ozma, Oh Ozma of Oz.

(*The rescue party arrives at the stage and OZMA alights from the litter.*)

DOROTHY: Here I am. Help me please!

OZMA: Who are you?

DOROTHY: I'm Dorothy Gale. Are you Ozma?

OZMA: I am Ozma of Oz, and I have come with ·my Army.

GENERAL: I'm the General.

ARMY: And I'm the Army.

DOROTHY: Is that all your Army?

OZMA: It's all I need. We have come to find the Tic Toc Man. We went to the cave and followed the tracks here. I know he has been started again.

DOROTHY: How did you know?

GENERAL: Because now there is day in Oz.

ARMY: And now there is night.

OZMA: In the darkness, the Gnomes can walk upon the surface. Roquat's forces have totally conquered the land of the Wheelers.

DOROTHY: I'm sorry. My Uncle and I started Tic Toc.

OZMA: That was a dangerous thing to do.

DOROTHY: We didn't know what we were doing. Hey, could you rescue me? I'd feel so much better if I was rescued.

(*OZMA nods to General.*)

GENERAL: Leave it to us. Army, rescue her.

ARMY: Yes, Sir!

(*ARMY makes a great show of attempting to bash in the door and fails.*)

OZMA: Leave it to me.

(*OZMA crosses to the door and pulls the bars apart easily.*)

DOROTHY: (*Impressed*) Thank you.

OZMA: You're welcome.

(*As soon as DOROTHY steps outside of the prison, an alarm goes off. LANGWIDERE, NANDA and GUARD enter at a run. LANGWIDERE wears the "Country Western" head.*)

LANGWIDERE: GUARD, Stop them!

(*The GUARD rushes at OZMA, who subdues him in a brilliant display of the martial arts.*)

LANGWIDERE: Nanda! Attack!

(*NANDA goes after OZMA. OZMA subdues her as well, but much more gently. ARMY and GENERAL applaud.*)

GENERAL: Very Good, Ozma!

OZMA: Tie them up, men.

GENERAL: Army, tie them up!

(*ARMY leads them off.*)

LANGWIDERE: (*Covering, sweetly*) Ozma, what ever are you doing here?

OZMA: Langwidere, if I'm not mistaken. Of course with you, it's sometimes hard to tell.

LANGWIDERE: Why-ever have you bashed up my servants?

DOROTHY: What have you done with my Uncle?

LANGWIDERE: I see you have met my . . . guest.

DOROTHY: You mean your prisoner! Where is my Uncle?

OZMA: And the Tic Toc Man!

LANGWIDERE: Whatever do you mean?

OZMA: Men, look around!

GENERAL: Army, look around!

(*ARMY enters and exits again.*)

DOROTHY: You know perfectly well.

LANGWIDERE: Oh, you mean my other guests. Why, they left early this morning. They were in such a hurry, so I gave them a nice big breakfast of flapjacks and cornbread and a nice hot cup of coffee . . .

OZMA: Langwidere, I can see a lie right through your eyes.

LANGWIDERE: (*Closes her eyes tightly*) You're right. I didn't give them breakfast. They just left. And they didn't even leave a note saying "Thank you for the lovely time."

(*OZMA fixes her with a stare and raises her arm slowly.*)

OZMA: I can make you tell me the truth.

(*There is a magical sound, as OZMA uses her power. LANGWIDERE resists, but is drawn toward her; as OZMA almost touches her, the facade cracks.*)

LANGWIDERE: No . . . Don't use . . . I was so frightened. I don't want to grow old.

OZMA: What have you done with them?

LANGWIDERE: I sold them.

DOROTHY: Sold them?

LANGWIDERE: To the Gnome King. He came here, in the darkness. He promised to turn off the Tic Toc Man. He promised to stop time. What else could I do?

DOROTHY: (*Incredulous*) You sold my Uncle?

OZMA: Why did you sell the Uncle?

LANGWIDERE: I couldn't stand to look at him.

(*OZMA releases her from the power. The magic sound stops.*)

LANGWIDERE: What are you going to do with me?

OZMA: Nothing. Time will do far worse to you than I ever could. Now, go!

(*LANGWIDERE exits.*)

DOROTHY: Where has the Gnome King taken them?

OZMA: To his Kingdom underground. If he has the key, we are lost.

DOROTHY: He doesn't. I do. Tic Toc told me never to give away the key. We were coming to find you.

OZMA: Good girl, Dorothy!

DOROTHY: Ozma, my Uncle hasn't been very well. He's a very old man, and he's in a wheelchair, and we've got to do something. We've got to find him before . . . .

(*ARMY enters, excited.*)

ARMY: Permission to speak?

GENERAL: Granted.

ARMY: Sir, Sir, there are fresh wheel tracks and foot prints leading north toward the mountains.

GENERAL: Thank you.

ARMY: You're welcome.

(*GENERAL Crosses to OZMA and uses ARMY'S exact inflection.*)

GENERAL: Permission to speak?

OZMA: Granted.

GENERAL: Ozma, Ozma, there are fresh wheel tracks and foot prints leading north toward the mountains.

OZMA: Thank you.

GENERAL: You're welcome.

DOROTHY: That must be them!

OZMA: We shall follow the trail and rescue them, or my name's not Ozma of Oz!

(*The troops assemble. OZMA sits on the litter. Theme music begins; OZMA motions to DOROTHY to join in the procession. ALL march off singing the "OZMA March."*)

ALL: The sun has the day
The moon has the night
And youth belongs to the stars
The sky has the way
The sea has the might
But the truth belongs to Ozma
Ozma of Oz
Defending the good and upholding the laws
Ozma, Ozma, Oh, Ozma of Oz.

(*As they march, scenery shifts and lights change.*)

Scene IX: A Pass in the Road

OZMA and entourage march around the rear of the house. Two huge crashing rocks appear on stage. They open and crash together in regular intervals, the cadence rumbles ominously. As they approach the stage OZMA signals a halt. The rocks are dimly lit, the rescue party is lit more brightly.

OZMA: Halt.

DOROTHY: What's that terrible sound?

OZMA: What's that terrible sound?

GENERAL: What's that terrible sound?

(*ARMY runs ahead a few steps to see.*)

ARMY: (*To General*) Sir, Sir, up ahead are two huge boulders crashing together, directly in our path.

GENERAL: Thank you.

(*GENERAL Crosses to OZMA and copies ARMY'S inflection exactly.*)

GENERAL: Ozma, Ozma, up ahead there are two huge boulders crashing together, directly in our path.

OZMA: Thank you. The Gnome King's defenses.

(*To General*)

Can we go around them?

GENERAL: (*To Army*) Can we go around them?

ARMY: No.

GENERAL: (*To OZMA*) No.

OZMA: Can we go over them?

GENERAL: Can we go over them?

ARMY: No.

GENERAL: No.

OZMA: Can we go under them?

GENERAL: Can we go under them?

ARMY: No.

GENERAL: No.

OZMA: Then we shall have to go through them.

BOTH: NO!

GENERAL: They will pound us to powder, crush us to crumbs, smash us to smudge.

ARMY: We're liable to get hurt.

OZMA: All we have to do is to wait for them to open, run through, and get out before they close. Right?

BOTH: Wrong!

GENERAL: In battle we are wonderfully courageous. But battle is one thing and being pounded into pancakes is quite another. Naturally, we are a bit hesitant.

OZMA: Then we shall have to go alone. Come on Dorothy.

   (*She starts off and ARMY runs to her.*)

ARMY: I'll go with you, Ozma!

OZMA: Good brave Army!

GENERAL: Remember your rank. You are supposed to report only to me!

OZMA: General?

GENERAL: Oh . . . very well.

OZMA: Forward!

   (*They move toward the sound and lights come up on the boulders.*)

OZMA: I'll go first to see if it's possible. If it is, come along. If not, try anyway!

   (*OZMA waits for the crucial second, then does a cartwheel through.*)

I made it! Now Dorothy, you try.

DOROTHY: I'm not very good at this sort of thing.

(*DOROTHY waits, dashes, and makes it.*)

OZMA: Well done!

GENERAL: Army, forward, march!

ARMY: Remember my rank, General! After you!

GENERAL: That's an order!

ARMY: Yes sir.

(*ARMY waits for the beat and runs.*)

OZMA: Good job! Come on, General.

GENERAL: (*Terrified*) Can't you order it to slow down?

OZMA: You can do it, General. 1 . . . 2 . . . 3 . . . GO!

(*GENERAL Starts, hesitates, and trips.*)

DOROTHY: Oh, NO!

(*OZMA dashes in and holds the rocks apart with her bare hands.*)

OZMA: Get up, General!

(*He scurries to safety, OZMA heaves the rocks apart, steps out, and they crash together loudly.*)

GENERAL: You saved my life.

OZMA: (*Modestly*) It was nothing.

DOROTHY: That was wonderful!

OZMA: (*Honestly, without bragging*) Yes it was. Now forward! On to the Gnome King's Cavern!

(*They march forward in a time step and the stage darkens in strange colors. The sounds of laughter can be heard, and strange rock-like shapes appear around them.*)

OZMA: Look, you can see where the Gnomes have been. Everywhere they go, they leave a silicate slime and every living thing withers and dies and turns to rock.

(*The laughter grows and the shapes arrange themselves into huge doors to ROQUAT's Cavern behind them.*)

DOROTHY: What's that sound?

OZMA: Gnomes. Night is coming. We must be very careful.

(*The stage darkens to a single spot on the party. From the darkness ROQUAT'S VOICE booms.*)

ROQUAT'S VOICE: So you have breeched my defenses, Ozma! I see you are still quick as quicksilver.

(*His laughter echoes.*)

OZMA: Roquat! We have come to rescue those whom you have taken prisoner! We shall fight you and defeat you!

DOROTHY: (To GENERAL) Should we say that to him?

GENERAL: Ozma always tells the truth.

OZMA: Come out, Roquat! Come out and face me!

ROQUAT: Not before dark; have patience, my dear.

OZMA: Then we are coming in.

(*ROQUAT laughs and the laughter echoes.*)

ROQUAT: Still brash as bronze. Very well, you may enter. But those of you who have fear in your hearts may go no further. The doors to my domain will open only to those brave enough to enter freely of their own will.

(*More laughter echoed by GNOMES. GENERAL nearly collapses in fear, his knees knock, metals jangle, etc.*)

GENERAL: Ohhhhh, Ozma, can I have a word with you?

OZMA: I understand, General, you will stay here.

ARMY: I'll go with you, Ozma. I'm brave, I swear it, I really do . . . .

OZMA: Army?

ARMY: I would follow you anywhere.

(*OZMA raises her hand, and the sound of her power is heard. ARMY is drawn toward her.*)

ARMY: I'm brave enough to follow you through darkness, through fire, through . . .

(*OZMA touches his palm.*)

I'm scared to death!

(*She releases him from the power.*)

OZMA: You will stay here.

ARMY: But Ozma.

OZMA: To protect the General.

GENERAL: That's an order!

ARMY: Yes, Sir!

OZMA: Dorothy?

DOROTHY: I'll admit it. I'm scared too, but I have to find Uncle Henry.

OZMA: (*Takes her hand*) Very well. ROQUAT! We are ready. Open your doors!

(*The cavern opens to the sound of low and evil laughter. ARMY and GENERAL exit. DOROTHY and OZMA pass through the doors and into the cavern.*)

Scene X: In the Gnome King's Cavern

OZMA and DOROTHY wind through the passageways of the cavern. It is a deep mine, filled with rich gems and ore. It has a luminescent quality about it. The path is twisted and difficult, the scenery shifts around DOROTHY and OZMA, as they make their way toward the throne room. A large gem studded throne indicates this space. ROCK PEOPLE, who seem to be part of the scenery, dart here and there and give the space a constantly changing appearance. Laughter echoes everywhere.

DOROTHY: I can't see anything.

OZMA: Our eyes will become accustomed to the darkness in a moment. Stay close, Dorothy; my powers are not at their strongest down here.

ROQUAT'S VOICE: Ozma . . .

(GNOMES echo her name in raspy whispers.)

Welcome to my dominions, Ozma.

OZMA: Roquat, where are you?

ROQUAT: Here, somewhere.

OZMA: But where?

ROQUAT: You shall have to find me.

(Rocks and sounds shift about.)

OZMA: Games, as always, Roquat. We will not play! We will simply stand here until you appear before us.

ROQUAT: As you wish.

(There is a flash and a figure appears on the throne, he gestures as ROQUAT speaks but the voice comes from everywhere.)

ROQUAT: Why have you come?

DOROTHY: To find my Uncle Henry and the Tic Toc Man.

ROQUAT: I do not have them.

DOROTHY: I beg you, give me my Uncle. He's a very old man and he needs special . . .

OZMA: You are wasting your breath, Dorothy.

DOROTHY: Why?

OZMA: Because that is not the Gnome King. Roquat, come out at once!

(ROQUAT laughs and GNOMES whisper "OZMA".)

Then I shall have to find you!

(ROCKS shift, shadowy figures dart about. OZMA moves from rock to rock placing her hand upon them until finally . . .)

HERE! Now, come out!

(ROCK swings aside and ROQUAT enters.)

ROQUAT: Bi-tuminous and lignite, you did it. Still sharp as sulphur, I see. Allow me to introduce Feldspar, a mineral of many uses.

(Indicates the figure who was on the throne. FELDSPAR makes an ugly, rasping sound.)

ROQUAT: Now, Ozma, it seems an eocene since last we met. How are you my semi-precious?

OZMA: Very well, if it is any concern of yours.

ROQUAT: And who is this little gem you have brought with you?

DOROTHY: My name is Dorothy Gale, and my Uncle, Henry Gale, is the old man who you have . . .

ROQUAT: Sit, my dear. You must be quite eroded from your journey.

(He snaps and FELDSPAR becomes a chair.)

OZMA: (*Suspicious*) You are very friendly, Roquat.

ROQUAT: I am sorry for our little quakes of the past. Perhaps I'm just a sedimentary old fool, but I do hope we can be friends.

OZMA: You and I are enemies, and that will never change.

ROQUAT: Surely now, there is time enough for both of us in Oz.

OZMA: You speak to us of friendship, yet you still hold two prisoners.

ROQUAT: Prisoners? They aren't my prisoners . . . They are my possessions!

DOROTHY: What?

ROQUAT: Feldspar, my treasure chamber!

(*FELDSPAR wheels on a large display chamber with several oversized objects.*)

OZMA: What have you done?

ROQUAT: Your Uncle was no use to me as a human, but he does make a rather amusing gem crack.

(*DOROTHY gasps loudly.*)

Like carbon into diamond, sap into amber, sand into glass. I have merely transformed him into one of those beautiful objects of nature.

DOROTHY: UNCLE HENRY!

ROQUAT: Quite painless, I assure you. In fact, he is still intact, somewhere. But only I know where.

(*ROQUAT laughs uproariously.*)

OZMA: What of the Tic Toc Man? Have you transformed him as well?

ROQUAT: You and I both know he is too valuable for that! Listen.

(There is the sound of ticking.)

OZMA: Where is he?

ROQUAT: Wouldn't you like to know? He's here too. Somewhere.

(ROQUAT laughs again.)

DOROTHY: Please release my Uncle from the spell. Please, I beg you.

ROQUAT: Certainly, but first my dear little ingot, I believe you have something I want.

DOROTHY: The key?

ROQUAT: Precisely. You give me the key, and I will release your Uncle.

OZMA: Don't trust him. I see a lie.

DOROTHY: But my Uncle.

ROQUAT: Then perhaps you will agree to a little guessing game. I do love games!

OZMA: *(Suspicious)* Go on.

ROQUAT: You see before you four objects: an egg, a leaf, a piece of petrified wood, and a lump of quartz crystal.

DOROTHY: Yes.

ROQUAT: One of these objects is the true shape of your Uncle. I have not changed his substance, only his form. The hint is: what HE is. If you, Dorothy, can guess the correct object and place your hands upon it and call out "Uncle Henry", he will return to his human form and you will all go free.

DOROTHY: And if we fail?

ROQUAT: You will give me the key and I will turn you both into pig iron.

OZMA: This is just another trick.

ROQUAT: It's a GAME.

OZMA: I don't believe the Uncle is here at all. I don't believe you have transformed him into anything.

ROQUAT: Oh, you don't?

OZMA: Then prove it! I demand that you change him back, right here in front of us.

ROQUAT: Oh you do? No such luck! This is my game and you will play. But I will give you yet another hint, a little demonstration of my power. Dorothy, I believe that you had another companion at one time. What was that companion's name?

   (*ROQUAT hands the egg to DOROTHY.*)

DOROTHY: Bill.

   (*There is a flash and BILL appears.*)

BILL: Well, it's about time!

DOROTHY: Bill! It's really you!

ROQUAT: Round One to Dorothy! Now do you believe me, Ozma?

OZMA: Yes.

ROQUAT: See how simple it is? If you know your Uncle at all it should be child's play. Now, since we have time again in Oz, you have three minutes!

   (*FELDSPAR turns over a huge hourglass. ROQUAT and FELDSPAR exit. Cavern doors slam behind them.*)

BILL: So he got the old geezer too . . . figures.

OZMA: Dorothy, I have never seen this Uncle of yours. Tell me about him.

DOROTHY: Well, he's an old man . . .

OZMA: Old? What's that?

BILL: You know, like elderly, getting along, senior citizen, the golden years, you know . . .

OZMA: No, I don't. No one is old in Oz. You will have to tell me what that means.

DOROTHY: Old is just . . . old, that's all.

OZMA: You'll have to be more specific. Are you old?

DOROTHY: No.

OZMA: Am I? Is Bill?

BILL: Oh no!

DOROTHY: Old is different from us. We're young and he's . . . .

ALL: Old.

OZMA: Are any of these objects old?

DOROTHY: This leaf looks old. It has wrinkles and lines.

BILL: All withered up and dry . . . That's him!

OZMA: So old is wrinkled and withered, and that's all?

BILL: Yep!

DOROTHY: Well no, not exactly.

OZMA: Go on.

DOROTHY: This quartz crystal, I can't tell if it is old or not; it doesn't seem to have any age.

BILL: Forget about the crystal. Go on to the wood.

DOROTHY: This petrified wood, I know it's old, very, very old.

OZMA: How do you know that?

DOROTHY: Because once it was wood and now it has turned to stone.

BILL: That's it!

OZMA: So old is turning into something else?

BILL: You get all stiff and rigid, like a rock.

OZMA: And you only change when you're old?

DOROTHY: No, you change when you're young too.

BILL: It's the wood! No, it's the leaf! No, it's the wood!

OZMA: All you have told me about is the outside of these things. Is old just the way something looks?

DOROTHY: I don't know.

BILL: Time's half up!

DOROTHY: OZMA, I don't know! Help me, please!

OZMA: Dorothy, sit here and close your eyes. Just hold each of these objects and tell me what you feel.

   (*DOROTHY sits and OZMA takes her hand. The sound of OZMA'S power is heard. BILL hands DOROTHY the leaf.*)

DOROTHY: This is light and dry and brittle. It feels as though it would break apart if I closed my hand too tightly. It's fragile.

OZMA: Is Uncle Henry fragile?

DOROTHY: Yes . . . but sometimes he's strong too. On the journey through the desert he was so strong.

OZMA: Try the wood.

   (*BILL hands DOROTHY the wood. OZMA works her power.*)

DOROTHY: This feels cold and hard.

OZMA: Is Uncle Henry cold and hard?

DOROTHY: He's stubborn. He never does what I tell him to. But sometimes he's gentle. In the prison he was gentle.

BILL: Come on, Dorothy.

OZMA: Try the crystal.

(*BILL hands her the crystal.*)

DOROTHY: Ow! There's a jagged edge. It hurt me. Take it away.

OZMA: (*Recognizing something*) Does Uncle Henry hurt you?

DOROTHY: Sometimes I get so mad at him. I didn't want to go to Australia. I didn't want to leave home!

BILL: The sand is almost gone!

OZMA: (*Urgently*) Look into the crystal. Tell me what you see.

DOROTHY: Myself. I see a reflection of myself.

OZMA: Look beyond yourself. What do you see in the crystal?

DOROTHY: So many things.

(*The sound of OZMA'S power is heard.*)

OZMA: Go on.

DOROTHY: I see colors and light. Everything shimmers.

OZMA: Look deeper.

DOROTHY: Inside there are rainbows and sparks of color, shooting everywhere. They are moving, changing. The colors are alive and they're caught inside the crystal.

OZMA: Look into Uncle Henry.

DOROTHY: There's so much. There's so much alive inside of him. Outside he's old, but inside he's . . .

OZMA: (*Whispering*) Dorothy . . .

DOROTHY: UNCLE HENRY!

(*There is a flash and UNCLE HENRY appears.*)

UNCLE HENRY: You found me!

BILL: I knew it was the crystal!

(*DOROTHY runs to him and hugs him. He hugs her back.*)

DOROTHY: Uncle Henry, are you all right?

UNCLE HENRY: I'm all right! Dorothy, you found me.

DOROTHY: It was Ozma, she helped me see.

UNCLE HENRY: Thank you.

OZMA: So this is old . . . very interesting.

(*Suddenly the doors open and ROQUAT bursts in, followed by FELDSPAR.*)

ROQUAT: So you found him. That was very bright of you, bright as a fire opal; and it was very stupid of me to let you try.

OZMA: Roquat, release us!

ROQUAT: Not a chance!

DOROTHY: But that's not fair!

ROQUAT: I never said I was fair! Feldspar, kill the girl and fetch the key.

OZMA: No!

(*FELDSPAR advances on DOROTHY. OZMA steps into his path. FELD-SPAR flips OZMA, reaches for the key, and is repelled by the force field.*)

ROQUAT: So it's true! It cannot be taken. Very well, I can wait. I have all the time in Oz. I shall seal you in this cavern and you will starve. Then I shall have the key and time will be mine!

(*ROQUAT and FELDSPAR exit. The doors slam shut behind them. OZMA makes a rush for the door, but she cannot break it down.*)

BILL: We're doomed.

DOROTHY: Ozma, what happened?

OZMA: My powers are weakened down here. Roquat has placed a spell upon those doors and he is the only one who can open them. I wish I could give you some hope, but I can't lie.

BILL: We've had it.

OZMA: And we've lost the Tic Toc Man.

(*The ticking sound can be heard, but only Uncle Henry seems to hear it.*)

UNCLE HENRY: Maybe not.

DOROTHY: There must be miles of caverns down here.

UNCLE HENRY: Quiet!

BILL: We'll never find him!

UNCLE HENRY: We might, if everybody would just be quiet!

(*There is a hush as UNCLE HENRY follows the ticking sound.*)

UNCLE HENRY: The ticking comes from here.

(*OZMA crosses to the rock and pushes it aside with some difficulty. TIC TOC enters.*)

TIC TOC: Big Wheeler, you saved me! Dorothy, are you here too? And Ozma, at last!

BILL: I hate to interrupt this touching reunion, but does anyone realize that we are trapped down here and we are all probably going to starve?

TIC TOC: Hello, Bill.

BILL: We gotta get out of here! There's no bugs down here!

OZMA: Even if we could get out, it wouldn't do us any good. It's night out there by now and the Gnomes are on the surface.

UNCLE HENRY: Are you sure it's night?

OZMA: It was dusk when we arrived; by now the Gnomes are everywhere and Oz is lost.

UNCLE HENRY: But night can turn to day.

OZMA: You have a plan don't you?

UNCLE HENRY: Just a thought.

OZMA: Go on.

UNCLE HENRY: If you could lead Roquat up to the surface, all of you, Tic Toc too, then you could speed up time, make it day, and catch Roquat in the . . . . No, it's too crazy . . .

DOROTHY: Wait a minute, why not?

BILL: There's just one problem. How are we going to get him up there? He won't even open the door!

DOROTHY: (*After a beat*) He will to get the key!

OZMA: But you must never give him the . . .

DOROTHY: I won't really, I'll just tell him that to get him to open the door.

OZMA: But that's lying.

UNCLE HENRY: No, it's not; it's tricking.

OZMA: You don't understand. I can't lie. I'd like to, but I always tell the truth. It's part of me.

BILL: I tell you what, you just stand there and keep your mouth shut, and let Dorothy do the lying.

UNCLE HENRY: (*Hurrying them, but retreating himself*) As soon as he opens the door, get to the surface as quickly as you can.

DOROTHY: What about you?

UNCLE HENRY: I'm staying behind.

DOROTHY: What?

UNCLE HENRY: (*Covering*) As a . . . decoy. It's part of the plan. Captain Cook would have done it this way. It's part of the plan, I tell you, part of the . . .

OZMA: Look at me, Uncle.

(*She fixes him with a stare and works her power on him.*)

UNCLE HENRY: I'll slow you down. I'm an old man in a wheelchair and I'll just slow you down.

DOROTHY: No, you won't! You're our Captain and I won't leave without you.

UNCLE HENRY: But the chair . . .

OZMA: Use it, like a chariot!

(*The magic sound stops.*)

BILL: Hold it! It's coming! It's coming!

DOROTHY: The Gnome King?

BILL: No, an egg. I think I'm going to lay an egg!

UNCLE HENRY: Well, hold it! We haven't got time for that now!

(*BILL crosses her legs and waddles.*)

UNCLE HENRY: Tic Toc, you hide behind the throne. Go ahead, Dorothy. Call him.

DOROTHY: Roquat! Roquat of the Rock!

(*The doors swing open and ROQUAT and FELDSPAR enter.*)

ROQUAT: What?

DOROTHY: I wish to speak with you.

ROQUAT: Have we come to our senses, my little malachite midget?

DOROTHY: I have decided to give you the key.

ROQUAT: Have you?

DOROTHY: On one condition. You must lead us out of here and up to the surface. After I have given you the key, you must let us all go free.

ROQUAT: Very sensible. A little too sensible.

(*He turns swiftly on UNCLE HENRY.*)

Is this a trick?

UNCLE HENRY: Uhhhhh, no.

DOROTHY: As soon as we get to the surface, I'll give you the key.

ROQUAT: (*To BILL*) Is this true?

BILL: Uhhhh, yes, cross my heart.

DOROTHY: All we want is our freedom.

ROQUAT: Very well, proceed. The door is open.

(*ROQUAT gestures and the doors open, but FELDSPAR stands in the doorway with a large spear. They take a step or two toward the door.*)

ROQUAT: Wait! Ozma, I know you can't lie. Is she telling the truth?

(*ROQUAT faces her down. OZMA struggles to lie, but she cannot.*)

OZMA: No! We have no intention of giving you that key.

ROQUAT: I thought so.

(*Before he can move, BILL squawks loudly.*)

BILL: SQUAWK! Ready or not, here it comes!

(*BILL lays an egg.*)

Hey, Feldspar, how about a little egg in the face!

(*BILL throws the egg at FELDSPAR and hits him, knocking him out of the doorway.*)

UNCLE HENRY: The door is open! Run for it!

(*BILL and TIC TOC exit immediately. ROQUAT lunges for OZMA, she side-steps and throws him into the throne. DOROTHY races for UNCLE HENRY and takes hold of his chair. FELDSPAR begins to rise.*)

UNCLE HENRY: Get going, Dorothy!

(*He wrenches the chair away from her, extends his legs, and inadvertently hits Feldspar and decks him with his legs.*)

UNCLE HENRY: I'm all right!

ROQUAT: (*Up on the throne*) GUARDS!

(*Two ROCK PEOPLE appear in the doorway and rush at DOROTHY as she is trying to get out.*)

UNCLE HENRY: Duck, Dorothy!

(*DOROTHY ducks under their arms and exits. UNCLE HENRY rushes between the GUARDS, elbows them in their stomachs; as they double over, he whacks them with his canes, knocking them cold.*)

UNCLE HENRY: Hot Damn! I did it!

(*OZMA goes for ROQUAT, who leaps over her head. UNCLE HENRY rushes at him with legs extended, catches ROQUAT between the legs, and whirls him in a circle. OZMA grabs the back of the chair and assists.*)

OZMA: Well done, Uncle!

(*FELDSPAR begins to rise. OZMA and UNCLE HENRY whirl ROQUAT and throw him off. OZMA goes for ROQUAT and pins him. FELDSPAR rushes UNCLE HENRY.*)

OZMA: Look out!

(*UNCLE HENRY evades FELDSPAR and trips him with his canes. As FELDSPAR rises, UNCLE HENRY wheels around and hooks one cane into FELDSPAR'S belt. FELDSPAR runs about pulling UNCLE HENRY, who bonks him several times with his other cane.*)

UNCLE HENRY: Stand him up, Ozma!

(OZMA lifts ROQUAT up, just as UNCLE HENRY releases FELDSPAR and gives him a whack on the bottom with the cane. OZMA side-steps deftly, as FELDSPAR is propelled into ROQUAT; they both tumble.)

UNCLE HENRY: Let's get out of here!

(FELDSPAR helps ROQUAT up. OZMA grabs the back of UNCLE HENRY'S chair and they exit, as FELDSPAR and ROQUAT revive.)

ROQUAT: After them!

(ROQUAT and FELDSPAR exit, as the ROCK PEOPLE revive and follow them. In a single sweep, the chase brings all above ground. The scenery shifts throughout the chase.)

Scene XI: Outside the Gnome King's Cavern.

It is night. There are several large rocks comprising the entrance to the cavern. BILL, TIC TOC, and DOROTHY arrive first, out of breath and running.

DOROTHY: We're outside!

TIC TOC: We made it!

BILL: Whooeeeee!

(OZMA and UNCLE HENRY enter at a run.)

UNCLE HENRY: They are right behind us!

DOROTHY: Uncle Henry! You made it! Are you all right?

UNCLE HENRY: Of course I'm all right! But here they come!

(ROQUAT and FELDSPAR enter from the cave. Three other ROCK PEOPLE enter from the sides. They grab DOROTHY, UNCLE HENRY, and TIC TOC. FELDSPAR grabs OZMA.)

ROQUAT: Stop! You are surrounded!

(UNCLE HENRY and TIC TOC are caught on one side of the stage, DOROTHY, BILL and OZMA on the other. DOROTHY struggles to get the key to UNCLE HENRY, but she cannot.)

ROQUAT: My Gnomes are everywhere. There is no escape. The time for games of hide and seek are over. DOROTHY, GIVE ME THAT KEY!

DOROTHY: No!

ROQUAT: Then I shall order my Gnomes to crush all your friends, before your very eyes. And I shall begin with the chicken!

(*ROQUAT grabs BILL and shoves her between two ROCK PEOPLE, who close in slowly.*)

BILL: Ohhhh! Noooooo!

UNCLE HENRY: Dorothy, throw me the key!

DOROTHY: I can't.

BILL: Help me, Pleeeeeeeeeeease!

(*As BILL is being crushed, the others watch helplessly. Suddenly, a trumpet call is heard and the weird WHEELER sound. All look up. ARMY, GENERAL and the WHEELERS swoop in.**)

DOROTHY: What's that?

OZMA: It's the Army!

DOROTHY: And the General!

UNCLE HENRY: **And the Wheelers!

(*With their entrance, pandemonium breaks loose. In the melee, DOROTHY gets the key to UNCLE HENRY. OZMA and ROQUAT are engaged in a hand to hand battle center stage.*)

UNCLE HENRY: Where do I put it? What do I do?

TIC TOC: Wind me here and turn!

---

*If cast size is limited and Wheelers must be double-cast as Rock people, they need not enter here. Lines referring to the Wheelers are marked with ** and are optional.

(UNCLE HENRY turns the dial as ROQUAT is getting the best of OZMA.)

UNCLE HENRY: Not so fast, Roquat! Let's see how you feel about a little . . . DAYLIGHT!

(Lights and sound indicate that time is speeding up. The sun rises and catches ROQUAT and FELDSPAR and the ROCK PEOPLE in the light.)

ROQUAT: The Sun! The Sun!

OZMA: Keep him in the light.

(ROQUAT tries to escape, but OZMA and DOROTHY grab him by the cloak.)

ROQUAT: Noooooooo!

(ROQUAT turns to ash, leaving them with an empty cloak.)

UNCLE HENRY: *(Astonished)* It worked!

DOROTHY: You did it!

UNCLE HENRY: No, we did it!

WHEELERS: **Big Wheeler, you're safe.

UNCLE HENRY: **Nice work, men.

(He salutes them.)

ARMY and GENERAL: Ozma, you're safe.

OZMA: Nice work, men.

(She salutes them.)

BILL: Yoooo, Hooooo. Would somebody please get me out of here?

(OZMA pulls the rocks apart, releasing BILL.)

BILL: Whew! That was close!

UNCLE HENRY: But it worked! Hot Damn!

OZMA: Uncle Henry, the people of Oz humbly thank you for your wonderful plan.

(*All cheer.*)

Army, General, go ahead to the Emerald City and tell the people what has happened.

(*They salute and exit.*)

**Wheelers, return to your people and tell them they are free of the Gnome King forever!

(*They salute and exit.*)

And now we shall return to the Emerald City in triumph!

TIC TOC: I cannot go with you.

UNCLE HENRY: What?

TIC TOC: I must stay here. Ozma, you know what must be done.

OZMA: Yes.

TIC TOC: You must stop time in Oz.

DOROTHY: But now that the Gnome King is dead . . .

TIC TOC: My power is too great to be contained in Oz. As long as I am running there will be time. People will grow old and die, things will change.

DOROTHY: But that's just a natural process.

TIC TOC: Perhaps in your world, but Oz is not a natural place.

OZMA: In Oz there must be only day, it must be only now. We can't have change in Oz, we haven't the wisdom.

UNCLE HENRY: Tic Toc, do you want me to give your key to Ozma?

TIC TOC: Oh yes.

BILL: I can't look.

TIC TOC: Goodbye, my friends, I give you this moment forever. Now Ozma, stop time in Oz.

(*OZMA takes the key in her hands and holds it above her head. Slowly she breaks it in two. There is a jolt, strange lights, and sounds. Time stops. TIC TOC stands immobile.*)

BILL: Can I look now?

OZMA: Yes, Bill, it's done. Now we shall all return to the Emerald City.

DOROTHY: Ozma, Tic Toc said you have great powers, powers strong enough to send me home, back to Kansas.

OZMA: But you must stay here with us. You will be a Princess of Oz and you will stay young and strong forever.

DOROTHY: Thank you, but I don't think I want to be thirteen indefinitely. I want to go home.

BILL: Not me! I want to stay a spring chicken!

OZMA: Very well. But surely you, Uncle Henry, you will stay with us. You are an adventurer, a hero of Oz, and you have much to teach us. You will be Sir Uncle Henry, the Brave, the Resourceful, the Official Old of Oz.

(*She knights him with one of his canes.*)

DOROTHY: If you stay, Uncle Henry, you won't grow older, things will never change and you won't . . . die.

UNCLE HENRY: I know.

OZMA: Then you will stay with us forever.

UNCLE HENRY: I've got so many things I still want to do. I can't stay with you forever, I can't spare the time!

DOROTHY: What?

UNCLE HENRY: I'm going with Dorothy.

DOROTHY: But if you go back you'll . . .

UNCLE HENRY: Let's go!

OZMA: Where shall I send you?

DOROTHY: Where do we go, Uncle Henry? Back home to Kansas, or on to Australia?

UNCLE HENRY: Why don't you choose.

DOROTHY: You mean it?

UNCLE HENRY: Yep. High time you started making some of the decisions around here.

OZMA: (*To Dorothy*) Just hold the place in your mind and I shall see it there and send you. Have you chosen?

DOROTHY: Yes, Goodbye, Ozma.

OZMA: Goodbye, then.

(*She hugs DOROTHY and takes UNCLE HENRY'S hand.*)

OZMA: And thank you.

UNCLE HENRY: My pleasure.

BILL: Goodbye.

DOROTHY and UNCLE HENRY: Goodbye, Bill.

(*OZMA stands above them and places her hand on DOROTHY'S head and UNCLE HENRY'S shoulder.*)

OZMA: Hold the place in your mind. Hold the place in your mind. Hold the place in your . . . .

(*OZMA works her magic. There is a whirling effect in lights and sound. Oz whirls away and the scene shifts.*)

Scene XII: Shipboard

It is morning, the morning after the storm. DOROTHY lies unconscious on the deck. UNCLE HENRY is slumped over in his chair. STEVE and SAM are heard off-stage.

STEVE: I checked this cabin six times already. The door was open and there was water all over the place.

SAM: Maybe they're down in the cargo hold.

STEVE: I checked.

SAM: The galley . . .

STEVE: I've been all over this boat and I tell you they're not here.

   (*STEVE enters.*)

SAM: Kids and old people, I don't know why they . . . . .

STEVE: (*Sees them*) Hey, SAM! Here!

   (*SAM rushes in. STEVE runs to DOROTHY, SAM to UNCLE HENRY.*)

STEVE: But I checked here. She's out cold. He ain't . . . dead, is he?

SAM: (*Checking vital signs*) Naw, just out like a light.

STEVE: The kid's clothes are all wet.

SAM: Him too. They must have been out in that storm all night.

STEVE: But I checked here and I tell you they weren't . . . .

   (*DOROTHY wakes and sits up.*)

DOROTHY: Huh? Where . . .

STEVE: Take it easy kid, you're okay.

DOROTHY: Uncle Henry . . .

SAM: He's just knocked out.

DOROTHY: Can't you wake him up?

(*She crosses to them and shakes UNCLE HENRY.*)

Uncle Henry . . . . Uncle Henry . . . . Are you all right?

UNCLE HENRY: (*Wakes suddenly*) Everybody always wants to know if I'm all right!

SAM: Take it easy, Pop.

STEVE: You're all right.

UNCLE HENRY: I KNOW!

DOROTHY: (*Hugging him*) You sure are!

UNCLE HENRY: Hey, we're back on the boat. Dorothy, we're back on the boat!

DOROTHY: Yes.

UNCLE HENRY: You did that! You could have gone back to Kansas.

SAM: This boat's headed for Australia.

UNCLE HENRY: But we could have gone back to Kansas.

SAM: This boat don't go to Kansas.

STEVE: No boats go to Kansas. Kansas is land locked.

(*STEVE exits shaking his head.*)

SAM: I want you two to report to sick bay, looks like you been out in that storm all night.

(*DOROTHY and UNCLE HENRY exchange looks.*)

You know where it is?

DOROTHY: Uhhh, yes.

SAM: Can he manage?

DOROTHY: He can manage.

(*SAM exits.*)

UNCLE HENRY: But you could have gone back to Kansas. What about school and your friends, and what's his name . . . . Tommy . . .

DOROTHY: You know, Uncle Henry, in Australia there were all these adventurers and explorers, and what's his name . . . Captain Cook . . . .

(*UNCLE HENRY laughs and DOROTHY wheels him out with a garbled history of Australia. Over her words we hear the ticking of a clock.*)

CURTAIN!

Doors

Although *Doors* contains some of the elements found in Zeder's earlier writing—most notably a child protagonist who uses fantasy to deal with problems—there is new depth, seriousness, and structural complexity in this tightly written domestic drama not present in those earlier works. She also leaves the comfortable fold of the happy ending that we've seen in previous works and ventures into a situation in which many more uncomfortable questions are raised than are answered.

In comparison with her earlier works, Zeder gives increased attention to revealing more about all of the characters in the play rather than focusing on the child protagonist. However, Jeff is still the most fully developed character and the one through whose eyes we see the problems in the play unfold.

As with Ellie in *Step on a Crack*, much of Jeff's characterization and growth is revealed through his fantasies and the roles he plays in them. These reveal that his desire to take action to change his family's difficulties is equaled by his fear of doing so. The progression of his roles in these fantasies moves from passive victim to active agent as he moves psychologically closer to being able to deal with what is behind the door.

Given the fact that the first two-thirds of the play devotes so much time to developing Jeff's character through his fantasies, it is noteworthy that Zeder has also managed to make the other three characters multi-dimensional. This is especially true of Sandy. Sandy is the only "best friend" of a child protagonist in all of Zeder's works. He is drawn with a great deal of specificity. He is imaginative, energetic, and a born comedian. Though Sandy provides much comic relief, he also has a serious, sensible side. He is the catalyst that prods Jeff to examine what's happening, and he infuses Jeff with the will to risk facing the truth.

Even the parents are sketched in more detail than their predecessors in *Step on a Crack*, although much of their depth must still be found between the lines in the subtext. Ben is Zeder's first fully drawn adult male character. He has to struggle with his inner conflicts over wanting to get out of the marriage, but also wanting to maintain contact with Jeff. He thinks through what he is going to say far more carefully than Max in *Step on a Crack*, but he is an emotional man and not immune to angry outbursts. These contradictions make him interesting and give the actor playing Ben plenty of groundwork for making him true to life.

Of the characters in this play, Helen is in the most danger of being seen as too simplistic. She does struggle with the opposing desires of wanting a career in addition to being a wife and mother, and she gains some dimension by undergoing a change during the play in her realization that she no longer loves Ben. However, the actor playing Helen must fill in details to round her out.

In addition to more detailed characterization, Zeder achieves added depth and complexity in the arrangement of events in the play. In spite of the play being about a marriage coming apart, the structure in which these characters operate is almost symmetrically balanced. This symmetry is present, most notably, in Zeder's use of paired opposites in the role-playing and fantasy sequences. For example, Sandy's description of an argumentative but happy family car trip is balanced against Jeff's description of a silent but unhappy family drive. These two opposites are placed between Jeff's "silent break-fast" fantasy and his "perfect breakfast" fantasy. Paired opposites even show up on the level of individual lines when we see Ben and Helen using exactly the same sentence structure, but using key words that are opposite in meaning. In these instances the similarity in form serves to emphasize the difference in content and the opposition of viewpoints.

Zeder has skillfully structured the balance of opposing forces in the realistic scenes as well. The source of conflict between the parents often stems from each one having opposite interpretations of, or reactions to, the same event. Their viewpoints are equally weighted and equally valid so neither parent is a villian. Yet the overall impression given by the play is certainly not one of symmetry or balance. Just as this family is struggling to regain a balance that no longer exists, Zeder uses the underlying structural balance to emphasize the emotional imbalance that's breaking the family apart.

Zeder has created visual metaphors with carefully chosen scenery, props, and stage business to further emphasize what she's done with language and plot structure. Symmetry and balance are suggested in her description of the set seeming at first to be a normal bedroom with a large central door. On closer inspection, the room is off-kilter with odd angles and joints that don't quite meet. It is as if the room is coming apart like the family is coming apart. The oversized door suggests its importance as a carrier of meaning. It symbolizes Jeff's power to keep things out or let them in. The walls of scrim may appear to be solid, but they let in selected elements of chaos that are distortions of what the big door keeps out of the room.

Like the room that doesn't fit together, there is a model spaceship that everyone tries to put together which keeps falling apart. The dummy is another important prop that functions both to move the plot forward and to carry symbolic value by reflecting how Jeff feels about himself.

Zeder has stayed with many of the themes she has dealt with in earlier plays: the problems that occur when adults try to protect children by withholding information; how people refuse to listen to each other; the child's struggle to have a voice in parental decisions; and the function of fantasy in a child's working through of problems. However, she has done this in a far more serious way than in previous plays. When Ben closes the door to mark his final exit, there are no guarantees that things will work out. Jeff may not really have more of a voice in his parents' next set of decisions. He may or may not be able to maintain a strong relationship with both Ben and Helen in the future. He may have to leave all his friends and move to another city with his mother. Despite this, Zeder leaves the audience with some hope that the individuals in this family can both survive and grow in spite of or because of their pain. However, she offers only the possibility that answers can be found, rather than offering the answers themselves. She has left the door open, but made no guarantees about what will be found when people go through it.

Her experience with many *Doors* audiences has led Zeder to another important observation about the field of theatre for young audiences as a whole. She points out,

> "Although it is becoming more acceptable, I think the idea of the theatre being a place for catharsis for young audiences is still fairly radical. Some parents, teachers, and school administrators get a little bit frightened of emotional content and would prefer the theatre to be a safe place or a pretty place or a sweet place for young people—but certainly not a risky place. But to me, in theatre, risk is mandatory."

For those who are ready for a challenge and a risk, Zeder has opened up new territory with this play.

Doors

by Suzan L. Zeder

From the Playwright

This play began for me with a real child and a real divorce. A friend, whose marriage had recently exploded, shared a story about her ten year old son reaching out from his own pain and sadness to comfort her. It was an act of two human beings meeting in a moment of healing that went beyond the boundaries of a "social problem" into the realm of art. The story haunted me for years until I gave it a second life in the final lines of this play.

The next image that came to me was the door, and with it came the title. At first I didn't trust it. I thought the title needed to be something grander, more evocative. So I experimented with other titles such as *Separate Doors*, and *Through Separate Doors*. But the image was wiser than I, and the play must be called what it has always been, *Doors*.

The first production of this play in 1981 was its formative one. I am deeply grateful to Greg Falls for his initial commission and for the showcase production which gave the play its present substance and shape. Jim Hancock, my husband, was the director, but his role was that of a collaborator. This is as much his play as it is mine.

For fifteen years I have written plays about children, not from any social, educational, or therapeutic motivation, but simply because they fascinate me as a dramatist. I am profoundly interested in children as protagonists who find themselves in crises, who struggle against overpowering forces, and conduct themselves as heroes. I respect the efforts of parents and children facing troubled times with dignity and depth. I find these efforts to be legitimate and compelling dramatic territory.

I offer this play to you, not as an examination of a significant "social problem" but as a theatre experience which chronicles the journey of three individual survivors through a particularly difficult day.

Suzan Zeder
Dallas, Texas
1985

Dedication

For, with, and because of Jim

Doors was first commissioned by Gregory A. Falls and was show-cased by A Contemporary Theatre at the Bush School in Seattle, Washington in 1981, with the following cast:

Jeff .... Marco Sawrey
Ben .... William ter Kuile
Helen .... Theresa De Paolo
Sandy .... Chris Devore

The production was directed by Jim Hancock

CHARACTERS

Jeff: Eleven Years Old
Ben: His Father
Helen: His Mother
Sandy: His Best Friend

SETTING

Jeff's Room

TIME

The Present

Doors

A fragmentary set suggesting Jeff's bedroom. At first glance it seems to be the rather ordinary room of an eleven year boy; but there are odd angles, slanting doorways, and joints that do not quite connect. The whole room is slightly off-kilter.

The room is dominated by a large closed door, center stage. It is the door to Jeff's parents' bedroom. Down left is a smaller door to the rest of the house. The walls of the room are defined by large scrimmed panels. The panels are decorated with posters of movies, mostly science fiction adventure films, currently popular at the time of the production. The posters are oversized and made of a scrim material; they are also hinged so that actors can pass through them.

Also in the room are a small bed, a couple of chairs, a desk or work area, a T.V. set, a stereo, and an over-flowing laundry basket.

At rise, JEFF is alone on stage, seated at the desk. He is working intently on a large, complicated model of a spaceship. The model is almost finished. JEFF works with great concentration with the directions and a tube of glue.

*The first sounds we hear are muffled voices coming from Jeff's parents' room. They are arguing. This argument will be ongoing during most of the play; at times, specific voices and words will be heard, at other times, muffled sound, sometimes, nothing. Care should be taken to preserve the illusion that the argument is continuous without detracting from the primary focus which is to be on stage with Jeff and his actions.***

(JEFF tries to concentrate on his task of building the model, but he is obviously distracted and upset by the sounds coming from behind the door. He reads from the directions.)

JEFF: "When the glue is partially set, insert cockpit window flaps G and H into the main body of the craft."

**See production notes at the end of the script.

(The sounds of the argument grow louder and JEFF tries to concentrate harder.)

"Hold firmly in place for a few seconds until the glue sets . . ."

(There is another sound from behind the door. JEFF looks up, the part slips. He tries again.)

"When the glue is partially set, insert cockpit window flaps G and H into the main body of the craft."

(As JEFF lines up the parts, a series of angry bursts are heard, they register on his face, but he does not move.)

. . . "until the glue sets" . . .

(JEFF rises, turns on the stereo set, and returns to the model.)

"Insert wheel hub N into wheel rim O and affix wheel assembly to landing gear C."

(He looks all over the model.)

Where's the landing gear? Where's the landing gear? Where's that . . .

(Sounds from behind the door increase. JEFF picks up the model, looking for the landing gear and the cockpit falls off. The phone rings. JEFF looks at the door. The phone rings again. JEFF tries to return to the model, the phone rings again.)

"Insert wheel hub" . . yeah . . yeah . . . yeah . . . "affix to landing GEAR!"

(The phone continues to ring. Finally, JEFF rises and answers. The stereo is very loud.)

Hello? Just a second.

(JEFF puts down the phone, crosses to the stereo and turns it off. He returns to the phone.)

Sorry. Hello, Gramma. Yeah, this is Jeff. Yeah, we got out of school last week . . . No, I'm not going to camp this year . . . Gramma, they don't have camps for Grandmothers.

(*Sounds behind the door increase.*)

JEFF: Yeah, they're both here, but they can't come to the phone right now. They're in their room with the door closed and I don't think I'd better. . . . I'll tell them you called. I'm sure Mom will call you back later . . . Yeah, you too, Gramma. Bye.

(*JEFF hangs up the phone, and crosses back to the desk, on the way he turns on the stereo and the T.V. very loud.*)

Stop it. Stop it! STOP IT!

(*JEFF sits and buries his face in his hands; the sound is tremendous. After a beat, the large door bursts open and BEN enters angrily.*)

BEN: Jeff! Turn it down!

(*JEFF does not move.*)

For Christ's sakes, Jeff!

(*BEN crosses to T.V. and stereo and turns them off.*)

We can't even hear ourselves think in there. Why does it have to be so loud?

JEFF: I like it loud.

BEN: Well, you're blasting us out of the house.

JEFF: Sorry.

BEN: Your Mother and I are trying to . . . talk and that doesn't help.

JEFF: Sorry.

BEN: If you're sorry, then keep it down. You can listen, but keep it reasonable, okay?

(*BEN turns the stereo back on much lower and starts to exit back through the door. JEFF rises and stops him.*)

JEFF: Hey, Dad?

BEN: (*Turning back to him*) Yeah?

   (*JEFF turns the stereo off.*)

JEFF: Gramma called.

BEN: Oh . . . What did she want?

JEFF: I don't know, just to talk I guess.

BEN: (*Under his breath, with frustration*) Oh, Brother . . .

JEFF: What?

BEN: Nothing.

   (*BEN notices that JEFF is really "down".*)

Jeff?

   (*JEFF does not respond. BEN, not sure of what to do, assumes a wrestling stance.*)

Hey, Jeff?

JEFF: Oh, no, Dad!

   (*After a beat, JEFF responds with a wrestling stance, this is something they have done frequently. For a brief moment, they mock wrestle, or tickle, resulting in a much needed laugh for both of them. HELEN'S voice is heard off stage.*)

HELEN: Ben?

   (*BEN starts to go, JEFF stops him.*)

JEFF: Dad, can you have a look at this?

BEN: What?

   (*JEFF holds up the model.*)

JEFF: The cockpit keeps falling off.

BEN: That's really coming along.

JEFF: Mom painted the flag and the wing trim.

BEN: I was going to help you with that. I'm sorry, Jeff.

JEFF: Mom helped me with the body and the engine.

BEN: But things kind of got away from me.

JEFF: I can't get the cockpit to stay on.

BEN: Let me see it.

   (*BEN inspects the model.*)

Well, the flag is in the wrong place and the wing trim's crooked. But you put it together just fine.

JEFF: Really?

BEN: Oh, yeah. Have you got a razor blade?

   (*JEFF hands him a razor blade and watches as BEN scrapes the glue.*)

The surface has to be clean for it to seal. Now, the glue.

   (*BEN applies the glue and positions the cockpit.*)

JEFF: You've got to keep holding until the glue sets.

HELEN: (*Off*) Ben?

BEN: In a minute!

JEFF: Look out, Dad, it's slipping.

BEN: I've got it.

JEFF: Your hands are shaking.

BEN: They are not!

JEFF: You've got to hold it still.

BEN: I know!

   (*There is a pause. BEN looks toward the door, back at JEFF, and toward the door again. JEFF notices.*)

JEFF: Have a look at this.

(*JEFF shows him an old photograph.*)

BEN: Where did you get that?

JEFF: I found it.

BEN: That's our old house on Beachcroft. What are you doing with that?

JEFF: I just like to look at it sometimes.

BEN: You remember that place?

JEFF: I remember.

BEN: But that was years ago.

JEFF: I remember.

(*BEN takes the photo in one hand and holds the model in the other.*)

BEN: I built every inch of that house. Built it and rebuilt it.

JEFF: I remember my bedroom; it had clouds and stars on the ceiling.

BEN: We painted them for you when you said that you wanted to sleep in the sky.

JEFF: When I turned out the lights, the stars glowed.

BEN: That was a good house, Jeff, a good house. Solid foundations, thick walls, none of that stucco, pre-fab garbage. I can't build 'em like that anymore.

JEFF: How come?

BEN: I haven't got the time, and who's got the money, and nobody cares.

JEFF: I miss that house.

BEN: Yeah, so do I.

(*BEN puts down the photo and looks at JEFF.*)

BEN: Jeff, there's something going on here, something we all have to talk about . . .

JEFF: (*Interrupting quickly*) Dad, you've got to hold on to it!

BEN: Huh?

JEFF: The cockpit, it's slipping again. You've got to hold it in place or it won't work.

BEN: I've got it.

JEFF: You've got to hold it steady.

BEN: I am holding it steady.

(*HELEN enters and stands in the doorway.*)

HELEN: What are you doing?

BEN: I'll be right there.

JEFF: Dad's helping me with my model.

HELEN: But, Ben . . .

BEN: I said, I'll be right there!

HELEN: Jeff, honey, you spend so much time inside these days, and it's a beautiful day out there. Why don't you go on over to Sandy's . . .

JEFF: I don't want to go to Sandy's.

HELEN: But, I thought you two were going to work on the movie.

JEFF: He's coming over here later.

HELEN: It's a beautiful day and here you are all cooped up. . .

BEN: He said, he didn't want to go.

HELEN: It was just a suggestion.

BEN: You know, you could have waited.

HELEN: Ben, I have been waiting . . .

BEN: I'm talking about this model.

HELEN: The model?

BEN: I was going to help him with it, just as soon as I got a little ahead on the Carlson development.

JEFF: It's okay, Dad.

HELEN: He needed help and he asked me.

BEN: You could have waited.

HELEN: Sure, I could have waited, but he couldn't.

JEFF: It's almost done now.

BEN: Just as soon as I finished the bids and worked out the contracts, and . . . .

HELEN: And when would that have been, Ben? Next week? Next month? Next year?

BEN: I was looking forward to it!

(*The tension in their tone rises.*)

JEFF: (*Suddenly*) I don't feel well.

HELEN: (*Concerned*) What's the matter?

JEFF: I just don't feel so hot.

HELEN: Do you have a headache?

JEFF: I guess so.

BEN: He's all right.

(*HELEN crosses to JEFF.*)

HELEN: Do you have a temperature?

JEFF: I don't think so.

BEN: He's all right.

HELEN: (*To BEN*) How do you know he's all right?

BEN: (*To JEFF*) You're all right, aren't you?

JEFF: I'm all right.

HELEN: But you just said . . .

BEN: He just said he was all right!

JEFF: Dad, the cockpit's all screwed up again.

BEN: Helen, will you let me finish this?

HELEN: I was just . . .

JEFF: The glue's all over the place.

(*JEFF takes the model from BEN and returns to the desk with it.*)

HELEN: I'll be in our room when you're finished!

(*HELEN exits through the large door and slams it as she goes.*)

BEN: I'll be right there!

(*BEN paces in anger as JEFF returns dejectedly to the model.*)

JEFF: Hand me the razor blade?

(*BEN, distracted, does not answer.*)

Dad, can you hand me the blade?

BEN: Oh, yeah, sure; just kind of scrape it there . . . . it'll be all right.

JEFF: Yeah.

BEN: Just hold it firm until the glue sets.

JEFF: Yeah.

BEN: You're all right aren't you?

JEFF: Yeah.

   (*BEN crosses to the large door, hesitates for a beat, then exits. JEFF holds the model perfectly still during the next few lines, which we hear through the door.*)

HELEN: (*Off*) When we discuss this with Jeff, will you at least do me the courtesy of allowing me to be there?

BEN: (*Off*) We were talking about the model.

HELEN: (*Off*) When we do talk to him, we can't be emotional and upset.

BEN: (*Off*) I am NOT EMOTIONAL!

HELEN: (*Off*) Then why are you shouting?

BEN: (*Off*) I wasn't emotional then, now I'm emotional!

   (*JEFF slowly and deliberately pulls off the cockpit.*)

HELEN: Stop shouting!

BEN: Stop picking! You always have to pick at me, at Jeff!

   (*JEFF breaks off one wing. BEN and HELEN continue off stage.*)

HELEN: He said he didn't feel well.

BEN: He's all right.

HELEN: Just because you say he's all right, doesn't mean . . .

BEN: He said he was all right!

   (*JEFF snaps off the other wing.*)

HELEN: I was just concerned!

BEN: Can't you leave anything alone?

(*JEFF suddenly hurls the model at the door. It smashes onto the floor and breaks into pieces. JEFF rises and turns both the stereo and the T.V. on full blast. He returns to his desk and cradles his head in his hands. After a beat or so, SANDY is heard pouding on the smaller door.*)

SANDY: (*Off*) Jeff, you in there? Jeff?

(*SANDY enters through the small door. He is a bit put out and he lugs a life-sized dummy with him.*)

SANDY: Jeeze, Jeff, doesn't anyone around here answer the door? I've been out there about a half an hour ringing the bell and yelling. Hey, do you know the T.V. is on?

(*JEFF pulls himself together, but avoids looking at SANDY.*)

JEFF: Yeah.

SANDY: And the stereo, too?

(*SANDY turns off the T.V.*)

This much noise will rot your brain, at least that's what my Mom says.

(*SANDY starts to turn off stereo.*)

JEFF: Don't.

SANDY: Can I at least turn it down?

(*JEFF looks toward the large door. SANDY turns it down but not off.*)

JEFF: What are you doing in here?

SANDY: I knew you were home and the front door was unlocked so I . . .

JEFF: What do you want?

SANDY: We've got to finish the script, remember?

JEFF: Look, Sandy, this isn't a good time.

SANDY: Don't you even want to see what I brought?

JEFF: What's that?

(*SANDY holds up the dummy proudly.*)

SANDY: It's a body for the crash scene! I figure we could put ketchup all over it for blood and maybe some dog food for brains.

JEFF: That's gross.

SANDY: Wait until you hear how I got it.

JEFF: Sandy . . .

(*SANDY acts this out as he goes along.*)

SANDY: I was downtown in this ally behind Nordstroms and I saw this arm sticking out of a dumpster. . . . OH MY! I thought some bum had crawled in there and died, but then I figured out that it was a dummy. So, I asked this big goon by the loading dock, if I could have it. And he said, "It'll cost you a dollar." So, I grabbed it and ran down fifth like I was kidnapping it, or something. Then this number four-teen bus came along, and I hopped on. The driver said, "You can't bring that thing on this bus!" So, I said, "How dare you insult my younger brother!" And I paid two fares, sat it next to me, and talked to it all the way over here. Man, everyone on that bus really thought I was weird.

JEFF: You are weird.

(*JEFF turns away.*)

SANDY: You're the weird one. I thought that would really crack you up. All the way over here, I just kept thinking, "This will really crack Jeff up!"

(*No response.*)

What's the matter?

JEFF: Nothing.

SANDY: Your report card! Your parents hit the ceiling about that F in science.

JEFF: I never showed it to them.

SANDY: The dog! You finally asked them if you could have a dog, and they said no, and . . .

JEFF: I haven't asked them about that yet.

SANDY: Then what's wrong?

(*Sounds can be heard from behind the door.*)

JEFF: Sandy, I'll come over to your house later and . . .

SANDY: Did you get the video camera from your dad?

JEFF: Uhhhh, he's been out of town.

SANDY: You mean you haven't even asked him yet?

JEFF: I'll ask him.

SANDY: We've got to start shooting tomorrow!

JEFF: I'll ask him later.

SANDY: Alright! How's the star ship coming along?

JEFF: (*Pointing towards the door*) It's over there.

(*SANDY crosses to the door and picks up the wrecked model.*)

SANDY: What happened to the star ship?

JEFF: It got hit by a meteor shower!

SANDY: It got hit by something! Jeff, the wings are all broken and the frame is cracked! These things cost a lot of money!

JEFF: I'll pay you back! I'll buy you another one! What more do you want?

SANDY: Jeff, we are supposed to be doing this together and all you're doing is screwing up!

(*More sounds are heard.*)

JEFF: I don't want to do this today! Go home, Sandy. I'll call you later.

SANDY: I'm not leaving until we finish the script! And I'm turning that thing off!

(*SANDY switches off the stereo; for a second the sounds of the argument can be heard, SANDY hears it and chooses to ignore it. JEFF turns away. SANDY pulls some pages out of his pocket.*)

SANDY: Okay, we start with a long shot of the ship hurtling toward the death asteroid. Then we show the crash . . . This will work great!

(*He sarcastically holds the model up.*)

Then we show the crew, those who haven't been burned alive or had their heads split open . . .

(*He indicates the dummy.*)

. . . struggling out of the wreck.

(*SANDY acts this out as he goes along; JEFF watches, becoming more and more involved.*)

SANDY: Colonel McCabe is the first one out; that's me. Then comes Rocco, the navigator; that's Paul; and then the ship's doctor, old blood and guts; that's Rick; and finally comes the ship's robot computer, C.B. 430; that's you . . .

(*JEFF suddenly joins in.*)

JEFF: Suddenly, the robot computer starts acting strangely. His lights flash and smoke comes out of his ears. He walks toward the ship's Doctor and grabs him . . .

(*JEFF grabs the dummy.*)

He punches him in the stomach, hits him in the head, crushes him in his steel grip and throws his lifeless body to the ground.

(*JEFF beats the dummy and throws it.*)

SANDY: (*Laughing*) Rick's not going to like that.

JEFF: Then he whirls around and walks toward Rocco.

(*JEFF turns in a circle and grabs the dummy again.*)

He grabs him by the arms and twists them out of their sockets! He throws him on the ground, time after time, after time, after time.

(*JEFF beats the dummy on the floor.*)

SANDY: Jeff?

JEFF: (*Totally carried away*) He kicks him in the stomach, in the back, in the head, in the guts!

SANDY: Jeff, that's not in the script.

JEFF: Finally, he turns on Colonel McCabe.

(*JEFF turns on him and stalks him.*)

SANDY: Cut it out, Jeff.

JEFF: Coming at him, slowly, slowly . . .

SANDY: I said, cut it out.

JEFF: Closer and closer.

(*JEFF moves in and SANDY grows alarmed.*)

SANDY: Stop it!

JEFF: He raises his arm . . .

SANDY: Jeff!

(*JEFF backs him up until he is next to the bed.*)

JEFF: And zap! The death ray! Colonel McCabe collapses in agony.

(*SANDY is forced down on the bed. He is angry and confused.*)

SANDY: He does not.

JEFF: He does too.

SANDY: Colonel McCabe does not die! It says in the script, I don't die!

JEFF: You will if I want you to.

SANDY: I will not!

JEFF: Who's got the camera?

SANDY: I don't know, Jeff. Who does?

(*JEFF turns away.*)

You're such a jerk! I'm going home!

JEFF: Get out of here!

SANDY: I am!

JEFF: And take this piece of junk with you!

(*JEFF throws the dummy at SANDY.*)

Go home to your Mommy and your Daddy, clear out of here and leave me alone!

SANDY: You're a stupid jerk, Jeff. You've been acting like a stupid jerk ever since your parents first started . . .

JEFF: You shut up about my parents! You don't know anything about my parents!

SANDY: I know that they're yelling again. Jeff, I've heard them ever since I've been here. I could even hear them down on the street.

JEFF: Get out of here, Sandy!

SANDY: I know all about it.

(*JEFF turns away.*)

My Mom told me. Your Mom talks to my Mom; they gab all the time.

JEFF: (*Without turning to him*) What did she say?

SANDY: She said that there was trouble over here and I should keep my big nose out of it.

(*JEFF sits, upset. SANDY hesitates and approaches cautiously.*)

You want to talk about it in the pact?

JEFF: The pact?

SANDY: You remember the pact, Jeff?

JEFF: We were just little kids.

SANDY: You remember how we both pissed on that dead frog and buried it? How we both cut our fingers and spit and swore with our blood that we would always tell each other everything?

JEFF: We were just little kids.

SANDY: Yeah.

JEFF: (*After a pause*) I don't care anymore, Sandy. They can scream at each other until they're hoarse, I don't care. They can slap each other around all day, I don't care. I just want it to stop.

SANDY: Do they really hit each other?

JEFF: I don't know. I don't care!

SANDY: Jeeze, I don't know what I'd do if my parents ever hit each other.

JEFF: I didn't say they did. I just said, I didn't care.

SANDY: Do you ever see them?

JEFF: I never see anything, it's always behind the door.

SANDY: Do they ever come down for breakfast in the morning, you know, with black eyes or bruises?

JEFF: Blow it out your ear, Sandy.

SANDY: Do you know what it's about?

JEFF: Nobody tells me anything.

SANDY: Do you know when it started?

JEFF: I knew something was up when they started having all these appointments. When I'd ask Mom where she was going, she'd say, "Your Father and I have an appointment."

(Lights change and the posters are lit so the scrim becomes transparent. Behind each poster we see BEN and HELEN. The following scene is played as though they are each speaking to an off-stage counselor. The boys continue with their dialogue, seemingly oblivious to the words of BEN and HELEN. Underneath this scene there is sound which is not really music, but sets it apart from reality.**)

BEN: It all started about two years ago, Doctor. She went back to college for her Master's degree.

HELEN: It all started about four years ago. He stopped building houses and started building condominiums.

JEFF: *(To SANDY)* But it really started last Tuesday. Dad left and was gone for two days. Mom told me he was on a business trip, but he wasn't.

HELEN: "Condominiums", he said, "that's where the money is!" But the time? Time for electricians, carpenters, and clients; no time for us. So, I went back to school.

BEN: A Master's degree in Psychology? Why didn't she study something useful? What kind of work is psychology?

JEFF: When he came back, they tried to pretend everything was all right. But it wasn't. Everything had changed.

HELEN: I changed into someone neither of us had anticipated. I discovered I have my own ideas, feelings, needs . . .

BEN: I need her to be with me while I'm building something, something for all of us.

**See production notes at the end of the script.

JEFF: Now, everything's different.

SANDY: But do you know why?

BEN: I don't know why. She talks to me now, I don't understand what she's saying. She tells me I'm not giving her enough. Enough of what?

HELEN: When Ben gives, he gives things. When I give, I give things up.

JEFF: Something's happened, Sandy, I'm afraid it's something big.

HELEN: I won't give this up! It's my one chance to make something of my own.

BEN: I can't! I can't start all over again from scratch! This isn't just a job, it's my life!

JEFF: They hardly ever look at each other.

SANDY: Yeah?

BEN: We're tearing each other apart.

JEFF: They almost never talk to each other.

SANDY: Yeah?

HELEN: I want to put it back together again, with all the same pieces, but I want them to fit together differently.

JEFF: And they never ever smile at each other.

BEN: I want out.

   (*Lights out behind the posters. They appear to be solid again.*)

SANDY: Jeeze.

JEFF: Every night, when they think I'm asleep, Dad gets in his car and leaves. By morning he's back at the breakfast table. Every morning we eat breakfast in silence.

(Lights change, sound comes in. The walls become transparent and then swing open. BEN and HELEN enter in fantasy. HELEN carries a tray of utensils which transforms JEFF'S desk into a breakfast table.**

(The scene is played with great tension and counterpuntal rhythms of the various utensils. JEFF sits at the middle of the table. HELEN stirs a pot of hot cereal. As BEN enters she stops, they glare at each other. HELEN continues to stir as BEN pours coffee, sits, and opens a newspaper. HELEN stirs the pot in an ever increasing rhythm. BEN is bothered by the sound but ignores her. Finally she crosses to him, stirs faster and faster until she dumps a spoonful into his bowl. BEN looks at her and then at the bowl and half sighs, half grunts in response. JEFF is aware of the tension, but doggedly eats his cereal, scraping the bowl loudly with every bite. HELEN pours herself some coffee, and stirs it with her spoon clinking on the cup. The sound annoys BEN, he shoots her a look and retreats to his paper. JEFF, aware of the cross currents, eats quietly and retreats to a comic book. HELEN speaks to JEFF but looks at BEN.)

HELEN: Don't read at the table, Jeff! It's rude.

(BEN crumples his paper. JEFF stops reading and begins to tap his foot in a habitual nervous gesture. After a beat, HELEN taps her foot in a similar rhythm. BEN speaks to JEFF, but looks at HELEN.)

BEN: Don't tap your foot, son. It's very annoying.

(HELEN glares at BEN, he picks up a piece of toast and scrapes it into his cereal bowl. JEFF eats, noticing everything, but pretending to see nothing.)

BEN: *(Meaning the opposite)* Don't you just LOVE cream of wheat, Jeff?

(HELEN rises and clears the table. She clears all the dishes, including BEN'S coffee, leaving him with the spoon twirling in the air. BEN rises and leaves the table. There is a moment of wordless confrontation before they both exit through their posters. JEFF beats his hand down on the table as the lights return to normal.)

JEFF: I hate breakfast.

SANDY: Maybe you shouldn't have read at the table.

**See production notes at the end of the script.

JEFF: It wouldn't have made any difference.

SANDY: My parents do that kind of thing all the time. It's like they have a secret code or something; they don't even have to talk, they read each other's minds.

JEFF: It used to be that way with my folks too; but now it's like they are screaming at each other, but their voices are so high pitched that only dogs can hear them.

SANDY: Jeeze.

(*There is a pause and voices can be heard from behind the door. JEFF turns away. SANDY is a bit curious.*)

SANDY: Jeff, do you ever, you know, listen?

JEFF: Huh?

SANDY: I mean, when they fight, do you, you know, try to hear what they're saying?

JEFF: Sandy, I spend most of my time trying not to hear.

SANDY: Well, sometimes my folks argue, they don't really fight or anything; but when they argue, part of me tries to shut it out and part of me really wants to know what's going on.

JEFF: (*Not unkindly*) You little creep!

SANDY: No, but the weird thing is, the really weird thing is, whenever I listen, it all sounds so stupid! Like last year, you know, we all went down to Puyallup, to the fair. We go every year, and every year the same thing happens.

(*SANDY uses a couple of chairs to set up a "car" and he plays out the following.*)

My Dad always drives and my Mom sits next to him and does needlepoint. Julie, Carrie, and I sit in the back seat and argue over who has to sit on the hump. After we have been driving for about a half an hour, my Mom looks up and says, "We always go this way and we always get lost."

Then my Dad says, "You got a better route?"
And my Mom says, "Back there at the service station, I told you to turn left."
"But thats the way all the traffic goes."
"That's because we're going to Auburn."
Then, Julie says, "But I thought we were going to the fair!"
And they both say, "Be quiet, Julie."
And my Mom says, "Daddy's trying to drive."
And Dad says, "What that supposed to mean?"
So, my Mom says, "It's not supposed to mean anything. I am just trying to get us to the fair. If you'd listen instead of charging ahead, we wouldn't be lost."
Then, Dad says, "Who's lost? I know exactly where we are."
And Mom says, "Okay, where are we?"
And we all say, "WE'RE LOST!"
Then they both turn around and yell at US.

JEFF: Did you get to the fair?

SANDY: Yeah.

JEFF: How was it?

SANDY: It was great.

JEFF: With my folks we'd never get there.

   (*JEFF takes SANDY'S place and acts out the following.*)

JEFF: My Mom would say, "The reason you're driving this way is because you really don't want to go to the fair."
And my Dad would say, "What?"
"You didn't want to go last night when I suggested it and you didn't want to go this morning, while I was packing the picnic. That's why you didn't help."
"You said, you didn't need any help."
"Still, it would have been nice."
"Nice? I'm being nice: I'm taking you to the fair aren't I?"
"Only because you feel guilty."
"Guilty?"
"Because you didn't take us last year."
"But I'm taking you this year! I am taking you to the god-damned fair when I should be at the office."

"See, I knew you didn't want to go."
Then we'd turn around and all the way back to Seattle all you'd hear would be the sound of ice melting in the cooler.

SANDY: Did that really happen?

JEFF: No, but that's what would have happened.

SANDY: How do you know?

JEFF: I know, believe me, I know.

SANDY: What do you know?

JEFF: I know that's what would have happened.

SANDY: That's not what I mean. What do you know about what's happening?

JEFF: I don't know.

SANDY: You don't know what you know?

JEFF: No! What are you talking about?

SANDY: Look Jeff, if you can figure out what's going on, then maybe you can do something about it.

JEFF: I've tried.

SANDY: Well, try again! What are the facts?

JEFF: You sound like something out of Magnum P.I.**

SANDY: I'm just trying to help.

   (*SANDY leaps to his feet and becomes a detective.*)

Come on, man, what do you know?

JEFF: I know my Dad's not sleeping at home at night.

_____

**Update to any popular police or detective show and have Sandy imitate the lead character in his inquisition.

SANDY: Okay, where does he go?

JEFF: I don't know.

SANDY: Well, if he's not sleeping at home, he has to be sleeping somewhere else.

JEFF: Brilliant.

SANDY: Have you asked him?

JEFF: No.

SANDY: Why not?

JEFF: I can really see me going up to my father and saying, "Where you been sleeping these days, Dad?" Get real.

SANDY: We may have to tail him.

JEFF: I'm not going to do that!

SANDY: It was just a suggestion. Say, Jeff, do you think he's got a . . . girlfriend.

JEFF: No.

SANDY: Why not?

JEFF: He just wouldn't!

SANDY: Okay, scratch that. What else do you know?

JEFF: I know they fight a lot.

SANDY: What about?

JEFF: Everything. . . . Anything.

SANDY: You must have heard something in particular.

JEFF: This afternoon, I heard my Mom say, "I'm not giving up."

SANDY: Giving up what?

JEFF: I couldn't hear.

SANDY: Smoking! Your Dad wants her to give up smoking!

JEFF: She doesn't smoke.

SANDY: When my Mom tried to give up smoking, she threw a whole plate of spaghetti at my Dad. She said it slipped, but I knew she threw it.

JEFF: I said, she doesn't smoke.

SANDY: You sure?

JEFF: She's my Mother!

SANDY: What else did you hear?

JEFF: I heard my Mom say something about a job.

SANDY: YOUR DAD LOST HIS JOB!

JEFF: I don't think . . .

SANDY: That's it! Jeff, I saw this thing on "Sixty Minutes," about how all these people are losing jobs. First they lose the job, then they go on welfare, then everybody starts fighting with everybody and . . .

JEFF: My Dad works for himself, he's a contractor.

SANDY: Oh no, Jeff! That's the worst.

JEFF: But he just started a new project over in Bellevue . . .

SANDY: Don't take my word, ask Mike Wallace!

JEFF: Do you really think. . . .

SANDY: Here, I'll show you.

   (*SANDY grabs the dummy and mimes the characters with it.*)

Here is your Father, sitting around reading his paper. And your Mother comes in and says, "Well, I certainly hope that you're looking for a job." And he says, "Job, I have a job." And she says, "I mean a job with some money!"

"Maybe if you wouldn't spend so much on cigarettes and panty hose . . ."

JEFF: I told you, she doesn't . . .

SANDY: And she says, "Me spend so much? You're such a cheapskate . . ."

JEFF: Sandy . . .

SANDY: And that really makes him mad so he hauls off and . . . Bam! SLAP! POW! THWACK!

(*SANDY makes the dummy punch the air. JEFF grabs it from him.*)

JEFF: I never said they hit each other!

SANDY: I was just trying to . . .

JEFF: I've never seen them hit each other. They're not like that at all!

(*There is a pause.*)

SANDY: Hey, Jeff, why don't you just ask them what's going on?

(*JEFF tenderly carries the dummy over to the bed.*)

Ask your Mom, she'll tell you something. My Mother always tells me something.

JEFF: I just want it to stop, Sandy. That's all I really want. Every night when I hear them in there, I put the pillow over my head, so I can't hear them and I try to imagine what it would be like if they would just stop fighting. I try to make myself dream about it. If they would just stop fighting, everything would be perfect.

(*JEFF covers the dummy's head with a pillow during this speech. Lights change and there is music as we move into his fantasy.*)

It would be morning; and the first thing I hear would be Mom, in the kitchen making breakfast. The first thing I smell would be bacon frying. The first thing I feel would be sunlight on my face.

(*LIGHTS come up on the poster to the right of the door. HELEN appears behind it.*)

HELEN: Jeff, time to get up! Time for breakfast!

JEFF: So, I'd get up, and I'd come downstairs.

(*JEFF manipulates the dummy out of bed, and brings it to the desk which will serve once again as a breakfast table. The poster swings open and HELEN enters with utensils. JEFF enters the scene with the dummy. He manipulates the dummy and all relate to it as though it were him.*)

HELEN: Morning.

JEFF: Morning.

HELEN: Sleep well?

JEFF: Very.

(*JEFF seats the dummy at his place.*)

HELEN: Ben, breakfast is ready.

BEN: I'll be right there.

(*Poster swings open and BEN enters the scene. He takes his place at the table. In this scene there is no tension initially, everything is warm and loving, unreal and exaggerated.*)

HELEN: Morning.

BEN: Morning.

HELEN: Sleep well?

BEN: Very.

(*HELEN hands BEN a plate with obvious pleasure.*)

BEN: (*Delighted*) Eggs over easy, hash browns, bacon, toast, coffee with cream and two sugars. Thank you, dear.

HELEN: You're welcome, darling.

BEN: (*To the dummy*) Morning, son.

JEFF: (*Nodding the dummy toward BEN*) Morning.

BEN: Sleep well?

JEFF: Very.

   (*HELEN sits at table and all mime eating.*)

JEFF: (*To SANDY*) In this family everyone eats breakfast.

HELEN: This afternoon, I thought we'd all go to the circus. I've called for the tickets. They're at the box office.

BEN: This afternoon, I thought we'd all go to the Sonics game. I've called for the tickets, they're at the box office.

HELEN: But, Dearest, the circus . . .

BEN: But, Darling, the Sonics . . .

HELEN: Circus.

BEN: Sonics.

   (*Tension begins to build.*)

HELEN: CIRCUS!

BEN: SONICS!

JEFF: In this family there is NEVER any arguing.

HELEN: We'll go to the Sonics!

BEN: We'll go to the Circus!

JEFF: In this family there is ALWAYS a solution.

SANDY: In this family there is a dog!

   (*SANDY enters the scene as a boisterous slobbering dog. He bounds around the room.*)

HELEN: Who let the dog in?

BEN: He's all right! Here, Boy! Atta Boy! Good Dog. Good Boy!

HELEN: (*Pleasantly*) Ben, that's a hunting dog; don't you think he should really be outside?

(*SANDY bounds playfully over to BEN, jumps on him and they tussle.*)

BEN: Hey, Jeff, have a look at this. Fetch, Boy.

(*BEN throws an imaginary object and SANDY bounces after it.*)

HELEN: Please, Ben, not in the house.

JEFF: Sandy!

BEN: Good Dog! Bring it here. Good Boy!

(*SANDY fetches it and knocks into the table.*)

HELEN: Ben, he's knocking over the table.

BEN: Oh, he's just a puppy.

JEFF: Sandy . . .

(*BEN throws the object again.*)

BEN: After it, boy!

(*SANDY leaps onto the bed and kicks up the covers.*)

HELEN: He's tearing up the house.

HELEN: Stop it, Ben.

JEFF: Stop it, Sandy.

(*SANDY knocks over the hamper, scattering the contents.*)

HELEN: (*Very angry*) Ben, that dog just made a mess on the living room carpet!

BEN: Don't yell at me, I didn't do it!

JEFF: Stop it, Sandy!

HELEN: He's tearing up my house.

BEN: Your house? I thought this was my house, too!

HELEN: Well, if it's your house, then you can clean it up!

   (*HELEN exits behind her poster.*)

BEN: I'll have MY dog in MY house any damn time I want!

   (*BEN exits behind his poster. The lights return to normal.*)

JEFF: You spoiled everything! There aren't any dogs in this house!

   (*JEFF kicks SANDY who yelps like a dog, and dives under the bed.*)

SANDY: You kicked me!

JEFF: Why did you do that?

SANDY: I was just fooling around and you kicked me.

JEFF: Come out of there.

SANDY: Not until you say you're sorry.

JEFF: I'm sorry.

SANDY: You don't really mean it.

JEFF: I said I was sorry.

SANDY: Get down on your knees and say it.

   (*JEFF gets down on his knees, reluctantly.*)

JEFF: I'm sorry, I'm sorry, I'm sorry! Now, come on out!

   (*Just as SANDY starts out, the large door opens and HELEN enters in reality. SANDY ducks back under the bed.*)

HELEN: Jeff!

JEFF: (*Startled*) Huh?

HELEN: What are you doing?

JEFF: Nothing.

HELEN: What happened to your room?

JEFF: I'll clean it up.

HELEN: Never mind about that now, I didn't come in to talk about your room. Your Dad and I need to talk to you.

JEFF: What about?

HELEN: About all of us.

JEFF: Why?

HELEN: Just come on in. I think we'll be more comfortable in there.

(*HELEN indicates their room, JEFF pulls away.*)

JEFF: I'm cleaning my room.

HELEN: That can wait.

JEFF: I'm busy.

HELEN: Jeff, we need to talk to you now.

JEFF: I just want you to leave me alone.

HELEN: We've left you alone too much, but now we need to talk. Daddy's waiting . . .

(*JEFF pulls away and kicks the remains of the model which has wound up on the floor.*)

Your model? What happened to your model?

(*HELEN picks up the smashed model.*)

JEFF: I broke it.

HELEN: How?

JEFF: I just did. I smashed it.

HELEN: But you were so careful.

JEFF: I made it and I can smash it if I want!

(*JEFF lunges for it and HELEN holds it out of his grasp.*)

HELEN: Not after we worked so hard on it.

JEFF: What do you care?

HELEN: I care.

JEFF: (*Explodes*) Oh yeah, you care a lot, a whole damn lot!

(*HELEN, exhausted, sits on his bed.*)

HELEN: I am so tired of fighting, Jeff. I don't want to fight with you.

JEFF: Then don't. Just go away and leave me alone!

HELEN: Jeff, do me a favor. Just sit here with me for one minute and let's not talk, let's not even think.

JEFF: Why?

HELEN: Please.

(*JEFF sits, sullen at first. HELEN sighs. After a few seconds, HELEN starts to say something; JEFF catches her eye and looks at his watch; she is silent. HELEN reaches out to him and he slides closer to her. They relax in a moment of mutual comfort. In the silence, JEFF's anger is defused, for the moment. HELEN holds him and her face betrays her sorrow, pain, and concern. After a beat, JEFF speaks.*)

JEFF: Are we on welfare?

HELEN: What?

JEFF: Did Dad lose his job?

HELEN: No. What ever gave you that idea?

JEFF: Just something I heard.

HELEN: Heard? Heard where?

JEFF: (*Nods toward the large door*) I heard you guys yelling something about a job.

HELEN: Oh, Jeff, I'm sorry; I didn't want you to hear about it like that. I wanted to tell you myself as soon as I was sure.

JEFF: Tell me what?

HELEN: I've been offered a job with a Community Mental Health Center in Portland.

JEFF: Portland?

HELEN: It's a good job, a very good job, and it could be important to both of us.

JEFF: You aren't going to take it, are you?

HELEN: I haven't decided yet.

JEFF: So that's what it's all about, I mean with you and Dad.

HELEN: What's happening with us has very little to do with this job. There are other things, much more serious things.

JEFF: You have to tell them no. Tell them you have to stay here with Dad and me.

HELEN: If I thought that would solve anything, I would. I'd turn it down in a second if I thought it would change things with us. Your Dad and I have problems, serious ones. They don't need to be your problems, but they do affect you, so we need to talk.

JEFF: I don't want to talk, anymore.

HELEN: If you would rather talk here, I'll go get your Dad and we'll talk right here in your room.

(*HELEN starts out.*)

JEFF: Why don't you get a job here?

HELEN: That wouldn't help.

JEFF: You could find a job here!

HELEN: That wouldn't change anything.

JEFF: There must be all sorts of jobs here that you could . . .

HELEN: IT'S NOT THE JOB!

JEFF: I don't want to talk to you.

HELEN: Jeff . . .

(*JEFF turns away.*)

JEFF: I won't listen to anything you say!

HELEN: Stop it!

(*JEFF claps his hands over his ears.*)

JEFF: I can't hear you.

HELEN: I want you to stop this right now!

(*SANDY sneaks out from under the bed and tries to slip out the door. HELEN catches sight of him.*)

HELEN: Sandy!

SANDY: (*Embarrassed*) Excuse me.

HELEN: I didn't know anyone was here.

JEFF: I said, I was busy.

SANDY: I uhhhhhhh, gotta be going.

HELEN: (*To JEFF*) Why didn't you tell me?

SANDY: I'm sorry, Mrs. Stuart.

HELEN: Sandy, Jeff's Dad and I need to talk to him.

SANDY: Yeah, I know.

HELEN: I think you had better . . .

SANDY: I'm going right now, Mrs. Stuart.

JEFF: Can I at least say good-bye to him?

HELEN: Yes.

JEFF: Alone?

HELEN: Come into our room when you're done. Good-bye, Sandy.

SANDY: Bye, Mrs. Stuart. Uhhhh, Mrs. Stuart?

HELEN: Yes?

SANDY: I didn't mean to listen. I didn't hear much.

HELEN: Good-bye, Sandy. Say hello to your mother for me. We'll be waiting, Jeff.

JEFF: I'll come when I'm ready.

(*HELEN exits through the large door. SANDY picks up the dummy and starts toward the small door.*)

SANDY: Bye, Jeff. See you tomorrow.

JEFF: Don't go.

SANDY: You heard what she said.

JEFF: Don't go!

SANDY: But, Jeff . . .

JEFF: Please, Sandy, just for a little while.

SANDY: They're waiting for you.

JEFF: I know.

SANDY: I feel weird.

JEFF: I'll go in there when I'm ready, not right now.

(*SANDY sits and looks at JEFF. There is an awkward moment between them. SANDY looks at the door and then at his watch.*)

SANDY: When do you think you'll be ready, Jeff?

JEFF: Something's got to happen. Something big, something so she won't take that job.

SANDY: Didn't you listen? She said it wasn't the job.

JEFF: Something to make them stop fighting.

SANDY: Like what?

JEFF: Like if something happened to me: Like if I got hit by a truck or something.

(*JEFF jumps up, makes a wailing sound, grabs the dummy and runs around the room. He dumps the dummy face down on the desk and lights begin a gradual change as he moves into fantasy. SANDY does not join the fantasy as quickly.*)

SANDY: Jeff?

JEFF: Doctor, we have a very serious case here, a very serious case.

SANDY: Jeff . . .

JEFF: I said, Doctor we have a serious case here, a very serious case.

SANDY: I gotta go home.

JEFF: Please, Sandy! We have a serious case here.

(*SANDY reluctantly crosses to the desk, which has become an operating table, and joins in.*)

SANDY: Name?

JEFF: Jeff Stuart.

SANDY: Age?

JEFF: Eleven.

SANDY: Pulse?

JEFF: Weak!

SANDY: Heartbeat?

(*JEFF listens at the dummy's chest.*)

JEFF: Going, going, GONE!

SANDY: EMERGENCY!

(*Both boys pound frantically on the dummy's chest.*)

SANDY: Hold it!

JEFF: What is it?

SANDY: It's started again. He's better now.

(*SANDY tries to leave the fantasy, JEFF pulls him back.*)

JEFF: No, we have to operate!

SANDY: Operate?

JEFF: OPERATE! Knife!

(*JEFF holds up an imaginary knife SANDY assumes the role of the Doctor. JEFF slaps the knife into his hand.*)

SANDY: Knife!

(*SANDY mimes the operation, JEFF makes sound effects. SANDY opens the "patient."*)

SANDY: Oh, gross!

JEFF: Look at his guts.

SANDY: All twisted up.

JEFF: Look at his liver.

SANDY: That's disgusting.

JEFF: He's losing a lot of blood!

SANDY: TRANSFUSION!

   (*SANDY stands with one arm raised and his hand cupped, like a plasma bottle. JEFF jabs SANDY'S other arm at the dummy's arm.*)

SANDY: Glub, glub, glub . . .

   (*SANDY slowly closes his hand as though the bottle were emptying.*)

We saved him again; he's better now!

   (*SANDY tries again to leave the fantasy; JEFF won't let him.*)

JEFF: No! The parents have to be notified.

SANDY: (*Dropping the fantasy*) Jeff, this isn't going to help.

JEFF: Sandy, we have got to call the parents!

   (*JEFF crosses to the phone, picks up the receiver and hands it to SANDY*)

Tell them to come right away!

   (*JEFF makes SANDY take it.*)

Ring! Ring!

   (*Lights come up on posters; BEN and HELEN are seen each holding a phone receiver.*)

BEN and HELEN: Hello.

JEFF: (*To SANDY*) Tell them!

SANDY: This is the hospital! We have your son here. You'd better come right away.

BEN and HELEN: Oh, my God!

   (*Posters swing open and BEN and HELEN enter the scene. They each take a chair and establish a waiting room. JEFF crosses to them, SANDY hangs back and watches.*)

JEFF: Mr. and Mrs. Stuart?

HELEN: Is he going to be all right?

JEFF: Too soon to tell.

BEN: Is he going to make it?

JEFF: That all depends.

BEN and HELEN: On what?

JEFF: On what you do now. We've done everything that medical science can do for him. Now, you take him home and take good care of him. He needs rest and peace and QUIET!

(JEFF crosses to dummy and picks it up, he gives one end to SANDY and both boys race around the room like an ambulance. They dump the dummy on the bed.)

SANDY: *(Out of the fantasy)* Jeff, I'm going now.

JEFF: You can't; this is the best part!

(BEN and HELEN rise and cross to the bed. They kneel on either side of it. JEFF takes the two chairs and places them near the bed. JEFF and SANDY sit on the backs of the chairs with their feet on the seat, overlooking the scene. In this scene, everyone treats the dummy as JEFF.)

HELEN: Jeff, Jeff, this is your Mother.

BEN: Son, we're right here.

SANDY: He seems to be in a coma.

JEFF: But he can still hear you.

BEN: You've got to get well, son.

SANDY: So, he gets well and everybody lives happily ever . . .

(SANDY starts off the chair, JEFF pulls him back.)

JEFF: Not yet.

BEN: How do you feel son?

HELEN: Where does it hurt?

BEN: Can you hear us?

SANDY: No, he can't! His ears are filled with wax!

JEFF: Yes, he can! Go on!

HELEN: We promise things will change.

BEN: We'll do anything.

SANDY: Get him some soup! Get him a comic book!

JEFF: No, don't. Keep talking.

BEN: From now on, we'll be a family again.

JEFF: He's starting to come 'round.

SANDY: Still looks out of it to me.

HELEN: We'll all stay together, right here, we promise.

JEFF: He's definitely beginning to come 'round.

HELEN: If only we'd listened to each other.

BEN: If only we'd taken more time.

BEN: If only your Mother had paid more attention.

HELEN: If only your Father had been home more.

SANDY: There they go again.

JEFF: Hey, he's back in a coma!

BEN: (*To HELEN*) This is all your fault, you know.

HELEN: My fault? Why is it always my fault?

JEFF: Will you look at your son?

HELEN: At least I tried, I helped him with his model and that's more than I can say for you.

BEN: Oh yeah, well, I would have helped him, if you'd just given me a chance!

JEFF: He's dying!

HELEN: I can't talk to you, you're impossible!

BEN: I'm impossible? You're impossible!

(They both storm off and exit through their posters. JEFF and SANDY sit, looking at the patient for a long beat. SANDY jumps down and begins to march around the bed singing the FUNERAL MARCH.)

SANDY: Dum dum dee dum, Dum dee dum dee dum dum dum.

JEFF: Cut it out, Sandy.

(The phone rings. SANDY continues. The phone rings again. JEFF makes no move to answer it. The phone rings again.)

SANDY: Jeeze, Jeff, doesn't anyone around here ever answer the phone?

(SANDY answers the phone.)

Hello? Stuarts' residence . . . Oh, hi, Mom . . . Yeah, this is me . . . Obviously, I'm still here if I answered the phone . . . No, what time is it? . . . Aw, do I have to? . . . Yeah, I know . . . Yeah, I know . . . Yeah, I know . . . Okay, right away . . . Yeah, I know! Bye.

(SANDY hangs up and turns to JEFF.)

I gotta go. I have an appointment with the orthodontist.

JEFF: Orthodontist?

SANDY: I hate it when my Mom makes me dentist appointments during vacations. I don't even get to get out of school.

JEFF: Do you have to go?

SANDY: Yeah.

JEFF: Can't you tell her you're sick or something?

SANDY: Then she'd just make me come home and go to bed.

JEFF: Can't you tell her I'm sick?

SANDY: She'd be afraid I'd catch it, she'd still make me come home.

JEFF: Can I come with you?

SANDY: To the orthodontist?

JEFF: Sandy, I need you to stay with me, just five more minutes.

SANDY: What good would it do? Jeff, you can't change anything by not talking to them.

(*JEFF turns away.*)

Things will be better when it's over.

JEFF: When what's over?

SANDY: After you've talked to them.

JEFF: Are you sure?

SANDY: No. Bye, Jeff. See you tomorrow.

JEFF: Yeah.

SANDY: (*On his way out*) Hey, take it easy.

JEFF: Okay.

(*SANDY exits, JEFF turns away. JEFF sees the dummy and runs after him.*)

Hey, Sandy, just a minute, you forgot . . .

(*JEFF exits through the small door, but he returns immediately dragging the dummy behind him.*)

Damn!

(*JEFF dumps the dummy on the floor and looks at the large door, he paces back and forth across the room. On each pass, he kicks the dummy out of the way.*)

Can't feel that, can you?

(*He continues to kick the dummy.*)

Or that! Or that! You can't feel anything!

(*After one last savage kick, JEFF picks the dummy up in his arms and hugs it tightly. He places it tenderly on the bed. JEFF crosses to the large door. It is the longest walk he has ever made. He opens the door but stands in the doorway and looks into the next room.*)

JEFF: What are you doing?

BEN'S VOICE: Packing.

JEFF: Another business trip?

BEN'S VOICE: Not this time, son.

(*JEFF turns away and steps back into his room.*)

BEN'S VOICE: Jeff, come back in here.

JEFF: I don't want to!

BEN'S VOICE: I'll get your Mother. She's making coffee. You wait right there.

(*JEFF stands near the door for a moment and then bolts into his parents' room. He returns to his room immediately with a suitcase.*)

Hey, what are you doing?

(*BEN enters and faces JEFF. JEFF holds the suitcase defiantly.*)

JEFF: Why are you packing?

BEN: I've got to get out of here and let things settle down for a while.

(*JEFF drops the case on the floor, falls to his knees and begins pulling articles of clothing out of the case.*)

JEFF: You can't take these, they're dirty. I'll wash them for you!

(*JEFF throws a handful of clothing on the floor.*)

BEN: Hey!

JEFF: Can't take these, they've got holes in them.

BEN: What are you doing?

JEFF: Can't take these, they're too old. Just rags! Can't take rags!

BEN: Easy, Jeff.

   (*JEFF rises with the case and dumps the rest on the floor.*)

JEFF: You can't take them! They belong here!

   (*JEFF hurls the empty suitcase to the ground.*)

BEN: For God's sake, Jeff!

JEFF: You can't leave! We've got to all stay here, together!

   (*BEN reaches out to JEFF.*)

BEN: Let me talk to you!

   (*JEFF pulls away viciously.*)

JEFF: Don't touch me!

BEN: Oh, God, Jeff!

JEFF: And don't you DARE cry!

BEN: Please, try to understand.

JEFF: Understand what?

BEN: Your Mother and I fight all the time, you must have heard us!

JEFF: I just turn up the T.V. and I don't hear anything.

BEN: That doesn't mean it isn't happening.

JEFF: I don't have to hear this!

(JEFF starts to try to leave. BEN stops him.)

BEN: Yes, you do! Now, sit down.

(BEN sits him on the bed.)

It's happening and it has been happening for years, and you know it!

JEFF: No, I don't!

BEN: Yes, you do! There hasn't been peace or quiet or comfort in this house for a long time, and you know that, too.

JEFF: How do you know what I know?

(HELEN enters and stands in the doorway with two coffee cups.)

BEN: We can't go on like this, any of us. It has to stop sometime. Now, I know how you feel but . . .

JEFF: You don't know what I feel!

HELEN: Jeff, honey, please listen to us.

JEFF: Mom, ask him not to go!

(BEN and HELEN look at each other. She can't do this and they both know it.)

BEN: Jeff, about a week ago, I moved into a hotel, just temporarily, until I could find an apartment.

JEFF: Is that where you've been sleeping?

BEN: Yes.

HELEN: *(Astonished)* You knew?

JEFF: I've seen you go every night.

BEN: *(To HELEN)* I knew we shouldn't have done it this way, we should have told him when I first left.

HELEN: Ben . . .

JEFF: But every morning you'd be back for breakfast.

BEN: (*To HELEN*) I told you this wouldn't work.

HELEN: Alright, Ben!

HELEN: (*To JEFF*) Why didn't you say something?

JEFF: Why didn't you?

HELEN: I still hoped that we could work things out. We were seeing a counselor and I thought if we could just solve some of the . . .

BEN: It was a dumb thing for us to do and we're sorry.

HELEN: (*Angrily to BEN*) I thought it was best, Ben!

JEFF: I can help!

HELEN: No, Jeff there's nothing you can do.

JEFF: I can help around the house more. I can be quieter. I can stay out of the way more.

HELEN: You are not responsible for this in any way.

JEFF: From now on, I'll clean up my room. I won't play the T.V. loud or the stereo . . .

HELEN: Jeff . . .

JEFF: Just tell me what I did wrong and I'll fix it; I will!

BEN: Jeff, you are the one really good thing in our lives. You were never the problem.

HELEN: That's right, honey.

BEN: What's happening here is between your Mother and me. It's not your fault.

JEFF: So, why are you doing this?

HELEN: It's complicated . . . there are so many reasons.

JEFF: Like what?

HELEN: Things we thought we wanted when we got married, just don't seem to be the things we want now.

JEFF: What things?

BEN: Jeff, I need . . . want, your Mother to be the kind of wife she just can't be to me anymore. And she wants . . . needs, things from me that I just can't give her.

JEFF: I don't understand.

BEN: Sometimes, adults have to make decisions all their own. Now, they might not sound like good reasons to you but . . .

JEFF: You are changing everything in my whole life and you can't even give me one good reason why?

BEN: We can't keep living this way, Jeff!

JEFF: Because you fight? So what?

HELEN: It isn't only the fighting, Jeff.

JEFF: So, just stop! Stop fighting! Everything would be okay if you'd just . . .

BEN: It's why we fight.

JEFF: (*Very belligerent.*) Oh, yeah? Why?

BEN: (*Blurts it out*) We just don't love each other anymore.

   (*HELEN is shaken by this.*)

HELEN: Ben.

BEN: (*Realizing it himself for the first time*) That's it, isn't it, Helen?

HELEN: I have never heard you say that before.

BEN: That's what's really wrong, isn't it?

HELEN: I don't know.

(*HELEN crosses away from him.*)

BEN: Don't you?

HELEN: If we could just solve some of the problems.

BEN: (*Simply*) Helen, do you love me?

HELEN: I don't think we should talk about that here.

BEN: I do.

HELEN: But Jeff . . .

BEN: That's why we have to. Do you love me?

HELEN: There are things I love about you.

BEN: That's not what I . . .

HELEN: I know what you asked me.

BEN: And?

HELEN: (*Inaudible*) No.

BEN: Helen?

JEFF: Mom?

HELEN: No.

(*There is a long pause.*)

JEFF: Will you get a divorce?

HELEN: (*After a beat*) Probably.

JEFF: And what I think doesn't matter?

HELEN: It matters very much.

JEFF: And if I don't want you to?

BEN: I'm sorry, Jeff.

JEFF: You don't care.

BEN: That's the hard part, we do care, maybe not enough, maybe not about the same things, but we do care.

JEFF: But you're getting a divorce.

BEN: Not from you.

(*BEN tries to touch JEFF who pulls away.*)

BEN: This day, Jeff, this day is the hardest. Things will be better for all of us when this day is over.

JEFF: And then what happens to me?

HELEN: You'll stay here with me for now and then we'll . . .

JEFF: I mean, who do I live with? Will I have to go to Portland? What if I don't want to go? Will I have to leave all my friends?

BEN: We'll settle all that later.

JEFF: Who decides what happens to me?

HELEN: We all will, together.

JEFF: How do I know you aren't lying to me again?

HELEN: Lying?

JEFF: What do you think all that sneaking around was?

BEN: (*Very firmly*) Just a minute, sport, we may not have told you everything that was going on, but we never meant to lie to you.

HELEN: And when I tried to talk to you, you wouldn't listen. You just turned away and tuned me out.

BEN: This is a hard time for all of us. All of us, Jeff.

JEFF: From now on, will you tell me things?

BEN: Yes.

HELEN: From now, will you listen?

JEFF: (*Softly*) I'll try.

HELEN: And so will we.

BEN: We've got two whole months to figure this Portland thing out, so let's just take it a step at a time. Okay?

JEFF: Do I have a choice?

BEN: Come on, Jeff. I think you'll like my apartment. It has a room for you, and an elevator, and a pool . . .

JEFF: Can I have a dog?

(*Both BEN and HELEN laugh.*)

BEN: We'll see.

JEFF: Will you ever decide to get back together again?

(*They are caught off-guard and hesitate.*)

BEN: I don't think so.

JEFF: Mom?

HELEN: No.

(*There is an awkward pause.*)

BEN: Well, if I'm going to get moved in, I'd better get with it. I still have to check out of the hotel and take my things from there. . . .

(*He checks his watch.*)

I'd better get with it. I'll come back for this stuff, Helen, okay?

(*HELEN nods. BEN takes a card out of his pocket and writes on it.*)

BEN: Jeff, let me write down the address of the apartment for you. Come see me anytime. I've got a phone, so just call and I'll come for you.

JEFF: (*Turns away from him*) I can take the bus.

BEN: Anytime, Jeff, I'll come for you anytime . . .

(*No response from JEFF.*)

I'll call you.

(*He stands there for a moment, uncertain.*)

Jeff?

(*He holds out his arms, JEFF crosses to him and hugs him. Before the hug is really completed, JEFF pulls away.*)

JEFF: See ya.

(*JEFF turns away. BEN looks at HELEN, she is looking away.*)

BEN: Helen? . . . Take care.

(*He starts out.*)

HELEN: You too.

(*BEN exits through the small door. Both JEFF and HELEN look toward the door as we hear BEN'S footsteps disappearing. A final door shuts off-stage and the sound shudders through HELEN'S body.*)

HELEN: (*After a beat to compose herself*) You okay?

JEFF: (*Shrugs*) You?

HELEN: Lousy.

JEFF: Me, too.

HELEN: Well, at least we're lousy together.

JEFF: Yeah.

(*After a beat.*)

I hate this.

HELEN: I know. I hate it with you.

(*JEFF turns to her and looks away. HELEN moves toward him slightly and speaks from her own need for comfort as much as his.*)

Jeff, what do you do when you feel rotten? What do you do when you're really depressed?

JEFF: I don't know . . . Nothing . . . Sometimes I take a walk and just look around for something I like. Something like a leaf or a piece of glass or something, and I just look at it for a while.

HELEN: (*This is a risky question for her*) Want to take a walk?

JEFF: (*His voice says "yes", his body says "no".*) Okay.

HELEN: I'll get the house key.

(*HELEN exits to her room. JEFF crosses to the desk and picks up the card, he looks at it and then at the small door. He puts the card in his pocket. Finding release in activity, he gathers up BEN'S clothes, and puts them in the suitcase. HELEN enters and stands in the doorway.*)

JEFF: After we get back, I'll take these over to Dad's.

(*JEFF indicates the dummy.*)

And then I'll take this over to Sandy's.

HELEN: Okay.

(*JEFF starts out the door, HELEN waits, unsure. JEFF turns and really sees her for the first time since BEN'S exit.*)

JEFF: Let's go, Mom.

(*He holds out his hand to her. She takes it and they exit out the small door. There is music. Lights dim to black.*)

CURTAIN

Production Notes

Off-stage Argument:

I have deliberately not written specific dialogue for the off-stage argument. In an earlier draft I did try to sketch it out, but I felt it tended to limit and constrain the actors, and sounded artificial.

It is my intention that the argument should be created improvisationally by the actors and the director, and that the improvisational quality be maintained in production.

Some guidelines might be helpful:

It should be a real argument, and not random words or sounds. The actors should decide what specific circumstances and previous action have led Ben and Helen to this particular moment and each should have specific and conflicting motivations and objectives.

The dynamics of the argument must be modulated to work with the primary action on-stage. Off-stage sounds must never overwhelm what is happening on stage, but should underscore action, and provoke reactions from Jeff and Sandy. At the same time, there must be variety, build, and flow to the off-stage sounds.

When Ben and Helen enter a scene on-stage in "reality" they must bring some of their previous offstage actions with them. When they enter a scene in "fantasy" they are primarily projections of Jeff's thoughts, fears, hopes, and feelings.

Treatment of the Fantasies:

Perhaps the most important direction for my intention concerning the fantasies is to keep in mind that they are grounded in Jeff's needs in real life. It is this relevance to reality, rather than a departure from the real world, that gives these scenes their power.

Every director will interpret this in a different way, and will make his or her own stylistic choices. This is as it should be. I feel that light and sound can be important elements in introducing and underscoring these scenes. It must be clear that they are somehow different visually, rhythmically, and emotionally than the scenes "in reality"; but they must move the dramatic action of the play forward, rather than divert it.

If Jeff's motivations and objectives are the springboards for fantasy, then the best stylistic choices can be made.

A Final Note:

The words and actions of this play provide all the essentials for production; but much of the depth and intensity of this script must be found between the lines, in subtext, and in silence. The story yields only the uppermost layer and there is much to be discovered and created by actors and directors. I urge you to be bold in your emotional choices, to be clear and specific with the development of all relationships, and to bring the same emotional intensity to both the words of the text and the thoughts and feelings which remain unspoken.

Mother Hicks

In *Mother Hicks* Zeder breaks new ground, both for herself as a writer and for the field of theatre for young audiences. This play is the culmination of some of her deeply felt concerns and a synthesis of distinctive theatrical elements that appear in her earlier scripts. In looking at the whole body of Zeder's work, *Mother Hicks* can be seen as a pivotal play. Up to and including *Mother Hicks*, Zeder focuses primarily on child characters facing adulthood. In the plays that come after, adult characters struggle with problems of their literal childhood or their figurative children.

Zeder feels that *Mother Hicks* moved with a special power of its own from the beginning. She says, "It knew more about where it was going than any of the others. It was as if it came from somewhere else and simply came through me to find its way into the world." The play also took its own time to be born. It was not influenced by the pressures of production deadlines until well into its creation. The play's setting, characters, and plot grew out of interests she began to discover in 1972 when she was doing research on the folklore of witches for *Wiley and the Hairy Man*. It then stayed in the back of her mind for eleven years, growing and changing as she wrote and learned from the five preceding plays in this collection. This may account, in part, for the richness of its themes, characters, and relationships, and for the intensity of its dramatic action. The familiar thematic issues and theatrical elements that Zeder has explored in these earlier works reach an even fuller development here.

Many of Zeder's young protagonists deal with the real or potential loss of a parent and the fear of abandonment. But in *Mother Hicks*, Girl has already lost both real parents. Through most of the rest of the play she goes through a series of losses, including nearly losing her own life. Her physical and emotional obstacles are as difficult as any that a child has to face. Like Ellie and Dorothy, Girl learns to understand the effect of her actions on others. But Girl goes on to discover something that eludes most adults and certainly eludes the townspeople in this play. She learns that one must search for and create one's own identity, that identity cannot be completely defined by being part of a family, or having a particular job, or through owning material possessions. Girl realizes she must find her own name.

The function of fantasy in the child protagonist's life is another familiar theme that is strong in *Mother Hicks*, but it is presented in quite a different way than in Zeder's other scripts. In the earlier plays the protagonist's fantasies are visible to the audience, but Girl's fantasies about her real parents remain internalized and are revealed only in brief scenes in which she describes them to Ricky and Wilson Walker. The audience also sees how a new fantasy about her real mother grows as Girl gets to know Mother Hicks. Girl is both driven and blocked by her fantasies as much as Wiley, Ellie, or Jeff.

Zeder's interest in the dilemmas people get themselves into when they don't listen to each other is another issue found in every one of her previous plays. But the difficulty of meaningful and accurate communication between individuals that Zeder has explored in domestic settings takes on societal dimensions in *Mother Hicks*. The townspeople, ruled by fear and wanting easy explanations for disastrous events, force Mother Hicks out of town. They make no effort to listen to her, even when she confronts them directly with the truth. The presence of a deaf character adds yet another kind of difficulty to the already problematic communication in this town.

Stylistic and structural elements in *Mother Hicks* are reminiscent of earlier works, but they show Zeder's growth as a writer. Her use of the chorus, with its strongly rhythmic and musical language, is similar in many ways to the chorus in *Wiley and the Hairy Man*. Both choruses establish a threatening mood with a rhythmic chant at the play's opening and repeat the same chant at the end with a twist to comment on the progression that has occurred. But in *Mother Hicks*, the chorus serves a more complex purpose. She uses it to establish the atmosphere of fear in this town and as the force against which Mother Hicks and Girl must fight. However, each chorus member also moves in and out of one or more individual roles, as specific characters in the play, rather than having only a group identity. Although their time on stage as individual characters is relatively short, they are not stereotypical. One of Zeder's growing strengths as a writer, which emerges strongly in this script, is her ability to create minor characters with dimensionality.

Zeder's use of language in this script again shows her love of strong, simple rhythms, repeated phrases, and alliteration, but the addition of sign language brings a new layer of richness and complexity. The fact that Zeder has written Tuc's narrations as poetry, full of strong visual images, and the fact that the voicing by the chorus members must slow down to synchronize with Tuc's signing means that audience members have extra time to savor and appreciate the beauty of both languages.

Along with all of these familiar elements, Zeder stretches new muscles as a writer in this play. Mother Hicks is the most fully drawn adult character in all of Zeder's plays. The character began to take shape in Zeder's imagination as she did research for *Wiley and the Hairy Man* and discovered how women who were midwives and healers in remote, rural communities were often accused of being witches. But Zeder can also trace some of the earliest seeds of this character back to her childhood and a handyman on a neighboring farm who had an uncanny ability to attract wounded wild animals and nurse them back to health. This man's connection to the forces of nature made a deep impression on her and eventually became an important aspect of Mother Hicks' personality. Another direct root of Mother Hicks was Mary Ellen Bridges, the grandmother of Zeder's husband, Jim Hancock, and the woman to whom the play is dedicated. This wise country woman raised Jim. Although Zeder never met her, she came to know her through her husband's vivid descriptions. Mary Ellen often said, "Wish in one hand, spit in the other, and see which gets full first," and Zeder gave the saying to Mother Hicks. But perhaps her most important contribution was the freedom and support she gave Jim to create his own identity. Her impact on Jim found its way into Mother Hicks' impact on Girl.

The specificity of these influences helped Zeder create a character in Mother Hicks who is archetypal in stature, but also vulnerable and human in a unique, individual way. The mystery about her past creates the potential for ambiguity about her personal desires and motives. This maintains suspense for the audience and makes the subtext, especially in the last scene between Girl and Mother Hicks, some of the richest in all of Zeder's plays.

Tuc, as a character, is another new phenomenon in Zeder's work and perhaps a new phenomenon in contemporary theatre. He is one of a very few deaf or disabled characters in American dramatic literature who is important in his own right and not just important for his deafness. He is defined in terms of his abilities rather than his disability. Zeder states that she was surprised when he suddenly appeared in her mind. She was even more surprised when he spoke in verse, since she had never planned to use verse in this play. But she discovered, as Tuc revealed himself to her imagination, that he had a way of seeing the world in essences and needed language unencumbered by the need to be linear. Poetry was the leanest and clearest way for him to express himself.

Tuc's function in the play is that of a linking force. As storyteller, he literally brings the audience into the world of the play. He is also the link that brings Girl and Mother Hicks together. He is similar to

Mother Hicks and Girl in being an outsider and in having to put up with misunderstanding from others on a daily basis. He is also like both of them in having experienced death and loss. Not only has he lost his parents, but, in having lost his hearing as a child, he has also lost—and regained in a new form—his sense of identity. Unlike Girl and Mother Hicks, he seems to have very little bitterness about what has happened to him. He can still reach out to people, where Mother Hicks will not do so unless they are in desperate danger. Tuc's ability to "listen" so fully with his eyes makes a strong impression on Girl, which helps her discover what it means to listen to and understand other people.

In *Mother Hicks* Zeder feels she completely moved away from any notion of structuring the play for a child audience and "went with what the play demanded." She recalls how terrified she was when she saw kindergarteners at the preview of the first production. But she was surprised and pleased when the play held them spellbound.

Although Zeder receives a lot of letters from audience members and from the people involved in productions of her plays, the letters she has received about *Mother Hicks* have been entirely different in depth and dimension. This play touches people in a more personal way than her others.

One particularly articulate letter came from an eighth grade girl who had seen a 1988 production of *Mother Hicks* at the Nashville Academy Theatre. The girl was born sighted, had become blind, and was just learning to express herself in braille when her class attended the play. In her letter, she stated:

> "The way the play was written, it gave me visions that my eyes could never see. It helped me realize that people believe whatever they allow themselves to. To me, the play pointed out that you can't change what people think of you by just saying that's not true. You must prove to them that it is not true. Some people still won't change, but its not anyone's fault, just their own misconception."

> Cindy Miller

Zeder reports that the play seems to have a similar effect on all kinds of audience members. Girl's quest, Mother Hicks' power, and Tuc's wisdom are both specific and universal and have meaning for people of all ages who are on a similar journey and in need of help along the way. In the long run, *Mother Hicks* may be seen as Zeder's most important play. At this point in her career it is the most important one to her because it gave her visions that her eyes had never seen.

Mother Hicks

by Suzan L. Zeder

From the Playwright

This play came from somewhere and passed through me on its way to somewhere else. The idea first presented itself after I read a collection of oral lore from the W.P.A., Federal Writer's Project, written during the Depression. I was struck by the number of witch tales which provided supernatural explanations for natural disasters, and by the need of communities to create witches as scapegoats in troubled times and landscapes.

The writing of this play has been a joyous voyage of discovery for me. The witch stories, locations, and details of place and period are real and historically accurate. The characters and storyline are original and have shaped themselves through me. This play has always moved with its own power. It has told me where it needed to go next, and whenever I came to my desk there were characters waiting to talk to me.

I have one deep and serious production concern with this play. I strongly urge potential producers and directors to cast a deaf or hearing impaired actor in the role of Tuc. Although it may take a little extra time and effort to find and work with this actor, the benefits are overwhelming. It is the difference between someone copying choreographed movements and someone dancing in the language of their soul. The use of sign in this play is a language as precise as any of the words spoken aloud. If sign language is to have dramatic impact it must have meaning; it must be real and specific if it is to have emotional eloquence and physical poetry.

I have had a special relationship with this play. I wish you the same. May it help you "see the sharp sting of honey and taste the sunrise."

Suzan L. Zeder
Dallas, Texas
1986

Dedication

MOTHER HICKS is dedicated to Mary Ellen Bridges, whom I never met, but feel as though I know.

The premiere production of *Mother Hicks* was presented on May 6, 1983 at Poncho Theatre in Seattle, Washington with the following cast:

Tuc .... Keith Dahlgren
Girl .... Emily Jenkins
Mother Hicks .... Toni Cross

CHORUS

Keith Cavanah	Carmen Roman
Brian Faker	Sheri Lee Miller
Cecilie D. Keenan	Christopher Tolfree

The production was directed by Rita Giomi

From November 12–24th 1985, the Asolo Touring Theatre, Sarasota, Florida, was invited to perform *Mother Hicks* at the John F. Kennedy Center for the Performing Arts in Washington D.C.

The production was directed by Robert Miller

CHARACTERS

Tuc: A deaf man, in his 20's
Girl: A foundling, 13 years old
Mother Hicks: An ageless woman in her 40's

A chorus of at least two women and three men who speak the words
of Tuc's sign language and play the following roles:

Jake Hammon   Wilson Walker
Izzy Sue Ricks   Alma Ward
Ricky Ricks   Hosiah Ward
Clovis P. Eudy

SETTING

The town of Ware, in southern Illinois:
Act I: Various locations in and around town
Act II: Dug Hill, the store, a street, the graveyard.

TIME

Late Spring, 1935

Mother Hicks

Act One

The set consists of a large open area on a gently raked stage. Downstage there are two tall telephone poles with terminals and cables. The wires stretch diagonally upstage and connect with another smaller pole. There is a feeling of uncluttered vastness reaching toward a disappearing horizon.

Opening music is a folk song of the Depression, an upbeat kind of song, not too city, not too country; that reflects the tension and trouble of the time. House lights fade with the music and a tinkling bell is heard in the silence of the darkness. A rosey hued cyclorama floods the stage.

A figure is seen silhouetted against the cyclorama. TUC pulls a large wagon, ringing the bell as he crosses downstage. As lights come up we see that the wagon is loaded with odd pieces of furniture, hung with miscellaneous costume pieces, and rigged with a variety of props. From this wagon will come many of the costume and prop pieces used by the CHORUS as they take their various roles and move the action from scene to scene. TUC pulls the wagon to a spot center-stage, and steps into a bright pool of light. The CHORUS enters behind him.

(TUC signs in silence for a beat or two, then the CHORUS speaks his words.)

CHORUS: Mother Hicks is a witch, people say.
And she lives all alone at the top of Dug Hill
And she works her magic on the town below.

When cracks is seen in the dry creek bed
When the corn burns up
When a calf's born dead
Mother Hicks is a witch, people say.

When a child falls sick
And there ain't no cause
And there ain't no cure
Then everybody knows that it's witched for sure.
Mother Hicks is a witch . . . people say.

(*During the following, CHORUS members come forward, speak a few lines, take an article of clothing from the wagon, and exit. TUC continues signing.*)

CHORUS: This time is Spring in 1935
A year of fear in the Great Depression.
This place is Ware. W.A.R.E.
The Mississippi River's over there.
This is southern Illinois,
But we call it Egypt.

(*A single CHORUS member remains; comes forward and shares the edge of the spotlight with TUC. All subsequent translations of sign language will be handled this way: the interpreter shares the light, but gives focus to the sign.*)

CHORUS: My name is Tuc.
I cannot speak. I cannot hear.
I use my hands and the words appear.
I hang these words in the air for you
To tell a story that I know is true;
'Cause I heard every word with my eyes.

It is deep in the early,
Just before dawn.

(*Lights fade to blackout, a low throbbing electrical hum pulsates in the darkness. The sound is pierced by the shrill sound of a whistle. Lights come up on GIRL at the top of the telephone pole.*)

GIRL: A dare is a dare and done. Dare and double dare, to sneak over the fence at the power station and fetch the quarter that Ricky threw there. Up and over the fence and then drop down into the cool wet grass.

(*She drops down a rung.*)

Then I heard it, that stinging, singing sound; racing through them wires, and round them coils and cables; like the electricity wanted to be out like lightning bolts. It's true fact, that I do dares of mortal danger. Things that no one else in town would dare to do, or dare to tell they'd done 'em.

A dare is a dare and done!

(From out of the darkness, a voice is heard off-stage. It is RICKY RICKS, a boy about GIRL's age.)

RICKY: Girl! Hey . . . You here, Girl?

(GIRL ducks behind the pole and hoots like an owl. RICKY enters.)

Dang it, Girl come out! If my Ma finds out I'm not in bed . . .

(GIRL jumps out of the tree and startles him.)

You just made me jump to Jesus!

GIRL: You should have guessed, Ricky, them hoot owls live in trees.

RICKY: It's five o'clock in the morning, and I don't exactly feel like guessing!

(GIRL flips a quarter in the air and catches it.)

GIRL: A dare is a dare and done!

RICKY: My quarter!

GIRL: Nope, my quarter.

RICKY: I was sure you'd get electrocuted doing that dare.

GIRL: A dare ain't a dare unless there's danger. You got the money?

RICKY: I don't know why we had to do this so early. Why couldn't we wait 'till . . .

GIRL: Cause I need the money now!

RICKY: Then hand 'em over.

GIRL: (*Evasive*) Uhhh Ricky, you know how you always wanted a pet, but your Mama wouldn't let you have a dog cause it'd slobber up the house?

RICKY: Yeah.

GIRL: Well, I decided to sell you my frogs.

RICKY: Your frogs?

GIRL: I raised them since they was squiggles, they're good hoppers, and they all got names.

RICKY: Names?

GIRL: I figure frogs with names is worth more than regular.

RICKY: A deal's a deal! You promised to sell me your Tom Mix Wrangler Badge, the Buck Rogers pocket watch, and the Orphan Annie Secret Society code book.

GIRL: I did a million dares to get all that stuff.

RICKY: . . . AND all the seals you collected from the Ovaltine jars.

GIRL: I had to go through all the garbage in the whole city dump to get those . . .

RICKY: Deal's a deal! I also want the Jack Armstrong Whistle Ring!

GIRL: But Jake gave me that whistle, he sent for it with Wheaties box tops.

RICKY: No whistle, no deal.

GIRL: But it's the only thing that ever came through the mail just for me.

RICKY: (*Turning to leave*) Guess you don't want my money.

GIRL: I need that money, Ricky, I need it bad.

RICKY: Not bad enough.

GIRL: You can have the whistle! Hell-fire! You can have anything you want except my quilt piece.

   (*GIRL takes off her whistle-ring and gives it to him. She unfolds her quilt piece which contains her treasures in a small bundle.*)

RICKY: Who'd want that dirty old thing?

GIRL: That shows how much you know! This here's fine embroidery on these here initials: I.S.H. fine embroidery, by someone's own hand!

RICKY: Let's go see those frogs, maybe I'll buy 'em for a penny a piece.

(*RICKY starts out, GIRL follows.*)

GIRL: Penny? They's worth at least a nickle!

RICKY: I kin catch'em myself.

GIRL: With names? Kin you catch them with names . . . and trained?

(*GIRL and RICKY exit. Lights pick up TUC and a CHORUS member. TUC signs.*)

CHORUS: A baby girl found in town.
About thirteen years ago.
People took her in and raised her
Here, and there, and all around.
And so, she goes . . .
In and out of people's houses,
Like so many times before.
She rests a while inside a family,
Until they can't keep her anymore.
And then . . . she goes again.

(*There is the sound of distant thunder. From off stage JAKE is heard.*)

JAKE: Girl! You come here, Girl!

(*He enters carrying a duffle.*)

I want to get off before the storm!

(*GIRL enters at a run, she is clutching an old sock.*)

GIRL: I got it. Jake! I got it!

JAKE: (*Not listening to her*) Now, I told you, I need to be in Cairo by this afternoon and I can't go until I see you safely to the Wards.

GIRL: Sit down, Jake.

JAKE: Ellen and Becca packed up all your things, all they could find.

GIRL: Sit down.

JAKE: No, Girl. This is one time you're not going to get me buffaloed. I've got to get going.

GIRL: No, you don't!

JAKE: Girl, I told you.

GIRL: I got it for you. I got the money.

JAKE: What?

GIRL: I been collecting bottles at a penny a piece; I run groceries for Mr. Eudy, pulled weeds for Miz Snipes, and sold some stuff. I got six dollars and forty-three cents.

(*GIRL hands him the sock proudly. JAKE sits on a stump.*)

JAKE: Girl, that's real fine; and Ella and me, we're grateful, but I need a bit more for the mortgage.

GIRL: How much?

JAKE: Two hundred and fifty six dollars.

GIRL: (*Simply*) That's a lot of frogs.

JAKE: Huh?

GIRL: I kin earn it. I kin get me a real job . . .

JAKE: It's over. They took the farm and they'll sell it for back payments. I can't stay where I can't work.

GIRL: Bob Ricks digs ditches on the county road, Ricky told me.

JAKE: That's a WPA job. WPA stands for "we piddle around!" I wouldn't take a handout from those crooks in Washington if my life depended on it. There are jobs in Cairo, real jobs.

GIRL: (*Pleading*) Take me with you.

JAKE: I can't.

GIRL: I could get a job in Cairo. I could give you and Ellen all the money.

JAKE: I wish we could take you. Hell, I like you better'n some of my own kids. But you're not kin and I can't take responsibility for another living soul right now.

GIRL: I won't take up much room and I won't eat hardly nothing.

JAKE: Girl, neither God nor nature ever sent me anything before that I couldn't handle. Last year, when the flood came, I built a wall with sandbags. When we had that tornado, I knew how to get everyone in the shelter and wait it out. Even a war's got enemies with bullets; but there's something happening in this country now, like a terrible silent storm. I can't see it, or hear it, and I don't know how to fight it, and it scares me.

(*There is a pause. GIRL knows she can't change his mind. He hands her back her money.*)

GIRL: (*Very vulnerable*) I got used to your family, Jake.

JAKE: Hush, now.

GIRL: I never got used to anything before.

(*JAKE pulls out a plug of Red Man chewing tobacco. GIRL holds out her hand for some too.*)

JAKE: Chewing tobacco is one bad habit you'll have to break. Alma Ward will probably have a heard attack first time you spit.

GIRL: (*Suddenly angry*) I ain't going to live with no grave digger.

JAKE: Mortician.

GIRL: He digs graves, don't he?

JAKE: At least, Hosiah Ward will never be out of work.

GIRL: I won't go to the Wards. He smells like chemicals and she's got a face like somebody's foot.

JAKE: Alma Ward is a nice woman and they can afford to give you a good home.

GIRL: I won't go!

JAKE: They're the only one's in town who'll take you. You just about used up everybody else.

GIRL: I'll run away. I'll hitch me a ride to Cairo and I'll find my people.

JAKE: I told you, Girl, we can't . . .

GIRL: I mean my real people!

JAKE: (*He has heard this before*) Oh, Girl . . . You better roll up that tired old dream and put it away. Your people are long gone, or never were.

GIRL: (*Very upset*) That's all you know! Maybe they're rich, Jake! Maybe they got a truck bigger'n yours; maybe they got a family, better'n yours! Maybe they got jobs and lots of money!

JAKE: If they're so rich, how come they never found you?

GIRL: 'Cause I'm hard to find!

   (*She throws the money at him and runs off. He picks it up and takes off after her.*)

JAKE: Dang it, Girl! You come back . . .

   (*Lights return to TUC and CHORUS member. TUC signs.*)

CHORUS: There's a certain kind of spell
In the air, everywhere.
You can tell, very well, that it's fear.
Things begin to disappear.

Gone is the money in the bank.
Gone are the jobs.
Gone are the homes, and the families and their plans.
But they seemed so safe!
But they seemed so sure!
All of a sudden, everybody's poor.

Where did it go?
Who took it all away?

Mother Hicks is a witch, people say.

(*RICKY RICKS enters at a run from the opposite side and nearly collides with TUC. RICKY backs off, frightened, and ducks behind a tree stump. From off-stage his Mother, IZZY, calls.*)

IZZY: Ricky Ricks, you get back here and eat your oatmeal! You'll get it for supper, see if you don't!

(*She enters, sees TUC, shouts and waves to him.*)

TUC! Oh, Tuc, I've got something for you!

(*To herself.*)

I don't know why I do that. I know perfectly well that boy is as deaf as a fire plug, but I always call out to him!

(*She exits as TUC crosses, RICKY pops up and takes aim at TUC with his sling shot. IZZY enters again with a sack of old clothes. RICKY ducks out of sight. IZZY shouts at TUC when she speaks to him.*)

IZZY: (*Shouting*) This here's clothes . . . OLD CLOTHES!

(*She pulls out some overalls.*)

I swear you can see daylight through the knees of these overalls, but I expect you'll find some use for them.

(*TUC takes it, nods, and verbalizes a sound of thanks. He places the sack in his cart.*)

They say he reads lips, but I ain't so sure.

(*IZZY exits, RICKY pops up again and lets a stone fly from the sling shot. It hits TUC in the leg. Just as RICKY is aiming the next shot, TUC turns and catches him. TUC makes a face, RICKY screams and runs off. TUC smiles and comes forward and signs. A CHORUS member speaks for him.*)

TUC: Handed-down people and
Handed-down clothes
Passed from one to another
When the wear starts to show.

They give to feel good,
and then go on their way
They don't know how it feels
To be given away.

(*As TUC has been signing, the rest of the CHORUS sets up CLOVIS P. EUDY'S GENERAL MERCANTILE: a counter with cash register and candy jars, a few barrels, etc. CLOVIS enters with a crate. Whenever he talks to TUC he uses a loud exaggerated tone. TUC reads his lips.*)

CLOVIS: And these crates here, move them over there. Here to there. Understand? Comprendez? Got it?

(*TUC nods. WILSON WALKER enters, just as a horn is heard off-stage.*)

WILSON: (*To CLOVIS*) Excuse me, could you tell me if this place is called Ware?

CLOVIS: This place is called Clovis P. Eudy's General Mercantile; the town's Ware. . . .

(*Horn honks again.*)

. . . and that's the mail truck.

(*CLOVIS exits, WILSON Crosses to TUC who is moving crates.*)

WILSON: I beg your pardon; my name is Wilson Walker and I'm from the University at Carbondale. I'm doing some research on folklore.

(*TUC continues to work, unaware that WILSON is talking to him.*)

I'm collecting tales and legends and stories and sayings, that kind of thing, for a book about this region.

(*TUC notices him and hands him a card which Wilson reads.*)

"My name is TUC. I am deaf and mute."

(*Embarrassed, shouts at TUC.*)

Oh, My God, I'm sorry!

(*TUC turns the card over and hands it back to him. Wilson reads.*)

"Please do not shout. If you speak slowly I can read your lips."

(*Clovis enters.*)

CLOVIS: Leave him alone, he's working.

WILSON: I'm sorry, I didn't realize.

CLOVIS: What do you want?

WILSON: Information.

CLOVIS: Figures; information's free.

WILSON: My name is Wilson Walker and I'm from the Federal Writer's Project.

CLOVIS: From the government?

WILSON: Sort of.

CLOVIS: I've got nothing to say.

(*CLOVIS turns away. Before WILSON can respond, GIRL bursts into the store.*)

GIRL: Mr. Eudy, Mr. Eudy, afternoon mail here yet?

CLOVIS: Still in the bag.

GIRL: Anything for me?

CLOVIS: You think I got X-ray eyes?

GIRL: I'm expecting a very important letter from Jake Hammon; see he promised to send for me, just as soon as he got to Cairo . . .

CLOVIS: Girl, you seen the last of that dirt farmer and his family. Now, the Wards is nice people and you've got a good home . . .

GIRL: It ain't my home!

CLOVIS: Well, you go along there anyway.

GIRL: I can't!

CLOVIS: Why not?

GIRL: They sent me for groceries! Here's the list from the stiff house!

CLOVIS: Girl . . .

GIRL: And one more thing that should be on this list, a plug of Red Man.

CLOVIS: Girl, I can't sell you chewing tobacco. I'll check the mail.

(*CLOVIS touches TUC and hands him the list. They exit. GIRL scopes out WILSON.*)

GIRL: Hi.

WILSON: Hi.

GIRL: You're new around here.

WILSON: Just passing through.

GIRL: You chew?

WILSON: Huh?

GIRL: (*Meaning tobacco*) I don't suppose you chew, do you?

WILSON: Oh yeah, sure. . . . .Have a stick of Wrigley's.

(*WILSON hands her a stick of gum, she takes it but is obviously disappointed.*)

GIRL: Thanks. What's your name?

WILSON: Wilson Walker.

GIRL: Two last names? That's dumb.

WILSON: (*Amused by her*) Oh, yeah? What's yours?

GIRL: Girl.

WILSON: I can see that, what's your name?

GIRL: (*Touching her quilt piece*) Iswa Shunta Ho.

WILSON: Huh?

GIRL: It's a Cherokee name, you know, like these initials here on this Cherokee Indian blanket. I'm practically three quarters Cherokee.

WILSON: So how'd you get over here to Illinois, Cherokee?

GIRL: In a trunk.

WILSON: A trunk?

GIRL: My people was Vaudeville and they was always having babies in trunks and . . .

WILSON: I thought you said they were Cherokee Indian.

GIRL: They was Cherokee vaudeville.

WILSON: Oh! . . . So, where is everybody today, or is the town usually this dead?

GIRL: They're all at the funeral. Zollie Phelps got himself witched.

WILSON: Witched?

GIRL: That's what everybody says.

WILSON: Looks like I came to the right place.

GIRL: Oh, yeah.

WILSON: I hunt witches.

GIRL: Oh, yeah?

WILSON: Yep, I figure I've hunted down fifteen, maybe twenty witches between Carthage and Karnack.

GIRL: What do you use to hunt them with? Cross, silver bullet, holy water, Bible?

WILSON: I trap 'em here in this notebook and hold 'em tight in these pages, so people can read about 'em forever.

GIRL: You talk like a loon.

WILSON: I'm with the WPA . . .

GIRL: WPA? I wouldn't take a handout from those crooks in Washington if my life depended on it!

WILSON: Handout? This is a job!

(*WILSON sits as CLOVIS enters with a letter and package.*)

CLOVIS: Hey Girl.

GIRL: He wrote! I knew he would!

CLOVIS: This letter's for Hosiah and the package from Chicago's for Alma. You might as well take it home with you.

GIRL: I told you it ain't my home.

(*RICKY RICKS enters.*)

RICKY: Afternoon, Mr. Eudy, is my Ma here yet? I'm supposed to meet her here after the funeral.

CLOVIS: She'll be along. I expect they're just getting to the Amens and Hallelujas.

(*CLOVIS turns his back to RICKY who steals a licorice whip, CLOVIS turns just in time to see him.*)

CLOVIS: Did you get any hail over to your place?

RICKY: Yes, sir. Hail stones big as knucklebones.

CLOVIS: Queer time of year for hail.

RICKY: "Hail in June is a Devil's moon", that's what my Ma says.

CLOVIS: I'll check on your order, Girl.

(CLOVIS, exits. RICKY swipes another piece of licorice. He sees GIRL and brandishes his Jack Armstrong whistle ring with a flourish and blows it.)

RICKY: Hey, Girl, want to see a neat ring I got here?

GIRL: Not especially.

(RICKY blows it again just to tease her.)

Hey, Ricky, how about if I come to live at your house for a while?

RICKY: You give me back my quarter?

GIRL: Yeah . . .

(GIRL tosses him the quarter. RICKY takes it.)

RICKY: You kin sleep with the baby. She don't do nothing but cry and make bad smells.

GIRL: Ricky!

(RICKY sniffs in her direction.)

You got a cold, boy?

RICKY: I just wondered if you smelled like the dead yet.

GIRL: Get out of here.

RICKY: Well, you've been staying over to the grave diggers.

GIRL: Ricky, I'm going to bust you one if you don't . . .

(GIRL stops and sniffs herself.)

GIRL: Do I?

RICKY: *(Seriously)* Not so I can tell, of course I never smelled the dead.

GIRL: Neither have I!

RICKY: *(Teasing)* They make you sleep in a coffin?

GIRL: Shut up, Ricky.

RICKY: You ever see any . . . bodies?

GIRL: I'm warning you.

RICKY: Alright!

(*RICKY turns away steals a licorice whip just as IZZY enters.*)

IZZY: Ricky, stop stealing those licorice whips, you know I always wind up paying for them later.

RICKY: I like snitching them better!

IZZY: Ricky!

GIRL: Miz Ricks, I'm going to come and live with you for a while. Ricky said it was okay.

IZZY: But you're staying over with Alma and Hosiah Ward.

GIRL: You don't want me, huh?

IZZY: (*Simply*) We can't afford you, not now, I'm sorry.

(*GIRL turns away. CLOVIS enters.*)

CLOVIS: Morning, Izzy. You feeling any better today?

IZZY: Oh, not hardly. I feel like I'm something sent for that couldn't come. If I didn't know better I'd swear I'd been hexed.

CLOVIS: How was the funeral?

IZZY: Poor old Zollie, he sure did look . . . Oh, I don't know . . . dead. It was witch-work, Clovis, witch-work.

CLOVIS: You think?

IZZY: I know! Last time she come to town, Zollie cursed her for making his cows go dry. From that day on, he was a dead man.

GIRL: Zollie Phelps was a drunk.

IZZY: You watch your mouth, Girl. He was my cousin.

GIRL: Jake Hammond always said, witches was bunk.

IZZY: Well, Jake Hammond didn't know everything, young lady. There's not a sane person in this town would make light of witches, not in witch weather.

GIRL: Witch weather?

IZZY: When its cold like this, long past time for summer; when the thunder clouds roll in and the hail comes like frozen pieces of lightning, then it's Mother Hicks, up to her old tricks.

(*WILSON crosses down to them.*)

WILSON: Excuse me, did you say Mother Hicks?

IZZY: What if I did?

WILSON: My name is Wilson Walker, I'm with the Federal Writer's Project.

IZZY: Federal Writer's Project. I've heard of that! I heard Mrs. Roosevelt talking about it on the radio!

WILSON: Yes Mam, I'm with the Folklore Division: my subject is witchcraft.

CLOVIS: Witchcraft, you say.

WILSON: I was on my way to Jonesboro but I decided to stop and see if I could find out about this Mother Hicks.

IZZY: Well, you better look up on Dug Hill. You won't find her down here in town.

WILSON: People say this Mother Hicks is a witch.

IZZY: Mother Hicks is a witch alright, and she lives all alone at the top of Dug Hill. And most every night at midnight she comes to the graveyard and casts spells with devil dolls and tiny little clothes and tiny little shoes.

WILSON: People say she used to be a midwife.

IZZY: Until she stopped birthing babies and started witching them.

CLOVIS: Babies got sick.

IZZY: Babies died!

CLOVIS: People say she used to have a child herself once.

IZZY: A little girl, but she gave that child to the Devil.

GIRL: Gaw!

   (*RICKY and GIRL listen agape.*)

IZZY: (*Tweeking RICKY'S ear*) Now, don't these little pitchers have the biggest ears?

RICKY: Cut it out, Ma.

GIRL: What about you, Two Names, do you believe in witches?

WILSON: I've collected five notebooks full of stories.

GIRL: Stories or lies?

WILSON: The people who told them, told them as true. I believe every voice in these notebooks.

   (*GIRL takes a notebook from WILSON and glances through it. TUC enters with a box. He works as they talk about him.*)

CLOVIS: You see that poor unfortunate boy?

WILSON: Yes.

CLOVIS: Mother Hicks witched him, when she came to nurse him through the fever.

   (*A hooded figure with a walking stick slowly approaches the STORE. The others, wrapped up in IZZY'S story, do not notice.*)

IZZY: First she nursed him, then she witched him. When he cried that fever cry, she touched his throat and caught that cry; then she looked at him with the evil eye and sucked up his sounds into silence. Mother Hicks is a witch alright.

GIRL: Mother Hicks IS a witch!

WILSON: People say . .

(*The FIGURE raps sharply on the counter with the walking stick. All look up, startled. The FIGURE walks directly to CLOVIS and hands him an empty box of shotgun shells. IZZY and RICKY turn away as she passes. GIRL is frightened but curious. WILSON is confused at first, then fascinated.*)

WILSON: What's going on?

IZZY: Shut up, you damn fool.

WILSON: That's HER, isn't it?

(*WILSON starts to speak to MOTHER HICKS, but she turns toward him and his mouth is dry as ash. She turns back to CLOVIS who hands her a full box of shells. She pays him and exits swiftly.*)

WILSON: (*Starting after her*) I want to talk to her.

(*IZZY grabs his arm.*)

IZZY: Then you go up Dug Hill, all by yourself! Don't you see, she's down here because of the funeral. She must have smelled it all the way up witch mountain.

(*When TUC finishes he touches GIRL who is startled and yells.*)

GIRL: Ahhh!

(*They all jump.*)

You just made me jump to Jesus!

CLOVIS: Your order's ready, Girl. You take the sack and I'll send TUC along later with the heavy things. Now go straight home!

(*CLOVIS exits.*)

WILSON: How do I get to Dug Hill?

IZZY: Just up the Jonesboro road.

WILSON: Good, that's the way I'm headed.

IZZY: But you won't find her, unless she wants to be found. Come on, Ricky. Good-bye, Mr. Wilson.

WILSON: (*Correcting*) Walker.

IZZY: (*Flustered*) Walker . . . Wilson . . . whatever! Goodbye.

(*IZZY exits.*)

WILSON: Thank you, you've been most helpful.

(*WILSON starts out. GIRL still has one of his notebooks.*)

GIRL: Wait!

WILSON: What?

(*GIRL makes a decision to keep the book and hides it.*)

GIRL: Uhhhh, good luck, Two Names.

WILSON: So long Cherokee!

(*WILSON exits. GIRL starts out.*)

RICKY: Hey, Girl, I know the dare of dares, the dare of dares!

GIRL: What?

RICKY: Go to the graveyard late tonight and touch Mother Hicks if she comes.

GIRL: Shut up, Ricky!

RICKY: Dare and double dare?

(*He spits on his hand. Pause.*)

GIRL: Dare and double dare!

(*She spits on her hand and they shake. They exit.*)

(*TUC comes forward and signs. CHORUS member translates.*)

CHORUS: That Girl never does what she is told
Instead she does a dare or two.
Like going down to the railroad track
When the Rock Island Rocket rips through,
Or going down to the quarry pool
Diving deep into cold black wells.
And nobody tries to stop her
Because there's nobody there
To tell her to be careful.

(*During this speech the CHORUS has set up the WARD'S DINING ROOM. ALMA puts the finishing touches on the dinner table. HOSIAH ties his tie, very precisely, looking in a mirror. He checks his watch.*)

HOSIAH: That's it, Alma. We start without her.

ALMA: Just five more minutes, Hosiah. I'm sure she'll be along.

HOSIAH: I've got to be there for the memorial service by 6:55.

ALMA: I'm sure she'll be . . .

(*GIRL enters clutching the bag and the package.*)

Finally, Girl! I was getting worried.

GIRL: (*Heading straight for the table*) Oh, good! Supper's ready! I'm starved!

(*ALMA takes the package from her.*)

Sorry about the package, it got a little ripped up on the barbity wire over to the quarry.

(*ALMA exits into the kitchen with the groceries, she leaves the package on stage.*)

HOSIAH: Do you have any idea what time it is?

GIRL: (*She doesn't*) Uh uh.

HOSIAH: It's 6:08.

GIRL: So?

HOSIAH: In this house dinner is served exactly at six o'clock.

GIRL: Why?

HOSIAH: Because that's dinner time.

GIRL: At Jake's, dinner was whenever you got to the grub.

(*ALMA enters with a plate of food.*)

ALMA: Do you want to change for supper?

GIRL: Change what?

CHORUS: (*A bit amused*) Never mind. You can wash up in the kitchen.

GIRL: Don't need to. I been swimming over to the quarry.

CHORUS: (*On her way back to the kitchen*) But the quarry's closed.

HOSIAH: And there's a big sign saying "No Trespassing."

GIRL: I wasn't trespassing. I was swimming.

HOSIAH: (*Calling out to ALMA*) Remember that memorial service, Alma. They can't get started without the ashes.

GIRL: That's disgusting.

HOSIAH: It's a business.

GIRL: That's disgusting.

HOSIAH: What are we supposed to do, let people decompose wherever they drop dead?

(*ALMA enters with biscuits and hears this.*)

CHORUS: That's disgusting.

(*HOSIAH starts to dish up food with a serving fork.*)

GIRL: I don't see how you can do that.

HOSIAH: Do what?

GIRL: Touch food with hands that have touched the dead.

HOSIAH: I use a fork.

CHORUS: (*Heading off an argument*) Shall we say a blessing?

(*ALL take hands, except GIRL who reaches over HOSIAH'S hand to his wrist. They bow heads.*)

HOSIAH: Bless us, Oh Lord. . . .

(*GIRL isn't used to grace and starts for her food. ALMA catches her eye.*)

. . . For these thy gifts . . .

(*GIRL starts for food again.*)

Which we are about to receive through thy mercy.

GIRL: Now?

CHORUS: Now.

(*GIRL digs in and begins to wolf down her food.*)

ALMA: I heard a queer thing from Izzy today. Folks are having trouble with their milking. Cows have gone dry morning and evening.

GIRL: (*Talking with her mouth full*) I heard how a . . .

HOSIAH: Don't talk with your mouth full.

(*In all innocence, GIRL spits her food into her hand and finishes her sentence.*)

GIRL: I heard once how a witch can milk a cow a mile away by wringing milk out of a clean white dish rag.

(*She pops the food back in her mouth and wipes her hand on her knee. It does not go unnoticed by HOSIAH. ALMA just shakes her head.*)

ALMA: There is entirely too much witch talk in this town.

GIRL: Did you ever see Mother Hicks? People say she comes to the graveyard at midnight and does spells with . . .

ALMA: I don't want you going into the graveyard, Girl, not at night.

HOSIAH: Not at any time. You kids are always knocking over the gravestones and tearing up the plots. If I catch you in that graveyard, you're going to wish I hadn't.

(*GIRL pushes away from the table and pouts.*)

ALMA: Can I give you another biscuit, Girl?

GIRL: No.

HOSIAH: (*Prompting*) No what?

GIRL: No biscuit. I'm not hungry.

(*To break the tension ALMA hands GIRL the package.*)

ALMA: I was going to wait until after supper, but you might as well have this now.

GIRL: That package was for me?

ALMA: Since you've been so careless with this, I've half a mind not to give it to you.

(*GIRL tears into the package and pulls out a new dress. She buries her face in it and smells.*)

GIRL: This is new ain't it?

ALMA: Yes.

GIRL: I kin tell because it don't smell like somebody else yet. I never had a new one, not one of my own.

ALMA: You need a new dress before you start at the big school next fall.

GIRL: I got no use for school. I'm going to Cairo to sell costume jewelry at Woolworths.

HOSIAH: Oh?

ALMA: You'll do no such thing; and speaking of school, we'll have to do something about your name.

GIRL: What about my name?

ALMA: If you're going to the big school you'll have to have a proper name.

GIRL: Why are you always trying to change me?

ALMA: I'm not trying to change you.

(*GIRL tosses aside the dress.*)

GIRL: I like my old things better.

HOSIAH: (*To GIRL*) Pick it up.

ALMA: (*Picking up the dress herself*) I just want you to be comfortable here.

GIRL: How can I be comfortable with you pickin' and peckin' at me all the time. I feel like a bird feeder.

HOSIAH: Young Lady, that is enough!

ALMA: It's alright, Hosiah . .

HOSIAH: It is not alright! She comes into our house like a tornado and acts like a hooligan when you are just trying to give her something.

GIRL: I don't want anything! I don't want anything from YOU!

HOSIAH: Go to your room.

GIRL: It ain't MY room. I'm going out. There's something I've got to do.

HOSIAH: The only thing you're going to do is to get to your room, before I let a spanking teach you some manners! Do you understand?

(*There is a moment of stand-off before GIRL storms off.*)

HOSIAH: (*After a beat*) I told you this wouldn't work, Alma.

ALMA: It might if you weren't so hard on her.

HOSIAH: Hard on her?

ALMA: It will work, we just have to be patient.

HOSIAH: We are just too old to be starting again with children.

(*ALMA turns away, stung by his remark.*)

And that one will tear you up! Alma, that kid was born bad and there's nothing you can do to break her of it.

(*GIRL returns, sneaking out, but she hears the following.*)

ALMA: I can try.

HOSIAH: I give it another week, but then she goes.

ALMA: There's no where else for her to go.

HOSIAH: There's the State Home.

(*GIRL hears this, and exits.*)

ALMA: Not while I have breath.

HOSIAH: The State Home is where that child belongs.

ALMA: Not while I have breath.

(*Lights change and TUC steps into a spot. CHORUS member translates.*)

CHORUS: So I go and follow her.
I have followed her before,
As she runs down darkening streets,
Until she can't run anymore;
Or climbs a huge pecan tree
To try to touch a star.
I am there below in shadow
Never seen, but never far,
Should she fall
Or suddenly be frightened.

Out late, deep into night
She goes to the graveyard
In the pale moonlight.

(*During the last speech the stage has been cleared of everything but the telephone poles. This scene begins in deep shadow. In the distance there is the hooting of an owl and the cry of a loon. Crickets can be heard, softly at first, providing an understated tension. The lighting is eerie in the GRAVEYARD.*)

(*GIRL enters, slowly, frightened. She moves through the graveyard with the utmost care. She stops for a moment and realizes that she is standing on a grave.*)

GIRL: Oh my Lord! I'm standing on one . . . Sorry!

(*She steps aside gingerly.*)

There's no such thing as spooks! There's no such thing as spooks!

(*Far downstage, to one side, GIRL sits and wraps herself in the quilt. She hums softly to herself. TUC enters and watches the following at a distance, from the shadows.*)

(*For a few beats there is only the sound of the crickets. Far upstage left the shrouded, hooded, figure of a woman enters and crosses downstage. She walks neither quickly nor slowly through the graveyard to a specific spot. She carries a basket. Under her breath she is muttering; only the rhythm and an occasional sibilant sound can be heard. The chirping of the crickets grows louder.*)

(*The woman kneels and carefully clears the ground in front of her, meticulously smoothing the earth. She removes a tiny baby dress from the basket, shakes it out, and places it on the ground. She removes a sweater from the basket, shakes it out and places it on top of the dress. A knitted cap, and two tiny soft moccasins are placed precisely in a human form. Suddenly, the women stretches out her arms, catches her breath and slowly lowers herself onto the ground over the clothes. The cricket sound grows.*)

(*GIRL rises slowly and moves toward the woman with an outstretched hand. The woman starts to rise, is aware of the presence and stops. GIRL draws back into the shadow, but she drops her quilt piece. The woman kneels, GIRL makes two feeble attempts to reach the piece and pulls back.*)

(*The woman gathers up the clothes quickly and turns toward the GIRL'S hiding place. She crosses slowly to the quilt piece, stops and picks it up. GIRL is frozen with fear. The woman steps toward GIRL and holds the cloth out to her. The crickets are deafening.*)

(*GIRL reaches for the cloth and there is a split second when they both hold it. GIRL looks up and they make eye contact. The woman drops the cloth, turns and exits back where she came from.*)

(*Gradually the cricket sounds lessen, GIRL steps out of the shadow, looks at the quilt piece and speaks.*)

GIRL: My heart is pounding. Louder than thunder, louder than Jesus. I close my eyes and see her eyes, shooting sparks. A witch can kill with a look. But then I see it, like a match, flare up inside her eyes, like she recognized me, like she knew me forever. And then her eyes go deep as wells and fill up with a kind of sadness.

She recognized me and I recognized her, too. She looked at me and knew me all my life.

(*She looks at the quilt piece.*)

I.S.H . . . H, for Hicks?

(*A loon cries in the distance. HOSIAH and the other CHORUS members appear in the shadows.*)

HOSIAH: I thought I told you to stay out of the graveyard!

GIRL: (*Startled*) Oh.

HOSIAH: Girl, I warned you.

(*HOSIAH turns her over his knee. He spanks her in a stylized manner. He mimes three or four blows; his hand stops short of hitting her as the others clap providing the sound of blows.*)

(*Lights dim all but a spot on GIRL.*)

(*GIRL rises slowly and looks toward the spot where HOSIAH stands in shadow. She pulls out Wilson's notebook.*)

GIRL: Witches are never lonely or afraid because they got the power.

(Light dim. In the dark there is the sound of running water. Lights rise on TUC and a CHORUS member.)

CHORUS: Early one morning, just before dawn,
I hitch up my cart and come down the long road.
Down to the town, from the hill where I stay.
I don't usually see much, but on this one day
I come to a clearing, near a stream and a tree,
And I saw the strangest thing I ever did see.

(The water sound is louder as GIRL enters with a sack. She carefully kneels and mimes the edge of the stream. She tests the cold water with her finger tips and shudders. She takes a white pan and a red knife out of the sack. She opens Wilson's notebook.)

GIRL: *(She opens the notebook and reads)* "This how you get to be a witch . . . Every morning just before dawn from Sabbath to Sabbath, go to a clear cold stream where the water runs east. Take a new white porcelain pan and an old knife gone red with rust. Wash that knife in water and pour a full pan of cold, clear water over your head and give your body to the Devil, saying . . . ."

(GIRL goes through the ritual as she speaks.)

GIRL: I swear that I do give
Everything betwixt my two hands
To the ways of witchcraft.
And I swear to do anything
The witch power asks of me.

(GIRL remains in her position and continues to mime the ritual as the scenes of her "witching" are played around her. It should be clear that she is responsible for the various tricks and pranks, but she need not go through the actual business. TUC signs. CHORUS member speaks.)

CHORUS: That very next day
I followed the Girl as she wandered around.
Strange things started happening
All over town.

Day One. Monday.

(GIRL reads from the notebook.)

GIRL: "To make a witchball, gather up some cow hair, licked with cow spit. Mix with salt and tallow. Get some ashes from a burned down church, gather moss from a tombstone, and roll it all, in a ball, around a little piece of razor."

(*Upstage IZZY enters with a picnic basket. She looks in the basket and screams. ALMA enters quickly.*)

IZZY: Oh, my Gawd! Oh, my Gawd!

CHORUS: What in the world's the matter?

IZZY: Look there, what do you see?

ALMA: Why, Izzy, it looks like your supper for the church social.

IZZY: No, there, on top of the pecan pie! Look on top of the pie!

ALMA: Euuuuuuwwwww, it looks like a bug, a big, black, bug.

IZZY: It's a ball, it's a witch ball!

(*GIRL laughs. She remains in her position and repeats the ritual as the scenes of her witching are played behind her. TUC signs each day as it passes.*)

CHORUS: (*For TUC*) Day Two, Tuesday.

GIRL: (*Reading from the notebook*) "A spell is done by placing a witch wreath inside the hat of the person fer hex. The spell will grow around the person's head and he is sure to go mad."

(*Lights up on HOSIAH and CLOVIS.*)

HOSIAH: It's a what?

CLOVIS: A witch wreath, made with feathers from a black hen.

HOSIAH: And you pulled that thing out of my hat?

CLOVIS: I think those headaches will stop now, Hosiah.

HOSIAH: You mean to tell me that bunch of feathers did a spell that caused my headaches?

CLOVIS: Nope, made your hat fit too tight.

CHORUS: (*For TUC*) Day Three, Wednesday.

GIRL: (*Reading*) "A witch can turn herself into a black panther cat and prowl around unnoticed. If that cat steals something from someone, the witch will have power over them for sure."

(*GIRL looks devilish and meows. IZZY crosses to CLOVIS.*)

IZZY: I tell you it was a cat, a big black panther cat, an unnaturally large panther cat and I heard it prowling around my washline and it stole a pair of my . . . personals.

CLOVIS: Now, let me get this straight. A cat stole your drawers and ever since, your vision's blurred, there's a ringing in your ears, you've got the chills, the shakes, the faints, and gas?

IZZY: That's right, Clovis.

CLOVIS: But Doc Gunner says there's not a thing wrong with you.

IZZY: That's how I know I'm doomed. When the Doctor can't find a thing wrong it's a sign that a person is witched. She's up to her old tricks.

CLOVIS: Mother Hicks?

IZZY: Mother Hicks!

(*From here to the end of the scene, a low muttering of "Mother Hicks" builds.*)

CHORUS: (*For TUC*) Day Four, Thursday.

GIRL: (*Showing signs of illness*)
I swear that I do give
Everything betwixt my two hands
To the ways of witchcraft . . .

(*ALMA crosses to CLOVIS.*)

ALMA: When I woke the Girl for school yesterday, she was burning up with fever, her hair was all wet and she was cold and clammy.

CLOVIS: What does Doc Gunner say?

ALMA: He's afraid it's pneumonia.

CLOVIS: Put a silver bullet in a bag and tie it around her neck.

ALMA: Whatever for?

CLOVIS: To protect her from witches.

ALMA: Doc Gunner says it's pneumonia.

(Muttering increases. GIRL is really ill as she goes through the witch ritual.)

CHORUS: *(For TUC)* Day Five, Friday.

GIRL: I swear that I do give . . .

(IZZY crosses to CLOVIS, ALMA turns away.)

IZZY: It just has to be Mother Hicks, Clovis. We've all been hexed by Mother Hicks.

CLOVIS: It's just like it was in 1925.

IZZY: But in 1925 they all died!

(Muttering increases, ALMA, very upset, crosses to HOSIAH.)

CHORUS: *(For TUC)* Day Six, Saturday!

ALMA: Girl is going to the hospital, and she is going today!

HOSIAH: Doc Gunner say's she's better off here at home.

ALMA: But she's delirious! This morning she woke up screaming something about witchcraft!

(Muttering increases to a chant of "Mother Hicks . . . Mother Hicks" TUC signs.)

CHORUS: *(For TUC)* Day seven, the second Sabbath!

(GIRL is nearly delirious, she kneels by the stream and forces herself through the ritual. Throughout the next few lines, TUC signs the numbers 1–7 as the scene builds in intensity.)

GIRL: I swear that I do give
Everything . . .

IZZY: It's a witchball!

GIRL: Everything . . .

HOSIAH: I got these headaches!

GIRL: Everything . . .

ALMA: It's pneumonia!

GIRL: Everything!

CLOVIS: They all died!

GIRL: Everything betwixt my two hands
To the ways of witchcraft

   (*Chanting builds to a crescendo.*)

And I swear to do anything
The witch power asks of me!

ALMA: (*Rising above the others*) THIS HAS GOT TO STOP!

   (*Silence. GIRL picks up the notebook and reads, she is ill.*)

GIRL: "Take a rust red knife
And cut the head off a living thing
Where the blood falls
The Devil will appear
And welcome you as a witch."

But I don't want to be that kind of witch, the kind of witch that kills
things.

   (*She is exhausted and wraps her arms around her knees and holds herself
together. She spies a flower growing nearby.*)

A flower is a living thing!

   (*She plucks the flower and holds it in front of her as she brandishes the
knife.*)

I swear that I do give
Everything betwixt my two hands
To the ways of witchcraft.
And I swear to do anything . . .

(*She brings the knife slashing down, misses the flower, but cuts a deep gash in her leg. It is a serious wound and blood flows down her leg. She grabs at her leg in shock.*)

GIRL: I cut myself . . . bad! I cut myself!

(*TUC rushes from the shadows where he has been watching her. She sees him and screams. She faints, he catches her and lifts her up in his arms. Just as he turns upstage, a spot comes up on the shrouded figure from the grave-yard. MOTHER HICKS holds her arms out as TUC turns toward her. BLACKOUT.*)

End of Act I

Act Two

MOTHER HICKS' cabin on Dug Hill.

With the addition of poles and canvas panels, TUC'S wagon is transformed into the cabin. All around are ceramic pots, baskets, jugs and small cages. Atop one of the poles is a wren roost. The area is lit by firelight from a large permanent campfire and several kerosene lamps around and about. A large smoking cauldron hangs above the campfire. Near the cauldron is a rocking chair.
Stage left is a makeshift pallet. GIRL is asleep, wrapped tightly in blankets. She wears an old flannel shirt and sleeps fitfully. Near the pallet, TUC squats on his heels and watches GIRL. He has been there some time, keeping a silent vigil.
GIRL stirs and moans and begins to cough deeply. TUC rises and fetches MOTHER HICKS from the cabin. She crosses to the steaming cauldron and stirs a smoking cupful of the brew into a bowl. She crosses to GIRL and hands the bowl to TUC who puts it to GIRL'S lips.

MOTHER HICKS: Drink this.

GIRL: Don't hurt me.

MOTHER HICKS: Hesh.

GIRL: Where am I?

MOTHER HICKS: Dug Hill.

GIRL: I know who you are! You're . . .

MOTHER HICKS: (*Cutting her off*) Drink!

GIRL: No!

MOTHER HICKS: Drink it or you'll strangle on your own flem.

   (*MOTHER HICKS makes a sharp sign to TUC; together they make GIRL drink the brew. MOTHER HICKS strokes GIRL'S throat the way she might help an injured animal to swallow.*)

GIRL: What is it?

MOTHER HICKS: Brew of scaley bark, pokeweed, and rattlesnake yarb.

GIRL: Tastes terrible.

MOTHER HICKS: Better'n dying.

   (*MOTHER HICKS bends over her and loosens the blankets.*)

GIRL: This ain't my shirt. It smells foul.

MOTHER HICKS: Greased it good with hog fat and nutmeg.

GIRL: Why?

MOTHER HICKS: Reasons.

   (*MOTHER HICKS draws back the cover and reveals the leg wound covered with a thick yellow mud.*)

Time again.

   (*MOTHER HICKS draws a large hunting knife and passes the blade through the fire. GIRL sees this and struggles.*)

Hold her.

(MOTHER HICKS signs as she speaks to TUC, she repeats both the sign and the words with urgency.)

HOLD HER!

(MOTHER HICKS approaches with the knife. GIRL struggles as TUC holds her down.)

GIRL: Don't touch me! Don't hurt . . .

MOTHER HICKS: Hold Still!

(In one swift motion, MOTHER HICKS flips the mudpack off revealing a long healing scar. She crosses to the fire and reaches into a small bowl.)

GIRL: What's that?

MOTHER HICKS: Hot yellow mud and vinegar, to draw the poison.

(MOTHER HICKS slaps the poultice on GIRL'S leg. GIRL cries out.)

GIRL: Owwwwww!

MOTHER HICKS: Hesh up, you're not hurt. You're not hurt are you?

(For the first time GIRL realizes that she isn't.)

GIRL: Some.

MOTHER HICKS: If I can't stop the festering, I'll have to cut it off.

GIRL: The mud?

MOTHER HICKS: The leg.

GIRL: No!

(GIRL struggles again. MOTHER HICKS signs to TUC to hold her.)

MOTHER HICKS: Now settle down and let that poultice dry. I'll have to tie you down if you don't.

(GIRL stops struggling and TUC and MOTHER HICKS wrap her up in the blankets. MOTHER HICKS rises and checks the sky. As she speaks to TUC, she signs.)

We'll leave her out here while the weather holds; inside smells like skunk.

GIRL: What are you going to do with me?

MOTHER HICKS: (*With a crooked grin*) Girl, I am doing with you now.

(*MOTHER HICKS exits into the cabin. GIRL sinks back down as TUC resumes his watch. Lights dim.*)

(*Pause.*)

(*In the darkness a shrieking sound is heard. It is just dawn, the sky is a bluish-red. MOTHER HICKS is kneeling over a large box. TUC sits in the chair holding a lantern over her work. The shrieking sound comes from the box as does a thumping sound of struggle.*)

MOTHER HICKS: Hesh, Sister Kicker, hesh. 1, 2, 3, 4, 5 alive and come this dead one stuck. There ain't no help for it, Sister Kicker, there ain't no help.

(*GIRL wakes and sits up. MOTHER HICKS pulls the lantern towards her and lifts the chimney, she passes the blade through the flame.*)

GIRL: What are you doing?

MOTHER HICKS: Stay away!

GIRL: What's happening?

MOTHER HICKS: I said, stay . . .

(*TUC is distracted and pulls the light away. MOTHER HICKS jerks his arm back.*)

Light, I need light!

GIRL: Stop it, please, whatever you're doing, stop it!

MOTHER HICKS: I can't.

(*At TUC's encouragement, GIRL inches toward them, horrified but fascinated at what is happening inside the box. MOTHER HICKS returns to the task at hand.*)

MOTHER HICKS: There, got it!

(*MOTHER HICKS hands the knife to TUC and returns her attention to the box.*)

Now, let 'em come. Snip, snip, snip and clip 'em off. Clip 'em clean!

(*After a beat, the sound subsides MOTHER HICKS wipes her hands they are covered with blood.*)

GIRL: There's blood.

MOTHER HICKS: There always blood at a birthing.

(*GIRL peers into the box.*)

GIRL: A rabbit?

MOTHER HICKS: Rabbits.

GIRL: I never heard a rabbit make such a sound before.

MOTHER HICKS: They only do when they're mortal scared or hurt.

GIRL: How many babies?

MOTHER HICKS: Five alive, three dead.

(*MOTHER HICKS tosses three tiny objects into a pail.*)

GIRL: (*Pulling at the box*) Can I see?

MOTHER HICKS: (*Protectively*) If she gets riled, she'll eat 'em.

GIRL: Eat her own babies?

MOTHER HICKS: (*Peering into the box*) Now, look at that, she's pushing them away, won't let them even get close to her.

GIRL: Why won't she nurse them?

MOTHER HICKS: Who knows why some critters don't take to their young? No reason, they just don't.

GIRL: Will she ever?

MOTHER HICKS: Likely not.

(*MOTHER HICKS stands and stretches.*)

MOTHER HICKS: Looks like the sky is getting ready to make itself a dawn. Come here!

(*MOTHER HICKS checks the fever. GIRL pulls away.*)

I said, come here! The fever's broke . . . Good. But get back to bed before it's light.

(*TUC carries her to the pallet.*)

GIRL: Can I name the rabbits?

MOTHER HICKS: No, but you can help.

(*TUC sets her gently down and hands her the quilt piece tucked under her pillow. She is very pleased to see it.*)

GIRL: My quilt piece!

MOTHER HICKS: Go to sleep!

(*GIRL goes back to sleep, lights dim.*)

(*Pause.*)

(*After beat there is the sound of chirping birds, lights rise on a morning scene. MOTHER HICKS kneels with several basins and baskets near her. She lifts an article of clothing out of a basin and wrings white liquid out of it. She shakes it out and we see it is a baby dress.*)

MOTHER HICKS: (*To the dress*) So, there you are, all fresh and clean; all fresh and clean to go visiting. Tonight we'll go, just like I promised. Tonight we'll go.

(*Accidentally she squirts some water on herself. GIRL wakes and listens.*)

None of that splashing, you hear?

(*She splashes more water and laughs.*)

And no spitting either!

(*GIRL sits up.*)

Now, stop, I say, stop! If you can't keep from dousing your own . . .

(*She is suddenly aware of GIRL.*)

What are you peeping at?

GIRL: Nothing.

MOTHER HICKS: You call me nothing?

GIRL: I didn't see nothing.

MOTHER HICKS: And if lies was food, there'd be no hunger in the world!

(*MOTHER HICKS lifts out another article and wrings soapy water out of it.*)

GIRL: I know what you're doing!

MOTHER HICKS: What?

GIRL: You're milking a cow by magic!

(*MOTHER HICKS pours a basin of soapy water into a bucket.*)

MOTHER HICKS: (*Gruff*) This here's laundry! I save the soapy water for my yarbs!

GIRL: Oh . . . If it's laundry I can help.

(*GIRL limps over to MOTHER HICKS and tentatively takes an article and wraps it in a flannel cloth.*)

I can take these flannel pieces and use 'em to wring the water out . . . These is baby clothes!

MOTHER HICKS: They is.

GIRL: There was all kinds of babies over at Jakes. Jakes is where I used to stay, and I used to love to play with 'em. They was all soft and white and plumped up, like dough before it's baked; soft little bread babies.

(*She works as she speaks.*)

This sure is fine linen, I can see right through it.

MOTHER HICKS: You be careful, mind?

GIRL: I mind.

MOTHER HICKS: Oncet there was a girl who wore that dress, and she had hair colored hair. You know how some folks go on about children and say they got hair blond as gold, or eyes blue as sky? Well, this little girl had hair colored hair, and eye colored eyes and she were beautiful.

GIRL: (*The question is important to her*) What happened to that girl?

MOTHER HICKS: (*Bitter*) Gone, taken with the rest.

GIRL: Gone where?

MOTHER HICKS: Just gone!

GIRL: Taken by who? Where was she taken?

MOTHER HICKS: (*Snaps at her*) Watch how you touch that piece, you're strangling the life out of it.

GIRL: But I want to know!

MOTHER HICKS: Well, wantin' ain't gettin'!

(*TUC enters at a run, laughing and gesturing to MOTHER HICKS.*)

What in the . . .

(*TUC signs something to her.*)

I don't know.

(*TUC signs something else and they both laugh.*)

GIRL: (*Mystified*) What are you laughing at?

MOTHER HICKS: This here fool.

GIRL: Jake always told me it weren't nice to laugh at him just because he's afflicted.

MOTHER HICKS: He told me a riddle.

GIRL: What?

MOTHER HICKS: He just made it up.

(*TUC signs as MOTHER HICKS speaks.*)

MOTHER HICKS: What looks just like half a chicken?

GIRL: What?

MOTHER HICKS: (*As TUC signs*) The other half.

(*They both laugh, GIRL is mystified.*)

GIRL: He told you that?

MOTHER HICKS: He did.

GIRL: How?

MOTHER HICKS: With them air pictures.

GIRL: You mean, all that fingering around means things?

MOTHER HICKS: (*Signs as she speaks*) They teached him that over to the State School where he learned to lip talk. After he left the school and his people died, he came around here and just stayed. He teached me some he learned at school, and I teached him some, I made up, and we just built ourselves a talking way.

(*TUC signs to her in a very animated manner, GIRL is a bit taken aback.*)

GIRL: What's he doing now?

MOTHER HICKS: He's talking to you.

GIRL: To me?

MOTHER HICKS: He's trying to tell you something, but you're too ignorant to understand.

GIRL: I am not ignorant!

MOTHER HICKS: In his talk you are. He said . . .

(*TUC signs and MOTHER HICKS translates.*)

You are my friend.

GIRL: Oh.

(*TUC continues signing.*)

What's he saying now?

(*TUC signs the following speech as MOTHER HICKS translates. She places emphasis on what is being said rather than a word by word translation of the signs.*)

MOTHER HICKS: You look at me and only see things I cannot do, things I cannot be; but I can taste the cool spring water and know what month it is, I can smell the difference between the smoke of hickory and apple wood. I can see the sharp sting of honey, and I can taste the sunrise.

GIRL: Doesn't he mean he can taste the honey and see the sunrise?

MOTHER HICKS: He means what he says, that's the trouble with you town folks; you see and you hear, but you don't know nothing!

GIRL: Down in town, nobody knows he stays up here.

MOTHER HICKS: (*Suddenly bitter*) I don't much care what they know in town.

(*TUC signs something.*)

GIRL: What did he say?

MOTHER HICKS: He asked if we could put your old shirt on. You smell like a buzzard egg gone bad.

GIRL: (*Sniffing herself*) I do.

MOTHER HICKS: Fever's broke, so I guess it will be alright. Go in, it's in the cabin.

(*GIRL starts limping to cabin.*)

Hey, watch how you step on that leg!

(*GIRL hops into the cabin, there is the sound of geese and other animals. TUC signs to her. She speaks and signs in response.*)

No, Tuc, as soon as she's well, she'll leave.

(*TUC signs.*)

She's just here for a spell.

(*TUC, agitated, signs again.*)

All critters come for the healing and then go.

(*TUC signs and she pats his cheek.*)

I know, Tuc, you stayed.

(*GIRL comes out from the cabin wearing her own shirt.*)

GIRL: There's a whole zoo in there!

MOTHER HICKS: Just the geese, a squirrel or two, and a family of skunks.

GIRL: Skunks?

(*TUC signs to GIRL.*)

Is he talking to me?

MOTHER HICKS: It appears that way.

GIRL: What's he saying?

MOTHER HICKS: I already told you that once! You got the memory of a piss ant.

GIRL: (*Understands*) OH!

(*She slowly repeats the sign.*)

You are my friend.

(*TUC signs "yes."*)

MOTHER HICKS: Look, I can't sit around here jaw jacking with you two. I got work to do.

GIRL: (*Curiosity peaked*) Are you going to do . . . secret things?

MOTHER HICKS: (*Mysteriously*) I am going to hang up this here laundry . . .

(*Sharply*) . . .

if that is any of your business!

GIRL: I just wondered . . .

MOTHER HICKS: If you want to make yourself some use you can feed the rabbits and see if you can find their names.

GIRL: But I want to name them myself.

MOTHER HICKS: Every critter's got its own name inside 'em; you can't just make it up, but if you watch 'em close enough sometimes you can find it.

GIRL: I don't understand.

MOTHER HICKS: Don't matter, the rabbits do.

(*MOTHER HICKS exits with laundry. GIRL and TUC cross down to the rabbit box. GIRL tenderly takes a tiny rabbit from the box and she and TUC feed it with an eye dropper and a bowl of warm milk.*)

GIRL: (*To TUC, pointing to the bunny*) Sure is ugly, ain't it? Looks like a rat!

(*TUC teaches her the sign for rat. With TUC'S help she feeds the bunny with an eye dropper.*)

Wouldn't it be something if you could remember that far back, when you was as young as they is? If you could remember lying there and all of a sudden you see this big old milk nipple coming towards you and WHAM . . . . supper!

(She squirts the rest of the milk into her own mouth.)

Sometimes I can remember back that far, I really can.

(She puts the bunny back in the box.)

I can just barely see hair colored hair and eye colored eyes . . .

(GIRL turns directly to TUC.)

You remember your people, Tuc? Your Paw and your Momma?

(TUC signs yes.)

They're dead ain't they?

(TUC signs yes.)

You're lucky . . . . Not on account of them being dead, that part's sad, but lucky you know where they are. You can close your eyes and see 'em live inside your mind. When you don't know about 'em . . . when you don't know, there's always something inside you that's hungry.

(GIRL notices TUC staring at her.)

When I see you staring at me, your eyes so big and round, I think I could fall right inside both your eyes and never be seen again.

(TUC looks puzzled.)

GIRL: Oh, don't mind me, I'm just talking loon talk. Loon talk, that's me!

(GIRL makes a circle near her ear and crosses her eyes, TUC copies her gesture rolls over and laughs. MOTHER HICKS enters and spreads out the flannels, pours the soapy water into a bucket and generally busies herself. GIRL crosses to her.)

GIRL: Will you teach me things?

(*MOTHER HICKS does not respond.*)

Teach me secret things?

MOTHER HICKS: Don't know any secret things.

GIRL: Some people call this place witch mountain.

MOTHER HICKS: Some people are stupid.

GIRL: I want to show you something, something special.

(*GIRL fetches her quilt piece and holds it out to her. MOTHER HICKS focuses on her tasks.*)

Have you ever seen this piece before?

MOTHER HICKS: Yep.

GIRL: You have?

MOTHER HICKS: When you first came, I practically had to pry it out of your hand.

GIRL: I mean before that, have you ever seen this before that?

MOTHER HICKS: (*Uncomfortable*) I don't know, maybe, maybe not.

GIRL: I had this with me ever since I was born and see these intials here, these are sewn on with someone's own hand, and they stand for my name, see here, I.S.H. . . . what do you think the H could stand for?

(*MOTHER HICKS crosses to the rabbit box, GIRL follows her.*)

MOTHER HICKS: (*Annoyed*) I told you, I don't know! Now, cut out the jaw jacking; You are gettin' these rabbits riled.

(*MOTHER HICKS places the eye dropper in GIRL'S hand and tries to get her to concentrate on the rabbits. GIRL still wants answers.*)

GIRL: You could teach me things.

MOTHER HICKS: (*Exasperated*) I wish someone had teached you how to feed a rabbit, you're squirting it up its nose! I swear of all the critters I got here you make the most noise and the least sense!

(*MOTHER HICKS stands and crosses to the bucket.*)

Now, I am going to water my yarbs and I want you to stay put!

(*She signs to TUC gruffly.*)

Watch her!

(*MOTHER HICKS exits, GIRL pouts and sits in the rocking chair.*)

GIRL: Is she always so mean?

(*TUC turns her face to look at his.*)

Is she always so mean?

(*TUC shakes his head no and signs something more complex.*)

I don't understand.

(*TUC signs "MOTHER HICKS," but GIRL does not understand until he mimes her movements and GIRL figures it out.*)

Mother Hicks!

(*TUC teaches GIRL the sign for "Mother Hicks."*)

GIRL: Mother Hicks.

(*TUC does the sign for "earth." GIRL does not understand, so he gives her hints with gestures.*)

Dirt.

(*He continues with different hints until GIRL guesses correctly.*)

Dirt, ground, world, earth!

(*TUC repeats "Mother Hicks" and "earth."*)

Mother Hicks . . . earth!

(*TUC nods and signs "and."*)

And.

 (*TUC nods and signs "air."*)

Wind, blow, all over, AIR!

 (*TUC nods and repeats all three signs.*)

Mother Hicks . . . earth and air!

 (*TUC nods and signs "and."*)

And . . .

 (*TUC signs "fire" and points to campfire.*)

GIRL: FIRE!

 (*TUC signs "and."*)

And

 (*TUC signs "water" and gestures.*)

Water!

 (*TUC nods and repeats all the signs. GIRL tries to copy but tries to go too fast. TUC laughs and slows her down.*)

Mother Hicks, earth, and air, and fire, and water . . .

 (*TUC signs "and."*)

And

 (*TUC signs "blood." GIRL finally guesses it.*)

Cut, ... blood!

 (*TUC signs "and."*)

And . . .

 (*TUC signs "tears," tracing a tear down his cheek and then down GIRL'S cheek.*)

Tears.

(TUC and GIRL repeat the whole sequence, as they do, the words and signs take on meaning and deep significance for her.)

GIRL: Mother Hicks IS earth, and air, and fire, and water, and blood, and tears. Mother Hicks is . . .

(TUC signs "everything." GIRL does not understand until he makes a more sweeping gesture.)

Everything!

(TUC signs "yes" as the lights dim.)

(Pause.)

(A spot comes up on TUC as he moves into it and signs. A CHORUS member enters and speaks.)

CHORUS: But soon there came the morning when
It was time for me to go to town again.
I didn't want to go.
I was afraid somehow they'd know
That Girl was here with us, and then
They'd make me bring her back again.

(TUC moves a bit nearer to her and watches her sleep.)

That morning, before I left,
I stood and watched her sleep.
I pressed my thoughts and feelings deep
Inside my memory.

(Lights dim on GIRL.)

(Lights quickly come up on another area of the stage which indicates CLOVIS' store. The following scenes are played in fragmentary rapid succession similar to the witching scene at the end of Act I.)

(TUC moves through the groups of townspeople catching fragments of their conversations.)

CLOVIS: (*To TUC*) And where in the blazes have you been? Take a little vacation did you? This whole town's been going to Hell and my stock boy decides to take himself a vacation!

(*ALMA joins them.*)

CHORUS: Morning, Clovis, any news?

CLOVIS: I went to the highway patrol station on my way in this morning. They haven't seen her, but they suggested you call the State Home, they keep runaways there sometimes. I'll call if you like.

ALMA: Thank you, Clovis, I'm grateful for your help.

CLOVIS: (*To TUC*) I got a week's worth of stock piled up, get with it, Boy!

(*Lights up on IZZY and ALMA.*)

IZZY: So, where's Hosiah off to in such a hurry?

ALMA: He's going to Cairo, he figures that's where Girl went looking for the Hammons.

IZZY: The whole time she was with them, they just let her run wild, let all those kids run wild, just wild things! Now, I'm sure that's where she went!

ALMA: She had pneumonia, she wouldn't have made it as far as the county line!

(*HOSIAH enters, ALMA rushes to him.*)

ALMA: Did you find her?

HOSIAH: Fool's errand! I been to the Cairo employment office, the welfare department, and I called every Hammon in the whole city and not one has ever heard of Jake or the Girl.

(*She turns away.*)

Alma, we've tried to find her.

ALMA: Not hard enough!

HOSIAH: There's nothing more we can do.

ALMA: When our boy was born dead, there was nothing we could do. When the scarlet fever took Sarah, there was nothing we could do, but this time, Hosiah, this time there *is* something we can do. We can keep looking!

(*TUC starts to exit and CLOVIS crosses to him and stops him.*)

CLOVIS: Hey, hey, hey! Where do you think you're going?

(*TUC tries to sign something.*)

Don't you go waggling your fingers at me.

(*CLOVIS finds a plug of Red Man chewing tobacco in TUC'S top pocket of his overalls.*)

Got yourself a new habit, Boy?

(*TUC shakes his head.*)

Help yourself, did you?

(*TUC indicates he paid for it.*)

What's the matter with you, boy. What's the matter with you anyway?

(*Lights dim to a spot. TUC signs, CHORUS member speaks.*)

CHORUS: Home late, long into night,
Winding up the trail in the pale moonlight
With a feeling deep inside
Makes me want to run and hide.
So, I turn . . . nothing.
And I turn . . . no one.
Then I turn and I see
There ain't no one there but me,
But I run anyway.

(*Lights come up on the cabin. MOTHER HICKS sits near the fire, braiding GIRL'S hair. We hear the sound of tree toads.*)

(*TUC enters at a run and grabs GIRL'S blanket and runs into the cabin with it.*)

MOTHER HICKS: Hey!

GIRL: What's going on?

MOTHER HICKS: I don't know, but I aim to find out!

(*TUC runs out of the cabin again.*)

Whoa! Care to tell me what you're doing?

(*TUC signs something.*)

She can't sleep in there 'cause I got a whole family of rackity coons that won't take too kindly to being disturbed just because you got the willies!

GIRL: What's the matter?

MOTHER HICKS: He's just got the jumps.

(*To TUC.*)

Now come and eat, you got black beans . . . burnt black beans. Now, sit and eat before you start making me feel goosey.

(*TUC takes his bowl of beans but keeps a watchful eye all around. MOTHER HICKS sits in her chair and weaves a basket. TUC tosses GIRL the plug of Red Man.*)

GIRL: Hey, thanks! You was over in town today?

(*TUC signs "yes."*)

Anything going on? Anyone say anything, you know, about me?

(*TUC pauses and signs "no."*)

Nobody?

(*TUC repeats the "no."*)

My whole life, I lived in that town and now, they don't even notice once I'm gone.

MOTHER HICKS: Down in town is a mighty measley place.

GIRL: But it's different here.

MOTHER HICKS: Here, my walls is made of tar paper, so creatures can come and go. There ain't no keepin' out and there ain't no holdin' in.

GIRL: (*Starting to take a plug of tobacco*) Why do the animals come here?

MOTHER HICKS: They come for the healing, when there's a fester to lance, or something broken to be bound up or cut away. They come when they can't do for themselves.

(*MOTHER HICKS crosses to GIRL and holds out her hand for the tobacco. GIRL gives it to her.*)

GIRL: And after? What happens after they's well?

MOTHER HICKS: Tuc and me, we watch 'em close and find their names, then they can go and we'll always know 'em again.

(*To TUC.*)

Now you bring back that bedding, so this little chicken can roost!

(*TUC exits into the house.*)

GIRL: What if an . . . animal doesn't want to go?

MOTHER HICKS: Sooner or later they do, they all do.

(*TUC enters with blankets and crosses back into the cabin.*)

GIRL: Will you wrap me up tight in them blankets, like when I first came here?

MOTHER HICKS: Why?

GIRL: I kinda feel like I'm a little tiny worm, all wrapped up in a cocoon.

MOTHER HICKS: Well, I ain't going to be expecting no butterflies at breakfast.

(*TUC enters with a shot gun.*)

MOTHER HICKS: And what do you think you're doing with that?

(*TUC signs "guarding."*)

MOTHER HICKS: Guarding? Against what?

GIRL: Something's wrong isn't it?

MOTHER HICKS: Sleep tight, Little Rabbit, and don't worry about nothing, lessen it's Daniel Boone over there shooting his own foot off.

(*There is a rustling sound.*)

GIRL: I heard something.

MOTHER HICKS: What?

GIRL: I thought I heard something over there.

(*CLOVIS steps out of shadow.*)

MOTHER HICKS: Who's there? I said, who's there?

CLOVIS: So it is you, and you've got . . .

(*TUC sees CLOVIS and shoots the shotgun in the air. CLOVIS turns and runs.*)

MOTHER HICKS: Tuc, you damned fool!

(*TUC starts to run after him and she snatches the gun away. TUC follows CLOVIS.*)

Tuc, it ain't no use!

(*Lights dim and come up immediately on the town. CLOVIS enters at a run. There is the sound of a bell ringing over and over. HOSIAH and ALMA cross over to CLOVIS.*)

ALMA: Clovis, that's the night bell, we only use it for emergencies.

CLOVIS: This is an emergency. I found her. I found the Girl.

ALMA: Where?

CLOVIS: Up on Dug Hill.

ALMA: Was she all right?

CLOVIS: I didn't get a good look.

ALMA: I am calling the State Police.

HOSIAH: Them state troopers don't take too kindly to witch stories or to trespassing!

CLOVIS: Trespassing? We are talking about kidnapping.

(*Lights up on IZZY she is holding a telephone receiver. ALMA and HOSIAH turn their backs.*)

IZZY: We are talking about witchcraft, Clovis.

(*CLOVIS steps into a pool of light. He also has a phone receiver.*)

CLOVIS: And then she said to Hosiah and me, "You can sit around here jaw jacking, but I'm going up that hill."

IZZY: Tonight? She's going up there tonight?

(*ALMA turns around.*)

ALMA: And don't you dare try to stop me, Hosiah Ward!

(*HOSIAH turns around.*)

HOSIAH: How do we know she was taken up there? How do we know she didn't just go.

ALMA: We won't unless we go up that hill.

(*ALMA and HOSIAH turn their backs.*)

CLOVIS: (*Into the phone*) And then she asked me to show her the way. When I hesitated she said . . .

ALMA: (*Turning front*) Clovis, I do believe you're scared.

IZZY: (*Into the phone*) It just makes sense to be scared when you're dealing with a witch.

CLOVIS: (*Into the phone*) Dealing with a shot gun!

ALMA: If you won't come with me, I swear I'll go alone.

CLOVIS: (*Into the phone*) So, I told her I'd go.

IZZY: (*Into the phone*) Clovis P. Eudy! If you think I'm going to go traipsing up witch mountain in my condition . . .

CLOVIS: (*Into the phone*) And miss everything?

(*Lights out on CLOVIS and IZZY. There is tension between ALMA and HOSIAH.*)

ALMA: You don't want her to come back, do you?

HOSIAH: Oh, Alma.

ALMA: Do you?

HOSIAH: Not if she's just going to leave again. I don't want her to hurt you that way.

ALMA: I'll be alright and I have to know that she's all right.

(*She touches his cheek. He nods.*)

HOSIAH: I'll need my climbing boots.

ALMA: Better bring mine too . . . And Hosiah, you better bring your gun.

(*He nods and exits as lights change back to the cabin.*)

(*GIRL is asleep on her pallet. MOTHER HICKS paces. TUC enters, out of breath and signing wildly.*)

MOTHER HICKS: Slow down, I can't follow you . . . slow down.

(*TUC takes a breath and signs.*)

When?

(TUC signs something.)

But why?

(TUC signs.)

But they ain't got no cause, they ain't got no right.

(GIRL wakes and sits up.)

GIRL: *(Alarmed)* What's going on?

MOTHER HICKS: *(To TUC)* And they've got guns? Damned fools!

GIRL: What is it? What's happened?

(TUC runs into the cabin.)

MOTHER HICKS: Tuc says some folks from town is on their way up here, he says they're riled and they got guns.

GIRL: But why?

MOTHER HICKS: Something to do with you.

GIRL: Let's witch 'em. All of 'em. Let's you and I witch 'em all.

MOTHER HICKS: What did you say?

GIRL: Let's throw them a spell to turn the road to slime and let 'em slide all the way back down to Main Street.

MOTHER HICKS: Hesh up, you fool.

GIRL: You can do it, and I can help. I know who I am.

MOTHER HICKS: You don't know anything!

GIRL: Yes, I do!

(Mimes the witch ritual.)

I swear that I do give
Everything betwixt my two hands
to the ways of witchcraft.

MOTHER HICKS: (*Angry*) Stop that jabbering!

GIRL: I want to be a witch, like you!

MOTHER HICKS: I'll tell you witches, I'll tell you witchcraft! When the fever comes and makes the babies scream and burn up in their beds and die, that can't be scarlet fever, it's a hex. When a child's born all crippled up, or blind, or deaf, it can't be because it's Mother took no notice of the measles, it's a spell! When the hand of God strikes a good man down, or takes away his job, it must be someone's fault, it must be witchcraft!

GIRL: But, Mother Hicks . . .

MOTHER HICKS: (*Turns on her*) Don't you EVER call me that!

GIRL: Why not?

MOTHER HICKS: Don't you ever say that to me again.

   (*She turns away from GIRL.*)

GIRL: (*Simply*) I know that I am your child.

MOTHER HICKS: My child was taken.

GIRL: They say you gave her to the Devil, but I . . .

MOTHER HICKS: I never gave her up! I held her when she screamed. I held her all the time she cried. I held her until she died of fever!

GIRL: She died?

MOTHER HICKS: And after, I held her in my own two arms, and then I laid her in the ground all by myself.

GIRL: (*Showing her the quilt piece*) But look at this, you know you've seen this before, it's my name here and the H . . . the H it stands for Hicks!

(*GIRL shoves the piece into her hands. MOTHER HICKS looks at her squarely.*)

MOTHER HICKS: It stands for Home.

GIRL: What?

MOTHER HICKS: Illinois State Home.

(*There is a pause.*)

I seen this piece before. I wrapped you in it just after you was born. Your Mother came here from the State Home, scared and all alone, hardly more than a child herself. I helped her with the birthing . . .

GIRL: (*In disbelief*) No.

MOTHER HICKS: She stayed a spell, but then one day she ran and took you with her. She must have left you in the town on her way to somewhere else.

GIRL: And so I am . . .

MOTHER HICKS: The orphan child of an orphan child.

GIRL: That's not true!

MOTHER HICKS: Yes it is, little rabbit.

GIRL: Witches is powerful, witches can make things happen, witches is never lonely or afraid, because they've got the power. I am your child and you are a witch!

MOTHER HICKS: I am not a witch!

GIRL: Then what are you?

MOTHER HICKS: I'm just a left over person, just like you!

(*TUC enters with the shot gun and an empty box of shells.*)

GIRL: That's not true!

MOTHER HICKS: (*To TUC*) I threw away the shells, I was afraid somebody would get hurt.

(*To GIRL.*)

Now, they are coming for you, and you'll go back to town with them, because that's where you belong!

GIRL: NO!

(*She turns and runs into the darkness. TUC starts after her. MOTHER HICKS grabs the gun.*)

MOTHER HICKS: Let her go, Tuc, let her go!

(*TUC pulls away and runs after GIRL. MOTHER HICKS paces for a moment and then pulls her chair around and sits with the shot gun in her lap, as voices of the townspeople are heard coming up the hill. After a beat, they enter with flash-lights.*)

MOTHER HICKS: Stop right there. One more step and you're on private property.

CLOVIS: (*Sees the gun*) Uhhhhh, beg your pardon. . . . Miz Hicks.

MOTHER HICKS: You got exactly three seconds to get your back-sides down this hill.

ALMA: We understand that you're holding a child here, against her will.

MOTHER HICKS: There ain't no one here.

CHORUS: The Girl's been missing over a week and . . .

MOTHER HICKS: That's no concern of mine.

CLOVIS: We just want to look around.

MOTHER HICKS: You got a warrant?

ALMA: (*Advancing on her*) Please, I need to see for myself. . . .

IZZY: Don't look at her Alma! She'll witch you!

MOTHER HICKS: (*To IZZY*) You never change, do you? What did I ever do to you, except give you a place to put your hate?

IZZY: (*Praying as a protection*) In the name of the Father and the Son . . .

MOTHER HICKS: (*Shouting and rising*) Be quiet!

CLOVIS: Can't stand to hear the word of God?

MOTHER HICKS: Prayers used that way is blasphemy!

IZZY: You cry blasphemy after witching our children?

MOTHER HICKS: I never hurt a child!

CLOVIS: But they died, you touched those babies and they died.

MOTHER HICKS: It was the fever!

HOSIAH: (*Gun at the ready*) Stand aside or use that gun, but we are coming in.

MOTHER HICKS: (*Raises the gun slightly*) What gives you the right? What gives any of you the right, to talk and talk and talk and call me witch?

ALMA: We just want the Girl!

MOTHER HICKS: (*Puts her gun down*) What's the use? You'll take whatever you want. You'll come in here with guns and call ME criminal!

ALMA: We just want the Girl.

MOTHER HICKS: She's not here!

ALMA: Let me look, please, I care for her.

MOTHER HICKS: (*After a long moment*) Then look, but just one. I won't have all of you trampling through my house.

(*HOSIAH starts.*)

Not the one with the gun.

(*ALMA starts and HOSIAH pulls her back.*)

ALMA: I'll go, I'm the one who started this in the first place.

(*ALMA slowly searches the place. She checks out the pallet and enters the cabin.*)

(*Animal sounds are heard as she enters, immediately she comes out, and steps aside quickly.*)

ALMA: She's not there.

CLOVIS: What?

ALMA: There's nothing in there but a bunch of animals.

IZZY: Her Incubus! The Devil animals!

MOTHER HICKS: (*This is the last straw*) That's right! You want a witch, then witch I'll be. When you look you see what you want to see!

IZZY: It's a spell!

MOTHER HICKS: (*Every bit a witch!*) Get out of here, before I lock your jaw and turn your blood to poison.

CLOVIS: We don't want any trouble.

MOTHER HICKS: Then get off my property!

(*She lunges at them. HOSIAH aims and cocks his gun. She faces him squarely.*)

MOTHER HICKS: And you better have a silver bullet in that gun!

(*There is a moment of tension.*)

ALMA: Hosiah.

(*He puts the gun down.*)

MOTHER HICKS: I'll count to five and if you're not halfway down the hill by then, I'll spell you all to Sunday! ONE!

(*IZZY bolts and exits.*)

MOTHER HICKS: TWO!

CLOVIS: We don't want any trouble.

MOTHER HICKS: THREE.

(*CLOVIS exits.*)

HOSIAH: Come on, Alma.

MOTHER HICKS: FOUR!

ALMA: I'll be right there.

(*HOSIAH steps aside but remains in the shadows waiting for her.*)

MOTHER HICKS: FIVE.

ALMA: She was ill. She had pneumonia.

MOTHER HICKS: Not anymore.

ALMA: (*Relieved*) When did she leave?

MOTHER HICKS: Not long ago.

ALMA: Where . . .

MOTHER HICKS: I don't know.

ALMA: If she comes back, if you see her . . . please tell her I care. Tell her I want her to come back.

MOTHER HICKS: I know . . . now, go.

(*There is a charged moment between the women as they look at each other. HOSIAH holds out an arm and ALMA exits with him.*)

(*Lights change and after a beat TUC steps into a spot. CHORUS member enters and speaks.*)

CHORUS: (*For TUC*)
    Four Days come and four days gone
    And she ain't here and she ain't there.
    This time the Girl has disappeared
    I know, 'cause I've looked everywhere
    And I am used to shadows, but she's not there

Or anywhere.

(*During this speech the stage has been cleared of everything except the graveyard.*)

CHORUS: It was just before midnight.
I was passing the graveyard
On my way home.

(*Lights are dim. The crickets and distant hooting and the sound of a loon are heard. TUC crouches in shadow. GIRL enters and moves to her hiding place as before.*)

(*MOTHER HICKS enters the graveyard and moves to the same spot she went to before. As she places the baby clothes on the ground, she speaks softly, but her words are audible.*)

MOTHER HICKS: So there you are, and don't you look something all dressed up to Sunday. Mind you don't get this pretty little dress dirty; I just washed it.

(*GIRL sits up.*)

The rabbits is fine and we got ourselves a whole family of racoons.

(*GIRL moves slowly, carefully near her.*)

Them coons got into rat poison, I reckon; but they're doing fine on sour milk and apple peelings . . . Oh, I wish you could see them.

(*With great grief and infinite tenderness, MOTHER HICKS starts to lower herself onto the ground. She is suddenly aware of GIRL and stops.*)

GIRL: I was afraid you wouldn't be here.

MOTHER HICKS: (*Without looking at her*) I didn't come looking for you. I had other reasons.

GIRL: I'm sorry for what I said to you.

(*No response from MOTHER HICKS.*)

I just needed it to be true.

(*No response from MOTHER HICKS.*)

Please, look at me.

(*MOTHER HICKS looks at her.*)

She's there isn't she? What was her name?

MOTHER HICKS: May-ry.

GIRL: Mary.

MOTHER HICKS: It ain't Mary and it ain't Marie. It's May-ry.

GIRL: May-ry.

(*There is a pause.*)

I'm sorry I ran away.

MOTHER HICKS: They always go when they's healed.

GIRL: But I'm not healed, not yet. But I do know one thing, I know one thing for positive sure; someday things are going to belong to me and I'm going to belong to them. But there's something I need first and I won't be healed until I find it.

MOTHER HICKS: You look all right to me.

GIRL: I'm talking about something inside me, like a piece of me left out and wanting.

MOTHER HICKS: (*Looks at her evenly*) You'll never find her. No matter how hard you look, you'll never find that poor scared rabbit that gave you birth.

GIRL: I know, that part of me isn't hungry anymore, it's just sad.

MOTHER HICKS: That woman, Alma, she cares. She wants you back.

GIRL: I know, but I can't go back there until I find what I need.

MOTHER HICKS: What?

GIRL: A name. I need a name. So, I wonder, could I have her name? Could I be May-ry?

MOTHER HICKS: That's her name, it ain't yours.

GIRL: But I wish it were.

MOTHER HICKS: (*Simply*) Well, you can wish in one hand and spit in the other and see which gets full first.

GIRL: Could you help me find my own name?

MOTHER HICKS: (*Looks at GIRL*) I reckon I could.

GIRL: Then I can stay with you 'til we find it, just for a while?

MOTHER HICKS: Creatures come when they need a healing spell, but when it's done, they go.

GIRL: I know.

(*TUC comes forward and signs. The CHORUS enters as a group as at the top of the play. As they speak, MOTHER HICKS gathers up the baby clothes. GIRL carefully folds the quilt piece and places it on top of the grave. She looks to MOTHER HICKS who nods. GIRL pats the quilt piece and leaves it behind. MOTHER HICKS rises and extends her hand to GIRL who reaches for it just as the CHORUS finishes their lines.*)

CHORUS: Mother Hicks is a witch, people say
And she lives all alone at the top of Dug Hill
And she works her magic on the town below.

When a child falls sick
And there ain't no cause
And there ain't no cure
Then everybody knows, that it's witched for sure
Mother Hicks is a witch, people say.

(*Lights dim to black.*)

CURTAIN

In a Room Somewhere

In a Room Somewhere marks a major departure for Zeder from the usual way she structures a play. It has five protagonists instead of one and is organized around bits of their five life histories rather than by a single story line. These five adults suddenly find themselves transported into a mysterious room with no windows or doors, a room in which time seems to be standing still, racing forward, or going backward simultaneously, and in which even gravity seems to be in abeyance.

This difference in structure is related to the fact that the process of developing this script was also very different from the way Zeder had worked in the past. Zeder had worked improvisationally with actors in creating *Wiley and the Hairy Man* and *The Play Called Noah's Flood*, but, in both those cases, she had worked with the actors using an already existing story as a starting point. With *In a Room Somewhere* Zeder started with information about the childhood experiences of many different people and no story line.

The development of the script was done with the professional actors of Metro Theatre Circus in St. Louis, Missouri and their artistic director, Carol Evans, who had commissioned Zeder to create a script with some focus on music and movement. As part of the exploration process, the Metro actors talked about what had happened to them as children. (A fuller description of the developmental process of this script appears in the appendix, since it is important to the play's structure.) Zeder and Evans discovered that they could ask just a few needling questions that would allow the actors, as adults, to step across a kind of threshold where they were not simply relating the past, but actually reliving it while still being fully themselves and remaining fully adult. Zeder describes this as a sort of "past-present" time and a shared adult-child space unlike any she'd ever worked with before. It became an important element in the structuring of this play and allowed her to further develop her interest and skill in putting multiple time frames on the stage at once.

Zeder is quick to admit that *In a Room Somewhere* has been the most difficult of all her plays to write. Selecting from and structuring a huge amount of raw material was a long, arduous process. At one point in the script, one of the characters says that they are stuck in a place where "little pieces of time get lost." This image of finding lost pieces of time from a person's life and putting the puzzle of that life together is not only a metaphor central to the deepest meaning of this script, but it also describes Zeder's lengthy and meticulous process in creating this play. The script went through eight drafts during Metro's rehearsal period and its first year of toured performances and seven more during subsequent productions before it was published in 1988. Each draft involved her reshaping the five characters by putting the pieces of their lives together in different ways, until the most important piece of information about each character finally presented itself to her imagination.

She accomplishes depth of characterization in a short amount of time a number of different ways. First, she pinpoints one particular set of conflicting desires within each character and a behavior pattern which manifests these conflicting desires. She then makes sure that this behavior pattern shows up clearly at the very beginning of the play and reappears each time the character is in focus. For example, Mason's tendency to protect himself from past emotional wounds by denying pain and by turning serious issues into jokes is visible at the very beginning of the show when he smashes his thumb with a hammer and denies that it hurts. Immediately after that he makes a joke. These two behaviors—denial and joking—recur in nearly every scene in which Mason appears. Each time the behavior pattern repeats Zeder reveals more about the childhood origins of his conflicts.

Zeder's choice of key personal objects from each character's past also helps create depth of characterization quickly. For example, Cat's glasses emphasize her ability to see what's going on inside of people. Michael's piano and his expressive playing of it underscore his gentle sensitivity. The fact that his watch is going backwards, while those of the other characters have stopped or are whizzing forward, points to his openness to his own past. Sometimes a character's personal object serves to reveal inner strengths and resources a character may have forgotten or never realized he had. Kurt's bicycle symbolizes his tendency to rush and push too hard, but it also reveals the understanding he had, even as a child, of the importance of having a safe way to release his anger. Dudleigh's tap shoes show us her fear of doing something less than perfectly, as well as her potential to let herself go and be freer and more confident.

Even the roles Zeder has each character play in other characters' remembrance scenes give them added depth. We see a different side of Mason when he plays the role of the understanding father in Michael's memory scene. When we discover the truth about Mason's father, the significance of his playing the role of a good father—one he probably would like to have had—increases our understanding of the pain he is denying. When Dudleigh voluntarily assumes the role of Kurt's mother during Kurt's remembrance, we see her giving Kurt advice that she needs to, but can't yet give herself.

The room itself behaves as a character. Its actions are an integral part of the plot's structure and help reveal the lives of each character by providing the major obstacle that forces them to confront unresolved conflicts from the past. However, it also provides the tools—mysterious aromas, over-sized dolls, and objects from each person's past—which the characters use to come to grips with their past experiences.

A room which represents an inner, psychological space is a device that Zeder has used before in both *Step on a Crack* and *Doors*, but in this play, the mental space is shared rather than being identified with just one character. Just as the walls of this room are invisible to the audience, each character creates and breaks through inner walls that may be invisible to other people, but which are very restrictive to the individual experiencing them. In this room, as in life, some people help each other to find their way out of psychological traps. Sometimes this help is intentional, as the characters illustrate when they consciously take on roles in each other's memories. But sometimes, what prods people on to new self-awareness is unintentional, accidental, and even dangerous. In the fight between Mason and Kurt, both men are transferring unresolved conflicts from their respective pasts into the present and not seeing each other as they really are. Their confrontation is a painful, but necessary, step for both of them to reach a greater understanding of themselves. Cat is related to this healing and growth process, but whether she represents an external source of help, such as a therapist or friend, or whether she represents the inherent, self-therapeutic drive for continuing growth within each individual, is a question that is left for the audience to ponder.

The mystery surrounding Cat is only one of several ambiguous points that Zeder has built into the play. She uses many different conventions to move characters in and out of the past-present time space, as well as in and out of each other's memories. This variety of conventions mirrors the endless variety of the human imagination in its often surprising leaps from experiences in the present to memories of the past. It also reflects the unconscious tendency in most people to project feelings from early family relationships onto strangers, friends, co-workers, and situations in the present. She has created a complex, multi-layered world within this room, and it is important for directors and actors approaching a production of this piece to avoid reducing or over-simplify that complexity. A key to doing justice to the world of the play is to trust the psychological truth of the inner lives of the characters and the simultaneity of past and present in the room which grew out of the original rehearsal process during the play's development.

In spite of the many ways in which this play differs from Zeder's other works, many familiar Zeder themes are still present. Most prominent is Zeder's belief in the healing properties of play and the imagination. Playfulness is present, in varying degrees, in each of the characters. Zeder hints at this visually by having each character take off outer layers of neutral clothing revealing bright colors underneath. The ability to acknowledge and value the child within themselves and to reconnect with the child's flexibility and willingness to imagine, dream, and play is crucial to each character finding a way out of the room.

One might assume that it would take an adult's ability to reflect on past experience in order to appreciate the play. However, Zeder has crafted this play in a way that makes it appeal across all age levels. She has chosen "lost pieces of time" for each of her characters in such a way that almost anyone in the audience, child or adult, can identify with at least one, if not several, of the characters' crises or challenges. Parental expectations affect most people throughout the whole span of life. Finding ways to release anger and forgive the intentional or unintentional wrongs done is a recurrent struggle for these characters as well as for many adults and children in real life. As a contrast to the hard lessons, Zeder had included the joy the characters find as they learn to free themselves from life's pressures. Whether it is through artistic expression like Michael's in playing the piano, or imaginative play and physical release like Dudleigh's in tap dancing, these ways of re-creating ourselves, discovered in childhood, often become more valuable as we grow older. The play has been tested during the long process of revision through hundreds of performances for all age levels, and although Zeder reports that it provides a more emotional experience for adults than children, even the very youngest children relate to it on their own terms.

More than any of Zeder's other plays, *In a Room Somewhere* finds the psychological and emotional issues that are common to both children and adults. It is the most direct statement of the very strong belief in the continuing importance of childhood that has informed Zeder's writing from the beginning. She speaks both to that emerging adult within each child and to the too-often ignored child within each adult using words and images that remind us that we need each other. In the face of all the forces that seem to be aimed at diminishing us, the deeper message of *In a Room Somewhere* is that it is the childlike, imaginative part of us, with its capacity for flexibility and wonder and it's passionate drive to grow, that is the inner power which adults relinquish only at their peril.

In a Room Somewhere

Book and Lyrics
by Suzan L. Zeder

Musical Score
by Daniel Paul Davis

From the Playwright

I am deeply grateful to the many people who gave so much of themselves to build this "room": to the Metro Theatre Circus, whose lives, thoughts and feelings formed the foundation; to Carol Evans who joined the parts together with passion and compassion; to Daniel Paul Davis who filled the air inside the room with music; and to my husband Jim, who taught me to believe in the healing power of this special place.

Each of you who will produce, present, or perform in this play will build your own room. I have provided a very specific blueprint to challenge and spark your imagination; but you will furnish it with your own personal metaphors and people it with your concept of these characters. In this quest, I urge you to look to the depth of your vision and to trust your audience, no matter what their age. Allow them to come to the room on their own level and to take from the room whatever they will. I have seen this play performed for audiences of pre-schoolers through senior citizens; the play works on entirely different levels for different ages.

I urge you not to try to simplify or literalize this "room," so "even kids will understand." There need be no artificial indications of what is past and what is present. The character of Cat is deliberately enigmatic: to make her the obvious "therapist" in the room is to diminish her, and to deprive your audience of the fun of figuring her out for themselves.

I am often asked: "What age is this play aimed at?" This play, more than any other I have written, is aimed at the child within the adult and the adult within the child that exists in all of us. The four years that I have spent in this "room" has given me an entirely new conception of time, not a chronological progression where childhood is something past and done with; but a cyclical whole deepened by the simultaneity of time.

Just as the adult tree is nourished by the sapling that still grows deep inside, this play has reaffirmed my faith in the power of that child space within us all.

Suzan Zeder
1988

Dedication

To the Metro Theatre Circus,
who helped me build "the room" for the very first time,
and to Carol who made it possible
for all of us to go there.

In a Room Somewhere was commissioned by and created with Metro Theatre Circus. It was rehearsed and performed over a three year period from June, 1984 until November, 1987. The original cast created the following roles:

Mason .... Nicholas Kryah
Cat .... Claudia Holzapfel
Kurt .... Scott Hanson
Michael .... Larry Pressgrove
Dudleigh .... Jan Feager Cosby

The production was directed by Carol Evans

Set Design by .... Nicholas Kryah
Costume Design by .... Clyde Ruffin
Original Musical Score by .... Steven Radeck

CHARACTERS

Mason Welch: A carpenter
Kurt Paxton: A salesman
Michael Waverly: A musician
Leigh-Ann (Dudleigh) Scott: A law student
Catlyn (Cat): A person in the room

Also four life-sized, soft sculptured doll-like creations, who will be used to represent various adults. There are three female dolls and one male doll. The females represent teachers and mothers. The male represents all fathers.

TIME

One hour of real time, right now.

PLACE

In a room somewhere

MUSICAL NUMBERS

Opening
Look for a Door .... Mason, Kurt, Cat
Think What I Think .... Michael, Kurt, Cat
Good Teachers/Wicked Teachers .... Company
Movin' to the Music .... Cat, Dudleigh, Michael
Ballad of the Bike .... Kurt
Saaa Boss .... Michael, Mason

In a Room Somewhere

The room is a mysterious place. On the stage floor are colored lines indicating the boundaries of the space. On all sides of the acting area are indications of four emphatic walls, invisible to the audience but solid to the characters. Walls are suggested by sharply angled corner pieces which seem to disappear into an upward infinity. The walls are there, and yet they're not.

Dominating the space is a large abstract sculptural piece. Primarily, it is a clock with no numbers and only one hand. This clock will keep practical time and the hand will make one full revolution during the action of the play. The piece is large enough for characters to move behind and out of sight. This structure should challenge the imagination of any set designer, as it must "deliver" various objects into the room during the action of the play: objects such as a pair of glasses, a large ball, report cards, tap shoes, a baseball, etc. Perhaps there are small trap doors which pop open to reveal objects, or chutes which propel objects into the room. Perhaps the whole structure turns almost imperceptibly and reveals nooks and crannies where objects are hidden. The structure itself should be of a neutral color; the objects should be brightly colored.

All around the room are lumpy objects covered by neutral colored sheets of silk. There are several small boxes and cubes of odd sizes and shapes; these are also neutral but underneath and within the inner recesses are vibrantly colored. A piano and bench are partially covered by a neutral sheet.

CAT, MASON and KURT are onstage. MASON and KURT are frozen in stop-action positions: MASON perched up on one end of the piano with a hammer raised above a non-existant nail, KURT stands with both arms raised in frozen excitement. If he were animated he would be yelling. CAT sits quietly, only her eyeballs move as she shifts her gaze from KURT to MASON. She is dressed in bright colors, MASON and KURT wear neutral colored pants and jackets which cover layers of bright clothing.

The "Opening" Music is heard and the sound of ticking.

CAT: Well?

(Mason brings the hammer down sharply, hitting his thumb.)

MASON: Ahhhhhhh! I can't believe I did that! JEEEZE!

(*He deals with the pain by denying it.*)

MASON: It doesn't really hurt, not really! It doesn't really HURT!

(*Cat crosses to Mason.*)

CAT: It would help if you would shout a very bad word very loud. If you keep it inside, your eyes will bug out and your ears will flap.

MASON: Who are you?

CAT: My name is Catlyn but you will call me Cat.

MASON: Where in the world am I?

(*Suddenly, Kurt comes to life, shakes his fists and shouts.*)

KURT: So, go on, shoot, shoot! SHOOT!

(*There is the sound of a buzzer.*)

BRIAN!!!!!

MASON: What is going on here?

(*Kurt realizes he is not where he thought he was.*)

KURT: Where's the team? Where's the court?

MASON: Where's the roof? Where's the house I was . . .

KURT: Where in BLAZES are we?

CAT: We're in a room somewhere.

KURT: Just a minute ago I was coaching my kid's basketball team, we're down by 16 points, and Brian, my own kid, is just standing with the ball. I nearly had a heart attack; he's just standing there looking stupid. So, I yell at him . . .

CAT: Maybe you died.

KURT: What?

CAT: I saw it on *Twilight Zone*; all these people were trapped in an elevator, except that really they were dead and they had to spend eternity going up and down between floors.

KURT: I didn't die. It was just the end of the quarter.

MASON: If he died, what am I doing here? I was up on the roof and just about to nail down a shingle . . . wait a minute, that was yesterday! I finished the roof yesterday! It's like a dream, I remember things in bits and pieces, like a dream.

KURT: What is going ON?

CAT: Extra-Terrestrials?

KURT: What?

CAT: I saw a movie about people who had been taken on a space craft. Once they were on board, the aliens stuck little flashlights in their noses to see inside their brains.

KURT: (*Uncomfortable*) I think you've seen too many movies.

MASON: The name's Mason . . . Mason Welch, pleased to meet you, Coach.

   (*Kurt flips a stack of cards out of his shirt pocket.*)

KURT: Kurt, Kurt Paxton, I just volunteer as a Coach, actually I'm a field rep for The Jock Shop, you know: uniforms, running shoes, basketballs . . .

CAT: I'm Cat.

   (*He hands cards to them.*)

MASON: (*Turning over the card*) Way to go, Coach.

KURT: What?

MASON: It's blank.

KURT: WHAT?

(*Mason shows him, Kurt pulls the stack from his pocket.*)

KURT: (*Astonished*) They're all blank! But they can't be.

CAT: Maybe they're blank so you can just make up whoever you want to be next.

KURT: (*Perturbed*) What kind of salesman has blank cards?

MASON: An air salesman?

KURT: I just looked at them this morning, they had my name on them. "Kurt Paxton . . .

MASON: Blank billboards?

KURT: . . . Field Rep., Jock Shop."

MASON: Donut holes?

KURT: I sell sporting goods!

MASON: If you say so, Coach.

KURT: Kurt!

MASON: Whatever.

KURT: Look, there has got to be a way out of here. Try to find a door, a window, anything.

MASON: You got it, Coach.

KURT: Kurt!

(*Music begins for "Look For A Door." Kurt and Mason speak/sing this number as they search the room. They explore the walls in very specific mime establishing the boundaries.*)

KURT: Look for a door.

MASON: Check the walls.

KURT: Check the floor.

MASON: Look around on the ground
For a trapdoor or a hatch.

KURT: There has got to be a catch
Like a keyhole or a latch.
Look for a window.

MASON: Look for a door.

KURT: Look for a window.

MASON: I'm looking for a door.

CAT: But there isn't any door.

MASON: There has to be a door.

KURT: Look for a window.

MASON: I'm looking for a door!

CAT: (*Sings*) You can look all day.
You can look until you drop.
You still won't find it,
So you might as well stop.
There isn't any window.
There isn't any door.
You can try, till you cry,
But I've tried it all before.
Look high, look low;
There is nowhere else to go.

KURT: Keep looking for a window.

MASON: There isn't any door!

CAT: There isn't any window.

KURT: I heard you before!

MASON: (*Spoken*) Wait a minute. No one would build a room with no windows and no doors! I know! I'm a Carpenter.

KURT: Okay, then, Mr. Carpenter, where is it?

MASON: The name is Mason, and I don't know!

KURT: Well, then, look harder!

(*Music continues.*)

KURT: Look for a door.

MASON: Check the walls.

KURT: Check the floor.

MASON: Look around on the ground
For a trapdoor or a hatch.

KURT: There has got to be a catch.
Like a trapdoor or a . . .

CAT: (*Spoken*) Wait a minute! There isn't any ceiling either!

KURT: What?

MASON: What?

KURT: Where?

CAT: There!

(*Sings*)

Up in the air
In the dark
Nothing there
Not a ceiling or a roof
I can show you; I've got proof!

KURT: Just because we can't see up there

MASON: Doesn't mean it can't be up there.

CAT: If you toss up a ball
You'd hear it hit before the fall.
Right?

MASON: Right.

CAT: Right?

KURT: Right!

CAT: (*Spoken*) Well, go ahead and try it!

(*Cat produces a small ball from her pocket. Mason tosses it straight up; it comes down. He throws it again, a bit higher. On the third throw, he palms the ball and tosses his empty hand in the air. The ball seems to disappear into the void. All this is reflected in the music.*)

MASON: (*In awe, spoken*) It's like watching it fall down a well.

ALL THREE: (*Sung*) There isn't any ceiling
. . . There isn't any door.
. . . . . . There isn't any window
. . . . There isn't any . . .

(*The music ends.*)

KURT: (*Calling*) Hey . . . is there anybody out there?

CAT: I don't think anyone can hear you.

KURT: Might as well try! Hey, Hey, Hey!

CAT: I tried.

MASON: (*To Cat*) How long have you been here?

CAT: I don't know, my watch is broken!

MASON: (*Checking his watch*) Mine's stopped.

(*Kurt checks his watch.*)

KURT: (*Amazed*) Look at that, the hands are whizzing around faster and faster.

MASON: How time flies when you're having . . .

(*Cat lifts one of the sheets and peeks under it. She gives a little shriek.*)

KURT: What is it?

CAT: A leg!

MASON: A leg?

CAT: A leg!

KURT: Oh, my Lord.

   (*Cat points to one of the lumps under a sheet.*)

CAT: There's a body under that sheet!

MASON: (*Indicating another lumpy object*) Uhhh, you mean like this sheet?

CAT: Just like that sheet!

KURT: Oh, my Lord.

MASON: So, what did this . . . leg look like?

CAT: Dead! It looked like a dead leg! Look for yourself!

MASON: Okay . . . I will! Sure . . . uhhhh Kurt, you check out that one, and . . .

CAT: Cat.

MASON: Check out that one.

   (*With trepidation they approach the objects and whip off the coverings. A magical sound is heard.*)

KURT: What the?

   (*They hold up life-sized figures. They are soft and stuffed and have no distinctly distinguishable faces.*)

MASON: Dolls! They're dolls!

KURT: They **are** dolls.

CAT: This one looks just like my fifth grade teacher.

MASON: (*Pointedly*) That is **not** your teacher.

CAT: Oh yeah, who is it?

MASON: It's a doll, just like this . . .

(*Mason removes the final sheet covering a lumpy object on the piano stool. Under this sheet is Michael, wearing formal evening clothes. As soon as the sheet is removed he begins to play: "Michael's Entrance." He plays as if in a trance.*)

MASON: HEYYY!

KURT: It's alive!

CAT: It's a person! Hey there! Hey there! Hey there!

KURT: How do we stop him?

MASON: I don't know.

(*Cat, crosses to Michael.*)

CAT: Please stop.

(*Music stops.*)

MICHAEL: (*Unaware of where he is*) I'll never get it; never!

CAT: Hello.

MICHAEL: (*He looks up and sees her*) I'm terribly sorry but I have this practice room signed out for the whole hour. If you want to use this room you've got to sign up for it with the Competition Coordinator.

MASON: Ahhhh, I don't think you are quite where you think you are.

MICHAEL: (*Realizing where he is or isn't for the first time*) Huh? Where am I?

KURT: We're all trapped in this room somewhere.

MICHAEL: Well, there's got to be a window, there's got to be a . . .

KURT: There isn't.

MASON: We looked.

MICHAEL: Who are all you people?

CAT: I'm Cat, he's Kurt, and that's . . .

MASON: Mason Welch. Pardon my appearance, I didn't realize this abduction was black tie.

MICHAEL: I'm Michael Waverly, and in exactly two hours I am supposed to play in the most important piano competition of my life.

(*He looks at his watch.*)

MICHAEL: What the . . .

(*He shakes his wrist and taps his watch.*)

KURT: We have got to get out of here. We're all going to starve to death!

(*There is a strange kind of music: "The Sound of Forgotten Smells."*)

CAT: What's that smell?

(*Others sniff, sound continues.*)

It's popcorn, like at the Saturday afternoon movies!

KURT: No, it's not! It's chocholate chip cookies, just like my Mom used to make.

MICHAEL: No, it's not! It's hay! That's just how the fields on my Dad's farm used to smell in the spring, just after mowing.

MASON: No, it's not!

CAT: What do you smell, Mason?

(*The sound stops.*)

MASON: Nothing!

(*There is another strange sound, as suddenly a door pops open on the structure or an object flies in through a chute.*)

MICHAEL: What's that?

(*Cat crosses to the structure and removes a pair of glasses.*)

CAT: My glasses!

MICHAEL: What?

CAT: My glasses.

KURT: Where?

CAT: I heard that sound and then I found my very first pair of glasses there!

MASON: Oh, come on, your very first pair . . .

CAT: I got them when I was eleven and I thought I'd die of shame.

(*She looks at them closely.*)

Now, I'm sure that they're the same, I stomped on them and cracked the frame.

(*She puts them on.*)

It was bad enough when I had to get braces and everyone at school called me tin grin, then I got these and they called me four eyes. When I refused to wear them, I kept bumping into things, and then they called me klutz. My body was ruining my life!

MASON: Hold it. Those can't be your glasses.

CAT: Why not?

MASON: How did they get here?

KURT: How did we get here?

MICHAEL: Where's here?

(*Michael slaps his hand down on the piano for emphasis, to everyone's astonishment Michael's piano plays by itself.*)

MASON: Heeeey!

CAT: It's playing.

MICHAEL: I just touched it.

KURT: You started it.

MICHAEL: I just touched it.

MASON: Do something.

MICHAEL: I just touched it!

CAT: Well, touch it again.

(*Michael touches the piano again it stops. Michael really looks at the piano.*)

MICHAEL: I don't believe this!

MASON: I don't either!

MICHAEL: This is my piano.

KURT: So?

MICHAEL: No, I mean this is MY piano.

MASON: Yeah, you were playing it when you . . .

MICHAEL: I was playing a Steinway in the practice room, but this isn't it. This is my own piano, the very first one I had when I was a kid.

MASON: You mean this looks like your piano.

MICHAEL: Look, here, there's a ring left by a glass of chocolate milk. I got a spanking for that. And I can feel where I used to park my gum while I practiced. Wait a minute . . . this can't be that piano.

CAT: Why not?

MICHAEL: I left it with my parents on the farm. Their house burned six years ago. They lost everything, including my old piano.

MASON: You have got to be kidding.

MICHAEL: But this is my piano alright!

KURT: (*Explodes*) We have got to get out of here! WE have got to . . .

(*The strange sound is heard again and suddenly a small two-wheeler bike is propelled into the room, straight into Kurt's outstretched hands.*)

KURT: Oh my Lord! It's the Flyer.

MASON: What?

KURT: The Flyer!

MICHAEL: (*Looking up from the piano*) Where?

KURT: I heard the sound and turned around and it came outta nowhere. This is the first bike I ever owned.

MASON: You mean it looks like the first bike you ever owned.

KURT: No, it's the bike! The very bike! I bent this rim popping wheelies and this paint got scratched up when my brakes failed and I smashed through the plate glass window at K-Mart! This is MY BIKE, I'd know it anywhere!

MASON: You are all out of your minds! I mean, glasses . . . there must be millions of glasses that look alike, . . . and bikes, I mean a bike is a bike . . . I mean, it's just a coincidence.

(*He moves to Michael.*)

Isn't it?

(*Michael removes his jacket revealing a colored cummerbund. He "plays" the melody for "Think What I Think."*)*

MICHAEL: When I was a kid I'd play this piano 3–4 hours a day. I couldn't wait to get home to practice. It was my own place. My secret space where I could really be myself. I could . . .

---

*This can be played live or recorded with Michael seeming to play as long as his hands are not visible to the audience.

(He sings.)

Think what I think, see what I see
Be what I am, and what I can be
And nobody could see me
And nobody could hear
There's nobody near
There's nobody here
But me.

(Cat puts on her glasses and wails unhappily.)

CAT: Right here on my face
Between my forehead and my nose
Is a frame, it's such a pain
That nobody knows
Four-eyes, they'll say at school
How can they be so cruel?
So I think I'll just disappear
Sit in my closet for a year

MICHAEL AND CAT: Think what I think, see what I see
Be what I am and what I can be.

(Kurt straddles his bike and pops a stationary wheelie.)

KURT: *(Sings)* Over the sidewalk
And whizzing down the street
Where I can fly past passersby
I am a blur, I am a streak
Faster than time, faster than air
So fast I'm gone before I'm there!
And even if they try to call
They never see me there at all!

(All but Mason.)

ALL: I can
Think what I think, see what I see
Be what I am, or what I can be
And nobody can see me
And nobody can hear
There's nobody near

There's nobody here
But me.

(*As the song ends Mason looks on with quiet contempt.*)

MASON: That is the most ridiculous thing I've ever seen.

CAT: What?

MASON: You, all of you! Glasses, piano, bicycles . . .

CAT: Maybe there's something of yours here, too.

MASON: There is nothing here of mine!

CAT: Maybe if you try to remember . . .

MASON: I don't remember! I don't remember anything about being a kid.

KURT: I remember riding home from school on this bike and there was this hill, killer hill. Nobody got up that hill without walking. Nobody but me!

MASON: *(With an edge to Kurt)* Don't you think you're a little big for that bike?

KURT: What?

MASON: I mean, look at it. It's not even a ten speed.

KURT: Well, yeah . . . but . . .

MASON: *(Chiding)* And it's got a little Disneyland USA license plate saying "KURT."

KURT: Hey, it's my bike, alright?

MASON: It's a wreck.

KURT: You shut up about my bike.

MASON: Make me!

KURT: Oh, yeah!

MICHAEL: Stop it! Stop it!

(*There is a magical sound as a trapdoor flies open on the structure and Dudleigh tumbles into the room. She is dressed in a conservative blue suit, she holds a pencil between her teeth and clutches a blue book. She reads from an exam paper.*)

DUDLEIGH: "A: Stare decisis!" (*Star-i De-sigh-sus*)

(*All are mystified, Cat is delighted.*)

CAT: Somebody else!

DUDLEIGH: "B: Res judicata!" (*Race judi-cata*)

MASON: What is she saying?

CAT: Maybe she's foreign.

DUDLEIGH: "C: Res ipsa loquitor!" (*Race ipsa low-qui-tor*)

CAT: Maybe she's speaking some ancient, dead language like Sanskrit!

DUDLEIGH: "D: A and C only." "E: None of the above."

MICHAEL: What does she want?

DUDLEIGH: (*Wails*) I don't KNOW!

MICHAEL: (*Touching her on the shoulder*) It's all right!

(*Dudleigh suddenly snaps awake and looks at Michael.*)

DUDLEIGH: Shhhhh! We are not supposed to be talking!

(*Dudleigh returns to her paper.*)

MICHAEL: Uhhhh, excuse me, but . . .

DUDLEIGH: (*Through clenched teeth*) This is supposed to be the honor system!

KURT: Look, here . . .

DUDLEIGH: What do you think you're doing? Sit down and be quiet!

(*All back off as Dudleigh returns to her paper.*)

KURT: This one's wacko.

DUDLEIGH: We are going to get kicked out if anyone catches us talking during a final!

MASON: You don't understand.

DUDLEIGH: You don't understand, I have to ace this exam or it's goodbye law school.

MASON: Well then, goodbye law school . . .

(*Mason gestures and Dudleigh looks around finally.*)

DUDLEIGH: What the . . .?

MASON: . . . and welcome to the room!

DUDLEIGH: But . . .

MASON: The same thing happened to all of us.

DUDLEIGH: But . . .

MICHAEL: We've all come from different places and wound up here . . .

KURT: But nobody seems to know how or why.

DUDLEIGH: You'll have to excuse me, but I must be getting back . . .

(*She crosses to where she thinks the door should be.*)

Uhhhh, well, have a nice day . . .

(*She tries again, no luck.*)

Uhhhh, I don't suppose you could tell me where the door is?

MASON: There isn't one.

KURT: There aren't any windows either.

MICHAEL: There's no way out.

DUDLEIGH: Of course! Now I understand!

ALL: You do?

DUDLEIGH: It's a dream.

KURT: What?

DUDLEIGH: I must have fallen asleep at my desk and you are all part of my dream!

MASON: We can't be your dream! We were here first!

CAT: Or maybe we're all dreaming, and I'm in your dream, and you're in my dream, and Kurt's in Michael's dream, and Michael's in . . .

DUDLEIGH: (*Bellows*) WAKE-UP!

(*They all turn and stare at her.*)

Sorry . . . I guess that was really stupid.

KURT: I'll say!

(*Dudleigh sits, defeated.*)

DUDLEIGH: Do you suppose they can flunk you for dematerializing during an exam?

CAT: What's your name?

DUDLEIGH: Dudleigh . . . I mean, Leigh-Ann, Leigh-Ann Scott. I haven't been called Dudleigh since the junior high. Why did I do that? What is this place?

CAT: It's just a room somewhere.

DUDLEIGH: What are we supopsed to do in here?

CAT: Whatever we like.

(*Cat picks up one of the female dolls.*)

DUDLEIGH: What is that thing?

CAT: What does it look like?

(*Cat turns it to her and Dudleigh bursts out laughing.*)

DUDLEIGH: Miss Parmaley!

CAT: Miss Parmaley?

DUDLEIGH: Whatever made me think of Miss Parmaley?

MICHAEL: Miss Parmaley?

DUDLEIGH: She was my English teacher in the third grade. I haven't thought about her in years!

MASON: (*Scoffing*) Miss Parmaley?

DUDLEIGH: When I was in the third grade I won a poetry contest. When she presented the award, Miss Parmaley told the whole school: "We expect big things from this little girl."

MICHAEL: I had a piano teacher like that . . .

(*Imitates her voice.*)

MICHAEL: "We expect big things from this young man."

MASON: (*Raises the tape measure like an aerial*) Earth to anyone . . . do you read me?

CAT: What about you, Mason, didn't you have a special teacher?

MASON: I don't remember.

DUDLEIGH: Well, I remember. I remember Miss Parmaley . . .

(Dudleigh hands doll to Cat.)

KURT: *(Groaning)* I remember school.

MICHAEL: *(Groaning louder)* I remember recess!

(There is the sound of a school bell and a ball is propelled out of a chute into the room. Kurt and Dudleigh begin a game of catch.)

MICHAEL: The thing I hated most about recess was kickball . . . and softball . . . and basketball, volleyball, soccer and spud!

(While Michael speaks he is trying to catch the ball as Kurt and Dudleigh play "moneky-in-the-middle" with Michael as the monkey. Cat stands with her back to the audience holding the Miss Parmaley doll.)

If you won you were the hero, if you lost, you were the goat! I mean what's with all this winning and losing? If someone has to win, then someone has to lose. So losing is just as important as winning, right? Got it!

(Michael catches the ball and expects to be let into the game. They continue with the game, using Kurt's shoe. Michael is still out.)

I guess winning was never that important to me. I mean it's only a game, right? And who really cares about . . . AH HA!

(Michael finally catches the shoes. They look at him and continue the game miming the ball. He can't win. He crosses to the piano and sits.)

I hate recess!

(A bell is heard. Cat turns around wearing the doll in front of her. She manipulates the doll and it appears as though the doll is playing the role. Michael "plays" the piano as music underscores this scene.)

DUDLEIGH: Miss Parmaley!

MISS PARMALEY: Dear Children! Sweet Children! Darling Children! I am pleased and proud to announce the winner of the poetry contest to celebrate "Teacher Appreciation Day" here at Peabody School.

KIDS: Yay!!!!!

MISS PARMALEY: This year's award of a one year subscription to *The Weekly Reader* goes to our own Leigh-Ann Scott!

KIDS: Yay, Dudleigh! Way to go!

(*Dudleigh comes forward.*)

MISS PARMALEY: In the future we expect big things from this little girl!

DUDLEIGH: Me, Miss Parmaley?

MISS PARMALEY: Yes, you, my dear! Now, perhaps you would like to share your poem with the class!

DUDLEIGH: Oh, yes, Miss Parmaley . . . "Good Teachers" by Leigh-Ann Scott.

(*Music swings into* 'Teacher/Teacher.')

DUDLEIGH: (*Sings*) Good teachers are always sweet and kind;
They make it so that you never mind
Going to school and obeying the rules;
If you act like a fool, they stay calm, they stay cool.
And even if you are dumb,

(*Others join in on*)

Dumb . . . dumb
It's still fun.

KIDS: Good teachers are always very nice;
They make it seem like it's paradise.
When you're in their class you know you will pass,
What they expect of you, you, you
You can do.

(*They nestle into a cozy group sitting at Miss P's feet and looking up at her with adoration.*)

MISS PARMALEY: (*Spoken*) And now dear children, I'll show you slides I took on my summer vacation to a tiny mountain village on the Isle of Skye. Then I will play the autoharp and sing you folk songs in Welsh; and then we will have a snack of gingerbread I baked just for you.

KIDS: We love you, Miss Parmaley!

MISS PARMALEY: I know.

KURT: Wait a minute! It isn't always like that. Sometimes you get a teacher who doesn't like you. Sometimes you get a teacher who hates you for no reason. Sometimes you get a teacher who's just plain wicked!

(*The actor playing Mason enters "wearing" a doll signifying The Wicked Teacher, who swoops in and forces Miss Parmaley to move aside.*)

WICKED TEACHER: What is the meaning of this? What is the meaning of this? Recess was over $3^1/2$ seconds ago. You should all be back at your desks sitting bolt upright in absolute silence!

KIDS: Yes, Teacher.

WICKED TEACHER: Do you all want to grow up to be ignoramusses?

KIDS: No, Teacher.

WICHED TEACHER: Then get your little fannies back to your desks!

KIDS: Yes, Teacher.

(*Music changes.*)

KURT: (*Sings*) Wicked teachers are super strict and super mean.
They eat children like popcorn;
They throw erasers and they scream;
They lock you in your locker, and throw away the key;
They send you to the principal until you're sixty–three;
And they never set you free.

KIDS: Wicked teachers have fingernails like dragon tails,
Long sharp noses and elbows.
They're thin as rails or big as whales.
They make you forget answers, even when you really know,
And if you have to leave the room they never let you go,
When you really have to go.

(*As the beat continues, the Wicked Teacher sneaks up on Kurt who mimes working at his desk humming to himself.*)

WICKED TEACHER: What is that sound?

KURT: Sound, Teacher?

WICKED TEACHER: That sound you were making?

KURT: Me, Teacher?

WICKED TEACHER: Yes, you!

KURT: I guess I was humming.

WICKED TEACHER: Humming?

KURT: Humming.

WICKED TEACHER: You must like that song a lot.

KURT: Yes, I do.

WICKED TEACHER: Well, then, maybe you'd like to share it with the class?

KURT: No thank you, Teacher!

WICKED TEACHER: SING IT!

KURT: But I don't know the words.

WICKED TEACHER: Then, HUM IT!

(*Mortified, Kurt stands and starts to hum. Mercifully, Miss Parmaley comes to his rescue.*)

MISS PARMALEY: No, no, NO! Everytime I get the chance, I tell my children dance, dance, dance!

(*Music swells into dance with Miss Parmaley and the Kids. Finally they coax the Wicked Teacher to join in; she protests at first and finally cuts loose and dances up a storm.*)

WICKED TEACHER: Whopppeeeee!

MICHAEL: (*Spoken*) You know, sometimes a wicked teacher is just a good teacher on a bad day.

(There is a big finish.)

(The bell rings again. Four folded cards shoot out of another chute.)

KURT: What's this?

CAT: Report cards.

MICHAEL: Report cards?

CAT: And they've got names on them.

(Cat hands out the cards.)

Leigh-Ann Scott, Michael Waverly, Kurt Paxton, Mason . . .

(Mason enters and refuses his card. He moves away. Dudleigh comes forward with her card.)

DUDLEIGH: Everybody says, "Leigh Ann's the smart one." "She may not be pretty, but by golly she's smart." "Straight A's again, Leigh Ann?" "Yes, Daddy." "That's my girl!" But I'm losing it. Even before I look, I know I'm losing it. I feel like every one of those A's weighs 100 pounds and is standing on my shoulders. I'm losing it. I'm going stupid or something. They didn't catch me last time, so it's got to be this time . . .

(She looks at the card. Her face brightens momentarily, but quickly clouds over again.)

They'll catch me next time.

(Michael opens his card and reads. Slowly a smile spreads across his face. He slyly shows his card to Mason.)

(Mason crosses, passing Kurt. On his way, he tries to sneak a peek at Kurt's report card. Kurt shields it. Mason laughs, moves away behind the structure or out of sight. Kurt is very nervous. He opens his card, as he reads his whole body reflects defeat.)

KURT: "Kurt is not working up to his abilities."
"Kurt lacks self control." "Kurt is such a bright boy, but he can't seem to concentrate. He just needs to try harder." Try harder! Try harder! Try harder!

(*He is near tears.*)

How does she know how hard I try?

(*Kurt tosses the card away and sits despondent. Cat picks up his card.*)

DUDLEIGH: I don't know which is worse, never being told you're smart enough or always being told you're too smart to be anything else.

MICHAEL: Either way you disappoint somebody.

CAT: (*Looking at the card*) This isn't your card.

KURT: Huh?

CAT: It says, "Brian Paxton."

KURT: Brian's my son . . . let ms see that!

(*She hands it to him, he looks at it in astonishment.*)

"Brian is not working up to his abilities."
"Brian lacks self control . . ."

(*Kurt realizes the others are looking at him. He covers shrugging it off.*)

Uhhhhh, well . . . Brian's a smart kid. He just needs to try a little harder.

(*He places the report card in his breast pocket.*)

(*Suddenly a deep, echoing voice booms out of an area away from the structure.*)

VOICE: This is it!

(*All look up, confused and a bit scared.*)

CAT: What?

VOICE: This is IT!

DUDLEIGH: Oh, no!

VOICE: This is the end!

KURT: The end of what?

VOICE: . . . of everything, Kurt Paxton.

KURT: Oh, my Lord, it knows my name!

MICHAEL: What do you want from us?

   (*From behind the structure comes a large threatening presence covered by a sheet. It zeros in on Dudleigh.*)

VOICE: Leigh Ann Scott, what have you got to say for yourself?

DUDLEIGH: Nothing.

VOICE: Are you sure?

DUDLEIGH: I don't know . . . well, actually, I'm not sure . . . I mean . . .

   (*The Voice begins to laugh. Cat pulls on the sheet revealing Mason with a megaphone.*)

CAT: Mason!

MASON: I really got you guys going! Look what I found back there!

CAT: That wasn't kind.

MASON: Yeah, but it was funny.

KURT: I have just about had enough of you.

MASON: Oh, take it easy, I was just kidding.

KURT: You are just like my kid, always got a smart mouth answer.

MICHAEL: (*To Kurt*) It's okay!

KURT: It is NOT okay.

MICHAEL: Take it easy.

KURT: I'm tired of him.

CAT: Take it easy.

KURT: And I am tired of people telling me to take it easy!

(*Kurt pulls away.*)

DUDLEIGH: I just about had a heart attack. Whenever I hear a voice like that, I'm just sure that I've screwed up again.

CAT: Why?

DUDLEIGH: Because I usually have.

MASON: I didn't think you guys would take it that seriously.

MICHAEL: So, what do you take seriously, Mason?

MASON: Nothing. Not if I can help it. Look, we're in here and sooner or later we're going to get out.

DUDLEIGH: And what if we don't?

MASON: (*Simply*) Well, then, I guess we don't.

(*A loud ticking is heard.*)

MICHAEL: What's that sound? That ticking?

DUDLEIGH: It comes from over there.

MICHAEL: Now it's over there!

KURT: Mason?

MASON: I don't know anything about it. I swear!

(*It changes direction. To the structure.*)

CAT: Now, it's over there!

MICHAEL: What is that thing anyway?

KURT: It looks like some kind of clock or something.

MASON: I'll check it out.

(*Mason and Kurt cross behind the structure. The hand moves.*)

CAT: The hand, it moved!

DUDLEIGH: It's a time bomb! Take cover!

CAT: Everybody down!

(*All dive for cover. One of the dolls pops up from behind the structure. It is a Music Person.*)

MUSIC PERSON 1: Practice time!

MICHAEL: (*Delighted*) Practice time!

DUDLEIGH: (*Despondent*) Practice time?

(*Music Person 2 pops up.*)

MUSIC PERSON 2: Practice time!

MICHAEL: My favorite time of day!

BOTH MUSIC PERSONS: PRACTICE TIME!

DUDLEIGH: (*To the beat of the ticking*) Do I have to?

MUSIC PERSON 2: Yes you have to.

DUDLEIGH: I have to go to the bathroom.

MUSIC PERSON 1: Later.

DUDLEIGH: I have to do my homework.

MUSIC PERSON 2: Later!

DUDLEIGH: I think I'm coming down with the flu.

BOTH MUSIC PERSONS: PRACTICE TIME.

MICHAEL: Great!

DUDLEIGH: Nuts!

(Michael starts playing scales on the piano as Dudleigh crosses to the structure and gets a pair of tap shoes. She puts them on.)

DUDLEIGH: Do you have to watch?

(During the following Michael plays scales as Dudleigh "tries" to practice her tap dancing. Whenever she makes a mistake she is frustrated. Michael, on the other hand, loves practicing.)

MICHAEL: Sometimes when I'm practicing I close my eyes and play and play, and play, and it's like the room disappears . . .

(Dudleigh stops and peers around her.)

DUDLEIGH: I have to keep checking to see if anyone's here . . .

MICHAEL: And then the piano disappears . . .

DUDLEIGH: . . . because if anyone's near they can see me practicing . . .

MICHAEL: And then I disappear.

DUDLEIGH: And if they see me practicing, they can see me making mistakes . . .

MICHAEL: And there's nothing left but the notes hanging in the air . . .

DUDLEIGH: If they see me making mistakes, they'll say . . .

(Music Person 1 pops up again.)

MUSIC PERSON 1: What's going on in there?

DUDLEIGH: It's just me.

MICHAEL: I'm practicing.

(Music Person 2 pops up.)

MUSIC PERSON 2: You are really coming along nicely, Michael.

MICHAEL: Thanks.

MUSIC PERSON 1: Leigh Ann, that's supposed to be step, ball, change, step, step . . .

DUDLEIGH: That's what I'm doing!

MUSIC PERSON 1: Oh . . .

MUSIC PERSON 2: When is that . . .

BOTH MUSIC PEOPLE: . . . RECITAL?

MUSIC PERSON 1: Next week?

MUSIC PERSON 2: Next month?

DUDLEIGH and MICHAEL: Tomorrow!

BOTH MUSIC PEOPLE: Well, you'd better PRACTICE!

MICHAEL: I'm never sure if I'm playing the music or if the music is playing me . . .

DUDLEIGH: I force myself to go on, and I do the same steps over and over again, because I'm afraid to try anything new . . .

MICHAEL: So, I just let it go.

DUDLEIGH: I feel like a klutz and I look like a cow!

(*Cat, who has been watching all this comes forward as Michael transforms the scales into a rag time beat.*)

CAT: Just a minute, you got that all wrong.

DUDLEIGH: I know, I just can't do all those steps.

CAT: I'm not talking about the steps, forget about the steps, forget about the recital, forget about everything but the beat.

(*Seductive drum beat begins.*)

DUDLEIGH: The beat?

CAT: The beat! Now, close your eyes. Can you feel it?

DUDLEIGH: Feel what?

(*Dialogue moves into:* "Movin' To The Music.")

CAT: The beat, the beat.
Nothin' but the beat.
Tingling in your fingers
Flowing to your feet.

Now the knees, please,
Nothin' but the knees.
Kinda sleazy, kinda breezy,
Let 'em go where they please.

And the hips and the thighs,
Let 'em be a surprise.
From your fingers to your toes,
Let it go where it goes.

Feelin' kinda smooth.
Feelin' kinda sweet.
Never mind nothin'
Don't you mind nothin'
But the beat.

(*Dudleigh stands with her eyes closed "feeling the beat"* . . . *and trying a few steps . . . sort of.*)

CAT: Can you feel it?

DUDLEIGH: How do I look?

CAT: Never mind how you look, can you feel it?

DUDLEIGH: I think so . . . I think so.

(*Music picks up tempo.*)

MICHAEL: Just close your eyes and see yourself on stage . . .

CAT: . . . wearing a solid gold dress . . .

MICHAEL: . . . in front of millions of people . . .

CAT: . . . and silver shoes . . .

MICHAEL: And they've all come just to see you . . .

CAT: Sold out! Standing room only!

MICHAEL: And the house lights go down . . .

CAT: And the spot light comes up . . .

MICHAEL and CAT: And the music starts . . .

(*Music swings into melody.*)

DUDLEIGH: (*Sings*) I feel the music coming to me,
Through me,
So free!
I got a feeling there's a new me,
Tingling from my fingers to my toes.

CAT: (*To Dudleigh*) And now you're standing in a spot light,
It's a hot light,
That's right.

You can be more than what you are
When you pretend that you're a star.

You can be what you want to be,
Let yourself go and then you're free.

MICHAEL: Practicing the piano's not a drag time,
Or a gag time
When it's rag time.

CAT: Never mind your Momma or the nag time.
Let your fancy fly and set you free.

BOTH: Who needs talent, who needs skill?
When you got imagination on overkill?

Let 'em smile, let 'em laugh.
Soon they're going to beg you for your autograph.
You can sock it to 'em, you can knock 'em dead,

Practicing the piano,

Prancin' and a dancin',
Movin' to the music in your head!

(*Music builds under dialogue.*)

CAT: Come on, Dudleigh, let's see what you can do.

DUDLEIGH: But I'm not any good.

CAT: Who said you had to be good, just do it! Come on, Michael, help us out.

MICHAEL: 5, 6, 7, 8.

(*Dudleigh does a few steps and then screws up and stops.*)

CAT: Go on, go on! That was great!

DUDLEIGH: Really?

CAT: Really!

DUDLEIGH: (*To Michael*) Really?

MICHAEL: Really!

(*Dudleigh dances again, her confidence growing.*)

CAT: You can be more than what you are,
When you pretend that you're a star.

DUDLEIGH: I can be what I want to be,
Let myself go and then I'm free.

ALL: Who needs talent, who needs skill?
When you got imagination on overkill?

DUDLEIGH: I can sock it to 'em, I can knock 'em dead.

ALL: Movin' to the music.
Prancin' and a dancin'.
Moving to the music in my head!

(*There is a big finish.*)

CAT: Girl, you were something!

DUDLEIGH: I got all screwed up in the middle there.

CAT: Who cares?

DUDLEIGH: Oh, I've got as much grace as a cow, eh, Mason? Elsie and the Borden Ballet?

MASON: You looked pretty good to me.

(Dudleigh is flustered at the compliment and turns immediately to Michael.)

DUDLEIGH: Uhhh, Michael, you really were something. I mean you're good, really good, you could play professionally.

MICHAEL: I do.

DUDLEIGH: You're a musician. I thought you were a waiter!

MICHAEL: I'd probably get farther as a waiter.

CAT: But you sounded so good.

MICHAEL: That's the trouble. I'm always good, but never quite good enough, to win a competition. I always get into the semi-finals then . . . nothing! I'm like a dog on an invisible leash, I get right up to the finish and . . . Aaakkk!

CAT: This time you would have made it.

MICHAEL: How do you know?

CAT: I just do.

(Softly in the distance we hear a man's voice calling "Saaaa Bosss.")*

MICHAEL: Listen, everybody, do you hear that?

VOICE: Saaaa Boss!

MASON: What?

---

*Pronounced Sah Boss.

MICHAEL: That sound. That's my Dad's voice, but it can't be. He's been dead three years.

(*Cat hands Mason the male "doll." After a beat, he puts it on.*)

MICHAEL: (*Returning the call*) Saa Bossssss!

(*To Cat and Dudleigh.*)

Every evening my Dad would call the cows in from the pastures for milking with that call.

(*The voice answers "Saa Bosss." Mason joins with the recorded voice and steps into the role of Michael's Father.*)

FATHER: Okay, Mike, you try it!

MICHAEL: Me?

FATHER: It's about time you learned.

MICHAEL: But I can't do it as good as you can.

FATHER: And I couldn't do it as well as my father and he couldn't do it as well as his father, but the cows came anyway. Go ahead . . .

MICHAEL: (*A weak high-pitched sound*) Sa Boss!

FATHER: Lower!

(*Michael squats and tries again.*)

MICHAEL: Sa Boss!

FATHER: I mean your voice. Lower your voice. Sa Bossss!

MICHAEL: Saaa Booooos.

FATHER: Sounds like a fog horn!

MICHAEL: (*Better, but not good enough*) Sa Booosss.

FATHER: Longer and lower!

MICHAEL: Saaa Bossss.

FATHER: Mike, at this very minute those cows are munching on clover, and slip sliding around in sweet, sweet mud. Now, your voice has got to make them want to stop what they are doing and hustle on home to be milked!

MICHAEL: But how?

FATHER: They have to know that you mean it!

MICHAEL: Sa Boss!

FATHER: That you expect them to come!

MICHAEL: Sa Bosss!

FATHER: That you won't take "no" for an answer!

MICHAEL: SA BOSSS!

FATHER: You got 'em!!! Look at that, down near the hedge trees, that's Betty in the lead. Let her have it again, son.

MICHAEL: (*Delighted*) SA BOSS!!!!

FATHER: We'll make a dairyman out of you yet!

   (*Father beams, Michael looks uncomfortable.*)

MICHAEL: Uhhhh Dad?

FATHER: What?

MICHAEL: I'm going to be late for my piano lesson.

FATHER: Huh?

MICHAEL: Mom said she could take me.

FATHER: Go ahead, Mike. Go ahead.

   (*Father turns away. Michael feels he should stay, but he really is late.*)

MICHAEL: Dad?

FATHER: (*Turns back*) Yeah?

MICHAEL: Nothing.

(*Father turns away again and exits as Michael watches. Michael starts to turn away, changes his mind, and turns back again.*)

MICHAEL: Dad? DAD!

(*Mason enters where Dad has exited.*)

MASON: What?

MICHAEL: Nothing, I, uhhh, was just thinking about my Dad.

MASON: Oh.

(*There is an awkward moment between them. Michael exits. Dudleigh, concerned, exits after him.*)

(*A small door opens in the structure and a baseball rolls in Mason's path. He looks at it, starts to walk past it, and makes eye contact with Cat. She holds his gaze for a second and exits. He turns back, picks up the ball, and tosses it in the air. Mason takes off his jacket revealing a brightly colored tee shirt.*)

MASON: I never did figure it out about my Dad. I had to have someone tell me and the way it happened was so stupid.

(*Kurt enters as Friend.*)

FATHER: Over here!

(*They start a game of catch, tossing the ball back and forth. Suddenly a Man's Voice yells:*)

VOICE: Get away from my car!

(*The boys stop, look toward the voice and resume their game.*)

MASON: We weren't doing anything wrong. Just tossing a baseball back and forth, and my Dad comes out and yells at us and as he goes back into the house, he trips on the door jamb. My friend looked away in disgust and it all came to me. Dad not coming home until late. Mom crying for no reason when we were sitting around watching T.V. Dad acting crazy, kissing us with a sort of slobber one minute, and a cuff to the ear the next. That smell, like chlorine in a pool, even at breakfast. And then my friend said . . .

FRIEND: Your Dad's a drunk.

MASON: And I just said . . . Yeah.

(Mason throws the ball very hard at Kurt; it slaps into his mitt. Mason exits behind the structure.)

(Kurt turns away, pockets the ball and removes a bat from somewhere on the structure. He mimes throwing the ball in the air and takes a swing.)

(Dudleigh enters, sees Kurt, picks up the female doll and enters as Kurt's Mom.)

MOM: Here you are.

KURT: Yeah.

MOM: What are you doing?

KURT: What does it look like?

MOM: Oh . . .

(Kurt tries again and misses.)

MOM: You've been at this for hours. It's getting dark.

KURT: Dad says I've got to try harder to keep my eye on the ball.

MOM: It would help if you could see it.

KURT: I can see it!

(He tries again and misses.)

MOM: Honey, everyone strikes out.

KURT: Three times, does everyone strike out three times in one game?

MOM: Well . . .

KURT: If the pitcher hadn't beaned me with that curve ball, I never would have gotten a base.

MOM: How's your head?

KURT: It's okay!

MOM: Come on in.

KURT: Dad told me to keep trying until I hit five in a row without missing.

MOM: Do you want me to bring your sleeping bag out here?

KURT: Mom, that's not funny.

MOM: Come on, Kurt, don't be so hard on yourself.

KURT: Just a few more minutes.

MOM: Let it go.

(*Kurt swings again and misses.*)

I made you some chocolate chip cookies.

(*Kurt swings again and misses.*)

Bonanza's on.

KURT: Mom!

MOM: Okay! Don't be long, honey.

KURT: Dad says it just takes practice.

(*Mom exits.*)

Okay, keep your eye on the ball . . . try harder . . . try harder . . . try . . .

(*He tosses the ball and swings, there is a crack as the bat makes contact, followed immediately by the sound of shattering glass.*)

MOM: (*Off-stage*) KURT!

KURT: I'm sorry, Mom, I'm sorry!

MOM: Your Father will want to talk to you just as soon as he gets back from the Rotary Club!

(*Music for "Ballad of the Bike" begins as Kurt paces in frustration.*)

KURT: I'm doomed! The last time I broke a window, he took away my allowance, AND grounded me, AND yelled at me for 25 minutes straight!

(*Music picks up tempo Kurt sings.*)

KURT: Go, I gotta go;
Feeling sad and mad and low.
Hit the road
Or explode.
Gotta get out, gotta go.

Ride, I gotta ride;
Or I think I'm gonna cry.
I'm ashamed
Of the pain
Gotta get out, gotta ride.

(*Kurt crosses to the bike.*)

(*Spoken.*)

And I head straight for KILLER HILL!!!

(*Kurt speaks/sings this as he creates the illusion of pedaling up "Killer Hill."*)

Gotta do it. Gotta do it.
Gotta just get through it.
Gotta get up to the top.
To the top, hot damn!
I'm the only one who can.
Can't stop, can't stop,
'Til I get up to the top.

Gotta try, gotta try.
'Til I think I'm gonna die.
Gotta push until I find
I can leave it all behind.
Can't stop, can't stop,
'Til I get up to the . . .

(*As he crests the hill, the music changes and Kurt mirrors in his body the joy of the dizzy downward ride.*)

KURT: (*Sings*) And I feel the air
On my face, in my hair,
And the worry and care
Disappear.

I dip and I sway
And the pain goes away,
And the wind starts to play
With my fear.

The hills they go up
And the valley's go down,
But the wheel's just go round
And around.

I soar and I glide,
Feel the healing inside
As I ride and I ride
And I ride.

(*Kurt pops a wheelie and dances a bit with his beloved bike. He is lost in his own world when Mason enters abruptly.*)

MASON: What do you think you're doing?

KURT: Riding my bike.

MASON: Why?

KURT: When I'd get really upset, it always used to make me feel better.

MASON: Why are you riding it here? Why are you riding it now?

KURT: I don't know.

MASON: Listen, Coach . . .

KURT: Don't call me that!

MASON: Don't you think this is all a little stupid? We should be figuring out how to get out of here, but instead we keep bringing up a lot of foolish, childish memories.

KURT: I thought this was no big deal to you.

MASON: I'm sick of this place; it no longer amuses me.

KURT: Your amusement? Is that what we're here for, YOUR AMUSEMENT?

MICHAEL: Stop it! This isn't getting us anywhere! If we don't figure out a way to work together, we're going to be stuck in here for the rest of our lives!

CAT: No, sometimes people get out.

MASON: (*Quickly*) What people?

CAT: The ones who got out.

DUDLEIGH: Where?

CAT: Here.

MICHAEL: When?

CAT: Before.

KURT: There were people here before us. Why didn't you tell us?

CAT: You didn't ask.

KURT: What kind of people?

CAT: Spies, explorers.

KURT: (*Explodes*) Oh yeah, sure!

MASON: You know what I think? I think you know more about this than you're telling.

CAT: Me?

MASON: Yes, you. I think you are a part of this . . .

CAT: No, I'm just like you, only I've been here longer.

KURT: I don't believe you.

MASON: I don't either.

CAT: Dudleigh, surely you believe me.

DUDLEIGH: I don't know. I'm not sure.

CAT: I don't know how to get out, but I do know where we are.

MASON: Where?

CAT: We're underneath a crack in the world. We're somewhere where little pieces of time get lost.

KURT: Now, cut out the double talk and tell us how to get out of here!

MICHAEL: Leave her alone. She can't tell us.

MASON: Oh, yeah? Then who can?

MICHAEL: Nobody, we have to find it ourselves.

MASON: (*Scoffing*) Pieces of time . . .

CAT: (*To Michael*) You just have to know which piece.

MASON: And you're both from the planet Xercon!

KURT: There has got to be something we haven't thought of, something we are overlooking . . . something like a . . . trap door!

MASON: That's it! Or a secret passageway.

MICHAEL: I remember . . .

(Michael stands still, center stage, as he remembers. The others swirl around him.)

I remember my eleventh birthday.

MASON: A systematic search, that's what we need, a systematic search!

MICHAEL: It was my birthday party and everyone was there. My Aunt Betty Lou . . .

(Dudleigh passes in front of Michael as she circles around and out of sight.)

MICHAEL: My Grandmother . . .

MASON: Kurt, you check around the floor line, where the walls touch the floor.

KURT: Got it!

(Kurt checks the floor and exits behind the structure as well.)

MICHAEL: My Mother . . .

MASON: Cat, check out the corners wherever two walls come together!

(Cat is listening to Michael.)

Cat? Cat, are you with us on this?

CAT: Uhhh, yes, sure.

(Cat crosses to a corner and then off.)

MICHAEL: And my father . . .

MASON: Michael? Michael? Earth to Michael! Earth to . . . Oh, never mind.

(Mason exits behind the structure.)

MICHAEL: My Aunt Betty Lou made her famous double chocolate cake with white icing. My Grandmother took pictures.

(One of the dolls pops up from behind the structure.)

GRANDMA: Say Cheese!

(Michael smiles and has his picture taken.)

MICHAEL: We always save the presents for last, like they are supposed to be a big surprise or something. My Grandmother always gives me clothes and they are always the same size, too big.

(Kurt enters with Grandma.)

MICHAEL: Thanks, Grandma! I need a new shirt for school.

GRANDMA: I hope it fits.

(Kurt exits with Grandma.)

MICHAEL: My Aunt Betty Lou always gives me a game, and it's always the same game.

(Dudleigh enters with Aunt Betty Lou.)

MICHAEL: A game of Clue!

AUNT BETTY LOU: I didn't know if you had that one.

(Dudleigh exits with Aunt Betty Lou.)

MICHAEL: My Mom always gives me socks and underpants, cause I always need socks and underpants.

(Cat enters with Mom.)

MOM: That should hold you until next year.

(Cat exits with Mom.)

MICHAEL: My Dad always gets me something special, and it's always something to do with the farm. This year I knew it was going to be a heifer calf that we saw at the county fair. I knew he wanted me to want it. But I didn't, and I didn't want to disappoint him . . . Not again. So, I didn't say anything and I dreaded my birthday.

(*Mason enters with Father.*)

MICHAEL: I wasn't surprised when my Dad said:

FATHER: Mike, we couldn't exactly hide my gift here in the house, so you'll have to go out to the back porch to see it.

MICHAEL: That walk to the kitchen door was the longest one of my life. I opened the door and . . .

(*Michael is near the piano. He turns and sees it.*)

A piano? You got me my own piano?

(*He runs and hugs his Dad.*)

FATHER: Play something, son . . . play. I'd like to hear you.

MICHAEL: You would?

FATHER: I would.

(*Michael sits at the piano and begins to play "Sa Boss" as Father stands nearby.*)

MICHAEL: (*Spoken under the "Intro"*) I was . . . uhhh . . . kind of working on something, it's kind of a song, I mean it's not really finished or anything, I mean, it's just kind of begun, I mean, it's . . .

FATHER: Just play it, Mike.

MICHAEL: Okay . . .

(*Sung.*)

Sa Bosss . . .

FATHER: (*Spoken, laughing slightly*) Longer, lower. Like this . . .

(*Sung.*)

Sa Bosss . . .

MICHAEL: Like this?

   (*He tries again.*)

Sa Bosss . . .

TOGETHER: Cows come on home!

MICHAEL: Home from the pastures
Sweet with spring and flowers.

FATHER: Tracing trails
Through fields of frost.

TOGETHER: Never getting lost.

FATHER: (*Spoken*) Now, try it again!

   (*Sings.*)

Sa Bosss!

MICHAEL: (*On exactly the same pitch*) Sa Bosss!

FATHER: That's it!

MICHAEL: (*Moving towards Dad*) Following the sound
The sound of Father's calling.

FATHER: (*Lifts his arm to encircle Michael's shoulder*) Calling children
safely home.

MICHAEL: (*Steps back*) But I must go alone.

   (*Michael turns away and Dad exits slowly during this verse.*)

MICHAEL: And so I go
My separate way,
Forgiving you,
Forgive me too.
I hear you still
I always will
Sa Boss, Sa Boss!

(*Music ends as Cat enters and watches.*)

MICHAEL: I didn't remember that you gave me that piano. After all these years of wanting your approval . . .

(*There is a strange soft sound. He looks puzzled, and tentatively puts his hands on the wall.*)

MICHAEL: He gave me that piano!

(*Michael takes a deep breath and walks through the wall. Mason enters, and cannot see him.*)

MASON: Michael, we could really use your . . . Michael? Hey, Michael!

KURT: (*Entering*) What's the matter?

MASON: Have you seen Michael?

DUDLEIGH: (*Entering*) He was just here.

MASON: Well, he's not here now!

(*Michael exits.*)

MASON: Where was he standing?

DUDLEIGH: Right here.

KURT: Are you sure?

DUDLEIGH: He must have found the trap door, the passageway.

KURT: Are you sure?

CAT: Maybe it was just time for him to go.

DUDLEIGH: But I just saw him!

KURT: Are you sure?

DUDLEIGH: You know, I hate that! I really hate that.

KURT: What?

DUDLEIGH: "Are you sure? Are you sure?" I told you what I saw.

KURT: I was just asking.

DUDLEIGH: I had an uncle who used to do that to me all the time. Good old Uncle Bob.

(Music is heard. Dudleigh places a sheet over Michael's piano to turn it into a dining table. She hands Kurt the male doll and Cat the female doll. Mason observes from a distance.)

DUDLEIGH: He'd always pick some time when lots of people were around, like a family reunion, or a big holiday with all the relatives . . .

MASON: (*Sarcastic*) Oh yeah, family dinners!

DUDLEIGH: Everyone would be there including good old Uncle Bob and Aunt Ethel. And just as dessert was about to be served, good old Uncle Bob would start with the numbers.

(Kurt and Cat join her at the "table" with Uncle Bob and Aunt Ethel. Music underscores this scene.)

UNCLE BOB: Are you ready, Leigh Ann?

AUNT ETHEL: Let her finish her dinner, Dear.

DUDLEIGH: No, Aunt Ethel, it's okay. I'm ready.

UNCLE BOB: Are you sure?

DUDLEIGH: I guess so.

UNCLE BOB: Okay, what's 43 minus 18 plus 25 times 2 minus 10 divided by 3?

DUDLEIGH: Just a sec. Let's see, 43 minus 18 plus 25 times 2 minus 10 divided by . . .

UNCLE BOB: Three . . . Well?

(*Dudleigh computes in her head.*)

DUDLEIGH: 30!

UNCLE BOB: (*As if she has made an error*) 30? Are you sure?

DUDLEIGH: (*Suddenly unsure*) No, wait, wait! Let me try again, let's see it's . . . 43 minus 18 . . .

MASON: Hold it!

(*Everyone at the table freezes; Mason crosses to the table, takes the male doll from Kurt. Kurt, Cat and Dudleigh turn their backs. Music changes to a low, tense, hollow sort of sound. Mason props the male doll up against the table, it slumps over, but stays in place. It is Mason's father. He is drunk.*)

Family dinner!

(*One by one the company take their places at the table and eat in silence. Mason stands a bit apart, tossing the baseball and catching it.*)

BROTHER: Hey, Mason. We're eating.

(*Mason enters the scene. There is a breathless tension and elaborate politeness surrounding the scene.*)

SISTER I: Please pass the chicken, Mason.

(*Sister II mimes passing it.*)

Thank you.

SISTER II: You're welcome.

BROTHER: Could I have some rice?

(*Sister I mimes passing it.*)

Thank you.

SISTER I: You're welcome.

SISTER II: Pass the peas.

(Brother mimes passing it.)

Thank you.

BROTHER: You're welcome.

MASON: Can I have some salt, Dad?

(He looks to "Father" who does not move.)

I said, please pass the salt, DAD!

(Brother angrily hands Mason the salt.)

BROTHER: Just get it yourself!

MASON: It was right by him.

(They eat for a moment in silence. After a beat, Mason speaks again.)

MASON: So, Dad, you want to know what I got on my report card? They came out today and we're supposed to be sure we show them to BOTH parents? So, Dad, you want to see it?

BROTHER: Leave him alone, Mason.

SISTER I: Mom can sign it for you when she gets back from work.

MASON: But we're supposed to have BOTH parents sign.

BROTHER: Will you come off it?

MASON: Come off what?

BROTHER: You know.

MASON: When BOTH parents are home, BOTH parents are supposed to sign.

BROTHER: *(Whispers to him)* If you don't stop, he'll get mad and leave.

MASON: Are you kidding? He's too far gone to know what's going on around here!

SISTER I: Mason! Stop it!

SISTER II: Well, at least he's home!

MASON: Is he? Is he really?

(*Mason nails her with a look, and exits behind the structure. Kurt, Cat and Dudleigh turn their backs. Suddenly Dudleigh whirls around.*)

DUDLEIGH: Hold it!

(*Dudleigh hands Kurt and Cat the dolls.*)

This time I'm sure!

(*Upbeat music starts again as we return to her dinner.*)

Yes, I'm sure this time. The answer is 30, I'm positive!

UNCLE BOB: Are you sure?

DUDLEIGH: Well . . .?

UNCLE BOB: Are you absolutely sure?

DUDLEIGH: I guess so, I don't know.

AUNT ETHEL: (*This has gone on long enough*) Robert!

UNCLE BOB: Well, you're right! It is 30! Leigh Ann, you ought to stick up for what you believe in!

DUDLEIGH: How come even when I'm right, I still feel wrong?

(*Kurt and Cat turn their backs again. Dudleigh suddenly realizes something.*)

Ah Hah!

(*She whips the cloth off.*)

It was a set-up. It was a set-up all the time and I always fell right into it.

CAT: Always?

DUDLEIGH: Always. Even when I was absolutely sure I knew the answer, I still made myself feel stupid and dumb and out of it. It wasn't Uncle Bob . . . it was me!

(*Realizing for the first time.*)

I could have just said "yes!"

(*There is the strange soft sound. She looks at the wall.*)

Hey, look at the wall!

MASON: What about it?

DUDLEIGH: It looks different, like it's made of fog or something.

KURT: Are you sure?

DUDLEIGH: Well, actually . . . I don't know . . .

(*The sound stops.*)

KURT: (*Aggressively*) What did you see?

DUDLEIGH: I don't know . . . a soft spot . . . I'm not sure.

KURT: What if that's the way out of here? And you're not even sure what you saw? Come on, Dudleigh!

MASON: You were standing right there, Kurt, what did you see?

KURT: (*Kurt shoots him a look*) Nothing. Look, I've got an idea. Everybody push, right here, all of us, push against the soft spot, or whatever . . . Come on . . .

(*They form a group and push.*)

KURT: Come on let's go! 1 . . . 2 . . . 3 . . . Push!

(*Cat drops out.*)

Try again, 1 . . . 2 . . . 3 . . . PUSH!

(*Dudleigh drops out.*)

Once more, 1 . . . 2 . . . 3 . . . PUSH.

(*Finally Mason drops out.*)

1 . . . 2 . . .

MASON: It isn't budging.

KURT: If we don't get out of here soon, everything we know on the outside will be gone! No one is even trying to get out! No one but me!

CAT: It wasn't going to work.

KURT: Well have you got a better idea? Because if you have a better idea, I am sure we would all like to hear it.

DUDLEIGH: Leave her alone, Kurt.

KURT: Oh, so now you're siding with her.

DUDLEIGH: I am not siding with anyone. We're all trying the best we can!

KURT: Then do something! Check that corner.

(*He takes her by the shoulders and propels her.*)

DUDLEIGH: Don't do that.

KURT: What?

DUDLEIGH: I'll help you if you want, but don't push me.

KURT: I didn't!

MASON: Yes, you did, Kurt.

KURT: What do you know?

MASON: Face it, Kurt, you're just a pushy guy!

KURT: (*Blasts at Mason*) I am sick and tired of you standing around making smart ass remarks. I have had all I'm going to take from you, Brian.

MASON: Brian?

KURT: Mason.

MASON: You called me Brian.

KURT: I did not.

MASON: I know what I heard.

KURT: I know what I said.

DUDLEIGH: You called him Brian.

KURT: (*Shouting*) I did not!

MASON: So, is that what you do when you're wrong, yell at your kid?

KURT: You shut up about my kid. You don't know anything about my kid.

MASON: I know his father's a jerk!

(*Kurt throws a single punch and decks Mason.*)

CAT: You hit him.

DUDLEIGH: KURT!

MASON: What, do you punch him around too?

KURT: (*Horrified at his own action*) No!

MASON: I'll bet!

CAT: Are you alright?

MASON: (*It does*) It doesn't really hurt, not really, it doesn't really hurt!

KURT: Mason, look, I don't do that!

MASON: Yeah, yeah, I know all about it. My old man used to knock me around all the time!

KURT: I am not your old man.

MASON: And I am not your son!

KURT: I know. I don't hit him, Mason, I swear to God. Sometimes I feel like it, sometimes he makes me so mad, I could just . . .

MASON: Yeah.

KURT: But I don't.

MASON: Not yet.

(*There is a beat.*)

KURT: I want so much for him and he is so bright, so damn bright, but he doesn't try, he just doesn't try.

(*Mason takes the report card from Kurt's pocket.*)

MASON: (*Gently, handing him the card*) Are you sure you know how hard he tries?

KURT: (*To himself*) I'm doing it! I'm doing everything I hated as a kid. All the pressure, the push, push, I'm doing everything I swore I'd never . . . I don't have to do that!

(*The strange soft sound is heard. Kurt puts down the card and looks at the wall.*)

KURT: The wall . . .

MASON: What about it?

KURT: Dudleigh, it **is** different . . .

MASON: Looks the same to me.

(*Mason pounds on the wall.*)

KURT: You're trying too hard.

(*Kurt crosses to the same spot, extends his hand and it goes through the wall.*)

You just have to . . .

DUDLEIGH: But that doesn't make sense!

KURT: I know! Dudleigh, come on!

(*He offers her his hand and passes through the wall.*)

DUDLEIGH: Are you sure?

(*She stops half-way through.*)

Hold it! Hold it! I'm stuck! I'm stuck, I tell you.

(*Kurt is on one side of the wall, Cat and Mason on the other, and Dudleigh is frozen in the middle.*)

KURT: I've got your hand!

DUDLEIGH: I can't feel you.

KURT: What can you feel?

DUDLEIGH: Nothing!

KURT: What can you see?

DUDLEIGH: Nothing.

KURT: Can you hear me?

DUDLEIGH: Of course I can hear you, I'm talking to you aren't I?

MASON: Can you hear us?

DUDLEIGH: Faintly.

CAT: Can you see us?

DUDLEIGH: It's like a fog, everything is grey.

MASON: Try to come toward the sound of my voice.

DUDLEIGH: I told you I can't move!

MASON: Try holding your breath.

KURT: Try wiggling.

MASON: Try crawling.

CAT: Try jumping.

DUDLEIGH: Will everybody be QUIET! I can do this for myself!!

KURT: Are you sure?

DUDLEIGH: YES!

(*Suddenly she discovers that she is free. There is a sound as she passes through the wall.*)

KURT: You did it!

DUDLEIGH: We did it?

(*They exit together.*)

(*Inside the "Room," Mason is astonished and Cat is delighted.*)

MASON: How did they do that? I saw it, but I'm not sure I believe it!

CAT: They got out.

MASON: They must have found a passageway.

CAT: There isn't any passageway.

MASON: Why do you contradict everything I say?

CAT: I don't.

MASON: Yes, you do.

CAT: No, I don't. I just know what I know.

MASON: Then how do we get out of here?

CAT: I don't know.

MASON: You're hopeless!

CAT: I am full of hope!

(*Mason turns away from her in frustration. Looking up.*)

There are stars up there now.

MASON: (*Not looking*) Don't be ridiculous.

CAT: Dudleigh would have loved those stars.

MASON: Are you going to help me?

CAT: I am trying to. I am trying to show you these stars.

(*Mason has picked up a baseball and plays with it without noticing what he's doing.*)

MASON: I don't care about your bloody stars! I don't care about anything in this room. I just care about getting out like everybody else.

CAT: What's that?

MASON: (*Suddenly self-conscious*) A ball.

CAT: Who's is it?

MASON: It's mine.

CAT: Oh really?

MASON: Listen, you want to hear something really funny. My Dad, he gave me this ball but it was already mine.

CAT: Already yours?

MASON: (*Laughing*) Yeah, When I was ten he forgot my birthday, so he found this old ball in my closet, wrapped it up and gave it to me.

CAT: That's terrible.

MASON: (*Laughing*) It's funny.

CAT: No it isn't.

MASON: Ah, it doesn't matter. Not now. Not anymore.

(*Mason tries to toss the ball away. He is mildly surprised to discover it is stuck in his hand. He tries again to toss it, to no avail.*)

CAT: If it doesn't matter, then throw it away.

(*Mason tries again.*)

MASON: You want to know something really funny? I can't.

CAT: You can't?

MASON: It's stuck.

CAT: Stuck?

MASON: Like with glue or something.

(*Cat bursts into laughter. Mason tries harder to throw the ball. Cat laughs harder.*)

This is ridiculous.

(*Mason throws very hard and contorts his body. He is still laughing . . . sort of.*)

CAT: (*Still laughing*) If you could see how you look.

(*Mason tries again and again to get rid of the ball. He is becoming annoyed with Cat's laughter.*)

MASON: Come on, Cat.

CAT: Hey, Mason, toss me the ball.

(*Mason tries to throw the ball to her. It remains stuck.*)

MASON: Stop laughing at me.

(*Cat jumps up and down half-playing, half-goading him.*)

CAT: I'm over here . . . Come on, Mason . . . put it here . . . come on . . .

(*Mason tries to throw the ball AT her. Cat holds the male doll as a target for Mason.*)

MASON: (*Bellows*) STOP IT!

CAT: It's just a game, why are you so mad?

MASON: I'm so mad . . . so mad . . .

CAT: Don't yell at me, yell at HIM.

(*Cat tosses the doll at Mason. Finally, he blows his stack.*)

MASON: It's an old ball, Dad, an old ball! Didn't you think I'd notice? Didn't you think I'd care? Why did you bother? I didn't want anything from you, not anything.

(*He kneels down and grabs the doll with his free hand.*)

No, that's not true.

(*Simply.*)

It hurt, Dad . . . it really hurt.
I wanted you to remember.
I wanted you to remember and be glad I was born. I wanted you to look at me and see me. I wanted you to listen and hear ME. I wanted you to talk to me.

(*Between anger and tears.*)

Talk to me, Dad, just talk to me.

CAT: (*Tenderly*) He can't.

MASON: (*Vulnerable*) Why not?

CAT: It's just a doll, Mason.

(*After a beat or two, Mason comes back to reality.*)

MASON: Yeah.

(*He shakes the "doll" with a gesture that is a shadow of his former rage, then hugs it close to him.*)

Yeah.

(*The ball rolls from his hand, along the floor. They both watch it.*)

CAT: Mason, the ball . . .

MASON: Yeah.

(*After a beat.*)

Who are you, Cat? Who are you, really?

CAT: Who do you think I am?

MASON: (*Gently*) No double talk, just tell me.

CAT: (*Simply*) No double talk. I've told you all I know.

MASON: You've been in here too long. Come out of this room. Come with me.

CAT: No.

MASON: Why not?

CAT: It's not my turn.

(*She tosses him the ball. He looks up.*)

MASON: There are stars up there.

CAT: I know.

MASON: I hope you get out, Cat. I hope you do.

CAT: Goodbye, Mason.

(*Mason takes a deep breath, and we hear the strange soft sound as he passes through the wall.*)

MASON: There it is! The house, the house I was . . . Hey, you guys . . .

(*He turns back to the room. Astonished*)

The room, it's gone! The wall, the room, there's nothing there! It must have been a dream, it must have been . . .

(*Mason realizes he still holds the ball.*)

Huh!

(*He exits through the audience, shaking his head at the wonder of it all. Cat steps forward to the wall, the strange, soft sound is heard. With a motion like the parting of a curtain she passes through the wall and steps to the other side. She waves, but Mason is gone. She steps back into the room, and turns to the "dolls." Music begins.*)

CAT: Well!

(*She props the "dolls" up and cover them with sheets as at the beginning of the play. She sits, holding the final sheet, and looks around to be sure all is in readiness. She looks straight into the audience.*)

Well?

(*She billows out the final sheet. It falls over her, covering her completely.*)

CURTAIN

The Death and Life of
Sherlock Holmes

The fact that *The Death and Life of Sherlock Holmes* is the final play in this collection is significant beyond simple chronological order. This play marks a major turning point in Zeder's writing, born out of a period of intense questioning. She had been approached by Stage One Theatre in Louisville which wanted to commission the play, but she resisted at first. She felt that the Holmes material had been done to death, that it was too cinematic to be adequately translated to live theatre, and that she would have trouble finding anything of her own personal passion in the material. In addition to these factors, she felt she had come to a real crossroads in her creative life. The difficult process of clarifying *In a Room Somewhere* was weighing heavily on her, and she found herself suffering from, as she calls it, "that classic terror a writer feels when you've been very lucky and had a series of successes, but are plagued by a nagging fear that your luck will run out."

Early working notes she made as she was considering the commission reveal her attempt to weave the story around the character Wiggins. When she realized that she was forcing herself to make the child's perspective the heart of the material, she stopped abruptly. On top of her fears of creative burn out, she realized she was trapping herself in the box of her previous successes. "That scared me," she said, "and convinced me it was time to take a break from writing altogether."

When the Fulton Opera House in Lancaster, Pennsylvania joined Stage One in offering a commission for a play about Holmes, Zeder decided to take one last look at the material to see if she could find anything in it that connected with her personal concerns and interests. It was information about the author of the Sherlock Holmes stories, Sir Arthur Conan Doyle, which provided the key. Zeder learned that, at one point in his career, Doyle grew so tired of writing the popular Sherlock Holmes stories and was so eager to get on with other projects that he decided to kill his famous protagonist. This fact piqued Zeder's interest in the relationship between the author and his creation and gave her a point of entry into the material which was both organic to the original stories and which moved her into new creative territory that did not include any major child characters.

The way in which Zeder has constructed the complex plot of this play is another example of her ability to create fascinating puzzles. Nearly all the incidents and most of the dialogue is taken directly from the Sherlock Holmes stories, Doyle's personal letters, and incidents from Doyle's life. She orders events in such a way that the fit of the diverse Holmes stories with each other, with events from Doyle's life, and with Zeder's own original additions is almost seamless. The result is an elegantly crafted play that functions both as a detective adventure story and as a psychological drama. The linchpin that holds these elements together structurally is the character of Sir Arthur Conan Doyle. Doyle's struggles as a writer and his relationship to his fictional creation, Sherlock Holmes, become the thematic heart of the play.

Zeder's choice to have Doyle step into the roles of the villains he is writing is both psychologically truthful to the writer's process and theatrically exciting. It externalizes Doyle's inner conflict in all of its intensity. The audience can see the addictive exhiliration he feels while living out his stories balanced against the toll his writing takes on his health and on his relationships. Zeder also uses each villain role to deepen Doyle's characterization and to illuminate the increasingly urgent stages of his struggle to break out of a self-created trap. When Doyle becomes Moran, we see how his creativity, working at a subconscious level, comes up with an ending that even he doesn't expect. The role of Roylott shows us Doyle's vulnerability to psychic and spiritual forces. As Moriarty, Doyle gives his most articulate explanation of the negative aspects of having created Sherlock, describing how Sherlock has inconvenienced, persecuted, and nearly eclipsed him. In the final scene, when Doyle steps into his fictional worlds as himself, he reveals the positive aspects of creating Holmes, including the companionship Sherlock has provided and the way the stories represent pieces of his real life, both as it is and as he wishes it could be.

Some of the other characters, written but not role-played by Doyle, also reveal his inner life. The link between Doyle and Watson is established as they share the narration of the play, during which Watson reveals Doyle's deep affection for Sherlock. Sherlock himself shares Doyle's obsessive intensity and becomes an extension of the author's observational and analytical prowess.

Though most of the play grows out of the unfolding of Doyle's character, Mary's role provides the suspense and surprise that keeps the play mysterious and exciting. Paradoxically, Mary becomes a villain more powerful than Moriarty. She is the only character, other than Doyle, to appear both as a character in her own right and as one of Doyle's fictional creations. The fact that some of Mary's simple daily activities show up in Doyle's fiction, wonderfully transformed and heightened, gives us more insight into Doyle's creative process. But even more important than this, is the way Zeder uses Mary to articulate Doyle's "real life" problems. It is through Doyle's relationship to Mary that we guage how he grows and changes during the course of the play.

As different as *The Death and Life of Sherlock Holmes* is from the rest of Zeder's plays, there are still familiar elements. Zeder's interest in juxtaposing different planes of reality in the same stage space is certainly present here as she moves into and out of Doyle's fictional world. She artfully blurs the lines between the fictional world and the real world at times to increase suspense and illustrate how the creative process spills over and affects Doyle's life in unexpected ways.

Zeder's skill with language is just as evident here as in her earlier plays, although the demands of the material have required her to blend her voice with that of Sir Arthur Conan Doyle. In this she succeeds admirably. Her word choice and construction of dialogue make her own material so like Doyle's in tone that even Sherlock Holmes devotees will be hard pressed to tell the difference. She is also adroit in selecting which bits of dialogue to take directly from the original stories. Almost all the dialogue in the exchanges between Sherlock and the various villains is from the original stories, but it takes on a whole new layer of meaning when it issues from the mouth of Sir Arthur Conan Doyle as he enacts these villains. Moriarty's words, in particular, are so fitting for the character of Doyle one can't help thinking that Zeder has tapped into the real Doyle's underlying feeling while he was writing "The Final Problem," and that he would smile if he were to see them performed in this context.

Thematically this play extends Zeder's concerns in her earlier work into new areas. Doyle faces, on an adult level, a struggle not unlike Ellie's in *Step on a Crack* and Jeff's in *Doors*. These child protagonists discover that the fantasy that helped them work through their problems is also getting in their way. Ellie ordering her imaginary friends into the toy chest has some similarity to Doyle freezing Holmes and Watson at the top of the waterfall. But Zeder goes farther in this play in examining the potentially destructive elements in the creative process.

In the final scene, Doyle, disguised as Moriarty, is locked in mortal combat with Sherlock on the promontory overlooking the boiling waters of Reichenbach Falls. Both men are in equal danger of falling to their deaths in the terrifying abyss. The implication is clear: if the creation dies, then the creator is in danger of dying too. For Doyle, and for many artists, the very process of creating becomes a daily need as powerful as the need for food, but it requires an opening up of the self that allows the creation to take over. This process can be frightening and dangerous for some writers. For those writers who achieve success or become popular for a particular style or character, the public demand for more of the same and the lure of financial gain that goes with it can present another potential pitfall. Doyle, as conceived by Zeder, suffers from both in this play.

As Zeder wrote the last scene of the play she was surprised to find herself back in familiar territory, when, out of Mary's mouth popped the words of a jealous daughter: "But what of me? I'm your child!" This was followed instantly by Doyle's reply, "Aye, and so is he." Without ever intending it, Zeder found herself back in the realm of parent-child relationships. But this time she had come at it from a very different angle. In this play, the literary creation, Sherlock, is the child, and the world of the play is seen from the viewpoint of the parent—a complete reversal from Zeder's usual approach.

The Death and Life of Sherlock Holmes may well signal a change in the direction of Zeder's work. Although other of her plays were not written with a child audience in mind, this is the only one in this collection that seems too complex for the attention span and interests of some young children.

In the time that has elapsed since she started *Holmes* and the completion of this collection, she still does not know what will come next for her as a playwright, and she has taken a break from writing. She did not realize until after this play was completed what a parallel there was between Doyle's feelings of being suffocated by Holmes and her own feelings of being haunted, and even trapped, within her work. She says, "I feel sometimes like I am standing at Reichenbach Falls with Ellie, Wiley, Jeff, and Girl, but I don't know yet what is on the other side of the falls." She feels that something has changed but is not yet sure about what the change is or what it will mean for her future works. The fact that she is confronting and freeing herself from assumptions, categories, and limitations—both those that are self-imposed and those absorbed from outside influences—may well be opening her to new and deeper levels.

Even if her future plays do not include child protagonists, she has already served as a pioneer in theatre for young audiences. American dramatic literature has, for the most part, ignored, killed off, or in other ways minimized the complexity and humanity of child characters. Indeed, much contemporary American theatre shows parent/

child relationships as a hostile battlefield of blame and battering. The child within characters written by many well-known playwrights seems to be hurt and angry and screaming about past betrayals. The characters in Marsha Norman's *Getting Out* and *Night Mother* are examples, as are Sam Shepard's nuclear families after the holocaust, and Christopher Durang's cartoon figures whose searing anger pervades the comedy.

In contrast, the works in this collection provide a rich legacy of very real child characters. Along with Zeder's adult characters, they struggle to understand each other and to find affirmation and growth even when they make mistakes. This legacy has already begun to inspire other playwrights and producers to move beyond their preconceived assumptions about child characters and young audiences and to improve the depth and quality of dramatic literature about and for young people and families.

The Death and Life of Sherlock Holmes

by Suzan L. Zeder

Based upon the stories of
Sir Arthur Conan Doyle

From the Playwright

Writing a play is a bit like solving a mystery. The first clue comes as an idea, a character, or a concept. As it is shaped in draft after draft, more clues are found. The play develops like a photograph: images are clarified, themes are sharply etched, and meanings emerge out of action. In each production, the play is further shaped by directors and designers; it is brought to life by actors, and is given whatever relevance it has in the hearts and minds of audiences. Each creative force makes a contribution, each supplies a special part of the puzzle. But finally the play begins to speak in it's own voice, a voice that is louder and more articulate than any combination of the voices of all of us who made it. As time goes on, the play will have its own life; it will breathe with its own power; it will move with an energy far greater than all of our energies combined.

Writing this play has been like creating a puzzle without knowing exactly how to solve it. At its heart is a sometimes terrible, sometimes tender, always tentative relationship between creator and creation. Virtually every plot element, and character can be traced either to the Sherlock Holmes stories or to the life of Arthur Conan Doyle, but the pieces have been put together in a new way. It has been my task to weave Doyle's words and my own, Doyle's characters and my motivations, Doyle's thoughts and my conflicts, into a tapestry that is neither an adaptation nor a biography, but a new creation respectful of it's sources and mindful of its heritage. Finding the correct balance of mystery, psychology, and structure has been a continuing challenge.

I am grateful to Moses Goldberg of Stage One: The Louisville Children's Theatre and to Kathleen Collins of The Fulton Opera House, for commissioning this work. It has been an exciting, slightly dangerous mystery for my characters and for me. For I found myself, a bit like Doyle, looking back over all the plays I have written and wondering if I created them or they created me? If I have done my job well, people will remember the plays and the characters who dwell within them long after they have forgotten the color of my hair or the sound of my voice. That is as it should be, but it does make you wonder what and who is real after all.

Suzan Zeder
Tampa
1989

Dedication

This One,
at last,

For My Father

The Death and Life of Sherlock Holmes was co-commissioned by Stage One: The Louisville Children's Theatre, Louisville, Kentucky and the Fulton Opera House, Lancaster, Pennsylvania. The first production opened in February 1987 at Stage One, with the following cast:

Sherlock Holmes .... Bain Boehlke
Dr. John Watson .... Rick Munger
Arthur Conan Doyle .... Andy Backer
Mary Doyle .... Pamela White
Wiggins .... Bonnie Akimoto
Mrs. Hudson, Madame Bergolia .... Breton Frazier
Officer Hopkins, Messenger .... Steve Wise
Inspector Lestrade, Zoltan .... William Groth

The production was directed by Moses Goldberg.

The second production opened in January 1988 at the Fulton Opera House with the following cast:

Sherlock Holmes .... Steven Crossley
Dr. John Watson .... Robertson Carricart
Arthur Conan Doyle .... Orson Bean
Mary Doyle .... Holly Felton
Wiggins .... Shelley Delaney
Mrs. Hudson, Madame Bergolia .... Ann Hillary
Officer Hopkins, Messenger .... Gary Smith
Inspector Lestrade, Zoltan .... Ian D. Shupeck

The production was directed by Kathleen Collins.

CHARACTERS

Sherlock Holmes:
   Blind Begger (Disguise)
   Clergyman (Disguise)
   Achmed the Servant (Disguise)

Dr. John Watson:
   Sir Charles Altamont (Disguise)

Mary Doyle
   Mary Altamont

Arthur Conan Doyle:
   Colonel Sebastian Moran
   Dr. Grimsby Roylott
   Professor Moriarty

Mrs. Hudson

Lady of the Street*
Madame Bergolia*

Wiggins
   Orphan Girl (Disguise)
Inspector Lestrade
   Drunk (Disguise)

Zoltan*
John Clay*

Officer Hopkins

Holmes Apparition*
Swiss Messenger*

Characters playing other roles in disguise are indicated above.

   * Characters which may be played by the same actor are grouped together. If a larger cast is desired, these roles may be played by different actors.

SCENES

ACT ONE

London Street, Exterior: Baker St. and Empty Room.
Desk also visible.*
Windlesham, The Study: Interior
221B Baker Street: Interior
Windlesham, The Study: Interior and Exterior
221B Baker Street: Interior
Stoke Moran, Seance Chamber: Interior
Stoke Moran, Mary's Bedroom: Interior

ACT TWO

221B Baker Street: (Interior)
London Street: (Exterior)
221B Baker Street: (Interior)
Before the Ascent to Reichenbach Falls: (Exterior)
The Promontory of Reichenbach Falls: (Exterior)

*The desk seen at the top of the show and incorporated into the study at Windlesham should never leave the stage, but may be moved to far stage left or right.

It is suggested that projections of the original illustrations from the serialized stories be incorporated into the design; either as backdrops or as a transitional device between the scenes accompanying Watson's narrations. Wherever possible specific illustrations are suggested.

TIME

March, 1893

The Death and Life of Sherlock Holmes

ACT I

Scene I

AT RISE: The sound of Big Ben tolling midnight. Spotlight comes up on a small area downstage. DOYLE huddles over the DESK scribbling. He works feverishly as music begins and lights come up on the rest of the stage:

AN EXTERIOR OF A LONDON STREET on a foggy night in 1893.

Music of a hurdy-gurdy and a violin are heard.

On either side of the stage are two-story structures. Stage left: the facade of a London row house with a practical door. Above is a second-story casement window with wide ledge and a drain pipe leading to the street below. Stage right: 221B BAKER STREET features a second-floor bow window. The shades are pulled, behind them we see the familiar silhouette of SHERLOCK HOLMES. The windows of the two buildings face each other. Center stage: a street lamp flickers. Nearby is a large rubbish bin or rain barrel.

(On the street, a BLIND BEGGER turns the crank of a hurdy-gurdy. A police whistle is heard. WIGGINS enters at a run followed by OFFICER HOPKINS. WIGGINS dives into the rubbish bin, escaping the OFFICER. A LADY OF THE STREET saunters on and leans against a lamp post. OFFICER HOPKINS looks about for WIGGINS and nods to the LADY who returns the nod. The OFFICER raps once on the bin with his stick. The LADY takes out two coins puts them in the BLIND BEGGER'S cup. He nods twice in thanks. A DRUNK enters and stands directly in the LADY'S path; he steps to the right and then to the left; she steadies him and touches his cheek with three quick pats before exiting. In actuality they are passing a series of signals between them.)

(The DRUNK lunges at the BLIND BEGGER'S cup in an attempt to rob him, OFFICER HOPKINS intercedes just in time. The DRUNK staggers into the rubbish bin; WIGGINS pops up; the DRUNK pushes WIGGINS back down, before careening into the side of the stage-left building. OFFICER HOPKINS exits.)

(As this is happening, DOYLE finishes writing. He swivels in his chair and looks into a small mirror. He expertly applies a small goatee. He stands, puts on a cloak and a broad-brimmed hat, picks up a rifle, which he hides in his cloak, and blows out the lamp. He has become COLONEL SEBASTIAN MORAN. MORAN leaves the desk area and crosses stage left.)

(The DRUNK crosses from the opposite side and weaves into his path. MORAN narrowly avoids a collision, and enters the building. WIGGINS pops out of the bin once again and starts towards the BLIND BEGGER. The DRUNK takes a menacing step towards WIGGINS who returns quickly to the bin.)

(Above, the casement window opens. MORAN kneels holding the rifle. He takes careful aim at the bow window. WIGGINS ducks down inside the bin for safety. The DRUNK flattens against the side of the building.)

(DR. WATSON enters at a run.)

WATSON: For God's sake, somebody stop him!!

(Above, MORAN shoots, there is a small pop from the air gun. There is the sound of glass breaking. The silhouette falls behind the bow window. There is a scream. MRS. HUDSON opens the window and shouts to the street.)

MRS. HUDSON: Murder! Bloody MURDER!

(WATSON bolts into the building and up to the second floor.)

MRS. HUDSON: He's dead. Shot through the head! Sherlock Holmes is dead.

WATSON: You murdering swine!

(We see WATSON through the window. MORAN whirls around and they struggle over the gun. MORAN hits WATSON with the gun butt, he staggers and falls.)

(*MORAN goes out the window onto the ledge, and slides down the drain pipe to the street below. The DRUNK springs to life and struggles with MORAN. MORAN punches the DRUNK who falls like a nine pin.*)

(*WIGGINS leaps out of the rubbish bin and butts MORAN in the stomach, momentarily knocking him into a wall. OFFICER HOPKINS enters at a run.*)

OFFICER: Stop, in the name of Scotland Yard!

(*MORAN lunges for the BLIND BEGGER and grabs him from behind. He pulls out a dangerous-looking knife and holds it to his throat.*)

MORAN: One step more and I cut his throat.

(*The others stand at bay as the BEGGER simpers in terror.*)

MORAN: Shut up or I'll slit you a second smile.

BEGGER: (*Straightening suddenly*) That's not very civilized, now is it?

(*In three swift moves, the BEGGER disarms MORAN, flips him, and forces him onto his knees. In a brisk motion, the OFFICER takes charge of him as the BEGGER removes his wig and glasses revealing that he is SHERLOCK HOLMES.*)

MORAN: Sherlock Holmes!

HOLMES: Indeed!

(*To the Drunk.*)

That you, Lestrade?

(*LESTRADE removes his disguise.*)

LESTRADE: Yes, Mr. Holmes.

HOLMES: (*To MORAN*) Ah, Colonel, "Journey's end in lover's meeting" as the old play says.

MORAN: You fiend, you clever, clever fiend!

(*WATSON enters rubbing his jaw.*)

HOLMES: All right, Watson?

WATSON: Quite.

(WIGGINS runs to HOLMES.)

WIGGINS: J'you see me, guv? J'you see me plow him inna basket?

HOLMES: Well done, Wiggins! Run along now, they'll worry about you at home.

WIGGINS: Not bloody likely.

HOLMES: Wiggins!

(HOLMES gives a look; WIGGINS exits.)

HOLMES: Congratulations Lestrade, with your usual happy mixture of cunning and audacity, you have got him.

LESTRADE: Got him? Got whom?

HOLMES: This, gentlemen, is Colonel Sebastian Moran, the best heavy-game shot in the Empire. I believe I am correct, Colonel, in saying that your bag of tigers remains unrivaled!

MORAN: You may or may not have just cause for arresting me, but I shall not submit to the gibes of . . . this person!

HOLMES: Lestrade, what charge do you intend to prefer?

LESTRADE: Why the attempted murder of Sherlock Holmes!

HOLMES: I do not intend to press charges.

LESTRADE: You don't?

HOLMES: It won't be necessary, for there you have the man all Scotland Yard is looking for!

LESTRADE: I do?

(LESTRADE grabs MORAN'S arm.)

HOLMES: (*On one breath*) On the thirtieth of last month, Colonel Moran shot the Honorable Robert Adair with an expanding bullet from an air gun through the open window of the second floor of No. 427 Park Lane. A feat he tried to duplicate here tonight.

MORAN: You've got no proof, you Scotland yard jack-nape!

HOLMES: Proof enough is proof indeed.

(*WATSON hands HOLMES the gun.*)

Well, what is this? An air gun? A unique weapon! Noiseless and of tremendous power. As for the bullet . . .

(*He calls.*)

Mrs. Hudson?

(*MRS. HUDSON is seen at window.*)

MRS. HUDSON: How'd I do, Mr. Holmes?

HOLMES: Admirably, Mrs. Hudson! Did you observe where the bullet went?

(*She holds up a dummy with a large hole in the head.*)

MRS. HUDSON: It's spoilt your beautiful bust, the bullet passed right through the head and flattened on the wall. I've picked it up from the carpet with my tweezers. What do you want me to do with it?

HOLMES: After the Inspector is through with it, you may have it as a souvenir.

MRS. HUDSON: Lovely!

(*She closes the window.*)

HOLMES: Congratulations, Lestrade!

(*OFFICER frisks MORAN and a small piece of white paper falls from his pocket. WATSON picks it up.*)

LESTRADE: Yes, Sir! Thank you, Sir. It was nothing, Sir.

HOLMES: Quite.

MORAN: This is not the end, Holmes! Mark me well!

LESTRADE: Come on, you!

(LESTRADE, MORAN, and OFFICER exit. WATSON crosses to HOLMES.)

WATSON: *(Showing him the paper)* What do you make of this, Holmes?

HOLMES: It looks like a line of little dancing men.

WATSON: It fell out of Moran's pocket. It's probably nothing.

(HOLMES examines the paper with his magnifying glass.)

HOLMES: Nothing from that pocket is nothing. Colonel Sebastian Moran is the second most dangerous man in London. Come Watson, this bears a closer look.

*(HOLMES exits. Lights dim. WATSON steps into a spotlight.)***

WATSON: And so ended "The Adventure of the Empty House." To this day the famous air gun can be seen in the Scotland Yard Museum, and come what may, Colonel Sebastian Moran will bother us no more, thanks to the world's greatest consulting detective. No man who lives or has ever lived has brought the same passion, study, and natural talent to the detection of crime as Sherlock Holmes.

(There is the sound of a clock chiming the three-quarter hour as light comes up a bit on DOYLE back at the desk. He speaks this next line in unison with WATSON.)

DOYLE and WATSON: I am Dr. John Watson and it is my honor to be his chronicler, his Boswell, his friend.

(Lights out on Watson.)

**Projection: "Holmes Pulled out his Watch." Illustration from *The Adventure of the Greek Interpreter.*

DOYLE: (*Alone*) His friend?

(*Lights fade.*)

Scene II

Lights come up dimly on the DESK which has been incorporated into the STUDY. The area is lit by a flickering lamp and the glow from a small fireplace. In the shadows are book cases, a setee, a small table, and a set of heavily curtained double doors leading to a terrace.

(*As the lights come up DOYLE is scribbling furiously. MARY is heard offstage, pounding on his door.*)

MARY: (*Off*) Father! Father, are you alright?

DOYLE: (*Without looking up*) It's open.

MARY: Father!

DOYLE: I said, it's open!

(*MARY rushes into the room wearing a robe, carrying a lamp.*)

MARY: Are you alright?

DOYLE: (*Still scribbling*) Aye.

MARY: You were shouting something about bullets and a rare gun.

DOYLE: Air gun.

MARY: What?

DOYLE: It was an air gun.

(*He reads.*)

"A unique weapon, noiseless and of tremendous power."

MARY: Father, you promised no more . . .

DOYLE: (*Ignoring her*) But that's not the best of it, the best of it's the bust . . .

MARY: We're not even here a week and here you are . . .

DOYLE: . . . "made of wax, exact in every detail."

MARY: Father, it is almost three o'clock in the morning.

DOYLE: Then get you to bed, child.

MARY: Not until you put down that pen and . . .

DOYLE: For God's sakes, Mary, I'm writing!

MARY: (*Trying to cajole him*) I wish I had sixpence for every time I've heard that!

   (*She imitates him.*)

"A little less noise there, Mary, I'm writing!" "Not now, Mary, I'm writing!" "For God's sakes, Mary I'm . . .

DOYLE: (*Calling out*) Louise!

MARY: (*Taken aback*) Father!

DOYLE: (*Shouting*) Touie, Mary is in my study!

MARY: She can't hear you, Father, you know that!

DOYLE: Louise! I cannot work with this child in here.

MARY: (*Upset*) She's not here, Father. Not here to sharpen your quills, or to fill your inkwells; not here to mind the children or give you your precious quiet. She's dead, Father!

DOYLE: Touie, dead?

MARY: (*Firmly*) Mother died of tuberculosis.

DOYLE: But she was here!

MARY: (*As if to a child*) She died six months ago; you know that.

DOYLE: Here in this room, tonight!

MARY: You've tried so hard to call her back . . .

DOYLE: (*Raving*) I saw her! Here! Mary, I tell you she's calling to me from the other side . . .

MARY: Father! Stop it!

(*Mary holds him.*)

My God, you're burning up.

(*She feels his brow.*)

You're ill. Let me get you to bed.

(*She tries to take the pen.*)

Look at that. Your poor fingers have twisted round that quill so long that you can't even straighten them.

DOYLE: It's just a cramp.

(*MARY finds a piece of paper.*)

MARY: The dancing men?!!

(*DOYLE turns away.*)

Father, you are a known and respected writer, and yet your book on the Boar War lies unfinished and your history of spiritualism is long overdue at the publisher, all because you are obsessed with that man!

DOYLE: All England is obsessed with that man.

MARY: He takes your mind from better things.

DOYLE: The more I write the more they cry for more!

MARY: This has gone too far.

DOYLE: I close my eyes; I see his face.

MARY: This has got to stop.

DOYLE: I hear his voice inside my head.

MARY: You must make an end of it!

DOYLE: He plagues me by day and haunts my dreamless nights.

MARY: (*Tenderly*) In Switzerland you slept.

DOYLE: Aye.

MARY: Remember the day we went to Reichenbach, the picnic by the falls?

DOYLE: What do picnics have to do with . . .

MARY: You said at last you'd found a place . . .

DOYLE: (*Remembering*) Aye . . . a terrible place . . . a wonderful place . . . a boiling pit of . . . Good, Mary . . . very good . . .

(*Doyle consults a small black book and is lost again in thought.*)

MARY: Come to bed, Father.

DOYLE: (*Scribbling, without looking up*) Soon, Mary . . . Soon.

(*She picks up her lamp, starts for the door, and stops.*)

MARY: If you do not find a way to end it, Father, I promise you, I will.

(*MARY exits. DOYLE continues writing as the clock chimes three. A spot comes up on WATSON.*)

WATSON: Sherlock Holmes was a walking lexicon of crime, from forgery to felony, from murder to mayhem, from assassination to assignation, there was not one element of the criminal mind with which he was not familiar.

Nothing could exceed his energy when the working fit was upon him. He would go for days and nights on end, without food or rest, like a man possessed.

But now and again a strange reaction would seize him and for days on end he would sit in a basket chair, hardly uttering a word or moving a muscle from morning to night.

He was plagued by a silent foe, an enemy within against whom he was powerless . . . boredom.

(Lights dim and in the dark we hear three shots dispatched in a regular even tempo.)

Scene III

Interior of DRAWING ROOM at 221B BAKER STREET. It is a cozy room with a deliberate untidiness. There are two doors, one leads to the bedrooms, and the other to a hall leading downstairs to the outside. In one part of the room a table is set up with Holmes' chemicals and a series of pegs bearing his various disguises. There is a large fireplace and several comfortable chairs, including a large basket (wicker) chair. There is also a blackboard inscribed with the numbers 222 followed by a string of dancing men.*

(As lights come up, HOLMES is sitting on the top edge of the back of a large wing-backed chair, with his feet on the seat. He wears an old dressing gown but is fully clothed underneath. He holds a pistol in one hand and a mirror in the other, and uses the mirror to see behind his back as he shoots at the opposite wall. We see his bullet holes forming the initials V.R. He shoots the last blast to finish the R.)

(WATSON enters at a run.)

WATSON: Holmes! Holmes are you . . .

HOLMES: Bull's eye!

WATSON: What the devil is going on?

HOLMES: (*Laconically*) V.R. . . . Victoria Regina! Long may she reign!

(HOLMES salutes and sings softly.)

"Rule Britannia, Britannia Rules the Waves."

WATSON: I have always felt that pistol practice is a distinctly open air pastime.

HOLMES: "England never, never, never shall be slaves."

WATSON: Have you taken leave of your senses?

---

*See Notes.

HOLMES: Probably.

(*HOLMES slides down the back of the chair and sits with his knees drawn up under him.*)

WATSON: Neither the atmosphere, nor the appearance of our rooms is much improved by your little . . . decoration!

HOLMES: Give me work! Give me problems! Give me the most abstruse cryptogram, the most intricate analysis. I despise the daily dull!

WATSON: But you have the puzzle of the dancing men.

HOLMES: That was days ago, and since then . . . nothing!

(*He paces about.*)

My mind is like a racing engine tearing itself to pieces. Life is commonplace. The papers are sterile. Audacity and romance seem to have passed forever from the criminal world.

(*WATSON picks up a newspaper.*)

WATSON: There's nothing here?

HOLMES: Commonplace little murders, insignificant swindles, routine robberies. Even the agony column affords no relief. The London criminal is a dull fellow.

WATSON: (*Thumbing through the paper*) There have been a run of petty thefts.

(*HOLMES groans and collapses in the chair.*)

HOLMES: It is fortunate indeed that I am not a criminal!

WATSON: Indeed!

HOLMES: Suppose that I were Moran, or Moriarty, or any one of fifty men who would like to see me dead. How long could I survive against my own pursuit? A summons. A bogus appointment, and it would all be over.

(*HOLMES whips out the pistol and fires another blast at the wall, providing the period at the end of the R. WATSON nearly jumps out of his skin.*)

WATSON: HOLMES! Mrs. Hudson will be up with a meat cleaver if you don't stop!

HOLMES: Decapitation would be preferable to this insufferable suffocation.

(*There is a knock at the door. WATSON is raging.*)

WATSON: That is probably her now! I don't know how she puts up with you, Sherlock Holmes! I don't know how I put up with you, Sherlock Holmes. I don't know how anyone puts up with you . . .

(*He throws open the door, revealing a lady dressed in black and heavily veiled.*)

MARY: Sherlock Holmes?

WATSON: It's for you!

(*MARY enters the room as HOLMES bounds forward to greet her.*)

HOLMES: Good morning, madam. My name is Sherlock Holmes. This is my intimate friend and associate, Dr. Watson, before whom you can speak as freely as before myself. Pray draw up to the fire and let me get you some coffee, for I observe you are shivering.

MARY: It is not cold which makes me shiver.

HOLMES: What then?

MARY: It is fear. It is terror.

HOLMES: You must not fear. We shall soon set matters to right. You have come in by train this morning I see.

(*He leads MARY to a chair.*)

MARY: You know me then?

HOLMES: No, but I observe the second half of a return ticket in the palm of your glove. You must have started early, and yet you have had a good drive in a dog cart before you reached the station.

MARY: How did you know?

HOLMES: There is no mystery, my dear Madam. The left arm of your jacket is spattered with mud in no less than seven places. The marks are perfectly fresh and there is no other vehicle save a dog cart which throws up mud in that particular way.

MARY: You are perfectly correct. I left Windlesham by cart and took the train to Waterloo.

HOLMES: I can tell how and when, but I cannot tell you why you have come to see me.

MARY: I have no one to turn to, save the one I care for beyond all others, and it is about him that I come to you.

(*MARY removes her gloves.*)

HOLMES: Your father.

MARY: How did you know?

HOLMES: I see no engagement or wedding ring, and one reserves that particular tone for either lover or father.

MARY: You are quite right.

HOLMES: Pray go on, Miss Mary.

MARY: How did you know my name?

HOLMES: The initial M is stitched on your handkerchief, and Mary was an educated guess.

WATSON: Well done, Holmes.

MARY: Someone is trying to kill my Father and I come to you to prevent it.

HOLMES: Be assured that I will do everything in my power, my dear Miss . . .

MARY: Altamont, Mary Altamont. My Father is Sir Charles Altamont; you have heard of him?

HOLMES: Sorry . . .

MARY: He is very famous in our circle.

WATSON: And what circle is that?

MARY: A psychic circle. Sir Charles is, among other things, Special Investigator of The Society of Psychical Research.

HOLMES: Could you be a little more specific?

MARY: Seances, apparitions, poltergeists.

WATSON: Could you be a little more specific?

HOLMES: Ghosts.

WATSON: (*Laughs in spite of himself*) Surely you don't believe in all that twaddle?

MARY: (*Evenly*) With all my soul, and so does my father.

WATSON: I do apologize.

MARY: It's all right, Dr. Watson, we are quite used to skeptics. Indeed, it is my father's task to travel to the site of psychic occurrences and verify their truth or expose their fraudulence. That is why Dr. Grimsby Roylott wants to kill him.

HOLMES: Grimsby Roylott?

MARY: A supposed spiritualist, who seeks to profit from holding seances. He lives in his country house at Stoke Moran with his medium, Madame Bergolia, and her band of gypsies. My Father is determined to expose him!

WATSON: And this Roylott is a charlatan!

MARY: And dangerous as well! He has killed once; he will do so again.

HOLMES: (*To Watson*) A murder, Watson! This is good, this is very good!

MARY: I beg your pardon?

WATSON: Please continue.

MARY: Six months ago, my Mother died of tuberculosis. My Father was devastated and suffered a complete breakdown. In the midst of his grief, my Father received a letter from Dr. Roylott; enclosed was a message which Roylott claimed to have received from my Mother in the form of automatic writing.

WATSON: From your Mother?

MARY: From the world beyond.

WATSON: And the message was?

MARY: A curious pictogram, a row of little stick figures.

WATSON: A row of dancing men?

MARY: Yes, quite like that.

(*Watson and Holmes exchange glances.*)

Roylott claimed that only his medium, Madam Bergolia, could decipher their meaning and bid us come to Stoke Moran. But Father was too ill to travel, so I went in his place, alone, except for my maidservant, Lily.

WATSON: That was very brave of you, Miss Altamont.

HOLMES: Very brave or very foolish. Pray go on.

MARY: We began with a seance; at first it was all the usual sort of thing, knocking on the table, moans, cries and whispers, which all foretold that someone would be dead before morning.

(*Mary hesitates.*)

HOLMES: Go on, and be very careful not to leave anything out.

MARY: That night when we retired, Lily and I switched rooms. I was to sleep in the chamber Dr. Roylott had prepared for my Father, the room right next to his, but it had a large drafty window, and I am, you see, somewhat prone to chill.

Around midnight I heard strange music.

(*Strange music begins.*)

A vague feeling of impending misfortune impressed me. Suddenly, the stillness of the night was split with the scream. I sprang from my bed, and rushed into the corridor as Lily unlocked her door from the inside. She stood in the doorway, face blanched with terror, hair shot through with streaks of silver, hands groping for help. I ran to her, but her knees buckled and she fell. She murmured my name in a voice heavy with death. "Mary," she whispered "It was the band. The speckled band." A fresh convulsion seized her and she died.

(*MARY is overcome with emotion.*)

WATSON: Miss Altamont, can I get you some water?

MARY: You're very kind.

(*WATSON fetches water.*)

HOLMES: And what do you make of the allusion to a band, a speckled band?

MARY: A band of people?

WATSON: The gypsies! They wear dotted handkerchiefs around their necks!

MARY: Since Lily's death, my Father has been a man possessed, writing endless articles debunking Roylott as a fraud, a fiend, a malicious murderer! He writes all day, all night, with one aim: to destroy Roylott, by attacking him in print. Father's health is now quite ruined, and I fear for his sanity as well.

HOLMES: I beg your pardon, Miss Altamont, but it would seem that your Father has less to fear from Roylott than he does from himself. I suggest a long rest in a quiet place . . .

MARY: We are just returned from a rest cure in Switzerland, but last night he was up all night again, writing. I found this upon his desk.

(*She hands him a scrap of paper.*)

HOLMES: (*Showing the paper to WATSON*) A row of dancing men.

WATSON: Quite.

HOLMES: Something must be done, and it must be done now. The demon is within him and can only be exorcised by a murder solved and a fraud exposed at Stoke Moran.

MARY: That is precisely why I am here.

HOLMES: This is a very deep business, and there are a thousand details which I desire to ask Sir Charles.

MARY: I'm afraid that is impossible.

WATSON: Why?

MARY: That is the delicate part of this matter. My father is never to know that you are on this case.

WATSON: I should think it would give him peace of mind . . .

MARY: Nothing would cause him greater agitation. My Father would sooner lay down his life than expose his beliefs to your particular brand of scrutiny.

HOLMES: I don't give a fig for his beliefs, I am merely trying to save his life.

MARY: Please, I beg you, do not come to Windlesham in Surry. The mere mention of your name throws him into a great consternation. Be like a good guardian angel and protect him with an invisible grace.

HOLMES: Rest assured that Dr. Watson and I will do all in our power to protect your Father and you, for it occurs to me that you are in danger too. In the meantime, may I keep the dancing men?

MARY: Of course, have you ever seen anything like them?

HOLMES: There are very few things in this world that I have never seen anything like. I shall look into this matter. In the meantime, fear not.

MARY: I am so relieved! Good Day to you, Mr. Holmes.

HOLMES: Good day to you, Madam.

MARY: Good day Dr. Watson. Thank you. Thank you both!

(MARY exits. HOLMES crosses to the window, waves a lighted match.)

WATSON: Wiggins?

HOLMES: Wiggins.

WATSON: It seems to me to be a most dark and sinister business.

HOLMES: Dark enough and sinister enough.

(With a bound WIGGINS enters.)

WIGGINS: Yes, Guv?

HOLMES: The young lady who just left . . .

WIGGINS: *(Instantly on report)* The other side of twenty . . ., fair looker, genteel but not posh, mud spatters on her jacket, shows she trucks about inna dog cart!

HOLMES: That will be enough, Wiggins . . . Follow her to Windlesham in Surry and keep her under strict surveillance. Use the other lads, the Baker Street Irregulars, to watch round the clock. Here's a tanner for the tickets; don't let her see you.

WIGGINS: 'nvsible as air!

HOLMES: There's a good detective!

WIGGINS: YES SIR!

(WIGGINS exits.)

HOLMES: Well Watson, I think we shall amble down to Windlesham in Surry for a brief interview with Sir Charles.

WATSON: But you promised Miss Mary . . .

HOLMES: Not to worry, Watson. Sherlock Holmes won't be there!

(Lights dim and WATSON comes forward into a spotlight.**)

WATSON: He sat down at his little table and stood up a few moments later in the character of an amiable and simple minded Nonconformist clergyman. His broad black hat, his baggy black trousers, his white tie, his sympathetic smile and general look of peering and benevolent curiosity were the very portrait of piety!

It was not merely that Holmes changed his costume. His expression, his manner, his very soul seemed to vary with every fresh part he assumed. The stage lost a fine actor when Holmes became a specialist in crime!

(In the darkness we hear a clock strike the hour of seven.)

Scene IV

Interior and Exterior of the STUDY. Lights come up on the study and the terrace area immediately outside the French doors. The terrace is bordered by a hedgerow or a flower box or two.

(DOYLE is writing at the desk. The room is dim, the fire glows in the fireplace. As the clock stops chiming, MARY enters, dressed a bit differently from the previous scene. She carries a large hat box. She enters the room, sets the hatbox down and crosses toward the French doors.)

MARY: Still writing, Father?

DOYLE: Aye, Mary.

MARY: You'll turn into a mole if you don't get some light in here.

DOYLE: Leave it be.

MARY: Have you been up all night?

DOYLE: Is it morning?

(She pulls the drapes and sunlight streams into the room.)

MARY: Indeed it is.

**Projection: "A Simple Minded Clergyman," Illustration from *A Scandal in Bohemia.)*

DOYLE: Then I have.

MARY: And had no breakfast either?

DOYLE: No, Mary.

MARY: Shall I ring for Barrymore to bring you some?

DOYLE: Aye, Mary . . .

   (*She pulls a bell-rope. DOYLE notices her.*)

DOYLE: Do that again.

MARY: What?

DOYLE: Pull the bell-rope again.

MARY: I am quite certain that Barrymore heard it the first time.

DOYLE: Never mind. Hand me my day book.

   (*She hands him a small black book and he scribbles something in it.*)

MARY: I am off to the milliner, but I thought I had better see if you needed anything first . . .

DOYLE: (*Without looking up*) No thank you.

MARY: When I fetched my spring bonnet from the attic this morning, I discovered the most curious thing. Something has chewed a hole in my hat box and built a nest in there, can you imagine that?

DOYLE: No, Mary . . .

MARY: Probably a squirrel or a mouse.

DOYLE: Aye, Mary . .

MARY: (*Testing to see if he's listening*) Or maybe a python or a boa constrictor . . .

DOYLE: (*Without looking up*) Aye, Mary . . .

MARY: You haven't heard a word I've said.

DOYLE: I have . . . you've been nattering on about a hat box . . .

(*She feels his forehead.*)

Now, leave me be, girl.

MARY: The fever's broken.

DOYLE: I'm much better.

MARY: Last night you were burning up! Barrymore's turned down your bed for a proper rest.

DOYLE: (*Irritated*) I'm all right!

MARY: (*After a beat*) You called out to Mother again last night.

DOYLE: She was here.

MARY: She's gone, Father, and all the seances and automatic writing in the world can't bring her back to us.

DOYLE: She came with a warning.

MARY: What was it?

DOYLE: I don't know. I couldn't make it out.

MARY: It's the writing, Father. It took you from her; it takes you from me, and for what?

(*More gently.*)

Your gifts are so much greater than the use you put them to.

DOYLE: So you say.

MARY: So I know. And someday all of England will know.

(*After a beat.*)

Do you remember what we talked about last night . . .?

DOYLE: Aye, and I'm working on it! I promise you it will be done. By midnight tonight it will be done!

MARY: Why can't you just put down the pen and stop?

DOYLE: It's not that easy, Mary. Once the story is begun, you can't just stop, it has to be ended!

MARY: (*Flatly*) Then he has to die.

DOYLE: (*Picking up the pen*) Let me do this in my own way! Now, leave me be before you chase it all out of my head . . .

(*DOYLE starts writing and says the following almost to himself.*)

There is a clergyman out by the back terrace.

(*Lights come up to reveal HOLMES disguised as a CLERGYMAN on the back terrace.*)

MARY: Where?

DOYLE: (*Without looking up*) Just past the hedgerow, trampling the tea roses.

(*Mary crosses to the French doors. Although HOLMES is in plain sight, she can't see him.*)

MARY: I don't see him.

DOYLE: (*As he writes*) He removes his hat and fans himself with the broad brim.

(HOLMES removes his hat and fans himself.)

MARY: But I still don't . . .

DOYLE: See to him before Barrymore sets the hounds on him.

(*DOYLE hands her the hatbox and ushers her out the door.*)

MARY: You . . . rest!

DOYLE: For God's sake, Mary, I'm . . .

(*MARY joins in.*)

BOTH: . . . writing!

(*MARY shakes her head and exits. DOYLE returns to the desk as WATSON enters and HOLMES passes conspicuously close to the French doors.*)

WATSON: What are you doing?

HOLMES: Making sure he sees me. In my experience when a strange Vicar is seen at the back gate, the master of the house slips out the front.

(*DOYLE crumples some papers and throws them into his fireplace; strangely colored smoke billows out and DOYLE collapses.*)

HOLMES: (*While the action takes place inside*) I shall appear to be praying, that will dispatch him on the double, then we can examine his study.

WATSON: His study?

HOLMES: A man may tell a thousand tales, but his empty study never lies.

(*HOLMES crosses nearer to the window.*)

HOLMES: Hey ho, what's this? Watson come quickly.

(*HOLMES and WATSON crash through the French doors. Both put handkerchiefs to their mouths and rush to the unconscious DOYLE. They carry him out to the terrace.*)

(*WATSON examines DOYLE; HOLMES returns to the study and examines the room professionally.*)

(*MARY enters on the terrace, dressed slightly differently from the previous scene, perhaps in the same costume as her visit to Baker Street.*)

MARY: Dr. Watson, what in heaven's name . . .

WATSON: Someone tried to kill your Father. We got him out just in time.

MARY: Is he. . . .

WATSON: Just unconscious, I think.

MARY: I'll fetch some water.

(*MARY exits. HOLMES crosses to the desk and picks up some papers. He crosses to the fireplace and struggles against the smoke as he gingerly picks a page from the ashes. A cloaked FIGURE enters the study. HOLMES bends over the fire and does not notice. The FIGURE takes a wooden club from the wall and clobbers HOLMES. The FIGURE exits.*)

WATSON: Heartbeat . . . normal. Pulse . . . elevated, but within reason. Respiration . . . stronger and stronger. Well done, Sir Charles. Yes, we got him out in time, didn't we Holmes . . . Holmes?

(*WATSON realizes that HOLMES isn't there.*)

Oh, My Lord, he must still be inside!

(*WATSON crosses back into the study; he sees HOLMES on the floor and struggles to lift his dead weight.*)

(*While WATSON is inside the study, TWO SERVANTS enter the terrace area, followed by the FIGURE. The FIGURE motions and the SERVANTS carry off DOYLE. Finally, WATSON carries HOLMES to the terrace. The FIGURE disappears back into the house.*)

(*WATSON carries HOLMES to the terrace. He quickly opens a small vial and holds it to HOLMES' nose. MARY enters with the water.*)

WATSON: Come on Holmes,

MARY: Holmes?

WATSON: (*To MARY*) Quite!

(*To HOLMES.*)

There's a good man.

MARY: Spirits of ammonia?

WATSON: Gun powder! The smell of gunpowder always brings him 'round.

(*MARY looks to where her Father should be. She screams!*)

MARY: He's gone!

WATSON: Eh, what?

MARY: He's gone, my Father's gone! You were just tending to him.

WATSON: Until I went to fetch Holmes!

MARY: What can it mean?

HOLMES: (*Reviving instantly*) It means he has been kidnapped, unless I miss my guess.

MARY: Kidnapped?

HOLMES: Take comfort, Miss Altamont. He is obviously worth more to them alive than dead, otherwise they would have killed him there on the spot.

MARY: Somehow, that is not very comforting, Mr. Holmes.

WATSON: Are you all right, Holmes? Was it the smoke?

HOLMES: A Canary Island Bolo Club, more like.

WATSON: What?

HOLMES: The knots on my thick skull should match up exactly with the knots on the Canary Island Bolo Club that usually hangs on the wall of Sir Charles' study. I don't want to alarm you, Miss Altamont, but someone struck me.

MARY: I could not be more alarmed than I am this minute over the fate of my poor Father. Mr. Holmes, I'm so dreadfully afraid.

WATSON: The authorities should be notified. Perhaps we should call Scotland Yard.

MARY: Oh no! Do not call them, I beg of you!

WATSON: But a major crime has been committed.

MARY: I want my Father back alive, and I am certain that you and Mr. Holmes are the best equipped to accomplish that!

HOLMES: I am gratified by your confidence and will do all in my power to justify it. In the meantime, I wish to take a closer look at some fragments pulled from the fire and some scribbling on this note pad. I trust you have no objection?

MARY: But it's quite blank.

HOLMES: So it appears. One further question: has your father actually met Dr. Roylott?

MARY: No. They have corresponded but never met face to face. Do you suspect him?

HOLMES: I suspect no one. I suspect everyone. As for your father, I promise you we shall see to it that Sir Charles Altamont keeps his appointment with destiny.

MARY: Whose destiny, Mr. Holmes? His or yours?

HOLMES: Destiny, Miss Altamont, is destiny.

   (*HOLMES exits through the French doors.*)

WATSON: Good afternoon, Miss Altamont.

MARY: Good afternoon.

   (*MARY exits. Lights dim. WATSON steps into a spotlight.***)

WATSON: Sherlock Holmes was not very communicative on the long ride in the dog cart, nor on the train to Waterloo. He sat perfectly still with his eyes half closed, his fingertips just touching, and an expression which one less familiar with his features might mistake for repose, which I knew to be intense concentration.
   Later that afternoon, I awoke from my nap to the clean pungent smell of hydrochloric acid which told me that Holmes had spent the better part of the day in the chemical work that was so dear to him.

**Projection: "Holmes Working Hard over a Chemical Investigation." Illustration from *The Adventure of the Naval Treaty*.

Scene V

Interior of 221B BAKER STREET. The room is as before, only two inscriptions of the dancing men are written on the blackboard.*

   (HOLMES, wearing his dressing gown, is laboring over his chemical table. WATSON enters. HOLMES pours a steaming liquid into a beaker and it changes color immediately.)

WATSON: Well, have you solved it yet?

HOLMES: What?

WATSON: The dancing men?

HOLMES: At present I am more concerned about this fragment I pulled from Sir Charles' fireplace. I have tried every known chemical combination twice over and this formula escapes detection.

   (HOLMES sets up a burner and hands WATSON the beaker.)

Now, don't move for exactly 97½ seconds.

WATSON: Shall I ring for tea?

HOLMES: Not for 97½ seconds. While we wait, Watson, tell me what you observed about Sir Charles?

WATSON: *(Delighted to be asked)* He is a Caucasian male, forty-five to fifty years of age, well dressed . . .

   (WATSON tips beaker.)

HOLMES: Mind the beaker.

WATSON: I'm minding the beaker!

HOLMES: Pray, go on.

WATSON: I observed the symptoms of suffocation, reddening of the skin, constriction of the blood vessels. His pupils were not dialated. I had the general impression that drugs were not involved.

---

*See Notes.

HOLMES: 'Pon my word, Watson, you are really coming along wonderfully! It is true that you have missed everything of importance, but you have hit upon the method! You must go beyond your general impressions and concentrate upon details.

WATSON: What did I miss?

HOLMES: Sir Charles is a doctor by trade, a writer by avocation, and a devoted spiritualist. As a young man he sailed on whaling ships . . .

WATSON: Whaling ships!

HOLMES: . . . to the Arctic, and on the high seas of the gold coast of Africa. He has run for Parliament twice and was defeated both times. He suffers from chronic typhoid fever.

WATSON: You could tell all that from two minutes alone in his study?

HOLMES: His vocation and avocation are clearly reflected in the composition of his library; the sailing voyages by a harpoon-head paper weight. His political aspirations are chronicled by framed pamphlets, his defeat by the lack of congratulatory telegrams. A large bottle of quinine speaks eloquently of his illness. I could have told you a great deal more had my investigation not been so rudely interrupted.

WATSON: (*Feelings hurt, just a little*) Quite.

HOLMES: It's done. And as soon as it cools we shall have our answer.

WATSON: What answer?

HOLMES: Don't you think it curious that a smoking fireplace should have such a powerful effect on Sir Charles and relatively little on you and I?

WATSON: It stung my eyes.

HOLMES: Yes, but it nearly sent Sir Charles to join him compatriots in the spirit world.

WATSON: What do you suspect?

HOLMES: Devil's foot root.

WATSON: Devil's . . .

HOLMES: . . . foot root, An exotic poison, which in the first flash of incineration emits a deadly fume. After a few seconds the poison in the smoke disappears without a trace. I believe someone mixed the powdered root into ink and wrote Sir Charles this literal poison pen letter.

(HOLMES shows him the page.)

WATSON: *(Picking up the page)* It looks just like India ink.

HOLMES: Nevertheless it may be deadly when burned.

(WATSON puts the page down gingerly. HOLMES measures an eyedropper full of the liquid and squeezes it into a petrie dish.)

WATSON: *(Looking at the page)* Have you read that page?

HOLMES: I am more interested in what lies beneath its surface.

(WATSON picks up the paper with tweezers and examines it through the magnifying glass.)

WATSON: The paper's charred and I can hardly make it out . . .

HOLMES: *(Not really listening)* First, we must incinerate!

WATSON: . . . but I see ". . atson and . . olmes."

HOLMES: Uh, hummm

(HOLMES snips a section of the paper from the piece WATSON is reading.)

Now mind the fumes.

(HOLMES holds the snip of paper with tongs with one hand and a petrie dish with the other.)

WATSON: It says: ". . atson: It fell out of Moran's pocket. It's probably nothing . . . olmes: Nothing from that pocket is nothing . . ."

HOLMES: Inhale!

(*They take deep breaths as HOLMES touches the paper to the burner, the paper flares.*)

EXHALE!

WATSON: But Holmes, it said. . . .

HOLMES: I need total concentration!

(*HOLMES places the ash in the petrie dish and looks at it under the microscope.*)

WATSON: But . . .

(*HOLMES silences Watson with a look. He sits, tight with tension, peering into the microscope for a moment, then slumps in disappointment.*)

HOLMES: Blast! This is nothing but India ink. Not a trace of poison.

WATSON: But the words!

HOLMES: The words are obvious and you have to look beyond the obvious, Watson, beyond the obvious!

(*Another idea hits him.*)

Read me what is written on that memorandum pad I brought from Sir Charles' study.

(*WATSON crosses to the pad.*)

WATSON: It's quite blank.

HOLMES: Oh, sorry. Bring it here.

(*As he speaks HOLMES takes a pencil and passes it lightly over the pad.*)

If Sir Charles sent any messages this morning, and if he used a steady pressure with a firm, heavy quill, chances are that the impression of his writing may still be left on the pad. There!

(*HOLMES tears off the page and holds it up to the light.*)

HOLMES: What do you make of that, Watson?

WATSON: Dancing men!

HOLMES: As I expected.

WATSON: What does it mean?

HOLMES: We haven't enough information yet to make it out, but our material is rapidly accumulating. Copy it off onto the blackboard, while I try to make some sense of all this.

(*Suddenly, the door bursts open. A tall man wearing a hat, an eye-patch and cloak enters. It is DOYLE as GRIMSBY ROYLOTT.*)

ROYLOTT: Which of you is Holmes?

HOLMES: My name, Sir, but you have the advantage of me.

ROYLOTT: I am Dr. Grimseby Roylott of Stoke Moran.

HOLMES: Indeed, Doctor, pray take a seat.

ROYLOTT: I will do nothing of the kind. I'll not have you talking about me or my work!

HOLMES: How do you know I've been talking about you?

ROYLOTT: Every time I pick up a copy of *The Strand* I read about Mr. Sherlock Holmes. Your coming and goings are public property.

HOLMES: Ah, the tyranny of popularity!

ROYLOTT: But I warn you, stay away from Mary Altamont. There's danger there.

HOLMES: (*Smiling*) It's a little cold for this time of year, don't you think?

ROYLOTT: She is out of your depth.

HOLMES: But I have heard that the crocuses promise well.

ROYLOTT: You're playing with forces beyond your comprehension.

HOLMES: Do you expect an early thaw?

ROYLOTT: If you accept her case it will be your last, you Scotland Yard jack-nape.

HOLMES: (*Chuckling*) Your conversation is most entertaining. When you go out, please close the door as there is a slight draught.

ROYLOTT: I'll go when I've had my say! Don't you dare meddle in my affairs! I am a dangerous man to fall foul of!

(*ROYLOTT grabs a large firepoker and bends it double.**)

See that you keep yourself out of my grip.

(*He throws the poker down and strikes out the door.*)

HOLMES: He seems a very amiable person. Fancy him having the audacity to confuse me with the police force.

WATSON: (*Picking up the poker*) He bent it like butter.

(*HOLMES takes the poker, bends it back, and hands it to WATSON.*)

HOLMES: This adds more zest to our investigation. Watson, do you think Roylott got a good look at you?

(*WATSON subtly tries to bend it; it won't budge.*)

WATSON: I certainly hope not.

(*WATSON puts the poker back near the fireplace.*)

HOLMES: Excellent! I shall telegraph Miss Mary to meet us at Waterloo at nine tonight and to bring one of Sir Charles' suits for you.

WATSON: For me?

HOLMES: Unless you have something suitable for a Special Investigator for Psychical Research.

WATSON: Me?

---

*See Notes.

HOLMES: It's no good for me to be Sir Charles, as Dr. Roylott is all too familiar with my face.

WATSON: But if Roylott has kidnapped Sir Charles . . .

HOLMES: Think how confused he will be when another Sir Charles comes knocking at his door. It is our only way into Stoke Moran.

WATSON: But I don't know anything about Spiritualism.

HOLMES: All the better! You'll come to it without the slightest prejudice. But just in case, you would be wise to slip your service revolver into your pocket, Watson. And now, I must concoct something a bit exotic for myself!

(*HOLMES crosses to his make-up table as lights dim. WATSON comes forward and speaks.*)

WATSON: At Waterloo we were fortunate in catching a train for Leatherhead, where we hired a trap at the station inn and drove four or five miles to Surry. Miss Mary sat silent as a stone, her face pensive and pale in the moonlight. Holmes, disguised and distracted as usual, puffed on his pipe and gazed into nothingness. I, myself, was haunted by the face of Grimsby Roylott . .

(*A light comes up on the desk area. ROYLOTT, [DOYLE], sits there. On the opposite side of the stage, another spot comes up on HOLMES as he applies a moustache. For a moment the two men seem to be mirror images.*)

A large face, seared with a thousand wrinkles, burned a livid yellow, and marked with every evil passion. One eye, deep-set, bile shot, and his thin fleshless nose gave him the appearance of fierce old bird of prey.

(*Spot dims on HOLMES but remains on ROYLOTT.*)

Suddenly it loomed before us! Stoke Moran. We had arrived!

Scene VI

Lights come up on a small area surrounding the DESK. ROYLOTT (DOYLE) sits and writes for a brief moment. Without looking up he calls:

ROYLOTT: Madame Bergolia!

(Lights come up on MADAME BERGOLIA, dressed in full gypsy regalia.)

BERGOLIA: You call and I am here!

ROYLOTT: Is everything ready?

(He rises and takes off his cloak, revealing immaculate evening wear.)

BERGOLIA: I beg you to reconsider . . .

ROYLOTT: The seance chamber is prepared.

BERGOLIA: It could be dangerous.

ROYLOTT: It would be far more dangerous not to proceed. Remember, I know you, Bergolia. I know all about that bad business in Bohemia, the problem in Prague, the rumpus in Roumania.

BERGOLIA: Once I open the door to the spirit world, I cannot control what comes through!

ROYLOTT: You will call her and she will come.

BERGOLIA: I am the medium, the spirits speak through me, but I am only the channel.

ROYLOTT: She has a warning. . .

BERGOLIA: Once the forces of fate are set in motion, I am powerless to stop them!

(ZOLTAN, a strangely menacing gypsy, appears in a pool of light.)

ZOLTAN: Master, they are here.

ROYLOTT: Show them in, Zoltan.

(To BERGOLIA.)

Remember, I am watching you. I am always watching you.

(*BERGOLIA and ROYLOTT cross to the SEANCE CHAMBER, an exotic space dominated by a large round table and a chandelier which drops in from above. Various panels or screens hide the mechanisms for the special effects of the seance.*)

(*From another direction, ZOLTAN brings in WATSON, MARY and HOLMES. WATSON and MARY are dressed in evening clothes; HOLMES is in disguise as an Egyptian bodyguard; he wears a robe, a fez, a drooping moustance and an earring.*)

WATSON: Dr. Roylott, I suppose you know why we have come; I am Sir Charles Altamont.

ROYLOTT: (*Ironically*) Sir Charles, can it **really** be you?

WATSON: We are here despite the trouble at Windlesham earlier today.

ROYLOTT: Trouble?

WATSON: A person or persons unknown kidnapped my butler, Barrymore, this morning.

ROYLOTT: Your butler?

WATSON: Doubtless the fools thought they had kidnapped me.

ROYLOTT: Doubtless.

WATSON: We have every hope he will be found as soon as we finish our business here. I believe you know my daughter, Mary?

ROYLOTT: Better than you know, Sir Charles. Enchantez, Mademoiselle, as always.

WATSON: (*Presenting HOLMES*) This is my servant, Achmed; he joined my service when I was recently in Egypt.

ROYLOTT: Achmed, the servant?

WATSON: I'm afraid he has no English.

(*ROYLOTT bows and speaks a greeting in Egyptian. HOLMES bows and replies in flawless Egyptian.*)

WATSON: May we begin?

ROYLOTT: Of course. It is my honor to present you to our medium for this evening, Madame Bergolia of Bohemia Prague, and recently Roumania.

(*BERGOLIA crosses to him and takes his hand. WATSON starts to shake hands, but she peers at his palm.*)

BERGOLIA: Danger! I see great danger.

ROYLOTT: Bergolia!

(*She backs off.*)

Bergolia is a gypsy, drawn to the dark side of dramatics.

(*He leads them to the table.*)

And now, Sir Charles, Miss Mary, Achmed, your destiny awaits.

BERGOLIA: If you would be so good as to sit down.

(*They sit. BERGOLIA in the center. All place their hands on the table top as lights dim and strange noises are heard.*)

BERGOLIA: Denizens of the spirit world, hear my call. Shades and spectres, shadows of those beyond our ken. Come to us who come to you in friendship and in peace.

(*Lights change and strange sounds are heard. Those at the table are barely visible.*)

BERGOLIA: Is there anyone there?

(*Silence.*)

Is there anyone there?

(*Silence.*)

Is there . . .

(*There is a loud knocking on the table.*)

Have you messages for those assembled here?

(*There is another knock.*)

Is it for Miss Altamont?

(*Silence*)

For Sir Charles?

(*Silence*)

For Achmed, the servant?

(*There is a frantic, angry knocking.*)

SILENCE!

(*Silence*)

The spirits are very angry.

(*The table top begins to levitate. It moves up and then from side to side.*)

Come now, my Darlings. We mean you no harm.

(*The table descends to its original position.*)

That's better. Now, come to us. Show us yourselves. Appear in all your spectral glory.

(*Lights change abruptly to black light. A shower of colored flowers falls from above.*)

Thank you, that was beautiful. Can you materialize something else for us?

(*A beautiful bird with iridescent feathers flies across the room.*)

WATSON: Uhhh . . . Where did the bird come from?

DISEMBODIED VOICE: India, of course!

WATSON: What kind of bird is it?

VOICE: It is a jungle sparrow, ignoramus!

BERGOLIA: I'm sorry, Sir Charles, the spirits are not very polite.

ROYLOTT: BERGOLIA!

BERGOLIA: We must go deeper into the spirit world.

(*There is a discordant sound and strange lights; distant thunder rumbles.*)

We are no longer calling the spirits, they are calling us.

(*BERGOLIA'S head is thrown back sharply, then propelled forward as if by a force beyond her control. Lights and the quality of sound change as the seance moves deeper into a truly frightening dimension.*)

BERGOLIA: (*With deep power*) I see a woman. She is alone. She is crying.

(*APPARITION OF LOUISE appears. Her words are recorded, amplified, echoing and strange.*)

APPARITION OF LOUISE: Mary, I come with a warning.

MARY: Mother!

ROYLOTT: (*Speaking as DOYLE*) Louise!

APPARITION OF LOUISE: I come with a warning for you both!

MARY: Oh, Mother! It is you!

APPARITION OF LOUISE: The world will know him most for what he holds the least.

MARY: This has gone too far.

BERGOLIA: (*In her own voice*) I no longer have control.

MARY: This has got to stop!

ROYLOTT: (*Speaking as DOYLE*) I close my eyes and see his face.

APPARITION OF LOUISE: His fact will seem fiction as his fiction is believed as fact.

ROYLOTT: (*Speaking as DOYLE*) I hear his voice inside my head.

MARY: If you cannot find a way to stop it, I promise you I will.

(*WATSON'S recorded voice is heard.*)

VOICE OF WATSON: For God's sake, somebody stop him!

(*A shot is heard followed by the recorded voice of MRS. HUDSON.*)

VOICE OF MRS. HUDSON: He's dead! Shot through the head!

WATSON: (*Speaking aloud*) Mrs. Hudson.

BERGOLIA: (*In her own voice*) Hudson? Who is Hudson?

VOICE OF MRS. HUDSON: Sherlock Holmes is dead!

(*An APPARITION of SHERLOCK HOLMES is seen, wearing the deer-stalker cap. His voice is recorded and echoing.*)

APPARITION OF HOLMES: He killed me off for good and all.

WATSON: Who?

APPARITION OF HOLMES: The one who made me.

BERGOLIA: Spirits! Stop it! I command you!

APPARITION OF HOLMES: You can't kill me, don't you see? You can murder me if you like, but I will live forever!

APPARITION OF LOUISE: In the end he will sacrifice it all to the spirit world.

APPARITION OF HOLMES: I will return from the dead to bury you.

APPARITION OF LOUISE: Those who cheered will laugh. Those who praised will jeer.

ROYLOTT: (*Speaking as DOYLE*) No, Louise, No!

BOTH APPARITIONS: You will know the truth of the World Beyond. You will know the truth, but you will die for it!

(MARY screams and faints. The APPARITIONS disappear. The real HOLMES bounds up as lights return to normal. MARY has fainted. BERGOLIA and WATSON tend to her.)

HOLMES: This has gone quite far enough, don't you think, Dr. Roylott?

ROYLOTT: *(In his own voice as ROYLOTT)* I quite agree, Mr. Holmes.

HOLMES: I think we can put an end to this charade . . . Watson?

(Watson springs up to help.)

Once and for all!

(They pull aside the screens or panels where the APPARITIONS appeared. There is nothing there.)

ROYLOTT: Charade? I assure you, Mr. Holmes, all that you have witnessed here is quite authentic.

BERGOLIA: I take the lady to lie down.

(BERGOLIA helps MARY off.)

ROYLOTT: You have entered my house under false pretenses; I advise you to leave at once.

(ZOLTAN pulls a knife on them. WATSON reaches for his gun.)

ROYLOTT: It's no use, Dr. Watson. Zoltan relieved you of your service revolver when you entered this house. He is a gypsy with the lightest touch in the known universe.

(ZOLTAN reveals that he has WATSON'S gun.)

ROYLOTT: So, if you will be so kind . . .

(He motions towards the door.)

WATSON: Kindly fetch Miss Mary.

ROYLOTT: Miss Mary is resting comfortably in the room next to mine. She will remain here tonight.

HOLMES: If she's harmed in any way. . . .

ROYLOTT: I am a doctor, and I will take care of her. Zoltan, show them out.

(*HOLMES AND WATSON are led out. LIGHTS change as WATSON comes forward.***)

WATSON: We were prepared for just such an occurrence and had pre-arranged a signal with Miss Mary. Holmes told her to wait until the house had retired for the night, and to open her window for us to crawl through. She was then to place a lantern there as a signal and to withdraw with her belongings to seek safer shelter in a back bedroom.

Hours later, a single beam of light pierced the darkness shrouding the ancient Manor House.

"That's our signal," said Holmes, springing to his feet.

"The game's afoot," he whispered in a hoarse voice, and we were off.

Scene VII

Lights come up on MARY'S BEDROOM AT STOKE MORAN. It is a tiny space with a practical window and shutters. In the room is a bed, a small chest and a plain chair. From the top of the grid down to the bed, touching the pillow, is an ornate bell-rope. The room is empty, a lit lantern rests on the ledge on the open window. HOLMES and WATSON appear at the window, and enter the room.

WATSON: I see Miss Mary has followed your instructions to the letter.

HOLMES: Not quite, she has left behind a large hat box. I don't know why women insist on bringing a carriage full of luggage to an overnight engagement.

**Projection: "Holmes Lashed Furiously." Illustration from *The Speckled Band*.

WATSON: Perhaps it was too large to be easily removed.

HOLMES: I rest my case. We are in the very room where Lily, Miss Mary's unfortunate maid, met her end.

WATSON: But the doors and windows were locked and bolted from the inside.

(*They lock and bolt the doors and windows.*)

HOLMES: Locked . . .

WATSON: . . . and bolted!

HOLMES: Check for anything unusual about the room.

(*They examine the room.*)

Well?

WATSON: Well, what?

HOLMES: Well, what did you find?

WATSON: There is nothing in this room, save the bed, that chest, a chair, and Miss Mary's hat box, and all that seems to be in order.

HOLMES: Indeed, there is quite a bit out of order in this room.

WATSON: I didn't see anything.

HOLMES: That is because you don't know how to look, my dear Watson. You look with your eyes and see what you expect to see. I look with my mind and expect nothing, therefore I see a great deal more. For example, that ventilator connects with the room next-door, Dr. Roylott's room.

WATSON: Yes, it seems to.

HOLMES: What fool of a builder would open a ventilator into another room, when for the same trouble he could have opened it to the outside air? And this bell-rope. . . .

(*Holmes tugs on the bell rope. WATSON cringes.*)

WATSON: Don't, you'll ring the. . . .

HOLMES: It's a dummy. It's not even connected to a bell wire. It's fastened to a little hook there by the ventilator.

WATSON: I didn't notice that.

HOLMES: Quite. And the bed . . . it's bolted.

WATSON: Bolted?

HOLMES: To the floor. It cannot be moved. It must always remain in the same relative position to the bell-rope, to the ventilator.

WATSON: Holmes, I seem to see dimly what you are hinting at. We are only just in time to prevent a subtle and horrible crime.

HOLMES: Subtle enough and horrible enough. When a doctor goes wrong, he is the first of criminals. He has nerve and he has knowledge. We shall have horrors enough before this night is over.

(There is a sound and a shaft of light falls on them; it seems to come from the ventilator.)

Quick! Dim the light! Here Watson, we may have need of this.

(HOLMES hands WATSON his pistol.)

WATSON: But how did you. . . .

HOLMES: "The lightest touch in the known universe." Now, be alert, your very life depends upon it.

(HOLMES places his cane upon the edge of the bed and they both wait in breathless darkness.)

(After a beat there is the low sound of strange exotic music. A single flute weaves a hypnotic melody.)

WATSON: The music.

(A snake slithers out of the ventilator and down the bell-rope. HOLMES kneels on the bed with his cane poised.)

WATSON: *(Whispering)* What is it?

HOLMES: As I expected . . . a swamp adder, the deadliest snake in Egypt, sent through the ventilator from Roylott's room.

(*From behind HOLMES and WATSON, a second snake, a cobra, rises straight out of the hat-box. They do not see the second snake.*)

Hold perfectly still, Watson, perfectly . . .

(*The second snake hisses and WATSON sees it about to strike.*)

WATSON: My God, Holmes, there's another snake!

(*WATSON shoots the snake, just as HOLMES lashes furiously at the adder on the rope. The cobra is killed by the shot. The adder disappears up the bell rope.*)

WATSON: I got it! It's dead!

HOLMES: (*Still lashing*) This one is going up the rope back into the next room!

(*Suddenly there is a scream from off stage.*)

WATSON: What was that?

HOLMES: Take your pistol and we will enter Dr. Roylott's room.

(*HOLMES starts out the door of the room as the lights dim on the scene and a spotlight picks up WATSON.**)

WATSON: Dr. Grimsby Roylott sat in a wooden chair with his eyes fixed in a dreadful rigid stare, and round his brow he had a peculiar yellow band with brownish red speckles. We stepped forward and his strange headgear reared and spat at us with venomous fangs.
"The band! The speckled band! It is the swamp adder." I cried.

(*A spot comes up on ROYLOTT, dead in a chair, his arms akimbo, clutching a small piece of paper.*)

So ended the story of the Speckled Band with Dr. Roylott dead by the self-same snake he intended for Miss Mary. Clutched in his stiff-

---

**Projection: "He Made Neither Sound nor Motion." Illustration from *The Speckled Band*.

ening fingers was a small slip of paper inscribed with a single line of dancing men. But what of the second snake, the one in the hat box? For whom was it intended? That was the question that continued to plague Holmes by day and to haunt my dreamless nights.

(*Light on WATSON goes out. Spot remains on ROYLOTT.*)

(*After a beat, ROYLOTT rises, removes his wig and mustache.*)

DOYLE: Well done, Mr. Holmes! Once again!

(*He laughs a mad sort of laugh and stands menacingly as lights dim to black.*)

END OF ACT I

ACT II

Scene I

Spotlight up on the DESK, DOYLE sits, writing, as a clock chimes seven times. **

DOYLE: When Sherlock Holmes had an unsolved problem he would go for days and even weeks without rest, turning it over, rearranging his facts, looking at it from every point of view, until he either had it fathomed, or had convinced himself that his information was insufficient.

(*DOYLE picks up the day book from his desk, smiles and places it in his upper breast pocket, as lights dim.*)

Lights up on 221B BAKER STREET. It is as before except that an additional row of dancing men has been added to the blackboard.

**Projection: "The Pipe was Still Between his Lips." Illustration from *The Man with the Twisted Lip.*

(HOLMES sits on the floor atop a pile of pillows. He wears the blue dressing gown over his clothes and smokes his pipe as smoke swirls in clouds above his head. HOLMES speaks to himself, as WATSON enters.)

HOLMES: Insufficient information!

WATSON: Good Lord, Holmes! From the look of it you've smoked a pound and a half of tobacco. Have you been up all night again?

HOLMES: Is it morning?

WATSON: *(Opening the drapes of the bow window)* Indeed, it is.

HOLMES: Then, I have.

WATSON: And you've had no breakfast either.

HOLMES: *(Not really listening)* Mmmmmmm.

WATSON: Shall I ring for Mrs. Hudson to bring you some?

HOLMES: What day is it?

WATSON: March 29th, Thursday.

HOLMES: Three days I've sat here and I still can't make it out!

WATSON: What?

HOLMES: Roylott.

WATSON: Roylott's dead.

HOLMES: The second snake.

WATSON: Dead as well.

HOLMES: And once again, the dancing men.

(WATSON picks up a piece of paper and checks it against the new message on the blackboard.)

WATSON: Ah, yes, the ubiquitous dancing men!

HOLMES: And no sign of Sir Charles.

WATSON: "Aye, there's the rub," as the old play says.

HOLMES: We searched every nook and cranny of Stoke Moran and still no sign of him, no ransom demand, nothing!

WATSON: Not much to go on.

(*HOLMES pours himself coffee from a large beaker on his chemical table.*)

HOLMES: And the very lack of evidence is evidence itself! It is all part of a plan, a master plan, by a master criminal.

WATSON: Roylott?

HOLMES: Roylott was an amateur! Devious? Doubtless! Cunning? Completely! But the second snake, the second snake was the mark of a professional. You have never heard of Professor Moriarty, I suppose?

WATSON: Only from you.

HOLMES: And there's the genius and the wonder of the thing! The man pervades London and no one has ever heard of him.

WATSON: What has he done then?

HOLMES: He is the organizer of half that is evil and nearly all that is undetected in this great city. Again and again in cases of the most varying sorts, I have felt his presence. His agents are numerous and splendidly organized. He sits motionless like a spider in the center of its web, but the web has a thousand radiations, and he knows every quiver of every thread. He is the Napoleon of crime!

(*There is a knocking on the door.*)

HOLMES: That will be Miss Mary.

WATSON: Mary?

HOLMES: I sent for her last night and urged her to come by the first train this morning. Kindly let her in, Watson.

(*HOLMES goes to his desk to fetch some papers.*)

WATSON: Oh, yes, of course.

HOLMES: It is not safe for her to be seen here with us today!

(*WATSON crosses to the door and opens it. MARY enters quickly.*)

WATSON: Come in, Miss Mary, you're looking very well this . . .

MARY: I came as quickly as I could. You indicated it was urgent and extremely sensitive.

HOLMES: Urgent enough and sensitive enough. Come in, Miss Altamont. Were you followed?

MARY: Not that I could see.

HOLMES: Then you probably were.

WATSON: Would you care for some coffee?

HOLMES: I'm afraid, Watson, that there isn't time. Miss Mary will be leaving the country at once!

MARY: What?

HOLMES: I have arranged everything. Here are your tickets for the midday boat-train to Geneva, from there to Lucerne, then by pack mule up the Alps to Meiringen.

MARY: Switzerland?

HOLMES: A tiny town, totally remote and almost completely unknown. You must tell no one where you are going, you will register at the Enlischer Hof Hotel under the name of Hawkins. The Inn Keeper is my man and a trained marksman. I must have you out of the way, now that I know the identity of the mastermind behind this whole affair!

MARY: You know?

HOLMES: Beyond a shadow of a doubt.

MARY: Who?

HOLMES: It is better that you do not know.

MARY: If it concerns my Father, I must know.

HOLMES: My dear Miss Mary, do not worry your pretty head . . .

MARY: (*Sharply*) Do not condescend to me, Mr. Holmes. It has been three days and you still have not found my Father.

HOLMES: I am aware of that! But unless you leave immediately I may never find him. If you wish to save his life and your own then follow my instructions to the letter. You will leave from here. I have informed your servants by telegram that you will spend a few days in town. They do not expect you back.

MARY: You are very thorough, Mr. Holmes.

HOLMES: Go back to Waterloo on foot, from there go by coach to Victoria Station. Take neither the first, nor the second coach, the third will be driven by my brother Mycroft. He will have a suitcase containing what you need and he will put you on the Geneva train himself.

MARY: I don't know what to say.

HOLMES: Then say nothing and be on your way, Miss Altamont. Good bye and be brave.

MARY: (*With steely determination*) Believe me, Mr. Holmes, there is nothing I would not do to save my father.

WATSON: Good luck and God speed, Miss Mary.

MARY: Thank you, Dear Dr. Watson.

(*MARY exits.*)

HOLMES: In my own quiet way, I have been tracking the Professor. I have been gathering evidence step by step, crime by crime. One by one I have eliminated his henchmen: Colonel Moran, his second in command; and then Roylott and the vicious vipers. Now all that remains is to close the net on the spider himself. The key lies in the dancing men, if I can crack this code, I shall have proof of his handiwork in his own hand.

(Suddenly there is a loud commotion outside. MRS. HUDSON knocks on the door.)

MRS. HUDSON: Mr. Holmes! Dr. Watson! Come quick! A boy just come pounding on my door to say that the young lady who was just here has been run down by a carriage.

WATSON: Good Heavens, No!

HOLMES: Where?

MRS. HUDSON: He said, just round the block, on the way to Waterloo.

WATSON: Oh, My Lord!

MRS. HUDSON: Doctor, he says to bring your bag and hurry.

(WATSON exits with his bag.)

He says, Mr. Holmes should bring a blanket from the bed.

HOLMES: Yes, of course!

(MRS. HUDSON rushes out, as HOLMES disappears into the bedroom. MORIARTY slips into the room, [once again it is DOYLE]. He is clean shaven with sunken cheeks, wire rimmed glasses, thinning hair, and a cadaverous expression. MORIARTY sits in HOLMES' chair just as HOLMES emerges from the room and races toward the door.)

MORIARTY: Don't bother, Mr. Holmes.

(HOLMES stops short and whirls around to face his adversary.)

HOLMES: So it is you.

MORIARTY: Yes, it is I.

HOLMES: At last we meet face to face.

MORIARTY: You have less cranial development than I should have expected.

HOLMES: You are Professor Moriarty.

MORIARTY: If you say so.

HOLMES: And what of the young lady?

MORIARTY: Safely on her way and so they all will discover, but not before I've led them a merry dance.

(*HOLMES slips his hand inside the pocket of his dressing gown.*)

MORIARTY: It is a dangerous habit to finger loaded firearms in the pocket of one's dressing gown.

(*HOLMES draws out the gun, cocks it, and places it on a small table in front of him.*)

MORIARTY: You evidently don't know me.

HOLMES: On the contrary, I think it is fairly obvious that I do. Pray take a chair. I can spare you five minutes if you have anything to say.

MORIARTY: All that I have to say has already crossed your mind.

HOLMES: Then possibly my answer has already crossed yours.

(*MORIARTY claps his hand into his upper breast pocket. HOLMES reaches for the pistol and raises it. There is a moment of stand-off. MORIARTY draws the day book out of his pocket.*)

MORIARTY: Really Mr. Holmes, it's only my day book.

(*He opens it and checks pages.*)

You crossed my path on the fourth of December, on the twenty-third you incommoded me; by the middle of January, I was seriously inconvenienced by you; at the end of February, I was absolutely hampered in my plans; and now, at the close of March, I find myself placed in such a position that I am in positive danger of eclipse and all because of a Scotland Yard jack-nape.

(*HOLMES watches him carefully.*)

HOLMES: Where is Sir Charles Altamont?

MORIARTY: You disappoint me. He is under your very nose.

HOLMES: What do you want with him.

MORIARTY: Insurance that you will cease your persecution of me and my work at once. You must drop it, Mr. Holmes, really you must.

HOLMES: Not until I bring it to it's inevitable conclusion!

MORIARTY: I have come to warn you that unless you cease and desist your extravagant exploits you will place yourself in great danger.

HOLMES: Danger is part of my trade.

MORIARTY: If you are clever enough to bring destruction upon me, rest assured that I shall do as much to you.

HOLMES: If I were assured of the former, I would cheerfully accept the latter.

MORIARTY: I can promise you one, but not the other. So, you stand firm?

HOLMES: Absolutely.

MORIARTY: Then you are a dead man, Sherlock Holmes. I spared you before because you provided a certain intellectual stimulation, but now I see it will be necessary to eliminate you and Dr. Watson and all the brats of Baker Street.

(*MORIARTY turns on his heel and exits. HOLMES stands still for a second, then crosses to the window, lights a match and waves it as a signal.*)

HOLMES: The Baker Street Irregulars! What an extremely good idea! Thank you, Professor.

(*He sits at his desk, sketching quickly. WIGGINS enters.*)

WIGGINS: At your service, Mr. 'olmes!

HOLMES: Wiggins, did you see that singularly evil looking man who just left here?

WIGGINS: Yes, Sir. Nearly knocked me out of me rubbish bin, gave it such a good kick as he went by!

HOLMES: That gentleman has something which I want very much.

WIGGINS: Wot?

(*HOLMES removes a notebook from his top drawer.*)

HOLMES: This day book, or one just like it.

WIGGINS: You want me to pinch it for you?

HOLMES: I want you to arrange a little . . . substitution.

WIGGINS: Yes, sir!

HOLMES: And Wiggins, be extremely careful: broad daylight, lots of witnesses. This is a very dangerous man.

WIGGINS: Yes, Sir.

(*WIGGINS starts to go, HOLMES hands WIGGINS the tiny sketch.*)

HOLMES: And Wiggins, you'll be needing this.

(*WIGGINS nods and starts to go.*)

And Wiggins, be as quick as you can.

(*WIGGINS starts to go.*)

And Wiggins, do be careful.

WIGGINS: I will, Mr. Holmes. I swear I will.

(*WIGGINS salutes. HOLMES salutes in return. WIGGINS exits just as WATSON enters.*)

WATSON: Round Robin Hood's Barn! That's where we've been! Round Robin Hood's Barn.

HOLMES: I know.

WATSON: First I run down to the Brixton Road, and a whole crowd of rowdies tells me she's been taken to hospital. So I go to St. Bart's only to find they've never heard of her.

HOLMES: I know.

WATSON: It was all a ruse! An unkind, ill-considered ruse.

HOLMES: I know.

WATSON: How do you know, unless I tell you?

HOLMES: He was here.

WATSON: Who was here?

HOLMES: Moriarty.

WATSON: Oh, my Lord, Holmes! What are we to do?

HOLMES: Do, Watson? The only thing we can do. We wait. We watch for Wiggins. We hope that Mary gets safely away, and we pray for the soul of Sir Charles.

(Lights dim as WATSON comes forward into a spot**)

WATSON: And wait we did. The minutes weighed heavy as hours, and the hours seemed like days. Holmes paced around like a panther or sat in the basket chair and fumed in a brown study.
  "Data, data, data!" he cried impatiently, "I cannot make bricks without straw."
  Outside a thick fog rolled down between the lines of dun colored houses and the opposing windows loomed like dark shapeless blurs.
  But down in the street, the inevitable began to unravel.

Scene II

Exterior of a LONDON STREET. Lamp post and, perhaps, the rubbish bin are all that are really needed.

(JOHN CLAY, a pickpocket, loiters near the lamp post. OFFICER HOPKINS enters and walks his beat. CLAY turns to avoid being seen by him.)

OFFICER: Morning.

**Projection: "Professor Moriarty Stood Before Me." Illustration from *The Final Problem.*

CLAY: (*Disguises his voice*) Morning.

OFFICER: (*Not a bit taken in*) Right.

(*OFFICER continues on his way. MORIARTY enters, OFFICER walks toward him. MORIARTY tips his hat to the OFFICER in such a way as to obscure his face. OFFICER tips his nightstick to MORIARTY and continues. MORIARTY stops and reaches for his daybook, just as CLAY makes a grab to pick his pocket. MORIARTY is too quick for him and grabs his arm.*)

MORIARTY: It's no use, John Clay, you have no chance at all.

CLAY: (*Astonished*) How do you know my name?

MORIARTY: If your brain were as clever as your fingers, you'd know that I know everything.

CLAY: You don't know nothing!

MORIARTY: On the contrary, I know what you've done, what you're doing, and what you will do. I know your very thoughts before you think them.

CLAY: G'wan.

(*MORIARTY pulls out his day book and reads from it.*)

MORIARTY: "John Clay, thief, smasher, forger and petty pick-pocket."

CLAY: So you say.

MORIARTY: So, I know. Last month, you cracked a crib in Cornwall . . .

CLAY: (*Concerned*) Eh?

MORIARTY: . . . and the next week, pilfered an orphanage in Oxford . . .

CLAY: How did you . . .

MORIARTY: . . . And I am well aware of your plans for The Red-Headed League and the City Bank of London.

CLAY: (*Menacing*) I don't know how you know what you know, but don't you even think of going to Scotland Yard . . .

MORIARTY: Scotland Yard? If you cross me, John Clay, you'll wish with all your soul for Scotland Yard.

CLAY: (*Blustering*) I . . . I . . . warn you!

(*CLAY grabs MORIARTY'S lapel to threaten him.*)

You're playing a dangerous game.

(*In a single swift move, MORIARTY brings his cane sharply up and pins CLAY up against the lamp post.*)

MORIARTY: Dangerous? I'll tell you what's dangerous: trifling with me, that's dangerous; threatening me, that's dangerous; and touching me at any time, for any reason, that's dangerous!

CLAY: Who are you?

MORIARTY: That is no concern of yours.

CLAY: What do you want from me?

MORIARTY: A delivery. To some dear friends at 221B Baker Street, a little housewarming gift.

CLAY: Fire? I don't do fire! I do pockets, and now and then the odd safe, but no fire. People could get hurt.

MORIARTY: That is the general idea. I'll not take no for an answer. I know where you live, John Clay, I know everything about you.

CLAY: I ain't no fire bug.

MORIARTY: You'll be whatever I make you. I'll expect delivery around midnight. Now get out of my sight.

CLAY: Yes, Sir.

(*CLAY exits quickly. MORIARTY makes a note in his day book and puts it in his pocket.*)

(WIGGINS enters. This is the first time we realize that WIGGINS is a girl. She is dressed in a simple but fetching dress, a pinafore, long stockings, and ribbons in her long hair. She wears a locket around her neck.)

WIGGINS: *(To MORIARTY)* Father!

(MORIARTY turns to see who she's talking to. WIGGINS points directly at MORIARTY.)

WIGGINS: After all these years o' lookin!

MORIARTY: There must be some mistake.

(WIGGINS runs into MORIARTY'S arms to his amazement and his horror.)

WIGGINS: Me prayers is answered!

(MORIARTY throws her off.)

MORIARTY: What?

(WIGGINS dives back into his arms.)

WIGGINS: Don't you rec'gnize your own daughter?

MORIARTY: *(Throwing her off again)* Get away from me!

WIGGINS: *(Wailing)* Oh No! Do not make me go! Please, oh, please! No! No! No!

(OFFICER HOPKINS enters.)

OFFICER: What's going on here?

(MORIARTY tries to move away, but WIGGINS clamps on and will not let him go.)

MORIARTY: There must be some mistake. Get up! Get up, you . . .

(Vicious)

WRETCHED . . .

OFFICER: (*Warning*) Sir . . .

MORIARTY: (*Changing his tone*) . . . child.

OFFICER: Better.

MORIARTY: Officer, this poor demented creature is mistaken. I don't know what she is talking about.

WIGGINS: This is me dear old Da long lost at sea or something.

MORIARTY: I have never seen this child before in my life.

WIGGINS: Deny me if you will. Deny this is you can!

(*WIGGINS shows the OFFICER the picture in her locket. MORIARTY cringes when the OFFICER compares it to his face.*)

OFFICER: Well, it certainly is your portrait, Sir.

WIGGINS: Wet w' the salt of a thousand tears, as I cried meself to sleep for years and years!

MORIARTY: Officer, this is all a ruse.

WIGGINS: Mum's dead so you'r all I got in the world.

OFFICER: See here, Sir, round these parts we take our parental responsibilities very seriously.

MORIARTY: But . . .

OFFICER: It's a sacred trust, it is, a sacred trust and duty.

MORIARTY: But I . . .

OFFICER: Now I advise you take this child back to your bosom. Make it up to her. Go on home and forget these wandering ways . . .

MORIARTY: But . . .

OFFICER: Or you'll have me to deal with. Do I make myself clear?

MORIARTY: Perfectly.

OFFICER: Now go on . . .

(*MORIARTY reluctantly allows himself to be hugged as WIGGINS changes the books.*)

OFFICER: That's better. You'll not regret this Sir, she'll be a comfort to you in your old age, Sir. Good day, Missy. Right.

(*OFFICER exits smugly. MORIARTY maintains the hug as long as THE OFFICER is in sight. As soon as he is gone, MORIARTY grabs her and throws her to the ground.*)

MORIARTY: If you value your life, my girl, I advise you, never let me look on you again.

(*WIGGINS dives between his legs and gives him a swift kick as she exits.*)

WIGGINS: That suits me bleedin' beautiful. You're an old rotter, you are!

(*MORIARTY moves menacingly toward her. He suddenly stops and checks to see if his day book is still there. It is, he sighs and exits.*)

(*Lights dim as WATSON steps into a spot.***)

WATSON: The day book! The day book was the key! The day book was the clue to crack the code of this conundrum.
For Moriarty was a meticulous man, a mathematician with a mania for minutia. In his day book was a ledger listing all the criminal activity of his many minions, a complete account of checks and balances, of souls bought and bartered.
Holmes knew this for certain for when Moriarty brought out the daybook in his presence, Holmes caught a glint, a glimmer, a glimpse of the page reflected in Moriarty's glasses. HOLMES saw just enough to pique his curiosity and make his heart leap in his breast.

**Projection: "Holding it Only an Inch or Two from his Eyes." Illustration from *The Hound of the Baskervilles*.

Scene III

Interior of 221B BAKER ST. The sitting room is as before, but the DESK is littered with papers. On one blackboard the decoded messages of the dancing men are written. On another, the one message still to be decoded is written with the known letters filled in and the unknown letters left blank. *

(HOLMES sits at his desk scribbling, from time to time he moves back and forth between the two blackboards and his desk. WIGGINS enters the room, face smudged, ribbons askew, dress and pinafore rumpled. She is furious. She stamps into the room.)

WIGGINS: Nev'r again, Mr. Holmes! I won't do it, nev'r again!

(HOLMES leaps up from the desk.)

HOLMES: Wiggins, are you all right?

WIGGINS: 'ardly! I'm done for! I'm ruined.

HOLMES: Did he hurt you?

WIGGINS: Who?

HOLMES: Moriarty.

WIGGINS: It's me mates! They saw me all decked out in me dainties!

(HOLMES bursts out laughing.)

Go a'ead 'n laugh, but it ain't your ruination. I'll have to break every bleedin' head in the Baker Street Irregulars just to get back me self respect!

HOLMES: Did you get it?

WIGGINS: *(Handing him the day book)* Of course, I got it. But it come dear, it did.

HOLMES: You paid a noble price and did a noble deed! England is proud of you, and I am proud of you too!

---

*See Notes.

WIGGINS: You are?

HOLMES: Indeed I am!

WIGGINS: Cor, blimey!

(*WATSON enters.*)

WATSON: I didn't realize you had a client. Pardon me, young lady. . .

WIGGINS: Save your fancy talk for them wot needs it. Good to see you again, Doc.

(*WIGGINS exits.*)

WATSON: Who was that?

HOLMES: That, my good Doctor, was Wiggins!

WATSON: Wiggins?

HOLMES: And she . . .

WATSON: She?

HOLMES: . . . has been of inestimable help to us. I now have in my possession the key to this whole nefarious scheme!

WATSON: Pray it comes in time to save Sir Charles.

HOLMES: Quite! Now, Watson we have already determined that the dancing men constitute a code.

WATSON: Yes.

HOLMES: I am fairly familiar with all forms of secret writings, but I confess this one was entirely new to me until I realized that the symbols stood for letters . . .

WATSON: Of course!

(*As HOLMES goes through the explanation, he illustrates his points at the blackboards.*)

HOLMES: A vital key was provided by the very first message, this one dropped from Colonel Moran's pocket, see, the numbers 222 followed by a string of dancing men. I finally realized that the numbers referred to the house number directly across the street, the vantage point of the unfortunate Colonel, and that the ciphers stood for the rest of the address: "222 B. . .

HOLMES and WATSON: " . . . Baker St."

HOLMES: This was boon indeed for it gave me two vital vowels the A and the E, the two most common letters in the English language.

(*At the second blackboard.*)

The second message, brought to us by Miss Mary, and the third, obtained from the impression left Sir Charles' memoranda, are identical. What intrigues me here is the significance of the little men bearing flags, here, here, here, and here . . .

(*He points to the figures.*)

WATSON: What ho, perhaps they are used to break the sentence into words: Here, here, here, and here!

HOLMES: Capital, Watson. I must confess that notion had occurred to me, but your powers of observation are keen as ever!

(*Back to the first blackboard.*)

Now, the fourth message, clutched in the stiffening fingers of Dr. Roylott, was relatively easy to determine with the letters already known. Adder and Cobra refer to the choice of snakes employed in that particular escapade, and provide us with the key to letters D, C, and O.

(*Clutching the day book.*)

And now, unless I miss my guess, we will discover that Professor Moriarty's day book will provide the *coup de grace!*

(*He opens the book.*)

Just as I thought! It is written in code! The threads of his web are naught but a trail of dancing men, but now the tempo has changed and they will dance to our tune!

WATSON: Well done, Holmes!

HOLMES: (*Checking between the book and the blackboard*) Ah, ha! Hmmmmmm Well, well, well . . . Write this down, Watson. A.C.D.

WATSON: Yes.

HOLMES: That's it!

WATSON: What?

HOLMES: A.C.D. It is written all through here . . . You know what this is, Watson?

WATSON: What?

HOLMES: A blind alley. . . . which just leads us to another route . . . We'll check the very last entry, the one for today and see if we can find a number.

WATSON: (*Peers over the page*) There it is 29, March 29th, that's today!

HOLMES: Excellent, Watson! Now, the word 'March' gives us an 'M' here and here; and an 'H' here and here!

(*He fills in the letters on the second blackboard.*)

WATSON: Try an 'I' there!

(*Watson fills it in.*)

See? H.I.M. that's HIM. Him! What him?

(*HOLMES fills in a U.*)

HOLMES: (*Simply*) Murder.

WATSON: (*Excited*) That's it! Murder him . . . Murder him? Murder who?

(*HOLMES fills in the N.*)

WATSON: Murder him at Reichenbach . . .

HOLMES: Falls!

WATSON: That's wonderful!

HOLMES: It's terrible!

(*HOLMES dives into the text. He scribbles, madly translating the code as he goes.*)

WATSON: Holmes? Holmes, what is it?

HOLMES: I'll tell you in a minute.
(*HOLMES finishes the translation and looks up, very upset.*)

Great Heaven, Watson, he has beaten us!

WATSON: No, no, surely not!

HOLMES: The last entry, March 29th . . . "I have seen the wonderful waterfall at Reichenbach, a terrible place, a fearful place. The torrent plunges into a boiling pit of incalculable death. It will make a worthy tomb for him, even if I bury my bank book with him."

WATSON: Who?

HOLMES: Who else? Sir Charles!

WATSON: What?

HOLMES: Reichenbach Falls is near the tiny village of Meiringen. That's where Moriarty's been hiding Sir Charles.

WATSON: That's where we sent Miss Mary!

HOLMES: I've sent Mary to her death as well!

WATSON: Good Lord, no!!

HOLMES: By Heaven if the worst has happened, we'll see that they're avenged. Quickly, Watson, there is not a moment to be lost! We must take this book to Scotland Yard and then catch the 5:00 boat-train to Switzerland!

WATSON: But it left five minutes ago.

HOLMES: Then we'll catch it on the run.

(HOLMES grabs his deerstalker cap and races for the door as the lights dim and WATSON comes forward into the spot light.**)

WATSON: A carriage was waiting. The instant we stepped in, Holmes whipped up the horses and off we raced. Narry a word was spoken, narry a word was needed.

Through the streets we fairly flew, trailing sparks as the horses hooves struck flint on cobblestone. And then, ahead, the train! We pulled alongside even with the racing engine and we leaped aboard at Leatherhead.

(If projections are used, this journey can be indicated by changing images.***)

Holmes stood behind the stokers and shouted, "Heap it on, boys! Make her do all she can! The furnaces roared and powerful engines throbbed and beat like a great metallic heart. The train's bright beam split the evening air as plumes of steam billowed into the darkening sky!

(Projection changes.****)

London to Geneva, Geneva to Lucern, in record time; only to be halted on the road to Meiringen. No pack mules to take us up the Alps. It seems the last had been engaged the day before, by a tall thin Englishman.

I started up the mountain on my own, while Holmes waited below in the village for a telegram from Scotland Yard.

**Projection: "He Flicked the Horses with his Whip." Illustration from *The Man with the Twisted Lip.*
***Projection: "Holmes Gave a Sketch of the Event." Illustration from *The Silver Blaze.*
****Projection: "A Large Rock Clattered Down." Illustration from *The Final Problem.*

Scene IV

BEFORE THE ASCENT: The stage is bare.

(HOLMES enters clutching a telegram.)

WATSON: It came!

HOLMES: Yes, and I'm afraid the news is bleak indeed.

WATSON: Eh?

HOLMES: Someone set fire to our rooms at Baker Street right after we left.

WATSON: Good Heavens. Holmes!

HOLMES: Moriarty's men must have thought we were still there, otherwise why would they go to the trouble of incinerating our belongings.

WATSON: And the damage?

HOLMES: A total loss, it is as though we'd never been there.

WATSON: What of Mrs. Hudson?

HOLMES: Visiting her sister in Brighton, at my request.

WATSON: Thank God for that.

HOLMES: I was afraid that something like this might happen.

WATSON: This is intolerable, Holmes!

HOLMES: There is darker news yet. With the help of the day book, Scotland Yard captured the whole of Moriarty's gang, but the spider himself has escaped the net! He was last seen day before yesterday on the mid day boat-train to Geneva!

WATSON: The same train as Miss Mary!

HOLMES: If he has beaten us here, I fear that Miss Mary and Sir Charles are already at the bottom of Reichenbach Falls.

(After a beat.)

I think you had better return to England, Watson.

WATSON: Why?

HOLMES: You will find me a dangerous companion now.

WATSON: But there is danger for you as well.

HOLMES: I could not bear to have your life upon my conscience too.

WATSON: I prefer not to leave you, Holmes.

HOLMES: It may mean your death.

WATSON: Quite.

HOLMES: (*After a beat*) Then I suggest we make our way to the Falls. We have tarried here too long as it is.

(*After a beat.*)

Thank you . . . my friend.

(*WATSON nods. MESSENGER enters.*)

MESSENGER: *Mein Herren, Mein Herren*, I am sent to find two Englishmen by my Master Peter Steiler, Innkeeper of Englisher Hof.

HOLMES: Our trusted friend and ally!

MESSENGER: Ya . . Ya . . He sent me to fetch quick the Doctor Watson. An Englishwoman she is dying, she needs a doctor, right away.

(*Messenger hands WATSON a note.*)

HOLMES: That is the mark of the hotel.

WATSON: He says it's tuberculosis, the last stages. She's hemorrhaging.

HOLMES: The name, what is the name of the woman?

MESSENGER: My master say, Hawkins.

HOLMES: Miss Mary!

WATSON: But it can't be Miss Mary. I would have seen some signs of the disease before this.

HOLMES: Even if it is not Miss Mary, you cannot ignore the appeal of a fellow countrywoman, dying in a strange land . . .

WATSON: Then come with me.

HOLMES: My destiny awaits at Reichenbach Falls.

WATSON: I will meet you there, as soon as I. . . .

MESSENGER: *Schnell*, Doctor, *Bitta*, or we will be too late.

WATSON: Yes, of course.

(*WATSON starts to go.*)

HOLMES: Watson?

WATSON: (*Hesitating*) Yes?

HOLMES: Good bye, my friend.

WATSON: I'll meet you there. I **will** meet you there!

(*Lights dim. WATSON steps into a pool of light.***)

WATSON: It may have been a half an hour before I reached Meiringen. The Innkeeper was standing at the porch of his hotel. "Well," I said as I came hurrying up, "I trust she is no worse." A look of surprise passed over his face, and at the first quiver of his eyebrows my heart turned to lead in my breast.
"You did not write this?" I said, "There is no sick Englishwoman here?"
"Certainly not," he cried.
I waited for no more of the Innkeeper's explanation, I was already running down the village street, and making for the path I had so recently descended.

(*There is the sound of the rushing water of the Falls.*)

**Projection: "The Death of Sherlock Holmes." Illustration from *The Final Problem*.

Scene V

THE PROMONTORY OF REICHENBACH FALL: The stage is bare except for a two-story structure which has been stripped to a wooden framework suggesting the promontory overlooking the Falls.

(MORIARTY stands on top of the structure looking out toward the backdrop of rushing water. Smoke billows, suggesting tumbling water. There is the sound of the falls in the background. HOLMES enters.)

HOLMES: And there you are, Professor!

MORIARTY: So, Mr. Holmes, you have arrived?

HOLMES: I would travel to the ends of the earth to keep this appointment.

MORIARTY: You are tiresome. It is time to wind you up for good and all. You take my mind from better things.

HOLMES: There is nothing left for you in London, Professor.

MORIARTY: Arrogant fool! Do you think I am nothing, save in relationship to a dilettante detective?

HOLMES: Now, all London knows your name, but only because I have exposed you for what you are, for what I have made of you!

MORIARTY: You have made of me? You are nothing save what I have made of you. Your whole career is but the raveled edges of my imagination. Your reputation is based only upon what I have tossed to you to solve! Wretched creation, will you haunt me all my days?

(HOLMES starts up the steps.)

HOLMES: No, Professor, I am pleased to think that I shall be able to free society from any further effects of your presence.

MORIARTY: You know not what you do.

HOLMES: On the contrary, my dear Professor. I understand completely!

(MORIARTY lifts his cane to strike and the fight begins. It is a fearful struggle with one, then the other, almost falling over the edge.)

(*MARY enters with a drawn pistol.*)

MARY: Stop it! Stop it, at once! I have a pistol and I shall use it.

HOLMES: (*Delighted*) Miss Mary, thank God you are alive!

MARY: Very much alive, Mr. Holmes, and I'll thank you both to come down from that excessively dangerous place.

(*HOLMES starts down.*)

HOLMES: Watson and I had you as good as dead.

MARY: That was a trifle premature.

HOLMES: We'll take him back to the dock to stand trial.

(*He turns to MARY.*)

And now, my dear, I shall relieve you of that revolver.

MARY: (*Steely*) On the contrary, Mr. Holmes. I shall keep the revolver and relieve you of your misapprehensions. I think it is time you made the acquaintance of my father.

HOLMES: (*Thunderstruck*) Moriarty?

MARY: There is no Professor Moriarty. There never was. He is a fantasy, just as Moran and Roylott were fantasies, all of my father's invention.

HOLMES: I do not understand.

MARY: Of course you don't, because you are a fiction as well, limited in intellect and imagination to what he has given you. You Mr. Holmes are a sterile stereotype grown too powerful for your own good.

DOYLE: He cannot understand this, Mary.

MARY: Pray, come down Father, it worries me to see you so close to the edge.

(*DOYLE crosses to MARY as she keeps her gun trained upon HOLMES.*)

DOYLE: Must it be a gun?

MARY: Guns, knives, clubs, or poison, Father, you can throw him over the falls for all I care.

HOLMES: You, Miss Mary?

MARY: Yes, Mr. Holmes, it was I who supplied the second serpent at Stoke Moran, and as for the Bolo Club, I bludgeoned you myself!

HOLMES: So, the "Murder at Reichenbach Falls . . ."

MARY: Is your murder!

HOLMES: But why?

MARY: For what you have done to him.

HOLMES: But he's a criminal!

MARY: Silence, Mr. Holmes! That is what we need from you, now and forever. My Father is a physician, a novelist, a visionary! But does the world know him for who he is? No, they cry for your episodes! His honor is your accolade.

(*She points the gun directly at him.*)

You have overshadowed his brilliance with your little light long enough. Once the world is rid of Sherlock Holmes, it can discover Arthur Conan Doyle!

HOLMES: A.C.D. in the day book!

MARY: You know his name?

HOLMES: No, just his initials.

MARY: I thought as much!

DOYLE: Mary, don't. . .

MARY: It's time, Father!

(*WATSON enters at a run.*)

WATSON: For God's sakes, somebody stop . . . NO!

(*MARY shoots HOLMES at point blank range. He collapses. WATSON races to him.*)

WATSON: Holmes! Oh my God! HOLMES!

(*WATSON rips open HOLMES' jacket. He checks his vital signs.*)

There is no pulse, no breath, no heartbeat! He's dead, but I cannot find the wound!

MARY: Some wounds go too deep to be seen.

WATSON: (*Holding HOLMES in his arms*) Holmes. . . . please, God. . . . Holmes!

MARY: I assure you, Dr. Watson, he is quite, quite dead. He is dead, isn't he, Father?

DOYLE: I suppose so.

WATSON: Go ahead and kill me too, or I shall hunt you down. I can! I will! I know his methods!

DOYLE: I shan't let you. There will be no more stories of Sherlock Holmes, because I will not write them.

WATSON: What are you saying, Sir Charles?

DOYLE: My real name is Arthur Conan Doyle. I wrote the stories you lived. I invented Sherlock Holmes and I can be done with him as well.

WATSON: You can't do this.

MARY: On the contrary, my dear Doctor, it is done. Come, Father, you have other things to attend to.

(*She starts to lead him off.*)

WATSON: (*Grief-stricken*) Doyle!

DOYLE: (*Stops*) Yes?

WATSON: You cannot leave me thus. I was his friend!

DOYLE: (*Honestly*) I'm sorry.

WATSON: If you invented him, then you invented me as well.

DOYLE: Yes.

WATSON: Then take away the grief, take away the pain of his passing, take away the memories!

DOYLE: I can't do that.

WATSON: Why not?

DOYLE: (*With great kindness*) He was a fiction, but the memories are real.

(*They start away again. With infinite tenderness WATSON rocks the body of his comrade.*)

WATSON: (*Grieving*) He was the best and wisest man that I have ever known.

(*DOYLE stops, deeply touched.*)

MARY: Let it be over, Father. Let it be done!

DOYLE: Oh, Mary . . .

MARY: The story is finished! He's dead.

DOYLE: I should be so alone without him.

MARY: But what of me? I am your child!

DOYLE: Aye, and so is he.

MARY: Father!

(*DOYLE crosses to WATSON and HOLMES.*)

DOYLE: He was made from bits and pieces of me, people known and lost and found again in him. Bits and pieces of my life, what it was and what it wasn't and all I wanted it to be.

WATSON: Then he was you?

DOYLE: (*Looking directly at HOLMES.*) He walked around inside my mind, but his is and always will be, himself.

(*HOLMES stirs slightly and begins to breathe.*)

WATSON: I think he's breathing.

DOYLE: Yes.

MARY: Don't do this, Father, let it be done!

DOYLE: He's too much of me and I of him. You know that, Mary.

MARY: (*After a beat*) I suppose so. But if he's not to be dead, then just at rest. Give me time. Give yourself time for other things.

DOYLE: Aye, Mary! Done!

(*MARY hugs DOYLE. HOLMES stirs and sits up.*)

HOLMES: It seems that I have been asleep.

WATSON: HOLMES! You're alive!

HOLMES: Or clubbed, or drugged by some act of villainy, more like!

WATSON: I am overjoyed to see you!

HOLMES: (*Sees DOYLE*) Moriarty! Can it still be you?

WATSON: Holmes, for once, I beg you to be quiet. Your very life depends upon it!

(*SHERLOCK HOLMES rises grandly.*)

HOLMES: Professor Moriarty, you are under arrest!

MARY: No, Mr. Holmes, you are!

(*MARY raises the gun at him.*)

HOLMES: Miss Mary, I do believe you shot me.

MARY: That I did and will again, unless you give by Father time to write something else!

(*WATSON smoothly puts himself between HOLMES and the gun.*)

WATSON: We will. I promise you!

(*From another world a clock begins to chime twelve times.*)

DOYLE: Then you two shall remain in this place, suspended here in time and space, until I find that I can turn my mind to you again. Until then, I have provided you a pleasant place to wait.

(*He gestures grandly; HOLMES and WATSON freeze, and MARY exits. DOYLE looks at them and smiles. As the clock continues to chime, he crosses to the desk, still somewhere to one side of the stage. He removes the MORIARTY glasses, sits and begins to write.*)

DOYLE: (*As he writes*) "It is with a heavy heart that I have written of the final days of my friend . . . my friend, Sherlock Holmes . . ."

(*The chimes stop. He smiles and looks over at HOLMES and WATSON as they come back to life.*)

(*HOLMES, totally bewildered, runs to the top of the structure and looks out.*)

HOLMES: I do not understand.

(*WATSON climbs up to join him.*)

WATSON: It's alright, Holmes, I think I do. One day I shall explain it to you. It is, after all, elementary my dear Holmes.

(*DOYLE laughs and puts down the pen as lights dim and music begins.*)

CURTAIN

All messages with the dancing men.

1. 2 2 2 B B A K E R S T

2. _ _ R D E R _ _ _ A T
   R E _ C _ E _ B A C _ _ A L L S

3. _ _ R D E R _ _ _ A T
   R E _ C _ E _ B A C _ _ A L L S

4. A D D E R C O B R A

A: F: K: P: U: Z:

B: G: L: Q: V:

C: H: M: R: W:

D: I: N: S: X:

E: J: O: T: Y:

Notes

1. First, a note about the settings. Although there are a great number of locations, I encourage designers to find simple solutions and to indicate locations with furniture and set pieces, rather than full wagons for each set.

   Perhaps a way could be found to have WINDLESHAM and BAKER STREET share the stage, with a reversable fireplace shared by both locations. Perhaps a revolve could be used to whisk us to the various locations suggested with a minimum of scenery.

   In any event, the movement of the play as a whole is essential. WATSON'S narrations provide time to change sets behind a scrim displaying the projections. I encourage you to find ways to keep the actions moving, to prevent this from becoming a play about "moving lumber."

2. Roylott's bending of the fire-poker has been done in a number of ways, the most successful was simply by painting black a length of the flexible rod used for microphones, and attaching fireplace tools to the top and bottom. This material provides both weight and flexibility and it stays bent when released.

3. Special effects in the seance can be done with black light and flourescent paint. APPARITIONS which appear behind scrimmed paintings are also effective, as is film and projections. The easiest way to levitate the table is to build a very lightweight table and to have the actors wear hooks in their cuffs (Bracelets for MARY or BERGOLIA). The hooks slip under the table lip, and allow it to be raised and lowered by the actors with their palms flat upon the table top.

4. The snakes are always a problem. Here lies the true test of a prop person's ingenuity. Since this depends so totally upon the design of the set for Mary's Bedroom, I cannot be too much help here. A word of wisdom, learned the hard way: KEEP IT SIMPLE! Snakes jamming or getting stuck at this time in the play are disasterous.

5. Another note that probably does not need to be said, avoid another potential disaster by having a back-up gun in the wings in the event Mary's gun does not fire in the last scene. This is the

only ABSOLUTELY ESSENTIAL gun shot and I have seen it fail twice in two different productions. Without the "death" there can be no "life" for Sherlock Holmes, and without the gun shot Mary might be forced to kill him with poison spit!

Appendix
Development of the Plays

Suzan has found that, to do her best work, she must take her plays through quite a long developmental process, sometimes lasting up to five years or more. During this time she likes to see several productions of the play and make quite a number of rewrites based on what she has seen on stage and felt as part of the audience. She finds that being present at live rehearsals and performances provides a kind of dynamic growth that is born and bred of the theatre. Among other things, it allows the positive endings she has in many of her plays to be affirmations in the face of difficulty, rather than just sentimental or simplistic happy endings.

Suzan's first play, *Wiley and the Hairy Man*, certainly followed this pattern. It was begun in the spring of 1972 when Suzan was finishing her M.F.A. in playwriting at Southern Methodist University and was asked by faculty member, Charley Helfert, to work with him and a company of student actors to adapt the original folk tale of the same name into play form. The script she developed, working improvisationally with those actors, was very different than the one here, which was finally published in 1978. It took her five years and seeing quite a few productions before she found an ending to the play that satisfied her. Soon after the play was published a large national advertising effort and a tour of the production by Everyman Players, sumptuously designed by Irene Corey and directed by Marilee Hebert-Slater, brought the play to national attention and spurred many more productions of the play around the country. It is still one of Suzan's most often produced works.

The Play Called Noah's Flood also went through a lengthy development, although there were only a few productions upon which she based revisions. Suzan started the play in 1972, soon after the first production of *Wiley*, when she was hired by Ann Elgood to write a play with and for the teenage summer company of the Flint Youth Theatre in Flint, Michigan. Suzan knew she would be working with young actors who were being trained in all aspects of theatre and who were at different levels in terms of acting skill. She felt that medieval theatre, with its spectacle and its tradition of being done by amateurs for the love of doing plays, would provide a starting point that was vastly different in historical time from these young actors, but not so far distant from their emotional enthusiasm for theatre.

Suzan adapted the pageant-within-the-play from the original Chester and Townley cycle plays and outlined the play surrounding the pageant before arriving in Flint. She then worked with the young actors to improvise incidents that went together to form the plot, and she credits these young people with many of the ideas for specific incidents.

In spite of the success of that first production in Flint, the play remained in a drawer awaiting revisions until Suzan and I were both teaching at the University of Washington in Seattle in 1978. We found ourselves searching for the right script for a summer production with college students who had relatively little previous acting experience or training. Zeder decided it was time to take *Noah* out of that drawer and rewrite it for me to direct. It was during this production that the depth and refinement of relationship between John, Ira, and Petula was added, and a provocative, original musical score was written for the piece by my husband, Daniel P. Davis. Further revisions were made when the play was produced again at the Flint Youth Theatre in 1982 directed by Jude Levison. The play was finally published in 1984 and won the Distinguished Play Award of the Children's Theatre Association of America in 1985.

Suzan began writing *Step on a Crack* in the spring of 1974, and it developed more quickly than some of her others. While she was in Dallas writing up the results of her Fulbright research in England and waiting to begin her Ph.D. studies, she was hired to teach a class at Southern Methodist University focusing on Theatre-in-Education. I was a graduate student at SMU at the time and first met Suzan when I enrolled in that class. During that same semester, I was awarded a production slot to direct a play for my M.F.A. project. Zeder, eager to get back to playwriting, offered to write a play for me to direct for the project.

She completed the first draft during the summer of 1974. The play went through several more revisions before rehearsals began in the late fall of 1974 and even more revisions took place during both the rehearsal process and the twenty-performance run of the play during the spring of 1975. The play was published in 1976 and became her first published work. In 1977 the Poncho Theatre in Seattle (now Seattle Children's Theatre) scheduled a production of the play. Since Suzan liked the work of Poncho's composer, John Engerman, she decided to add songs to each of the fantasy sequences for this production. The songs became part of the second edition of the play and are optional for any production.

The Poncho Theatre production turned out to be a pivotal one in terms of making the play visible nationally. Soon after the company brought their production of the play to the national convention of the American Theatre Association in 1978, *Step* became one of the most often produced scripts handled by Anchorage Press.

Ozma of Oz, a Tale of Time also had one of the shorter developmental periods of the scripts in this anthology. It was commissioned in late 1978 by Poncho Theatre. The theatre wanted a title that was familiar and recognizable. Suzan picked *Ozma of Oz* because she had enjoyed the L. Frank Baum Oz books as a child. The play went through several revisions during the rehearsal process and opened in October of 1979. The play received a second production by the Honolulu Theatre for Youth the following year for which she rewrote three scenes. Two other productions followed and gave her opportunities to rewrite. The play was published in 1981.

Doors was commissioned in 1981 by Greg Falls, Artistic Director of A Contemporary Theatre in Seattle, one of the country's major professional regional theatres. The entire purpose of the commission and its workshop production was, according to Suzan, to allow her to write "any play she wanted." While Suzan's fee as a playwright was partially funded by the Children's Theatre Foundation, Falls supported the play's production costs and provided salaries for the two adult actors, a professional stage manager, and Jim Hancock, Suzan's husband, as director. The two child actors and much backstage help were supplied by Bush Middle School in Seattle where the play was rehearsed and performed. After making revisions based on this production, Suzan was involved with a production directed by Joan Lazarus at Arizona State University, with a staged reading at Stage One in Dallas, and, finally, with a production at Seattle Children's Theatre in 1985. All of these productions afforded Suzan many opportunities to revise and to learn from actors, directors, and, most importantly, from audience response. As a result the script went through an extremely thorough testing period before it was published in 1985. In 1983 *Doors* was produced by Carousel Theatre in Vancouver, B.C. under a working title *Separate Doors*. During the next three years the script swept through Canada with productions in Toronto, Manitoba, Winnipeg and Edmonton. Canadian response to the play was immediate and overwhelmingly positive. Response in the United States has been positive but a bit more cautious. In spite of this initial caution, *Doors* was awarded the Distinguished Play Award by the American Association of Theatre for Youth in 1986.

Mother Hicks had the longest gestation period of all of Suzan's plays. Her interest in the folklore of witches began when she came across WPA material on the subject while she was doing research for *Wiley and the Hairy Man* in 1972. In 1973 she sketched out an outline that included the characters of Girl, looking for a way to explain herself to herself, and Mother Hicks, a midwife blamed by the town for a variety of natural but unfortunate occurances. She put the outline away for several years, but the idea stayed in the back of her mind, resurfacing occasionally before returning to her subconscious. It was eleven years before *Mother Hicks* was shaped into a draft for its first production in the spring of 1983 at the Poncho Theatre in Seattle.

The script went through several more productions including one at the Fulton Opera House in Lancaster, Pennsylvania directed by Kathleen Collins in January of 1984 and another in February of the same year at the University of Wisconsin at Madison. Both helped her test various revisions. The 1985 Asolo Theatre production was invited to perform at the Kennedy Center in Washington, D.C., and the changes she made for that production resulted in the draft which was finally published in 1986 and which won the American Alliance for Theatre and Education Distinguished Play Award in 1987.

In a Room Somewhere began with a commission from Metro Theatre Circus of St. Louis, Missouri in 1983. The play was to go to rehearsal in 1985. The process began with a many-month-long search for a topic. Suzan and Carol Evans, Metro's Artistic Director, finally decided that *what* the play was about was not as important as *how* they went about working together as actors, director, and playwright in developing it. A foray into one of Suzan's picture files unearthed an interesting photograph of six very different children sitting on a bench. Suzan and Carol decided to go with a working title for the piece of "On the Bench," and to spend the next year finding out who the children were and why they were on the bench. That year included several residencies in which Suzan worked with the actors and director improvisationally and interviewed adults and children, showing them the photograph and asking them who they thought the children in the picture were. The photograph served as a sort of photographic Rorschach test through which actors and interviewees alike began telling about themselves. During the process of structuring the enormous amount of raw material generated in this process, Suzan gave up the idea of the characters being children on a bench and allowed them to be adults in a room instead.

The play was part of Metro's touring repertory for two full seasons, during which time, it went through eight complete revisions. It received another formative production, which included a new musical score by Daniel P. Davis, at the Asolo Theatre in the summer and fall of 1987. Even more changes were made at a production of the play at Arizona State University in the winter and spring of 1988. By the time the script reached its current form, it had been through fifteen drafts.

After twelve years of writing plays almost constantly, often on a commissioned basis, Suzan was feeling the need to take a break from playwriting, to get back in touch with her own needs and interests as a writer. But when Moses Goldberg of Stage One Theatre in Louisville offered to commission a work on Sherlock Holmes in 1985, and when Kathleen Collins of the Fulton Opera House in Lancaster, Pennsylvania joined Goldberg and doubled the commission, Suzan began research on *The Death and Life of Sherlock Holmes*. In the early drafts that led up to the first production of *Holmes* at Stage One in January, 1988 and Seattle Children's Theatre in May, 1988, Suzan tried to keep the audience from knowing, until the very end, that the many villains pursuing Holmes were really Sir Arthur Conan Doyle himself. As the play developed through another draft, in preparation for a production at Emmy Gifford Children's Theatre in Omaha, Nebraska in October, 1988, Suzan made Doyle's identity very clear from early in the play. This revelation allowed Suzan to make this both a good mystery adventure and a deeper exploration of a writer's creative struggles.

From reports by nearly all the theatre groups that have worked with her, Suzan is a collaborator in the best sense of the word. She regularly seeks out and uses input from the actors, directors, and designers working on early productions of her plays. She is often invited back and commissioned again by the same theatres because she is both an exciting artist who understands all aspects of theatre and an enjoyable and stimulating person with whom to work. Although Suzan has done much to cultivate healthy working relationships with theatre artists she respects, the professional, youth, and university theatres and directors who have given her the opportunity to write and rewrite her scripts for their productions deserve credit and thanks. Too often in American theatre, and especially in theatre for young audiences, the relationship between a theatre and a playwright is not long enough and continuous enough for scripts to reach their fullest development. The theatres named above, and others which may have gone unnamed but which have invited Suzan Zeder to develop scripts with them, have made a major contribution to the quality of American dramatic literature for family audiences.

Photo by David Stein

SUSAN PEARSON-DAVIS, Editor of *WISH IN ONE HAND, SPIT IN THE OTHER; A Collection of Plays by Suzan Zeder,* is an Associate Professor of Theatre at the University of New Mexico where she teaches children's theatre, creative drama, acting, and voice. Long active in children's theatre, regionally and nationally, she is a past Vice-President for Program of the Children's Theatre Association of America. She currently serves as Editor of the *Youth Theatre Journal.* Her B.A. was in English at the University of Washington in Seattle. She was assigned to teach drama as well as English in an Oregon junior high school. She felt impelled to learn more about her new responsibility and at the 1973 Aspen Theatre Institute she studied under Moses Goldberg and Dorothy Heathcote. She earned her M.F.A. in Theatre at Southern Methodist University, where she met Suzan Zeder. After two years teaching children's theatre and creative drama at the State University of New York in Plattsburgh, she joined Zeder as an Assistant Professor in the Child Drama program at the University of Washington, Seattle, for five years. In 1982, she moved to Albuquerque, where she lives with her husband, Daniel P. Davis, a composer who has created musical scores for two plays in this anthology.